Consumer Behavior

Consumer Behavior presents an autobiographical view of Morris B. Holbrook's contributions to the study of consumer behavior, describing his life and work over the past 60 years via a collection of subjective personal introspective essays. This new collection extends, enlarges, and elaborates on the insights garnered over Holbrook's career to provide a lively and thought-provoking exploration of the evolution of consumer research.

Using Subjective Personal Introspection (SPI), Holbrook shares aspects of his own journey in developing insights into such topics as the consumption experience, consumer value, the jazz metaphor, marketing education, and various controversies that have interested the scholarly community. Early chapters portray Holbrook's evolution in college, graduate school, and faculty membership, while later chapters trace his approaches to understanding the role of consumption as the essence of the human condition. Throughout, SPI is used to illuminate the ways in which academic struggles have led toward deeper understandings of consumers.

Readers with an interest in the autobiographical details of how ideas develop and emerge in an area such as consumer research – including doctoral students or faculty members in the field of marketing – will find enlightenment and inspiration in contemplating the (mis)adventures of a fellow traveler.

Morris B. Holbrook is now-retired W. T. Dillard Professor Emeritus of Marketing, Graduate School of Business, Columbia University, New York City. He received his Bachelor's Degree from Harvard College (English Literature) in 1965, his MBA from Columbia University in 1967, and his PhD in Marketing from Columbia in 1975. From 1975 to 2009, he taught courses at the Columbia Business School in such areas as sales management, marketing strategy, research methods, consumer behavior, and commercial communication in the culture of consumption. His research has covered a wide variety of topics in marketing and consumer behavior with a special focus on issues related to communication in general and to aesthetics, semiotics, hermeneutics, art, entertainment, music, jazz, motion pictures, nostalgia, and stereography in particular.

Routledge Interpretive Marketing Research

Recent years have witnessed an 'interpretive turn' in marketing and consumer research. Methodologies from the humanities are taking their place alongside those drawn from the traditional social sciences.

Qualitative and literary modes of marketing discourse are growing in popularity. Art and aesthetics are increasingly firing the marketing imagination.

This series brings together the most innovative work in the burgeoning interpretive marketing research tradition. It ranges across the methodological spectrum from grounded theory to personal introspection, covers all aspects of the postmodern marketing 'mix', from advertising to product development, and embraces marketing's principal sub-disciplines.

Gifts, Romance, And Consumer Culture
Edited by Yuko Minowa and Russell W. Belk

Food and Experiential Marketing
Pleasure, Wellbeing and Consumption
Edited by Wided Batat

Macro-Social Marketing Insights
Systems Thinking for Wicked Problems
Edited by Ann-Marie Kennedy

The Digital Coach
Stella Kanatouri

Consumer Behavior
New Essays on the Study of Consumption
Morris B. Holbrook

For more information about this series, please visit: www.routledge.com/Routledge-Interpretive-Marketing-Research/book-series/SE0484

Consumer Behavior

New Essays on the Study of
Consumption

Morris B. Holbrook

Routledge
Taylor & Francis Group

LONDON AND NEW YORK

First published 2025
by Routledge
4 Park Square, Milton Park, Abingdon, Oxon OX14 4RN

and by Routledge
605 Third Avenue, New York, NY 10158

Routledge is an imprint of the Taylor & Francis Group, an informa business

British Library Cataloguing-in-Publication Data
A catalogue record for this book is available from the British Library

ISBN: 978-1-032-90886-1 (hbk)
ISBN: 978-1-032-90885-4 (pbk)
ISBN: 978-1-003-56030-2 (ebk)

DOI: 10.4324/9781003560302

Typeset in Sabon
by Apex CoVantage, LLC

For Sally –

My Bear –

Who Has Shared All These Moments With Me

Contents

Figures

About the Author

Morris B. Holbrook is the now-retired W. T. Dillard Professor Emeritus of Marketing, Graduate School of Business, Columbia University, New York City (mbh3@columbia.edu; 212-873-7324; 140 Riverside Drive, Apartment 5H, New York, NY 10024-2605, USA). He received his Bachelor's Degree from Harvard College (English Literature) in 1965, his MBA from Columbia University in 1967, and his PhD in Marketing from Columbia in 1975. From 1975 to 2009, he taught courses at the Columbia Business School in such areas as Sales Management, Marketing Strategy, Research Methods, Consumer Behavior, and Commercial Communication in the Culture of Consumption. His research has covered a wide variety of topics in marketing and consumer behavior with a special focus on issues related to communication in general and to aesthetics, semiotics, hermeneutics, art, entertainment, music, jazz, motion pictures, nostalgia, and stereography in particular. His books and monographs include *Postmodern Consumer Research: The Study of Consumption as Text* (with Elizabeth C. Hirschman, 1992); *The Semiotics of Consumption: Interpreting Symbolic Consumer Behavior in Popular Culture and Works of Art* (with Elizabeth C. Hirschman, 1993); *Consumer Research: Introspective Essays on the Study of Consumption* (1995); *Consumer Value: A Framework for Analysis and Research* (ed. 1999); *Playing the Changes on the Jazz Metaphor: An Expanded Conceptualization of Music-, Management-, and Marketing-Related Themes* (2007); and *Music, Movies, Meanings, and Markets: Cinemajazzamatazz* (2011). He lives with his wife, Sally, on the Upper West Side of Manhattan, where he pursues such hobbies as playing the piano, attending jazz and classical concerts, going to movies and the theater, collecting musical recordings, taking stereographic photos, and being kind to cats.

Preface

Back in 1995, roughly halfway through my career as a Professor of Marketing at Columbia University's Graduate School of Business, I created a book entitled *Consumer Research: Introspective Essays on the Study of Consumption* (Holbrook, 1995b). This work focused on the evolution of consumer research as a field of study and treated this topic from the viewpoint of Subjective Personal Introspection (SPI) – that is, essays written to convey my own private idiosyncratic impressions of how this particular academic specialization had taken shape, developed, and changed during the years of my participation. In traversing this material, I touched on a variety of themes that interested me as a researcher. These included the shift from a neopositivistic rational information-processing decision-oriented perspective to the inclusion of a more humanistic interpretive experiential view; the nature of creativity in theory development; the demands for patience, persistence, and perseverance in pursuing a career as an academic consumer researcher; the difference between consumer research (oriented toward knowledge for its own sake) and marketing research (aimed at managerial relevance); the roles in the lives of human consumers of consumption experiences in general and of emotional responses in particular; the scope in consumer research for aspects of Romanticism, for insights drawn from Subjective Personal Introspection (SPI), and for contributions from psychoanalysis; the potential for feminist perspectives emphasizing the role of lyricism in studies of consumer behavior; the ultimate animal-based metaphor of marketing researchers as dogs (anxious to please their masters) versus consumer researchers as cats (driven by ceaseless curiosity) and the resulting tension between dogmatism (applied research) and catastrophe (pure research) in the development of marketing- and consumer-research studies; and applications of all this to the interpretation of musical consumption – especially the appreciation of jazz. In short, *Consumer Research* represented many or most of the ideas that I had been working on for two decades, as seen from the vantage point of my mid-career recollections (some might say, my mid-life crisis).

Some commentators on my work – including a few friends who perhaps should have known better – have treated my contributions as if they had stopped in the early 1990s or even sooner. For example, such pundits might cite one or two papers from early on – say, Hirschman and Holbrook (1982) on "Hedonic Consumption" or Holbrook and Hirschman (1982) on "The Experiential Aspects of Consumption" – and then give the impression that I had quit developing these ideas right after they had first flowered forth. Some commentators do not even extend their observations as far as my book on *Consumer Research* (1995b), and very few look past that point to wonder what I might have subsequently produced.

Yet a data-happy look at Google Scholar Citations (Scholar.Google.Com) shows that 3 of my top 5, 5 of my top 10, and 9 of my top 20 publications have appeared since 1994 (despite biases caused by lags in the appearance of such citations over time). From this, I infer that those who write commentaries tend to emphasize the earlier at the expense of the later work by those about whom they write these reviews. To offer a far-flung analogy, this constricted preoccupation with the past resembles the focus of a hypothetical sports writer who extolls the virtues of Henry Aaron's first year in the major leagues – during which he blasted 13 home runs and contributed 69 runs-batted-in with a batting average of .280 – without noticing that, in subsequent years, Hank went on to hammer out 755 HRs and 2,297 RBIs overall with a lifetime BA of .305. Obviously, despite whatever inappropriate vainglorious tendencies I might undeservedly harbor, I would never presume to compare my humble self to the magnificent Hammerin' Hank Aaron. Rather, I simply mention this grandiose analogy to emphasize my sense of neglect when my pre-1990s contributions are mentioned in ways that eclipse my latter-day efforts.

These feelings of self-pity have now inspired me to create and collect a series of essays that I hope present a fuller picture of my intellectual adventures and scholarly endeavors during the second half of my career (1996 to the present time). These new contributions now appear in the present book under the title *Consumer Behavior: New Essays on the Study of Consumption*. Here, I pick up where I left off in *Consumer Research* (1995b) and trace the development of my work over the entire course of my career with an emphasis on what has happened in the 30 years since 1995.

Originally, I had the opportunity to prepare these essays in response to kind invitations extended to me by several editors who deserve my warmest and most appreciative gratitude: Mark Tadajewski at the *Journal of Historical Research in Marketing*; Stephen Brown and Sharon Ponsonby-McCabe as editors for Routledge of *Brand Mascots and Other Marketing Animals*; Damien Chaney, Renaud Lunardo, and Rémi Mencarelli at *Qualitative Marketing Research*; Michela Addis, François Colbert, Alex Turrini, and Jennifer Wiggins at the *International Journal of Arts Management*; Arch Woodside at the *Journal of Global Scholars of Marketing Science*; Marin Marinov as editor for Routledge of *Value in Marketing: Retrospective and Perspective Stance*; Daragh O'Reilly, Ruth Rentschker, and Theresa A. Kirschner as editors for Routledge of *The Routledge Companion to Arts Marketing*; Adam Lindgreen, Piyush Sharma, Helen Alexander, and Richard Whitfield at *Marketing Intelligence & Planning*; Pauline Maclaran at *Marketing Theory*; Terry Witkowski at the *Journal of Macromarketing*; Stephen Brown and Sharon Ponsonby-McCabe again as editors at the *Journal of Customer Behaviour*; and Roger Marshall at the *Australasian Marketing Journal*. And, responding to no one in particular beyond my own restless curiosity, I have prepared an Appendix that contains over 600 examples of references to the consumption experience found in print advertisements, television commercials, and other promotional messages.

Taken together, these essays – now collected in the form of *Consumer Behavior: New Essays on the Study of Consumption* – provide a subjective personal introspective view of my life and work over the past 50-plus years (or even longer if you count the brief portions that reach back to my early childhood 80-plus years ago). In a few cases, I cover the same period of time in different essays from the viewpoints of different thematic concerns. In this, I hope to offer a portrait of someone committed to consumer research who aims to communicate with an audience of readers who pursue similar interests.

Publishers like to know what people and how many of them can be counted on to purchase a book that they plan to publish. With respect to the present volume, in all honesty, I cannot definitively answer those sorts of questions. According to Scholar.Google.Com, *Consumer Research* (Holbrook, 1995b) has received over 1,200 citations, and a subsequent collection on *Consumer Value* (Holbrook, ed. 1999) has been cited over 5,100 times. So somebody must be buying and reading these things. From the recent willingness of Sage to publish my life's work in 15 volumes under the title *Legends in Consumer Behavior: Morris B. Holbrook* (Holbrook, 2015c, ed. Sheth), I infer that someone out there – at least a few lost souls – might wish to pursue my stream of research. However, even the most sincere readers might balk at the rather steep price tag for the 15-volume series – currently on sale at Amazon. Com, depending on which vendor you select, for anywhere from $1,286.77 (used) to $1,505.33 (new). Challenged by this hefty price tag, understandably reluctant book buyers might appreciate a cheaper and more trouble-free path into the Holbrook-centered oeuvre and the Morris-oriented worldview as represented by some recent SPI essays (none of which appeared in the *Legends* series). So, for those select and no doubt slightly zany potential customers, the efficiency-conscious goal of comparatively inexpensive painlessness is exactly what the present book attempts to achieve.

The attentive reader may notice that passages from an earlier chapter sometimes reappear in a later chapter. Such repetitions result from the fact that the book collects essays that were originally published separately in various scholarly journals or academic books and that were intended as stand-alone contributions. I considered trying to remove the repetitions. But, on more careful reflection, I decided that they should remain so that a reader who wants to skip around in the text by reading just one or another chapter of interest will not miss out on key ideas that are needed to help the chapter make sense. In my view, a bit of redundancy should be forgiven where clarity is the main objective.

Thus, without further ado, let us march forth into the orbit of one consumer researcher (yours truly) who has tried to make a difference by being a bit of a nonconformist (viewed politely) or (less charitably) by being somewhat peculiar. But not without pausing briefly to thank the nice folks at Routledge who helped to bring forth this new book of essays – in particular, two anonymous reviewers (who offered helpful comments on an earlier draft); Mohana Chatterjee (who handled various publishing-related details); Promoth Jaikishan (who steered the production process); an anonymous copy editor (who made countless improvements); and especially Alex Atkinson (who provided encouragement and support along the way). Beyond that, I thank another gracious lady – my dear wife, Sally – to whom I dedicate this book with boundless love, with unlimited admiration, and with profound gratitude for her patience and support during the last 58 years of our always-exciting and ever-enjoyable marriage.

Acknowledgments

Beyond those already thanked in the Preface, I wish to express my gratitude to the following publishers and publications for permissions to include revised versions of the following articles and chapters in the present volume.

Holbrook, Morris B. (2013), "The Greedy Bastard's Guide to Business," *Journal of Macromarketing*, 33 (4, December), 369–385.

Holbrook, Morris B. (2014a) "Consumption Criteria in Arts Marketing," in *The Routledge Companion to Arts Marketing*, ed. Daragh O'Reilly, Ruth Rentschker, and Theresa A. Kirchner, London, UK and New York, NY: Routledge, 194–203.

Holbrook, Morris B. (2014c) "Morris the Cat or the Wolf-Man on the Upper West Side: Animal Metaphors and Me," in *Brand Mascots and Other Marketing Animals*, ed. Stephen Brown and Sharon Ponsonby-McCabe, London, UK and New York, NY: Routledge, 76–88.

Holbrook, Morris B. (2015d), "Morris B. Holbrook," in *Harvard and Radcliffe Class of 1965: Fiftieth Anniversary Report*, ed. John Paul Russo and Linda Smith Summers, Cambridge, MA: Class Report Office, Harvard University, 459–463. Reprinted with permission from the Harvard Alumni Association Class Report Office.

Holbrook, Morris B. (2015g), "The Marketing Manager as a Jazz Musician," *Marketing Intelligence & Planning*, 33 (7), 958–965.

Holbrook, Morris B. (2016), "Reflections on Jazz Training and Marketing Education: What Makes a Great Teacher?" *Marketing Theory*, 16 (4, December), 429–444.

Holbrook, Morris B. (2017), "Morris B. Holbrook: An Historical Autoethnographic Subjective Personal Introspection," *Journal of Historical Research in Marketing*, 9 (2), 144–190.

Holbrook, Morris B. (2018a), "A Subjective Personal Introspective Essay on the Evolution of Business Schools, the Fate of Marketing Education, and Aspirations Toward a Great Society," *Australasian Marketing Journal*, 26 (2, May), 70–78.

Holbrook, Morris B. (2018b), "Essay on the Origins, Development and Future of the Consumption Experience as a Concept in Marketing and Consumer Research," *Qualitative Marketing Research*, 21 (4), 421–444.

Holbrook, Morris B. (2020), "The Concept of Consumer Value: Development, Implications, Trajectory, in *Value in Marketing: Retrospective and Perspective Stance*, ed. Marin Marinov, London, UK: Routledge, 9–41.

Holbrook, Morris B. (2021), "Commentary: Consumption Experiences, Customer Value, Subjective Personal Introspection, the Photographic Essay, and Semiological/ Hermeneutic Interpretation," *Journal of Global Scholars of Marketing Science*, 31 (4), 663–675. Copyright © 2021 Korean Scholars of Marketing Science, reprinted by permission of informa UK Limited, trading as Taylor & Francis Group, www.tandfonline.com on behalf of Korean Scholars of Marketing Science.

Holbrook, Morris B. (2023), "Consumption Experiences in the Arts," *International Journal of Arts Management*, 26 (1, Fall), 6–17.

Holbrook, Morris B. (2024), "What for Art Thou, Marketing?" *Journal of Customer Behaviour*, 23 (1), 27–32.

Part I

Some Autobiographical Sketches

1 Morris B. Holbrook

An Introduction

Abstract

This introductory chapter comes from the *Fiftieth Anniversary Report* circulated at the time of the author's recent college reunion (Class of 1965). The autobiographical essay emphasizes the struggles he faced in rising to the challenges of the college experience and provides a subjective personal introspective account of how he suffered and emerged somewhat scathed.

I grew up in Milwaukee in a nice family with a loving mother, a caring-but-demanding father, a half-sister who was there for only part of the time, and an African American woman who worked for us and who was something like a second mother to me. My mom came from Montgomery and often took me down to Alabama for visits with my doting grandmother, my venerable great-grandfather, and other kind-and-sweet relatives. In Milwaukee, I had a paternal grandfather who was a natural-born storyteller, a master of the English language, a fine fly fisherman, a respected physician, a talented photographer, an animal lover, and a proud graduate of Harvard College (not necessarily in that order).

Like my dad, also a Harvard grad and a physician, my grandpop harbored a deep desire for other members of the family and especially yours truly to attend his alma mater, which, ultimately, I managed to do. To get me there, my father helped out as doctor for the local private boys' school (Milwaukee Country Day), where – because we were comfortable but not wealthy – I think he got for me a bit of a tuition discount in exchange for his medical services.

One such medical service involved his work as doctor for the school's football team. As such, unfortunately for me, he developed a deep desire to see his son in action on the gridiron – one of two or three paternal obsessions to which I caved in by going along with his misguided plan to turn me into a football player. Paradoxically, as a fine self-taught jazz pianist, my dad had also encouraged me to develop interests in that direction – never, apparently, noticing the contradiction between trying to become a pianist and having your fingers stomped on by aggressive members of the opposing team. I absolutely sucked at football, but I did develop some skills as a jazz pianist – later, also a vibraphonist – which I have tried to maintain in subsequent phases of

DOI: 10.4324/9781003560302-2

my progress. In this, I received patient guidance from Milwaukee's finest jazz pianist, Tommy Sheridan, who played a key role as the greatest and most inspiring teacher I have ever known (as described later in Chapter 10).

My second major concession to my father's ambitions for me involved my somewhat hesitant decision to choose Harvard over Princeton (where I was also accepted for admission). Obviously, I was blessed to have an opportunity at either school, let alone both of them. But I did face a rather difficult choice problem and resolved it in favor of my dad's wishes for his son's welfare. I don't know what the Princeton experience would have been like, but I can report with no fear of contradiction that I was absolutely miserable at Harvard – also that it was my own damn fault because Harvard College is a magnificent place where I was just simply way overmatched (sort of like the football field except that nobody stepped on my fingers).

I majored in English, which may not have been so wise given that I am one of the world's slowest readers. No, I'm not exaggerating. In high school, as a percentile, I did OK in comprehension, but I tested in the mid-teens in speed – meaning that 85 out of every 100 ordinary people from the general population read faster than I do. At Harvard, where the talent pool was anything but "ordinary," 99.999999 out of every hundred people read faster than I – a definite impediment when taking a course on (say) the Victorian novel with (say) a 700-page book by Dickens or Eliot or Thackeray to read every week. So in order to get good grades – which, despite my learning disability, I somehow managed to do – I needed to work several times harder than everybody else, making myself wretchedly unhappy in the process and enduring an around-the-clock fear of failure.

Also, my already beyond-slow reading habits were retarded still further, to a near halt, by the school's emphasis on the "close" reading of literary texts. In a class called "Hum 6," one of our professors told us to read every line as if it came from a precious love letter. Unfortunately, whatever its benefits on the romantic front, this practice insures snail-like progress when perusing a 700-page novel. Meanwhile, the number of English courses I needed to take for my major interfered with my ability to pursue other humanities courses in (say) music because I needed classes in the physical and social sciences to satisfy the various distribution requirements for the liberal arts degree. Because of my poor reading-and-studying skills, the courses I took in English and Music turned out to be difficult-and-unpleasant experiences, ruining the formal study of these subjects for me.

After that, I reasoned that studying something that I loved in a university setting tended to destroy it. So – my logic went – if I wanted to attend graduate school, it would make sense to pick a topic that I already hated (to avoid the potential destruction of something that had formerly brought me pleasure). Thus did I decide to attend business school – business being something that I have never liked and, indeed, that I tend to regard in its obsession with $$$$$ as pretty much the root of all evil.

After struggling my way to a fairly respectable academic record at the College – Magna Cum Laude, Phi Beta Kappa, and all that – I was pretty pissed off when the Harvard Business School turned me down cold for its MBA program (at the height of the Vietnam build-up in 1965, with a note from the admissions office saying that I lacked real-world experience and might benefit from joining the Army). Fortunately for me, earning my eternal gratitude, Columbia University's Graduate School of Business did accept me – which worked out well because my bride-to-be Sally was already attending the Columbia School of Social Work.

Sally and I had met the previous summer of 1964 on a tour of Europe – two months, going from one exciting and romantic spot to another (including the Iron-Curtain Countries, a stretch in those days) – and were wed, by coincidence, just one week before Lyndon Johnson lifted the automatic draft exemption for married people. Anyway, with the Milwaukee Draft Board breathing down my neck at the peak of the Vietnam War, I studied hard to keep my 2-S student deferment and to stay in school as an MBA and then a PhD candidate. Finally – on one of the happiest days I can recall, in roughly 1973, at about age 30 – I received a communication from my draft board with the news that, being way too old to shoot a gun (yes, reading it between the lines like a love letter), I was no longer of interest to them as a candidate for military service.

Even more happily, in 1969, we produced a bouncing baby boy (Chris). He has brought us many joys along the way. Today, he lives in Strasbourg, where he works as a filmmaker, writes plays, teaches English as a second language, and enjoys joint custody of his two small and delightfully charming children, Nathanael and Anika. Recently, Chris has had a couple of his plays produced in very-off-Broadway theaters – a real treat for his proud parents.

Paradoxically, after my unbearable labors as an undergrad at Harvard, the MBA program at Columbia seemed fairly pleasant – all the more because I fell under the spell of Professor John A. Howard and his exciting discoveries in what turned out to become "Buyer-Behavior Theory." In a sense, I found an aspect of business (loosely interpreted) that I actually did like and therefore continued in the PhD program (under John Howard's generous sponsorship, also described later in Chapter 10). Of course, I also needed to familiarize myself with the marketing-related side of things and realized that I liked some of that too – especially the parts that bear on larger social issues and questions of human welfare (what nowadays we would call "*macro*marketing"). These facets of marketing as a discipline remain somewhat neglected in the typical business-school curriculum (though there are partial exceptions at some of the more enlightened schools). As a broad generalization, I think it's fair to say that marketing academia tends to neglect issues related to the (often destructive) impact of business in general and marketing in particular on society and on the quality of human lives (as discussed in Part V).

Continuing in the PhD program at Columbia and in no hurry to lose my 2-S military deferment, I stretched my essentially cowardly strategy out for a full ten years, after which – through some kind of academic miracle and with plenty of help from my Guardian Angel (aka John Howard) – Columbia actually hired me (one of its own graduates) as a tenure-track assistant professor. Over the years, I worked my way up to a chaired position as the William T. Dillard Professor of Marketing (now emeritus). This reflected a whole lot of published research – mostly on consumer behavior and especially on consumers of cultural offerings or, in other words, audiences for the arts and entertainment – which the interested reader can find listed under "Morris B. Holbrook" on Scholar.Google.Com and throughout the remainder of the present volume.

I guess I should take a moment to preview and explain what, over these years, I might have contributed to the study of marketing and consumer research. Briefly, when I arrived on the scene, the study of buyer behavior – as developed by scholars such as my mentor John Howard – pursued a view of the consumer as a rational decision maker and studied consumption phenomena via various formal, experimental, quantitative, and data-driven approaches. A number of us began to rebel against this conventional wisdom by investigating a broader array of aspects involved in the consumption experience ("fantasies, feelings, and fun"), expanding our perspective to include consumer behavior associated with hedonic responses (pleasurable multi-sensory products) and aesthetic offerings (music, movies, plays, novels), and pursuing various qualitative methods drawn from the humanities and previously neglected in our field of inquiry (semiotics, hermeneutics, cultural studies, subjective personal introspection, psychoanalytic approaches). Gradually, tweaked by these subversive inclinations, a field once known as "buyer behavior" and concerned with rational purchase decisions evolved into "consumer research," with its emphasis on the whole consumption experience, the relevant emotions, the sources of consumer value, and the in-depth exploration of aesthetic responses and symbolic meanings. All these extensions and enlargements will be explained further in future chapters of this book.

So, when I retired in July 2009, I had been at Columbia University's Graduate School of Business since 1965 – roughly 45 years – first as an MBA student, then as a PhD candidate, and finally as a faculty member. Apparently, as gauged by revealed preference, I tend not to move around very much. During that time – due to work-related pressures – my family-inspired interests in such things as music, photography, creative writing, recreational reading, and being kind to cats tended to fall by the wayside a bit (though I did often draw on those sorts of avocations as topics for my consumer-related research). (By the way, as explored further by what follows in Chapter 2, a major impetus toward shifting my research interests in those directions came near the end of a six-year four-times-a-week-on-the-couch psychoanalysis when my analyst responded to my ceaseless kvetching about how bored I felt with some of the work I had been doing by inquiring why I did not devote more attention to the things I loved and to topics I found more engaging.)

Obviously, if you grab a guy whose main loves in life are music, photography, literature, movies, the arts, and such and if you make that guy teach courses in business strategy to the world's most unapologetically greedy MBA students, various sorts of frustrations and disappointments may result. Without belaboring the details (explored in Chapter 3 and Part V), I might summarize by saying that – by 2007 (just before the financial crisis, after which I probably would never have had the nerve to sign my retirement contract) – I had recognized the need to retire, perhaps to devote my energies to fooling around with various non-pragmatic arts-related activities.

So that's what I've been doing lately – playing some piano and vibes, reading some trashy detective novels, watching some low-brow films and TV shows, doing a little bit of writing – along with spending more time with Sally and working on a few unfinished scholarly projects. In 2015, I sent my warmest wishes to all my Harvard classmates, but I didn't get to the 50th Reunion because I was too afraid that no one would recognize or remember me. After all, I spent most of my college career in my lonely room at Dunster House, reading very slowly.

2 Morris B. Holbrook

A Historical Autoethnographic Subjective Personal Introspection

Abstract

This chapter describes the author's personal history and intellectual develop-ment as a participant in the field of marketing academics in general and con-sumer research in particular. The essay pursues an approach characterized by historical autoethnographic subjective personal introspection and interprets various aspects of key participants and major themes that emerged over the course of the author's career. The main implication is that every scholar in the field of marketing pursues a different light; follows a unique path; plays by idiosyncratic rules; and deserves individual attention, consideration, and respect . . . like a cat that carries its own leash.

I came into the world on November 7, 1943, at the Columbia Hospital in Mil-waukee, Wisconsin. (Starting with that, as we shall see, the name "Columbia" has tended to frame my activities on this planet.) My father – a local physician, affiliated with that hospital – missed the delivery because he had traveled to the Philippines to participate in World War II (WWII). At the time, he was 37 years old (a little elderly for military service), and the South-east Asian climate gave him a horribly debilitating skin rash. His commanding officers wanted to send him home, but he toughed it out and treated his skin problems by taking arse-nic pills. That was the sort of man, a master of tenacious self-discipline, who had a big influence on my life – much but not all of it in a good way.

My mother's brother had recently died aboard (I think it was) the *U.S.S. Oklahoma* when the Japanese attacked his ship during their assault on Pearl Harbor. So they named me after him – Morris Baldwin Holbrook. Unfortu-nately for me, I have never liked the name Morris. But – in my teenage years, when I thought seriously about changing it – my desire for a more normal moniker (say, Jack or Harry) produced such tears of anguish among the mem-bers of my mother's tribe that I reluctantly abandoned any such plans. In this, perhaps, I lucked out because my subsequent ability to identify with Morris the Cat proved instrumental in my intellectual connections with the more feline (as opposed to canine) community of scholars (Holbrook, 1989a).

The maternal tribe dwelled in Montgomery, Alabama, and my mother took me home to spend my first couple of years surrounded by doting women

DOI: 10.4324/9781003560302-3

(grandmother, aunts, female servants) who supplemented my mom's own assiduous care by tending to my every need, want, or whim. I imagine they had little better to do – all the men having left to fight in WWII – with the result that I was spoiled rotten by this overabundance of feminine attention and affection.

But the day before my father returned from the war, I managed to barge in on the mealtime of Chimmy – the family's huge collie dog and, until then, my good friend – who responded to my throwing my arms around his neck while he was trying to eat by biting me nastily on the cheek. So when my dad – the first man I had ever met – showed up at the railroad station, he found that his new bouncing baby boy wore an enormous bandage on his face. But, as the biblical saying goes, I had another cheek, and he rubbed his own face on it enthusiastically. Unfortunately, he had been riding on the train for a few days, and his week-old growth of beard scraped me painfully. I was shocked, threw a terrible-twos fit, and – as my six-year four-times-a-week-on-the-couch psychoanalyst would be happy to tell you – have never recovered. Indeed, the Oedipal dimensions of this trauma occupied my attention at length in a couple of my more self-revelatory (some would say self-indulgent) essays (Holbrook, 1988c, 1988e; see also Holbrook, 2015f).

When we returned to Milwaukee, we took along an African American woman named Ernestine or Teenie for short as my nurse. Extending the loving care of my own dear mother, Teenie treated me with such tender affection

Figure 2.1 Arthur Andrews "Sandy" Holbrook, Father of Morris, Early 1940s

Figure 2.2 May Baldwin Holbrook, Mother with Infant Morris, 1945

Figure 2.3 Infant Morris with Mother May and Father Sandy – Just Back from
WWII – 1945

that I regarded her as a sort of second female parent – one whom I grew to love with feelings that went far beyond the old cliché about being a "member of the family." Indeed, from knowing her, I learned that – if people from the South wanted to sustain their abhorrently outrageous level of racial prejudice – letting black folks raise their children was an idea that was bound to backfire. Believe me when I say that, under such circumstances, racial intolerance vanishes into thin air.

I found out about racism because, as a very young boy, my number one hero was . . . Jackie Robinson. I thought that he was the most handsome, talented, and impressive man I had ever seen. And – to this day, because of Jackie – I remain a fan of the old Brooklyn Dodgers (though not, needless to say, of the upstart Los Angeles team). But I did not know about the racially sensitive aspects of Jackie's situation. So, when I visited our local movie house to see *The Jackie Robinson Story* (1950) at age seven, I did not understand why various people treated him with such contempt and cruelty. I asked Teenie about this. And with the most immense tact and gentleness, she explained to me that some folks did not like people of color. As an illustration, she mentioned that, when she left our house after work to take the bus across town, the children of our neighbors often shouted insults and threw rocks at her. To this day, I become tearful when I recall that sorrowful moment of revelation

Figure 2.4 Young Morris with Teenie in Snow, Milwaukee, 1947

and the pain I felt to imagine that someone I loved so much could be treated with such hatred for reasons or excuses I did not begin to fathom.

Meanwhile, in a suburb of Milwaukee called Shorewood, we eased into my father's Midwestern way of life, and I immersed myself in many of his family traditions – the local school he had attended (Milwaukee Country Day), his circle of friends (not to mention grateful patients), his love of music (Fats Waller, Teddy Wilson, Nat Cole, Erroll Garner), his favorite vacation spots (the Brule River in Northern Wisconsin), and (perhaps less beneficently) his fierce sense of competitiveness (sports like tennis, squash, skiing, canoeing, and fly fishing), as well as his somewhat over-the-top achievement orientation (school, work, social status). The latter surfaced, for example, when my parents lobbied long and hard for my acceptance into a four-year kindergarten class at Country Day in which, at age three, I was the youngest member and should have been placed a year behind. In that class (where I remained, for 14 years, through 12th grade), I felt constantly challenged to keep up with the bigger boys – including, for example, F. James Sensenbrenner, Jr. (later a congressman and a very smart but politically conservative cookie), who showed up in kindergarten already knowing how to read. By contrast, as already mentioned in Chapter 1, reading always gave me great difficulty. I started out by struggling along in first and second grade – partly because, every time I picked up a book, I got a headache. The local ophthalmological geniuses figured out that this malady resulted from my inability to look cross-eyed and prescribed a regimen that required me to spend quality time zeroing in on the end of my toothbrush in order to train my eyes to converge. I finally learned to force my eyes to pivot inward, but I still retain a bit of residual exotropia, which greatly aids my skills at free-viewing the left-right 3-D images of a stereo pair, thereby facilitating my later obsession with stereoscopy (Holbrook, 1997b, 1997g, 1997h, 1997i, 1998a, 1998d, 1998e, 1998f, 1998g, 1999b, 1999f). Despite the toothbrush regimen, such difficulties with reading continued throughout my life and resulted in my becoming one of the world's slowest readers. In high school, they tested us constantly, and – though I performed OK on comprehension – I clocked in at about the 15th percentile when it came to speed. I took speed-reading classes (a la Evelyn Woods), but they didn't help at all. (Indeed, I regard them as something of a scam: Glance at the page and guess what was on it.) Later – as an English major required to read one or two 700-page Victorian novels per week – this handicap blighted my college years. And – to this day, when I read any sort of manuscript, article, or book – I involuntarily take the time to inspect every letter in every word; every word in every sentence; and every comma, semicolon, period, or apostrophe in every paragraph. This does wonders for my usefulness as a proofreader, but it drags my ability to absorb new material to a near standstill.

Not coincidentally, at an early age, my mother liked to read me children's books such as *Make Way for Ducklings*, *Babar*, *Bambi*, *Curious George*, *Little Toot*, and especially *The Little Engine That Could*, all about that annoyingly self-righteous ever-so-small train engine with the Big Mantra: "I think I can, I think I can, ... I thought I could, I thought I could." This slogan – so disturbingly preachy – embodied my mom's (unfounded) belief that no task exceeded her son's capabilities. If I complained that something seemed too difficult, she sweetly and cheerfully reminded me that "nothing worthwhile is ever easy." From this, by simple logic, it follows that nothing easy is ever worthwhile. But, worse, I also foolishly but predictably inferred the implicit-but-incorrect faux-corollary that "anything difficult must have merit." This dangerously invalid superstition guided many bad decisions that I made later in life – for example, my fruitless efforts (as a young boy) to play the trumpet when I had a mouthful of braces on my teeth; my sadomasochistic tendency (as a young man) to do viciously vigorous calisthenics past the point of reason; my ill-conceived attempts (as a doctoral candidate) to study difference equations; my vacation-ruining struggle (early in my career) to teach myself Fortran during the Xmas holidays; or my thankless endeavor (more recently) to comprehend an altogether impenetrable book by Jacques Lacan. If only I had realized and remembered that some difficult things are not necessarily worthwhile . . .. But . . . live and learn.

Thus challenged, I limped along through grade school and high school at Milwaukee Country Day – always facing the conflicting pressures of a reading disability pitted against the familial demands for academic success. Toward the end of my high school years, they tested us for aptitudes and skills in some sort of IQ-related format and then paraded their lack of good judgment by discussing with us our performances in detail. Specifically, they showed me an across-students scatter diagram of ability on the horizontal axis plotted against achievement on the vertical axis, and I found myself – putting it politely – to be something of an extreme over-achiever. In short, I was doing pretty well – but only because I was performing way better than would be expected, based on my modest ability. This pattern continued in college, where – as an English major – I became something of an expert on "close" (meaning, I'm sorry to say, very slow) reading (Holbrook, 1998b). (As shown in Chapter 1, I mentioned these dyslexic difficulties so poignantly and pathetically in my self-description for the 50th-anniversary college-reunion report that I received a sympathy letter from a classmate I had not heard from in five decades.)

During these childhood and teenage years, I made some wonderful life-long friends in the neighborhood (Harry Banzhaf, Steve Owen) and at school (Johnny Fuller, Peter Straub, Stew Sims). Over time, they have helped to preserve my ties to Milwaukee. Steve passed away a few years ago after a career as a flight instructor at the University of Illinois. Pete became a best-selling writer of horror stories and moved to a brownstone not far from us in New York City before eventually decamping to Brooklyn, where he recently died after a long illness. But we still see Harry (a highly respected retired investment counselor), Johnny (now Jake, a talented filmmaker), and Stew (who eventually masterminded the marketing of Rubik's Cube and Furby). Both Jake and Pete were voracious readers – capable of polishing off a thick novel in an afternoon and thereby highlighting, by counterexample, my own limitations along those lines.

Maybe all this partially explains why – fleeing from the printed page – I especially enjoyed courses in subjects like physics and math. Indeed, in high school, I learned some skills in algebra, geometry, trigonometry, and calculus that came in very handy later in my career when – with a lot of help from my more mathematically sophisticated colleagues – I started delving into multidimensional scaling and related techniques (e.g., Holbrook and Holloway, 1984; Holbrook and Huber, 1979b, 1983; Holbrook and Moore, 1982; Holbrook, Moore, and Winer, 1982). But – in the meantime – I played around with some family-endorsed diversions such as (1) sports and (2) music. The former proved to be a disaster, the latter a blessing.

1   As for sports, I've never been much of an athlete. Also, I took way too much pleasure in eating Teenie's excellent Southern cooking – fried chicken, vegetables swimming in butter, hot biscuits, grits, Apple Brown Betty, and all the rest – so that, by my senior year, I had put 190 pounds of flab onto a 5-foot-9.5-inch frame. Simply stated, I was fat. And, when I waddled out onto the football field, I had every reason to expect and did indeed consistently receive a merciless beating. I tried to quit the team. But, as mentioned earlier in Chapter 1, my father (who, as a physician, really should have known better) insisted that – after years of patiently waiting on the bench as the team doctor – he needed to see his son disporting himself out there on the gridiron. So – out of ill-advised filial respect – I subjected myself to that particular torture. And, no, it did not build my "character." It just made me miserable (Holbrook, 1989b).

2   My misery was amplified by the fact that I had developed a real devotion to music in general and to playing jazz piano in particular (an avocation that did not benefit from having opposing football players step on my frozen and exposed fingers when we routinely scrimmaged in several inches of Wisconsin snow). Musically, I started out at about age six with some traditional instruction in classical piano from a teacher who – though a kind person and a family friend – had no clue how to make her lessons amount to anything more than enervating drudgery. I found her assignments so frustrating that I literally bit the front lip of our Steinway's keyboard cover in my childish rage. (When my parents later moved from our house into a smaller apartment and sent the piano to us in New York City, it still bore the teeth marks that I had put there as a young boy. The expert technician who reconditioned this magnificent instrument years afterward found the scars that I had intentionally inflicted quite unusual and rather distressing.) So, after three or four years of unhappy and unsuccessful pianistic tutelage, my parents finally found for me a magnificent teacher – a local jazz pianist named Tommy Sheridan, who, as detailed in Chapter 10, embodied everything that is joyous in music and who, more importantly, knew how to convey this to his adoring students, including yours truly. With the greatest of enthusiasm, generosity, and kindness, Tommy taught me about jazz, the piano, the great songs, the master musicians, and other aspects of life in general. And, one day when I was about 15, his teachings were amplified

by a moment of epiphany in which, while I lay on the love seat in our living room and listened to the Modern Jazz Quartet's album called *Fontessa*, I suddenly found that the music – with all its flatted and augmented ninths, sharped elevenths, tritone substitutions, side-slipping, and other harmonic intricacies – made perfect sense. All at once – at the level of actual hearing instead of mere listening – I understood what Bird, Dizzy, Miles, Horace Silver, Chet Baker, Art Pepper, Paul Desmond, Oscar Peterson, Hampton Hawes, Bill Evans, and all the rest were doing. The scales had fallen from my eyes or the wax from my ears or whatever – mostly thanks to the training that Tommy had given me plus the serendipitous moment of Milt Jackson's solo on "Over the Rainbow" (currently available on YouTube.Com and, for my money, perhaps the greatest jazz solo ever recorded). Recently, I have (again) celebrated Tommy's pedagogical gifts in what I hope is something remotely approaching the tribute he deserves (Holbrook, 2016; please see Chapter 10 in what follows).

During these years, we formed a group called the Baywood Jazz Quartet (me from Shorewood on piano plus, from Whitefish Bay, Howard Schudson on guitar, Ken Schoeninger on bass, and Stu Langer on drums), which played for local parties and dances. Working with this combo in my mid-teens was the closest I ever came to being a professional musician. But we made barely enough money to buy ourselves corned beef sandwiches at Joe Plotkin's Deli after the gig. Howard (later aka Hod David) has passed away. Ken has disappeared, and – despite my most energetic Internet searches – I can't find him. But, via email, I remained in touch with Stu (who had also changed his name to David) until, so sadly, he too passed away after an immensely courageous battle with a long illness.

Peter Straub – who, beyond his literary skills, doubled as the world's greatest jazz fan – alerted me to musicians I needed to hear and accompanied me to concerts by any number of our favorite jazz artists: Dizzy Gillespie's Quintet with Junior Mance; Max Roach with Stanley and Tommy Turrentine; Dave Brubeck with Paul Desmond; the Modern Jazz Quartet with Milt Jackson; the Jazztet with Art Famer and Benny Golson; J. J. Johnson's Quintet with Freddie Hubbard, Clifford Jordan, and Cedar Walton; Cannonball Adderley's Quintet with Brother Nat; Shelly Manne's Group with Russ Freeman; the Duke Ellington Orchestra; Lionel Hampton's Big Band; Erroll Garner; Andre Previn's Trio; Gerry Mulligan's Quartet with Art Farmer; Ella Fitzgerald; Oscar Peterson's Trio with Ray Brown, Herb Ellis, and later Ed Thigpen; Lambert, Hendricks, and Ross. (Recently, when reading a collection of Pete's stories, I was honored to see my name mentioned in the acknowledgments along with many of these jazz greats. Pete was a true soulmate. I miss him so much!)

And Tommy's instruction prepared me at age 16 for a couple of weeks at the celebrated Lenox School of Jazz (run by John Lewis, other members of the Modern Jazz Quartet, Gunther Schuller, and such jazz luminaries of the time as J. J. Johnson, George Russell, and Herb Pomeroy). While at Lenox, I endured a fateful day when Lewis and Schuller decided to run an audition

for the piano players and told us to perform (1) a solo piece, (2) a trio rendition with jazz icon Percy Heath on bass, and (3) an accompaniment with
the rhythm section for tenor saxophonist J. R. Monterose. I did OK (for a
young teenager) on (2) "Blue Monk" and (3) "All the Things You Are," but
my performance on (1) turned out to be so disastrous – a rampant case of
stage fright screwing up my carefully prepared but badly botched climax to
"Someone to Watch Over Me" – that Lewis and Schuller solemnly advised
me against any hope I might have entertained of becoming a jazz professional. They were right, of course. Even jazz masters like J. J. Johnson (with
a sextet that, as mentioned earlier, included additional mega-stars) could not
make a go of it and, in his case, fled to the Hollywood studios to write film
scores. But, at the time, my comparative incompetence as a jazz musician
proved to be a bitter pill to swallow, and I returned to Milwaukee with a
damaged ego that received no bolstering from my next and final football
season. And, yes, I still have nightmares about football and about performing
Gershwin tunes in public. When, in 2015, our beloved son Chris requested
that I play "Someone to Watch Over Me" at his wedding in Strasbourg, it
took every ounce of courage I could muster to attempt to conquer my former
musical nemesis. This time, thank heavens, I did not screw it up – perhaps, in
part, because neither John Lewis nor Gunther Schuller was there to observe
but not to admire or, more likely, because God Himself was indeed watching
over me.

After slinking back to Country Day with my dreams of becoming the next
great jazz pianist shattered and a whole new football season to dread, I faced
the challenge of applying to colleges. Fresh from his triumph in mastermind-
ing my misbegotten football career, my father – with a little help from *his*
father, who never let anyone forget that he had attended Harvard College,
where he had studied under William James – applied all the pressure he could
muster to point me toward what had become recognized, if only by these
two erudite gentlemen, as a family tradition. (My mother's kin folks had
attended Princeton, but she remained discreetly silent on this topic.) With
mediocre SAT scores (probably due in part to my reading disabilities) but
with good grades plus a few symptoms of well-roundedness (jazz pianist,
football survivor, outrageously opinionated newspaper editor, enthusiastic
deb-party attendee) and with plenty of help from my family's school-related
connections (carefully nurtured over many decades of schmoozing), I managed to get accepted at my dad's alma mater (something I never could have
accomplished in today's much more competitive college-admissions climate).

So I entered Harvard College as a gridiron reject with an unrequited
avocation for music and a masochistic proclivity toward concentrating on
English literature. Though I had attained some success as an empirically
demonstrable over-achiever in high school, I now found myself even more
dauntingly over-matched in my new educational environment. If I ranked in
the 15th percentile in speed-of-reading among the general population, I probably ranked in the 1st percentile in the Ivy League. Or lower. Put simply,

everybody I encountered in Cambridge showed signs of being smarter, better prepared, more confident, and – especially – faster than yours truly. I managed to take quite a few courses in English literature and a couple of classes in music. Both were areas of study that I loved. But – in both cases – I found that the academic process at a prestigious institution robbed from them all semblance of the joy that I had hoped to find there. If the academic experience had destroyed something that I loved, I concluded that I would be better advised to direct my further studies toward something that could not be thus damaged because I already hated it – namely, business. Thus, as graduation approached, I applied to the MBA programs at Harvard, Columbia, and one or two "safety schools."

By this time, I had met my dearest bride-to-be – Sally Loring Milton, my true love, with whom I have recently celebrated our 58th wedding anniversary – and we had arranged to be married in Charlottesville, Virginia, at the UVA Chapel on August 14, 1965. Sally had already spent one year in the two-year master-degree program in social work at Columbia University. So we made a deal that, if I got accepted at the Harvard Business School, she would move to Boston but that, if I did not get into HBS but did get into Columbia, I would come to New York. So, as already lamented in Chapter 1,

Figure 2.5 Wedding of Morris and Sally, Charlottesville, 14 August 1965

guess who got rejected by the Harvard Business School (HBS) – with what struck me as a rather insensitive letter advising me that, due to my lack of real-world experience, I would be well-advised to spend some time in the army (this in 1965 at the height of the Vietnam build-up). I have never forgiven HBS – not because they rejected me (which probably made sense) but because they thought that I would make a good soldier (which did not). (Truth be told, I consider myself a pacifist and cheerfully admit to being a total coward when it comes to waging war.)

Honoring my commitment to Sally, I entered Columbia's MBA program in the fall of 1965. We needed a place to live, so – from the Columbia campus – we started walking north on Claremont Avenue past Barnard College, Union Theological Seminary, and the Juilliard School of Music. The first apartment building we passed on our side of the street presented a sign in the window that read "Apartment for Rent." So we went inside and leased a one-bedroom flat for $145 per month – forgoing a much more luxurious space with a gorgeous view of Grant's Tomb because, at $175, it seemed way too expensive. Suffice it to say that this sort of availability and pricing schedule has long since disappeared in the face of New York City's real-estate free-for-all.

In our new home, I applied myself to the study of business, while Sally continued her progress toward the MS degree in social work (later followed by extensive psychoanalytic training, a PhD in Clinical Counseling from NYU, and a long career as a psychotherapist). Actually – after English at Harvard – Columbia's MBA classes seemed easier than what I had experienced in Cambridge. I especially enjoyed my introductory course in marketing strategy (with Professor Al Oxenfeldt), marketing research (with Professor Abe Shuchman), and product management (with Professor Charles Ramond, then editor of the *Journal of Advertising Research*). But, most of all (as detailed in Chapter 10), I loved a course I took from John Howard in buyer behavior. This educational opportunity coincided with the fervent period of scholarly activity in which John and his protégé Jagdish Sheth worked on the book that would soon appear as *The Theory of Buyer Behavior*. Every day, John would appear in class carrying a mountain of mimeographed chapters, which he would distribute to the class members in anticipation of our questions and comments. The atmosphere around that course sizzled with intellectual excitement, and I found myself drawn into the world of buyer-behavior research with an irresistible attraction that shaped the remainder of my academic career.

Beyond his activities as an impassioned scholar and a fascinating teacher, John graciously assumed a role as my mentor – shepherding me through my buyer-related MBA studies, giving me a couple of much-needed summer jobs, and helping toward my acceptance into Columbia's PhD program in marketing, where I appreciatively studied the Howard-Sheth Theory under the men who had created it. I took my time – spending eight years as a doctoral student – partly because (as previously noted) I am very slow and partly because (as already hinted) I wanted to keep my draft board happy so as to retain my 2-S deferment (firmly believing that the Vietnam War was an atrocity in which, pacifist and coward that I am, I did not wish to participate). (Not surprisingly, given his resistance to the draft and to what many of us considered an unjust war, Muhammad Ali became another of my most-admired heroes – all the more when he returned from exile in 1974 to regain his championship title at the "Rumble in the Jungle" by defeating the formidable George Foreman, who later called him "the greatest man I've ever known.") So my progress in the PhD program was (as usual) painfully slow, stalled by self-doubts and fears of failure. After enduring countless sessions in which I bemoaned my own compulsively sloth-like movement through my doctoral studies – my psychoanalyst finally and quite justifiably issued the exasperated ultimatum in her learned Freudian vocabulary that I should "shit or get off the pot."

When I finally completed the doctoral program – ten years after starting as an MBA candidate – I had no job prospects in sight. Being superstitious and more than a little compulsive, I had vowed not to interview for possible positions until after receiving my degree. So I found myself at the end of December 1974 with a PhD degree but no job. By that time, we had a five-year-old child – Son Chris – so the situation seemed a bit dire, financially speaking. Once again, in the nick of time, John Howard came to my rescue. Subsequently, I have surmised that Columbia probably got turned down in the job offers they made that year. And so – right around Xmas 1974 (no doubt desperate to find a potential recruit) – John called me to ask if I would like to take a faculty position at Columbia, starting in January 1975. Relieved in the extreme, I did not bargain about salary, perks, course assignments, secretarial help, office furniture, parking spaces, or anything else. I just trusted John (one of my wiser instincts) and said, "Yes, please." At the time, I did not realize that hiring their own recent graduates was something that Columbia and other top-tier schools never did. Over the years, I learned that some of my future colleagues had deemed this a terrible idea and had voiced their opinions quite vociferously, but John and a few others stood by me (keeping anonymous but earning my everlasting gratitude). And at Columbia I remained – with the gracious help of John and other kind-hearted supporters – for the next 35 years. More recently, with immense appreciation, I have taken the opportunity to praise John's intellectual creativity, to acknowledge his supportive guidance, and to pay tribute to his generosity as a teacher, colleague, and friend (Holbrook, 1984c, 1989c, 1998c, 2001f, 2016; Holbrook, Lehmann, and Schmitt, 2016; please see Chapter 10 on "What Makes a Great Teacher?").

One of the reasons given for not hiring your own graduates hinges on the fear of intellectual incest in which a newly graduated hire might simply reproduce the teachings, opinions, interests, or attitudes of his or her former instructors. I confess that, in my first few published papers, I succumbed to just this sort of academic inbreeding. For example, after suitable

Figure 2.6 Sally and Baby Chris, New York City, 1969

revisions guided by the patient staff at *JMR*, I managed to publish a piece from my dissertation on advertising effects (Holbrook, 1975b) entitled "Beyond Attitude Structure: Toward the Informational Determinants of Attitude" (Holbrook, 1978a). In accord with the Howard-Sheth Model – based on the tenets of rational economic choice and a view of the buyer as an information-processing decision maker – this empirical study assumed that facts-oriented messages would be more powerful than feelings-oriented ads in building favorable affective responses toward a fictitious make of automobile (the Vendome, produced by Voisin Motors). This study incorporated what I believe to have been one of the first path analyses found in the marketing literature, and I feel a bit of pride that an old English major managed to make that kind of methodological leap. But, nonetheless, the conceptual basis for the paper – namely, the decision-oriented view – clung dangerously close to the information-acquisition framework that had inspired the Howard-Sheth formulation (based on a sequence of events from Information to Cognition to Affect to Behavior to Satisfaction or what I later called the ICABS Model). Other advertising-related work – stemming from my dissertation – included a fairly massive review of advertising research for the Federal Trade Commission (Holbrook, 1973a), a comparison of ad-effects measures (Holbrook,

1976), arguments for the use of content analysis in explaining message effects (Holbrook, 1977b), and a test of competing approaches to predicting Starch readership scores (Holbrook and Lehmann, 1980).

At that time, my greatest "strength" (the flip side of my slow-reading pro-clivities) came from my rather obsessive-compulsive penchant for reviewing and synthesizing the work of others, as in the case of the aforementioned FTC study on advertising research (Holbrook, 1973a). My mentor John Howard gave me opportunities to apply these tendencies in the direction of synthesizing a group of empirical studies based on the Howard-Sheth The-ory (Holbrook, 1974) and reviewing the then-extant literature on consumer behavior toward frequently purchased nondurables (Holbrook and Howard, 1977). The latter collaboration led us to a conference on "Aspects of Con-sumer Behavior" in Lake Geneva, Wisconsin – sponsored by the National Science Foundation and chaired by Bob Ferber – offering my first chance to meet many of the reigning stars in the academic community of multidiscipli-nary marketing-relevant researchers (Frank Bass, Harry Davis, Dave Gard-ner, Don Granbois, Flemming Hansen, Jack Jacoby, Kelvin Lancaster, Bill McGuire, Franco Nicosia, Everett Rogers, Subrata Sen, Bill Wells, and Jerry Wind, among many others). I think I was the youngest participant (as usual), so it felt like a huge honor to be included. As part of my chapter with John (Holbrook and Howard, 1977) and to update Copeland's famous classifica-tion of goods – Convenience Goods (low effort, low brand insistence), Shop-ping Goods (high effort, low brand insistence), and Specialty Goods (high effort, high brand insistence) – I invented a new fourth category of Preference Goods (low effort, high brand insistence). Much to my delight, Jerry Wind later included it in his textbook on *Product Policy*.

Also, while still related to my dissertation, my work strayed somewhat far-ther afield by pursuing another aspect of my doctoral research that – true to my egocentric preoccupation with reading disabilities – dealt with perceptual accuracy in the recognition of typographical errors. Specifically – drawing on Jerome Bruner's view of perception as a process of confirming hypotheses based on expectations – I produced a series of five studies tending to show by means of laboratory experiments that (1) visual dissimilarity (Holbrook, 1973b, 1975a, 1978b) and (2) verbal uncertainty due to complicated syn-tax (Holbrook, 1978c, 1979) tended to enhance one's ability to spot errors in the form of letter substitutions in a proofreading task. Obviously, such effects – though loosely linked to various arcane aspects of the Howard-Sheth framework – ranged fairly far from the conventional preoccupations of mar-keting scholars. Later, I discovered that – by pure coincidence and at about the same time – my colleague, friend, and close collaborator Robert Schindler had pursued a similar stream of research on letter recognition, putting the two of us (ironically, both now marketing academics) among the very few researchers who have ever cared deeply about these aspects of typographical perception. At any rate, I doubt that I would have developed this interest had it not been for my aforementioned reading-related handicaps. (To check on how you would perform in detecting typos, confirm whether you noticed the substitution of "becn" for "been" in the previous sentence. You probably didn't, which is why you can read faster than I can.)

Meanwhile, as my first teaching assignment at Columbia's Graduate School of Business (while still a PhD candidate), I had taught a course in sales management, and I continued to teach this course during my first years as a newly hired assistant professor. This pedagogical opportunity flew in the face of my total lack of experience as a salesman or sales manager – the closest I had approached those endeavors having occurred during the summer after my senior year in high school, spent on a Coca-Cola truck, giving away free samples of Coke to always-suspicious housewives (who kept asking me, "What's the catch?") on Milwaukee's West Side. These sales-related teaching responsibilities inspired me to develop a curiosity about interpersonal communication or what, more colloquially, we would call "salesmanship." So, during these early years, I worked on several papers with my colleagues Noel Capon, Mac Hulbert, John O'Shaughnessy, and Mike Ryan on various behavioral aspects of industrial purchasing in general and the personal selling process in particular (Capon, Holbrook, and Hulbert, 1972a, 1972b, 1977; Holbrook, Hulbert, and Ryan, 1978; Holbrook and O'Shaughnessy, 1976; Ryan, Holbrook, and Hulbert, 1978). Some of the work with Mike Ryan – generously sponsored by the National Association of Fleet Administrators or NAFA – involved lease-or-buy decisions in the management of automotive fleets (Holbrook and Ryan, 1982; Ryan and Holbrook, 1982a) – a topic that I pursued in deference both to the tastes of my senior faculty advisors and to my delight in working with a compatriot spirit such as Mike but that I found less than exciting from an intellectual point of view (lease-or-buy being a classic problem in introductory finance that I thought I had finished with in one of my lower-level MBA courses). These NAFA-related inquiries also produced the only bona fide full-length case I have ever participated in writing – to me, a futile exercise that I do **not** consider a feather in my cap (Farley, Holbrook, Hulbert, Lewis, and Ryan, 1975).

To escape from these doldrums, I began to honor calls by gurus like Phil Kotler and Sid Levy (1969) for a "broadening" of the marketing concept to include topics of inquiry related to such areas as the arts and entertainment. In this spirit, one of my first big breakthroughs involved measurement issues relating to a conventional multiattribute attitude model applied to the case of jazz singers (Holbrook, 1977a). When I mentioned to my psychoanalyst that I enjoyed this music-related research so much more than that addressing the dubiously significant problems of fleet managers, she broke her resolute Freudian silence just long enough to ask, "Well, then, why don't you do more work on the arts and entertainment?" This is why we spend countless hours and huge sums of money lying on the couch and talking about our petty selves, our picayune foibles, and our paltry problems for endless years of psychoanalysis. Put differently, hers was a passing comment that changed my life. Following her cue, I began to devote more and more of my attention to addressing marketing- and consumer-oriented issues related to music, movies, plays, books, poems, paintings, photography, sculptures, TV shows, sports, and other branches of the arts and entertainment.

When I first started on this new trajectory, I retained a firm commitment to the traditional decision-oriented choice models that I had absorbed from Howard, Sheth, and all those Fishbein- and Rosenberg-type multiattribute modelers plus the methodological refinements in multidimensional scaling and conjoint analysis introduced by folks like Paul Green, Jerry Wind, Vithala Rao, and their many psychometrician friends. Hence, we applied multidimensional scaling (MDS) to the case of jazz singers (Holbrook and Moore, 1980; Holbrook and Williams, 1978), jazz instrumentalists (Holbrook and Dixon, 1985), sweater designs (Holbrook, 1983a); radio stations (Holbrook, 1984b), and a broad spectrum of product categories (Holbrook, Lehmann, and O'Shaughnessy, 1986). Working with people like Joel Huber (PhD from Wharton), Bill Moore (Purdue), Russ Winer (Carnegie), Don Lehmann (Purdue), and Wayne DeSarbo (Wharton) – all of whom were far better trained than I in the various multidimensional scaling procedures and multivariate statistical methods – we used MDS to represent the preferences of radio listeners toward jazz musicians (Holbrook and Holloway, 1984; Holbrook and Huber, 1979b) and to map the market for jazz artists (Holbrook, 1982a). We compared principal components and discriminant analyses as approaches to building spatial representations of responses toward jazz performances (Huber and Holbrook, 1979, 1980). We built models of complementarity among leisure activities as uses of discretionary time (Holbrook, 1980a; Holbrook and Lehmann, 1981). We used conjoint analysis to compare visual versus verbal representations of product designs (Holbrook and Moore, 1981) and found a way to create market spaces with the help of canonical correlation (Holbrook and Moore, 1982). We applied pick-any procedures to the construction of preference maps for radio stations (Holbrook, Moore, and Winer, 1982) and for various breeds of dogs (Holbrook and Moore, 1984). We studied the biasing effects of affective overtones in the perception of saxophone solos (Holbrook and Huber, 1979a) and measured perceptual veridicality in the appreciation of saxophonists (Holbrook and Huber, 1983, 1994). Under the leadership of Wayne DeSarbo, we used a stochastic three-way unfolding model to represent the underlying dimensions of emotional descriptors related to various consumption experiences (DeSarbo, Lehmann, Holbrook, Havlena, and Gupta, 1987). And, with the help of Stephen Bertges (a classically trained concert pianist), we studied audience responses to the manipulation of stylistic features in piano performances of a piece from the *English Suites* by J. S. Bach (Holbrook and Bertges, 1981) with implications for a features-perceptions-affect model of evaluative judgments (Holbrook, 1981a) and relevance to the measurement of perceptual distortions due to halo effects (Holbrook, 1983c).

All such studies extended the typical marketing focus to embrace aspects of the arts and entertainment but continued to rely on traditional views of consumer choices as multiattribute purchase decisions modeled by conventional techniques of multidimensional scaling and multivariate statistics. Then, on one magical day in about 1979 or 1980, I met Beth Hirschman at a conference of the Association for Consumer Research (ACR). When I first saw Beth, as described further in Chapter 4, I found her in the midst of a presentation in which she was blithely and almost gleefully deconstructing our aforementioned article on "Separating Perceptual Dimensions from Affective Overtones" (Holbrook and Huber, 1979a). After the session, probably to her surprise, I went up and introduced myself. And, to her even greater amazement, I congratulated her on a very fine job of tearing our paper to shreds. We chatted, and I learned that Beth, who had recently moved her affiliation from Pittsburgh to New York University, lived two doors south of us on Riverside Drive. We decided to do some work together. And, from that, we evolved a productive partnership and lifelong friendship.

To this collaboration, Beth brought a sparkling intelligence and a stream of endlessly brilliant insights toward critiquing the inadequacies of the traditional decision-oriented information-processing choice models that I had been pursuing. Together, based on such subversive apostasies, we created an article about hedonic consumption first-authored by Beth (Hirschman and Holbrook, 1982) and a piece on the experiential aspects of consumption first-authored by yours truly (Holbrook and Hirschman, 1982). By extending the conventional ICABS formulation and expanding my own focus to include various aspects of "Fantasies, Feelings, and Fun," these two papers set my research agenda for years to come.

There followed a stream of articles and chapters dealing with concepts related to the consumption experience (Hirschman and Holbrook, 1986; Holbrook, 1987d, 1987e, 2008b; Holbrook, O'Shaughnessy, and Bell, 1990). Working with Columbia colleagues, I embarked on a series of empirical studies examining various aspects of experiential consumption. We investigated the role of emotions in the enjoyment of video games (Holbrook, Chestnut, Oliva, and Greenleaf, 1984). We compared methods for measuring the varieties of consumption experiences (Havlena and Holbrook, 1986; Havlena, Holbrook, and Lehmann, 1989). We developed ways to measure emotional responses to advertising (Batra and Holbrook, 1990; Holbrook, 1986c; Holbrook and Batra, 1987, 1988; Holbrook and O'Shaughnessy, 1984; Holbrook and Westwood, 1989). And we showed how emotions affect the zipping and zapping of TV commercials (Olney, Batra, and Holbrook, 1990; Olney, Holbrook, and Batra, 1991).

Along related lines – working with Bob Zirlin (a real PhD in Philosophy from Johns Hopkins) – I began to explore various conceptual and empirical aspects of consumption-based aesthetics (Holbrook and Zirlin, 1985) or what earlier we had called "Consumer Esthetics" (Holbrook, 1980b, 1981b, 1983b, 1987e). Toward this end – true to form – we continued to apply conventional measurement and scaling methodologies to issues involving the aesthetic responses of consumers to different versions of a pop song (Holbrook,

Moore, Dodgen, and Havlena, 1985), to art prints (Holbrook, Greenleaf, and Schindler, 1986; Schindler, Holbrook, and Greenleaf, 1989), and to other visual displays (Holbrook, 1982b, 1983b, 1986a). Punam Anand and I studied perceptual and affective responses to gradations of tempo in a pop song (Holbrook and Anand, 1990, 1992). Meryl Gardner and I examined the role of emotions in determining the length of time that people listen to a piece of music (Holbrook and Gardner, 1993, 1998) as well as how music-shaped moods get updated over time (Holbrook and Gardner, 2000). With Punam Anand and Debra Stephens, we explored the differences between left- and right-brained responses to musical versus verbal listening experiences (Anand and Holbrook, 1990b; Anand, Holbrook, and Stephens, 1988). And – turning to large publicly available data sets, with plenty of help from some unusually dedicated MBA students, who did heroic amounts of data entry and analysis – we investigated the impact of Oscar Awards on movie revenues (Dodds and Holbrook, 1988); the financial returns from including various actors and actresses in a film (Wallace, Seigerman, and Holbrook, 1993); the connections between popular appeal and expert critical judgments of films (Holbrook, 1999d); and – later, with my Italian colleague Michela Addis – the role of evaluations by ordinary consumers in mediating between expert judgments and popularity (Holbrook and Addis, 2007), as well as the different aspects of success related to artistic excellence versus commercial appeal in the motion-picture industry (Holbrook and Addis, 2008). All these studies entailed quantitative and/or experimental methods – that is, traditional neo-positivistic approaches – to investigating aspects of consumers' emotional and aesthetic responses to works of art and entertainment.

But then I met Mark Grayson – a brilliant Harvard graduate with a concentration in English and one of the finest students ever to occupy a seat in one of my MBA classes. Mark came to me one day to voice his desire to do an independent-study project on films. I reacted with enthusiasm and launched into suggestions about how we could collect a huge data set and massage it to a quantitative fare-thee-well. But Mark demurred, saying that what he had in mind involved a more interpretive approach – something akin to what we had both practiced in our English classes at Harvard (albeit, I don't doubt, with what was greater rapidity for him than for me). So I agreed, and pretty soon we chose the movie *Out of Africa* (1985) as a suitable vehicle for applying our semiological approach. This approach involved an analysis of marketing-related imagery and consumption symbolism toward the goal of gaining insights into the meanings of the film. We submitted our paper to the *Journal of Consumer Research* (*JCR*) and – despite its radical departure from the conventional methods of the day, with some gracious reviewing-and-editing help from John Sherry, Jerry Kernan, and Hal Kassarjian – managed to publish it in that outlet (Holbrook and Grayson, 1986; see also Holbrook, 1988d). There followed a series of papers in which I applied semiological approaches (Holbrook, 1987g, 1987h) to the interpretation of movies, plays, and other manifestations of popular culture – for example, the film *Gremlins* (Holbrook, 1988a), the Tina Howe play *Painting Churches* (Holbrook, 1988b), Tina Howe's *Coastal Disturbances* (Holbrook, Bell, and Grayson, 1989), the motion picture *Two For the Road* (Holbrook, 1989d), and the film *Mr. Holland's Opus* (Holbrook, 1998h). I also dabbled in the interpretation of various television productions such as the portrayal by Anne Bancroft of the shopping-related angst experienced by *Mrs. Cage* (Holbrook, 1996a) and – at considerably greater length – the hegemonic capitalism-reinforcing ethos embodied by such television game shows as *The Price Is Right* (Holbrook, 1993c, 2001b). And, intruding where even angels fear to tread, I braved the waters of literary criticism – pursuing a number of examples connected with Romanticism from Homer to James Joyce (Holbrook, 1991b). Ultimately – with Beth Hirschman (who had also embarked upon a series of interpretive studies directed toward understanding the marketing- and consumer-related aspects of popular culture – we collected many of these interpretive semiological pieces in a book entitled *The Semiotics of Consumption: Interpreting Symbolic Consumer Behavior in Popular Culture and Works of Art* (Holbrook and Hirschman, 1993). Beth and I did differ a bit in our orientations. She showed a primary interest, I believe, in examining how the semiotics of consumption symbolism could shed light on marketing-related phenomena. By contrast, I followed a Kennedy-like mantra that I sometimes paraphrased as "Ask not what semiotics can do for marketing but, rather, ask what marketing can do for semiotics." In other words, I cared mostly about how marketing imagery and consumption symbolism could elucidate the meanings of artistic offerings such as films, plays, novels, and so forth. Later (Holbrook, 2003a), I applied a similar logic to interpreting the role of jazz as film music in motion pictures such as *Sweet Smell of Success* (Holbrook, 2004a); *High Society* (Holbrook, 2005a); *The Fabulous Baker Boys* and *The Talented Mr. Ripley* (Holbrook, 2005f); *Young Man with a Horn, Paris Blues*, and *Mo' Better Blues* (Holbrook, 2005b, 2006e); *Heart Beat, The Score*, and *New York, New York* (Holbrook, 2007a); *Lady Sings the Blues, 'Round Midnight*, and *Bird* (Holbrook, 2007i); *Pete Kelly's Blues, The Cotton Club*, and *Kansas City* (Holbrook, 2008c); and *The Fabulous Dorseys, The Glenn Miller Story, The Benny Goodman Story, The Five Pennies* (based on the life of cornetist Red Nichols), and *The Gene Krupa Story* (Holbrook, 2009a). Ultimately, I revised and collected these interpretations in a book about jazz in films entitled *Music, Movies, Meanings, and Markets: Cinemajazzamatazz* (Holbrook, 2011).

The "ask not" mantra just mentioned embodied my inveterate preference for "pure" research directed toward the study of consumer behavior and marketing phenomena as a quest pursued for its own sake as an end in itself as opposed to "applied" research aimed at serving some useful purpose in the service of business managers. Over the years, this personal bias (shared by several editors of *JCR*, especially Hal Kassarjian) brought me into debates with people like Jack Jacoby on the merits of consulting as a dubious boon to scholarship (Holbrook, 1985; see also Holbrook, 1984a); on my tendency to label practitioner-oriented research as "banausic" (Holbrook, 1987f); on concerns raised, dangers recognized, and insights illuminated by my participation in the AMA Task Force on the Development of Marketing Thought (AMA Task Force, 1988; Holbrook, 1993b); and – most especially, harkening back to my identification with Morris the Cat – on the contrast between the more canine (master serving) and feline (curiosity satisfying) orientations to marketing or consumer research, positioned as "Dogmatism and Catastrophe in the Development of Marketing Thought" (Holbrook, 1989a, 1990a).

Similar to my advocacy of pure research as a cat-like endeavor aimed at satisfying one's curiosity via the pursuit of knowledge valued for its own sake, I also developed various highly opinionated views – some of them empirically supported – on what I deem an undesirable intrusion of business interests into the world of academia (Holbrook, 1985, 1993b, 2015b); on confusions between the objectives of applied marketing research versus scholarly consumer research (Holbrook, 1986e, 1986f, 1987j); on the ingratitude of (some) MBA students, as exhibited in the *Business Week* polls (Holbrook, 1993d, 2004c); on distortions embodied by the business-school rankings found in *U.S. News & World Report* (Holbrook, 2007d); on misapplications of the customer orientation to business education (Holbrook, 1995f, 1995g, 1998h; Holbrook and Day, 1994); on regrets over the decline of the scholarly community in academia due in part to an adoption by the universities of a business model that embraces a customer-oriented career-directed practitioner-targeted capitalism-dedicated subservience to an implicit but hegemonic trade-school mentality (Holbrook, 2004b; Holbrook and Hulbert, 2002b); on the misdirection of marketing education away from issues of relevance to social responsibility (Holbrook, 1995f, 2005d); on the misbegotten acceptance by the university of an ethos that Eisenhower presciently labeled the "military-industrial complex" (Holbrook, 2009d); and on the insidious abnegation of one's scholarly duty to pursue the truth at the expense of falsehoods that serve selfish interests such as those rampant in the world of business (Holbrook, 2005e) – not to mention the potential evils of a profit-oriented phony-academic institution such as Trump University (Holbrook, 2009d). To combat these wayward tendencies, I have advocated replacing the all-too-pervasive student-as-consumer analogy with a student-as-channel metaphor in which MBA graduates are viewed as conduits for distributing knowledge to the larger business community (Holbrook, 2006b; Holbrook and Hulbert, 2002b). I summarized many such issues, fairly politely (at the editor's insistence), in an invited review for the *Journal of Public Policy & Marketing* (Holbrook, 2007b) and, not so politely (thanks to a more lenient editor), in a more contentious piece for the *European Business Review* (Holbrook, 2008a). Ultimately, in perhaps too much painful detail for many readers to endure, I described the devastating personal impacts of the university's practitioner-centered customer-oriented business-obsessed trade-school mentality on my own experiences as a frustrated teacher and disillusioned former member of what had once been but no longer remained a dedicated community of scholars (Holbrook, 2012, 2014c).

While I dwell briefly at the fringe of politically tinged topics, I should mention that these sorts of macromarketing issues occupied my attention on many occasions and that – thanks to the generosity and tolerance of editors at the *Journal of Macromarketing* (especially Roger Dickinson and Cliff Shultz) and other publications (*Journal of Marketing*; *Journal of Marketing Research*; *Marketing Theory*; *Consumption, Markets and Culture*; *Journal of the Academy of Marketing Science*; *Psychology & Marketing*) – I managed to publish any number of book reviews that tapped the essence of my concerns related to issues of social responsibility, consumer welfare, and the ecological view of the firm as a Dynamic Open Complex Adaptive System (DOCAS). Indeed, I was honored to learn that there existed something that Rog Dickinson referred to as "a Holbrook-style book review" – by which, I guess, he meant a shamelessly opinionated piece of polemics that masqueraded as a critique of another's (or, more often, many others') literary output(s). In this spirit, I managed to present my personal views on such socially relevant topics as the positive-versus-negative effects of advertising (Holbrook, 1987c); aspects of elitism (Holbrook, 1995g); the nature of creativity (Holbrook, 1997a); April Benson's collection of essays on compulsive shopping (2001d); the Disneyfication of commercialized entertainment (Holbrook, 2001j); the growing literature on the consumption experience and its relevance to emerging trends in the American economy (Holbrook, 2000b, 2006g, 2007f, 2007g, 2007h); the symbiotic relationship between exhibitionism and voyeurism (Holbrook, 2001g, 2001i, 2002c); the evangelical aspects of consumer behavior (Holbrook, 2001h); Jerry Zaltman's insights into how consumers think (Holbrook, 2003c); some of my all-time favorite jazz musicians such as Chet Baker, Dave Brubeck, Ray Charles, Paul Desmond, and David Frishberg (Holbrook, 2001a); and my bookshelf of closely but slowly read treasures (Holbrook, 1998b, 2001–2002). Here, I have cited only a few of these book reviews. A complete listing or detailed summary would require too much space and take us too far afield. But the curious reader can get a quick taste or (more accurately) a big gulp by sampling an overview that I put together for the *Academy of Marketing Science Review* – namely "Adventures in Complexity: An Essay on Dynamic Open Complex Adaptive Systems, Butterfly Effects, Self-Organizing Order, Coevolution, the Ecological Perspective, Fitness Landscapes, Market Spaces, Emergent Beauty at the Edge of Chaos, and All That Jazz" (Holbrook, 2003b; a lengthy piece, available by Googling " 'Adventures in Complexity' Morris B. Holbrook"). Or, for a heavily satirical introduction to my somewhat idiosyncratic and potentially subversive opinions on social issues, the reader might try "The Greedy Bastard's Guide to Business" (Holbrook, 2013, revisited in Chapter 11).

The work mentioned in the last few paragraphs reflects my increasing drift in the direction of qualitative interpretive studies. Typical of my usual tendency to exaggerate everything – leading to frequent accusations of my being "hyperbolic," sometimes coupled with charges of "egocentricity" and "elitism" (none of which complaints I can dispute) – I began to push the qualitative interpretive approach in the direction of what I call Subjective Personal Introspection or SPI. Taking its justification from various trends in postpositivistic or postmodern thinking, SPI harkens back almost 500 years to Michel de Montaigne (1533–1592) – his invention of the essay form and his insistence that, being human, he was well-qualified to write about aspects of humanity. Or – to paraphrase – being a consumer, I am propitiously equipped to discuss consumption experiences in general and my own in particular (Holbrook, 1995d, 1997f). I first developed this approach in what I call my "ACR Trilogy" – which dealt with my love of jazz under the title "I'm Hip" (Holbrook, 1986d); my fanatic devotion to recorded music via a "25-Cent Tour of a Jazz Collector's Home" (Holbrook, 1987a); and a self-revelatory psychoanalytically oriented interpretive exegesis of the artistic objects in our country home (Holbrook, 1988c). The latter paper – plus a greatly expanded version subtitled "I Am an Animal" (Holbrook, 1988e) – captured some aspects of my participation in the Consumer-Behavior Odyssey (Holbrook, 1987b, 1991a, 2014b), and related themes from my writings with various other Odysseans (Russ Belk, Melanie Wallendorf, John Sherry, Jeff Durgee) appeared in the anthology prepared by Russ Belk in 1991 under the title *Highways and Buyways*. The CB Odyssey pioneered the use of ethnographic approaches in consumer research, and my own intentionally and admittedly solipsistic applications pushed the boundaries a bit further in the direction of *auto*ethnography. Later – in enough detail to fill a short monograph – Beth Hirschman and I explored related themes under the title *Postmodern Consumer Research: The Study of Consumption as Text* (Hirschman and Holbrook, 1992). And I continued to pursue my devotion to SPI – as in my essay on "Loving and Hating New York" (Holbrook, 1994d) and my various other exercises in autoethnographic self-exploration (Holbrook, 1992c, 1998e, 1998j, 2000c, 2003e, 2005c, 2006a, 2006d, 2014c).

Sometimes, I felt duty-bound to defend such qualitative interpretive autoethnographic approaches philosophically – as in my conceptual pieces with another one of my esteemed mentors, John O'Shaughnessy (Holbrook and O'Shaughnessy, 1988; J. O'Shaughnessy and Holbrook, 1988; see also Holbrook, 1992a), and in my various arguments on behalf of SPI (Holbrook, 1991b, 1995d, 1997f, 2006d). I collected many of my ruminations on SPI and related themes in what I consider to be the closest I have come to a *chef-d'oeuvre* – namely, my book entitled *Consumer Research: Introspective Essays on the Study of Consumption* (Holbrook, 1995b). Over the years – though embraced and advanced by numerous colleagues, as listed in Chapter 4 – SPI has been criticized by folks like Melanie Wallendorf and Merrie Brucks for being less than "scientific." *JCR* declined to publish my one-page poem in reply to Wallendorf and Brucks on the grounds that (1) those authors did not mention me by name in their attack and (2) the journal did not publish poetry. But my indignantly dismissive descent into doggerel does appear in the *Introspective Essays* (Holbrook, 1995b, p. 252). Since then, after going through most or all the usual postpositivistic justifications for SPI, I have slowly evolved toward a position that I now regard as self-evident – namely, "What's so great about science?" Anybody who has seriously considered the Philosophy of Science will know what I mean. Interestingly, I can find only a couple of examples of my saying this in print (Holbrook, 2006d, 2014b), though I remember loudly voicing my renegade opinion in public at a gathering of PhD students (right before they stopped inviting me to the AMA Doctoral Consortiums). Perhaps it happened in 2002 at my consortium talk entitled "Having Fun with Qualitative Methods or Interpretive Approaches" (Holbrook, 2002b). Or maybe at one of the talks entitled "Outside the Box: Alternative Perspectives and Opportunities" in 2003 or "The Dialectic Diaries: Be Introspective; Read My Biography; Don't Be Introspective . . . Yet" in 2004.

In this interpretive and qualitative frame of mind, during my first sabbatical in 1983, I decided to elaborate the notion of consumption experiences by developing the Concept of Consumer Value. This pushed me toward exploring the branch of philosophy known as Axiology (the study of value). And, in that spirit, I invaded the stacks in Columbia University's main library, Butler Hall, where musty old books on value-related themes (some of them donated by John Dewey himself) sat gathering dust and (judging from the check-out cards in pouches on their back covers) never having been read by a single human being (except maybe Professor Dewey himself in days of yore). These volumes carried so much foul-smelling grime, mold, and mildew that I needed to wear a surgical mask while Xeroxing them before I could settle down to the painfully slow task of reading these photocopies. But, from this ordeal, I developed a conceptualization of value – discussed further in Part III – as an interactive relativistic preference experience with eight major types characterized by their positions on three fundamental dimensions or distinctions (Extrinsic [E] vs. Intrinsic [I], Self-Oriented [S] vs. Other-Oriented [O], and Active [A] vs. Reactive [R]) – namely, Efficiency (ESA), Excellence (ESR), Politics or Status (EOA), Esteem (EOR), Play (ISA), Esthetics (ISR), Morality (IOA), and Spirituality (IOR) (Holbrook and Corfman, 1985) – later renamed as the *Eight E's* represented by Efficiency, Excellence, Exhibitionism, Elitism, Entertainment, Esthetics, Ethics, and Ecstasy (Holbrook, 2012, 2014a). Kim Corfman and I did a small empirical study along these lines and presented the theory and tests in our chapter for a book edited by Jack Jacoby and Jerry Olson from presentations at a conference on *Perceived Quality* that they hosted at NYU (Holbrook and Corfman, 1985). I recognized the need to develop the conceptual portion of this work into a full-fledged journal article. But, at the time, I felt so discouraged with the review process at our major journals (Holbrook, 1986b) that I could not bear to submit my brainchild (which I had labored so hard to produce and which I so strongly wished **not** to revise) for scholarly review by a revision-happy publication such as (say) *JM*, *JMR*, or

JCR. It took me ten years to find a suitable outlet for my first major paper on Consumer Value as a chapter in a book on *Service Quality* edited by Roland Rust and Rich Oliver (Holbrook, 1994f; for a more "popularized" version, see also Holbrook, 1994a). During that time and beyond, I took my value concept around the world as my traveling road show, giving talks on consumer-related axiology at the Universities of Utah, Michigan, Quebec, Illinois, British Columbia, Arizona, Texas, and Miami; at Ohio State University, Iowa State University, and the University of California-Los Angeles; at Columbia, Dartmouth, McGill, Rutgers, Baruch (CUNY), and Wharton (twice); and at Edith Cowan (Australia), Diamond (Japan), Hakuhodo (Japan), and the Japanese Marketing Association (Tokyo). In 1999 – based on a multi-participant session at ACR (Holbrook, 1996e) – we published a book on *Consumer Value* in which various colleagues provided chapters on the eight different value types (Holbrook, ed. 1999) and in which I presented introductory and concluding commentaries that summarized my own views (Holbrook, 1999a, 1999c). Subsequently, Bob Lusch and Steve Vargo were kind enough – in a book they edited on *The Service-Dominant Logic* – to let me argue for my position that the Concept of Consumer Value covered their viewpoint in a way that some might find more straightforward, economical, or even elegant (Holbrook, 2006f). I also adopted the vantage point of SPI to interpret a collection of my grandfather's photographs from the 1940s and 1950s as they revealed aspects of consumer value (Holbrook, 2005c, 2006a; please see Chapter 6) and to explain the multifaceted appeal of vibraphonist Gary Burton (Holbrook, 2014a; please see Chapter 8). Meanwhile, some of my European colleagues – especially Martina Gallarza and Raquel Sánchez-Fernández in Spain – began to refine the value concept and to test it empirically with mostly supportive results (Gallarza, Arteaga, Del Chiappa, Gil-Saura, and Holbrook, 2017; Gallarza, Gil-Saura, and Holbrook, 2011, 2012; Holbrook, Sánchez-Fernández, and Gallarza, 2020; Sánchez-Fernández, Iniesta-Bonillo, and Holbrook, 2009).

Speaking of European colleagues, I have been blessed over the years by the privilege of working with numerous compatriot spirits from the UK, Spain, Italy, France, India, and Japan (some of whom now make their homes in the USA and have indeed become at least as "Americanized" as I). The resulting outputs, as befits their international origins, have proven too multifaceted and diverse to categorize easily, much less to summarize succinctly. But, among many others (besides Martina and Raquel), these would include studies with (in alphabetical order) Michela Addis from Italy (e.g., Addis and Holbrook, 2001, 2010a, 2010b); Punam Anand from India (e.g., Anand and Holbrook, 1990a, 1990b; Anand, Holbrook, and Stephens, 1988); Pierre Berthon and Mac Hulbert from the UK (Berthon, Holbrook, and Hulbert, 2000, 2003; Berthon, Holbrook, Hulbert, and Pitt, 2007; Holbrook and Hulbert, 1975, 2002a, 2002b); Alan Bradshaw and Finola Kerrigan from the UK (e.g., Bradshaw and Holbrook, 2007, 2008; Bradshaw, Kerrigan, and Holbrook, 2010; see also Holbrook, 2006e); Arjun Chaudhuri from India (Chaudhuri and

Holbrook, 2001, 2002); Chris Hackley from the UK (Holbrook, 2003d); Gita Johar from India (Johar, Holbrook, and Stern, 2001); Takeo Kuwahara from Japan (Holbrook and Kuwahara, 1998, 1999); John O'Shaughnessy from the UK (Holbrook, Lehmann, and O'Shaughnessy, 1986; Holbrook and O'Shaughnessy, 1984, 1988; Holbrook, O'Shaughnessy, and Bell, 1990; O'Shaughnessy and Holbrook, 1988); Nicholas O'Shaughnessy from the UK (N. O'Shaughnessy and Holbrook, 1988); Ignacio Redondo from Spain (Redondo and Holbrook, 2008, 2010); and Michael Woodward from the UK (Woodward and Holbrook, 2013).

I should also give special mention to the often-unheralded editors who have helped me greatly over the years and to whom I feel immense gratitude – both from the USA (e.g., Chris Allen, Russ Belk, Jim Bettman, Pat Browne, Ray Browne, Gil Churchill, John Deighton, Nikhi Dholakia, Rog Dickinson, Bob Ferber, Ann Marie Fiore, Fuat Firat, Beth Hirschman, Keith Hunt, Shelby Hunt, Hal Kassarjian, Bob Lusch, Rich Lutz, Naresh Malhotra, Kent Monroe, Rajan Nataraajan, Jerry Olson, Lisa Peñaloza, Bob Peterson, Jonathan Schroeder, John Sherry, Jag Sheth, Cliff Shultz, Barb Stern, Jean Umiker-Sebeok, Alladi Ventkatesh, Terry Witkowski, Arch Woodside) and from abroad (e.g., Alan Bradshaw, Stephen Brown, Dougie Brownlie, Peter Earl, Chris Hackley, Finola Kerrigan, Adam Lindgreen, Pauline Maclaran, Mark Tadajewski). I am especially indebted to Stephen Brown (himself, probably, our finest writer), who has managed to uncork a veritable torrent of Holbrookian meanderings (Holbrook 1995c, 1996c, 1997i, 1998d, 2000a, 2000c, 2002a, 2006c, 2014c), with a little assistance from the poet John Sherry (Holbrook, 1998j, 2003e). Something similar might be said for Barb Stern (Holbrook, 1998e; Holbrook and Stern, 1997, 2000; Stern and Holbrook, 1994; Stern, Zinkhan, and Holbrook, 2002), who became a cherished colleague and a wonderful friend but, for whom, way-way-way too soon, I faced the immensely sad task of writing a memorial tribute to say that I miss her every day (Holbrook, 2009c).

I also benefited from collaborations not yet mentioned, working on topics too diverse to categorize easily, with many home-grown co-authors from the Columbia community. These included Neville Hughes (an MBA student) on projective techniques (Holbrook and Hughes, 1978); Karl Maier, David Velez, and Gerard Tabouret (MBA students) on an information-display sheet for studying information acquisition in the development of consumer attitudes (Holbrook and Maier, 1978; Holbrook, Velez, and Tabouret, 1981); Mike Ryan on multiattribute attitude models (Ryan and Holbrook, 1982b); Joel Huber on modeling esthetic judgments of real as opposed to artificial objects (Huber and Holbrook, 1981), on measuring temporal trends in consumer preferences (Huber and Holbrook, 1982), on situational influences that moderate preference functions (Huber, Holbrook, and Schiffman, 1982), and on contextual effects due to price sensitivity (Huber, Holbrook, and Kahn, 1986); Bill Moore on the predictive validity of joint-space models (Moore and Holbrook, 1982) and on the performance of conjoint analysis of objects with environmentally correlated features (Moore and Holbrook, 1990); Bill Havlena on generalizing multiattribute models from real to artificial product designs (Holbrook and Havlena, 1988); Donna Hoffman on quantitative citation analysis to assess the intellectual structure of consumer research (Hoffman and Holbrook, 1993; see also Holbrook, 1992b, 1993a); Mike Solomon and Stephen Bell (a PhD student) on the social and personality-related aspects of product-design preferences (Bell, Holbrook, and Solomon, 1991; Holbrook, Solomon, and Bell, 1990; see also Holbrook, 1992d); David Bello (an MBA student) on price premiums as indications of brand equity (Bello and Holbrook, 1995; see also Holbrook, 1992e); Elizabeth Cooper-Martin on the mapping of ethical consumption experiences (Cooper-Martin and Holbrook, 1993; see also Holbrook, 1994c); Alex Simonson (a PhD student) on permissible puffery in advertising (Simonson and Holbrook, 1993); Ellen Day on jazz as a metaphor for issues of relevance to teaching (Holbrook and Day, 1994); T. J. Olney (a PhD student) on romanticism as a personality trait that moderates consumer preferences (Holbrook and Olney, 1995); Cliff Shultz on sports statistics, anticipating "Money Ball," that assess the financial returns to player performance (Holbrook and Shultz, 1996; see also Holbrook, 1996b) and on aspects of social responsibility such as those associated with the "Tragedy of the Commons" (Shultz and Holbrook, 1999, 2009); Lauren Block and Gavan Fitzsimons (PhD students) on different types of beauty in personal appearances (Holbrook, Block, and Fitzsimons, 1998); Michael Weiss and John Habich (visiting scholars) on using the zip-code data analyzed by Claritas via its PRIZM system to map consumer tastes (Holbrook, 2001c; Holbrook, Weiss, and Habich, 2002, 2004; Weiss, Holbrook, and Habich, 2001).

Over the years, many people – usually doctoral students or younger faculty members – have asked me where the sorts of ideas that populate these studies come from. And, reluctant to give "blind luck" as my facile-but-nonetheless-accurate answer, I have sometimes found myself cast in the role of a person unqualified but still willing to offer inspirational advice on the subject of how to develop a career in consumer research or occasionally, with even less grounds for credibility, in some other field of endeavor. Thus, I have extolled the virtues of pure as opposed to applied research in consumer behavior (Holbrook, 1986f); the advantages of a feline curiosity-based approach as opposed to a more canine practitioner-oriented posture (Holbrook, 1989a); the need to keep plugging away, as in the cases of J. S. Bach and Mickey Mantle (Holbrook, 1989e); the near-thankless self-discipline associated with agonies experienced on the football field (Holbrook, 1989b); the merits of patience, persistence, and perseverance in the manner of Horton the Elephant as portrayed by Dr. Seuss (Holbrook, 1990b); the salubrious contribution of lyricism in research on consumer emotions – with a story about the nonpareil jazz singer Marlene VerPlanck, implications for the role of feminism in consumer research, and an illustration involving a brief performance of Hoagy Carmichael and Johnny Mercer's "Skylark" on the piano (Holbrook, 1990c; see also Holbrook, 1989b); the inspiration offered by contact with great jazz artists such as Dizzy Gillespie and Junior Mance (Holbrook, 1992c); the lessons learned from pieces of wisdom gleaned from key role models, near and far (Holbrook, 1995e); the need to try with all one's might, as in the case of a penguin attempting to fly (Holbrook, 1997e); the importance of boundary pushing as opposed to thinking outside the box (Holbrook, 1997d); and, again, the purposely contentious question "What's so great about science?" (Holbrook, 2002b, 2006d, 2014b).

Yet I cannot honestly say that I have usually or even often heeded my own advice. Rather, most of my little insights have emerged from ideas entertained while letting my mind wander, from random thoughts experienced in the shower, from passing comments by TV talk-show hosts, or from similar haphazard sources of serendipitous discovery. And I have no way of knowing where future ideas might originate. Or when . . . if ever. Such ideas come from beyond the realm of controllability or predictability. For example, one night Robert Schindler, Sally, and I were talking and drinking margaritas next to the three-story waterfall at a local restaurant called Caramba! The somewhat younger Robert commented that his musical preferences centered on the Beatles, recalled from his teenage years, whereas – a bit older – I countered that mine had already been formed by the time the Beatles came along and that, whereas I might have developed a fondness for Elvis, what really pleased me were such jazz stars as Chet Baker, Paul Desmond, and Art Pepper (all mainstays of the jazz scene during the late 1950s, when I was about 15 years old). It seemed to us, in our ever-so-slightly inebriated condition, that we had discovered an important phenomenon – namely the tendency for taste preferences in the arts and entertainment to solidify when one is in late adolescence or early adulthood and to remain rather stable thereafter. Pretty soon, we developed an approach to testing this nostalgia-related hypothesis using what we called the method of object-specific ages (Holbrook and Schindler, 1991) that we applied across time-dated stimuli to demonstrate age-related preference peaks in the general area of 15 to 24 years old in the cases of such products as popular music (Holbrook and Schindler, 1989), fashion models (Schindler and Holbrook, 1993), movie stars (Holbrook and Schindler, 1994), motion pictures (Holbrook and Schindler, 1996), and automobiles (Schindler and Holbrook, 2003) – with implications for the role of nostalgia in shaping consumer experiences (Holbrook, 1989f, 1991c, 1993e, 1993f, 1994e, 1995a; Holbrook and Schindler, 2003).

Other areas of programmatic research that developed over my later career – often in similarly serendipitous ways – involved (1) experiences with pets in general and cats in particular; (2) the impact of stereographic images for the three-dimensional representation of data; (3) the insightfulness of the collective stereographic photo essay; (4) the implications of a jazz metaphor for issues of relevance to marketing and consumer research; and (5) the determinants of consumer tastes – high- versus low-brow, refined versus ordinary, "good" versus "bad" – and their relation to aesthetic excellence as opposed to commercial appeal in the arts and entertainment. Let us briefly consider each of these five themes.

1. With respect to animal companions in general and feline pets in particular (please see Chapter 3), I celebrated the consumption-relevant aspects of our relationships with our cats Quarter and Rocky Raccoon (Holbrook, 1996d). I satirized some of the more straight-laced ethnographic approaches in the context of "Ethography, Felologies, and Unobtrusive Participation in the Life of a Cat" (Holbrook, 1997c). I interpreted *Breakfast at Tiffany's* from the perspective of Audrey Hepburn's cat (Holbrook, 1998i). I did a lengthy collective stereographic photo essay on aspects of animal companionship with four other animal lovers (Holbrook, Stephens, Day, Holbrook, and Strazar, 2001). And I presented my views on pets as companions (Holbrook, 2008d) in a special issue of the *Journal of Business Research* co-edited with Arch Woodside (Holbrook and Woodside, 2008).

2. In connection with stereographic representations of data, I fell in love with 3-D images first during the mid-1950s when my father took beautiful stereo photos with his then-popular David White camera (the same kind used by General Eisenhower) and again during the mid-1990s with the advent of the *Magic Eye* books (which made the process of stereopsis seem mysteriously profound). That second phase started one winter in about 1996 when we took a flight back to New York from Sarasota. The onboard magazine contained a random dot stereogram (RDS). As the countless fans of the *Magic Eye* displays came to appreciate, an RDS looks like a bunch of meaninglessly inchoate splotches on a page until – via the miracle of stereopsis – a coherent picture magically appears . . . in three-dimensional depth. Sally saw the 3-D image almost immediately, but I spent two and a half fruitless hours on the plane struggling to see the hidden picture. Finally, during the cab ride home from the airport, the image suddenly appeared in all its glory, and it provided a startling epiphany – namely, an in-depth three-dimensional representation, seemingly from nowhere. So I began to study up on all forms of 3-D imaging – stereograms, of course, but also stereo photographs. I had inherited my dad's old David White stereo camera, so I began to play around with that and with other approaches to stereo photography – including some progress I eventually made toward taking 3-D photos with two widely separated telescopic lenses. Gradually, it began to dawn on me that 3-D images – for example, stereo pairs presented side by side in the manner of the old stereopticons – would provide a viable means for enhancing the presentation of marketing-research data. So I wrote a general tutorial on the nature and types of all the different ways to present three-dimensional images (Holbrook, 1997g). To accompany this, I advocated the application of stereography to the social sciences in general (Holbrook, 1996f) and to marketing research in particular (Holbrook, 1997d). My chief claims on behalf of 3-D

imaging hinged on the ability of stereopsis to "break camouflage" by clari-
fying what would otherwise be the difficult-to-interpret confusion, clutter,
crowding, and/or complexity of a complicated visual representation. I presented these views both in the photography-oriented outlets (Holbrook,
1998a, 1999b) and in the marketing-relevant journals and books (1998d,
1998f, 1998g, 1999f; Holbrook and Kuwahara, 1999). My advocacy of
three-dimensional stereographic imaging even found its way to some commentaries published in Japan (Holbrook, 1999f, 2001e). But these 3-D
approaches to stereographic representation did suffer from some problems that seem to have prevented them from gaining the sort of traction
that I had hoped to encourage among my colleagues. Specifically, many
people find it difficult to "free view" stereo pairs. Further, they don't want
to bother with the readily available prismatic viewers; the red-and-green
glasses won't work with the black-and-white images typically found in our
academic publications; and the polarized displays used in movie theaters
require projection onto a silver screen of a type not available in home set-
tings. James Cameron, Steven Spielberg, and other big-time film directors
later latched onto 3-D motion pictures in a big way (using rapidly alter-
nating left-right images viewed through polarized glasses), but – to my
disappointment – comparable stereographic approaches do not seem to
have caught on in the community of marketing and consumer researchers.
3. Combining my faith in SPI with my appreciation for the revelatory power
of (stereo 3-D) photography – heavily influenced by the work of Deb Heisley and Sid Levy along similar lines – led to my celebration of the photo
essay in general plus its stereographic and/or collective forms in particular.
Basically, this method consisted of giving people stereo cameras, asking
them to take a 3-D photo that captured what was for them the essence
of some consumption experience, and instructing them to write a brief
subjective personal introspective vignette describing the meaning of the
photograph and its attendant consumer-related implications. The resulting 3-D photos and SPI vignettes permitted interpretive analyses in the
form of what we called a "Collective Stereographic Photo Essay." We
applied this approach to studying the experience of living in New York
City (Holbrook and Kuwahara, 1998) and to the study of animal companionship (Holbrook, Stephens, Day, Holbrook, and Strazar, 2001).
Sometimes, I dropped the requirement that the approach involves both
stereography and multiple vignettes – relying instead on ordinary mono-
graphic photos and/or on my own personal SPIs. Thus, I used my own
stereo photos to interpret the experience of animal companionship (Holbrook, 1995c, 1996c); to limn the significance in various contexts of
pushing the boundaries rather than stepping altogether outside the box
(Holbrook, 1997i); and even to satirize what I described, in the spirit of
parody, as the "ethnoscopic auto-auto-auto-driven" approach to charac-
terizing life in Kroywen – that is, New York spelled backward (Holbrook,
1998e). (As the Reader will discover in Chapter 11, I sometimes surrender

to an irresistible urge to blossom forth in the shape of satire or parody.) I also used ordinary non-stereo photos taken by a sample of informants to explore the meaning of beauty in their daily lives as consumers (Holbrook, 2005g). And I drew on my own subjective personal introspections to explore the autoethnographic meanings concerning consumption experiences and consumer value of photos that I took of my own record collection (Holbrook, 1987a), of shots representing the artistic objects in our summer home (Holbrook, 1988c), of the images found in a collection of my grandfather's photographs from the 1940s and 1950s (Holbrook, 2003e, 2005c, 2006a), and of pictures that I shot on a trip to the Phoenix Zoo (Holbrook, 2006d).

4. The jazz metaphor first appeared in my comparison of John Howard as the father of buyer-behavior theory with the work of Charlie Parker as the jazz saxophone genius known as "Bird" (Holbrook, 1984c). Over time – like other writers on marketing management, organizational behavior, and business strategy (e.g., Karl Weick, Noel Dennis, Steve Oakes, Michael Macaulay, Dougie Brownlie, Alan Bradshaw, and innumerable others) – I came to see the jazz metaphor as a lens through which to view such themes as the ups and downs of teaching (Holbrook and Day, 1994), the firm as a dynamic open complex adaptive system or DOCAS (Holbrook, 2003b), the nature of fruitful collaboration (Holbrook, 2010), the multiple types of consumer value as illustrated by the music of Gary Burton (Holbrook, 2014a; please see Chapter 8), the role of the marketing manager in developing new products (Holbrook, 2015g; please see Chapter 9), and the analogies between jazz training and marketing education (Holbrook, 2016; please see Chapter 10). These themes appear in some detail in my book-length monograph entitled *Playing the Changes on the Jazz Metaphor: An Expanded Conceptualization of Music-, Management-, and Marketing-Related Themes* (Holbrook, 2007e).

5. Apparently, a writer can find no faster way to attract dismissive charges of elitism – one of the nastiest epithets in our current atmosphere of political correctness – than to suggest that certain cultural offerings display more inherent quality than others and/or that certain consumers possess more refined capabilities than others for appreciating these merits. But, at the risk of enduring the slings and arrows of outraged populists who insist that everything in our culture is equally estimable, I have followed Pierre Bourdieu in believing (1) that different taste cultures exist (whether they pertain to the fine arts, classical music, jazz, rock, ballet, television soap operas, football, automobiles, clothing fashions, wok cooking, plumbing, or big game hunting); (2) that, within any given taste culture, some individuals (by virtue of formal education, on-the-job training, social influences, self-instruction, or other forms of cultural capital) have acquired a degree of refined understanding that exceeds that of ordinary folks; and (3) that this expertise allows them to appraise the excellence of the relevant cultural offerings (painting, symphonies, blues performances, touchdown

passes, SUVs, hemlines, soy sauce, sink drains, or elephant tusks) with an education- or experience-based degree of sophistication that eludes individuals who have not benefited from a similarly high level of the relevant intellectual cultivation. Put differently, I know more about jazz than most people – but vastly less about nose tackles, four-wheel drive vehicles, bathroom fixtures, or the Remington Model 700 than many folks who may never have heard of (say) Milt Jackson, Gary Burton, Bobby Hutcherson, or Joe Locke. Further, as a corollary, the effort to gain a larger audience for some cultural offering by making it more accessible to a larger number of consumers inevitably entails the need to dumb it down so that those with lower levels of cultural capital in that particular taste culture can appreciate it more easily. Thus – in my view and with reference to one or another taste culture – there is every reason for us to expect to find differences in tastes ("good" vs. "bad") among those with differing levels of cultural capital (refined vs. ordinary) and at different levels of the cultural hierarchy (high- vs. low-brow) with a concomitant tendency for greater (lesser) popularity **not** to accompany higher (lower) levels of quality or excellence in that particular cultural field. Over the years, in empirical work, I have investigated these inter-related phenomena in a number of ways involving the relationship of learning-by-exposure to connoisseurship in evaluating 20 graphic prints (Schindler, Holbrook, and Greenleaf, 1989), differences between the responses of (ordinary) listeners and (professional) critics in preference polls for 60 jazz artists (Holbrook, 1993g), the association between education and preferences toward 63 cultural products at different levels of the cultural hierarchy from highbrow (Dizzy Gillespie, Billie Holiday) to lowbrow (*Ozzie & Harriet*, George Bush) (Holbrook, 1995a), the demonstrably weak connection between expert critical judgments and the popular appeal of 1,000 films (Holbrook, 1999d), the relationship of cultural tastes to social classes (Holbrook, 2009b; Holbrook, Weiss, and Habich, 2002, 2004), the lack – according to an approach that I call Postmodern Statistics or PoMoStat – of a correlation between excellence and popularity in the market for 360,600 books (Holbrook, 2006c), the links between expert judgments and ordinary evaluations in accounting for the statistically significant but very weak associations between artistic excellence and the popular appeal of 219 motion pictures (Holbrook, 2005h), the levels of audience appeal among 200 recorded performances of "My Funny Valentine" (Holbrook, Lacher, and LaTour, 2006), the popularity of 219 and 192 movies from two different time periods (Holbrook and Addis, 2007), and the independence of artistic as opposed to commercial paths to success in a sample of 190 motion pictures (Holbrook and Addis, 2008).

I retired from teaching in the summer of 2009 and, since that time, have kept fairly busy with various projects such as the completion of my aforementioned book on jazz in films or *Cinemajazzamatazz* (Holbrook, 2011) and many of the articles and chapters described heretofore. With respect to the latter, various kind editors and friendly colleagues have given me the chance to publish my views on diverse topics such as the distortion or subversion of academic values in the customer-oriented university (Holbrook, 2009d; cf. Chapter 13), threats posed by marketing to vulnerable consumers (Shultz and Holbrook, 2009), the disconnect between artistic excellence and commercial success in the motion-picture industry (Addis and Holbrook, 2010b), the relationship of art to commerce in the marketplace (Bradshaw, Kerrigan, and Holbrook, 2010), the role of identification in the evaluation of films (Addis and Holbrook, 2010a), mechanisms by which jazz musicians achieve coordinated efforts in music making (Holbrook, 2010), the use of canonical correlation to model the appeal of movie features to various demographic segments (Redondo and Holbrook, 2010), the conceptualization of consumer value (Gallarza, Gil-Saura, and Holbrook, 2011; cf. Chapter 7); consumption symbolism in the cinematic portrayal of vampires (Hirschman and Holbrook, 2011), the dangers of running a university according to the business model (Holbrook, 2012; cf. Chapter 13), the nature and types of consumer value in the tourism industry (Gallarza, Gil-Saura, and Holbrook, 2012), the revisiting of the role of age-related preferences in markets for the arts and entertainment (Holbrook and Schindler, 2013), the interpersonal dialogue as a way of analyzing and interpreting the concept of consumption experiences (Woodward and Holbrook, 2013), atrocities attributable to the role of greed in our capitalistic economy (Holbrook, 2013; cf. Chapter 11), the nature and types of consumer value in arts marketing (Holbrook, 2014a; cf. Chapter 8), recollections of my experiences on the Consumer-Behavior Odyssey (Holbrook, 2014b), my use of animal metaphors as a basis for understanding consumer behavior (Holbrook, 2014c; cf. Chapter 3), the nature and importance of experiential consumption (Holbrook and Hirschman, 2015; cf. Chapters 4 and 5), the role of branding and its potential excesses (Holbrook, 2015a), recollections of my debate with Jack Jacoby on the merits of consulting (Holbrook, 2015e), the role of psychoanalytic approaches in consumer research (Holbrook, 2015f), a metaphorical view of the marketing manager as a jazz musician (Holbrook, 2015g; cf. Chapter 9), and analogies between the bases for excellence in jazz training and marketing education (Holbrook, 2016; cf. Chapter 10). So – aside from my increased rate of strolling around the neighborhood with Sally, traveling a bit to distant lands, visiting museums, going to the theater and restaurants, practicing the piano, taking a jazz-ensemble class and jamming with some of my fellow students (learning to play nicely with others), reading many of the trashy detective stories that I had no time for when I felt compelled to peruse the marketing journals, watching way too much television in general and Yankee games in particular, spending weekends with Sally in Montauk or the Poconos, visiting our son Chris in Strasbourg, and enjoying the company of our two boisterous and charming grandkids (Nathanael and Anika, who, we have reason to hope, will grow up in France speaking Czech, German, English, and French) – I have kept myself fairly busy with lingering academic pursuits. Also, Jagdish Sheth generously gave me the opportunity to re-publish most of my life's work in the form of 15 volumes included in his *Legends in Consumer Behavior* series (Holbrook, 2015c). Over 60 colleagues and friends kindly contributed to the completion of this project by writing volume introductions, providing commentaries, and conducting interviews with yours truly – all of which amounted to a heroic outpouring of collective energy graciously bestowed on my behalf. I appreciated this support more than words can convey, and it made me happy to imagine that my *oeuvre* might find its way into the Library of Congress via the *Legends* series. But the price tag for the 15-volume set is so high ($1,505.33 on Amazon.Com) that I doubt any but the most affluent university libraries will be able to afford it.

Some might wonder why I retired as early as 2009 at a "mere" 65 years of age. The short answer is that I felt threatened and even humiliated by some of the university-related problems mentioned earlier and explored in what follows – foremost among them, in my case, being my disastrous experience in teaching a standardized course on marketing strategy that, to put it mildly, the career-oriented MBA students at my School truly hated. And me along with it. Fortunately, after this disheartening episode, I spent a few terms teaching consumer behavior and again found myself surrounded by friendly faces – about half of them MBAs and the rest from other parts of the University (Psychology, Sociology, International Affairs, Law, Teachers College, Columbia College, Barnard College, and so forth). Unfortunately, the latter

Figure 2.7 Morris Playing "Someone to Watch Over Me" at the Wedding Rehearsal of Son Chris, Strasbourg, October 3, 2015

did not pay tuition to the Business School, so my success in attracting and pleasing them won me no favor with the School's administration. But it did allow me to leave with a fairly good feeling about things.

I spoke about all this at the wonderful farewell party that my terrific colleagues bounteously put together for me. And I concluded – with a little help from a few of my favorite animal metaphors and musical analogies – on what I regard as a rather happy note. I shall end Chapter 3 on "Animal Metaphors" with a lengthy quotation from the finale of my retirement speech. So, here, I shall merely emphasize that it acknowledges my faithful adherence to the goal of behaving like a cat who carries his own leash.

3 Morris the Cat or the Wolf-Man on the Upper West Side

Animal Metaphors and Me

Abstract

Various authors have dealt with the ways in which spokesanimals and mascots create symbolic meanings that shape or enhance brand images. Such inquiries tend to focus on how human qualities are attributed to various members of the animal kingdom. However, it also makes sense to explore ways in which animal characteristics are attributed to humans. This latter preoccupation has informed much of the author's own work, often through the use of animal metaphors – either to describe his own characteristics or to articulate his views concerning the perspectives adopted by others. The present essay revisits some of these examples of metaphoric animals in the author's writing on marketing in general and in his own efforts at self-branding in particular.

Introduction: Mascots and Self-Branding

Contributors to the volume on *Brand Mascots and Anthropomorphic Marketing* (ed. Brown and Ponsonby-McCabe, 2014) dealt at great length and in multifarious manners with the broad theme of anthropomorphism in marketing – that is, the ways in which spokesanimals and mascots have created symbolic meanings that shape or enhance brand images. In stressing the role of anthropomorphism, such inquiries tend to focus on how human qualities are attributed to various members of the animal kingdom – finicky felines (Morris the Cat), solicitous reptiles (the Geico Gecko), mirthful bovines (the Laughing Cow), and so forth. However, it also makes sense to explore ways in which animal characteristics are attributed to humans. And this latter preoccupation has informed much of my own work over the years.

Here, I refer to the manner in which I have tended to construct myself as a "brand" – that is, as a product offering intended for consumption by some relevant audience of marketing or consumer-behavior scholars. I need hardly mention the extent to which ways of promoting oneself have come to be regarded as a form of "human branding." In that light, my own efforts at self-branding have repeatedly drawn upon animal metaphors – either to describe my own characteristics or to articulate my views concerning the perspectives or stances

DOI: 10.4324/9781003560302-4

adopted by others. Thus, as a consumer researcher, I have identified with cats and have contrasted these feline proclivities with those of more canine marketing researchers. I have seen myself as resembling a turtle or a skylark. Under the heading "I Am an Animal," I have explained my own psychodynamics as threatened by wolves – hence, my titular reference to Freud's "Wolf-Man." I have compared my mentor John Howard to "Bird" (the jazz genius, Charlie Parker). I have conceived the consumer as an ASL-speaking gorilla. I have positioned my intellectual adversaries as bears. Speaking of bears, I have opposed the compromise-seeking sensibilities of Goldilocks. I have exalted the patience, persistence, and perseverance of elephants and have extolled the heroic aeronautic efforts of fictitious penguins. I have compared the judging of goats at a state fair to human beauty contests. And most of all, to repeat, I have identified with the curious and independent spirits of cats.

Subjective Personal Introspection and the Celebration of Self

In the present essay, I intend to revisit some of these examples of metaphoric animals in my writing on the subject of marketing and consumer research. I should warn the reader that my discussion will pursue an approach that I refer to as Subjective Personal Introspection (Holbrook, 1995b). That is, I shall focus primarily on myself and on my own writings as they have played upon animal-related themes in my own efforts at self-branding. I am, of course, aware that this way of describing the world comes across as self-centered, sometimes bordering on egomaniacal. Some might wonder why I do not dwell on the contributions of, say, Frank Bass, Philip Kotler, Shelby Hunt, John Howard, Beth Hirschman, Barbara Stern, or Stephen Brown – all worthy scholars who richly deserve the broadest and deepest possible interpretive treatments. The answers are, first, that these others have not dwelled on animal metaphors at any great length and, second, that these others have already attracted considerable attention of a sort that I shall receive if and only if I provide it myself. So – with apologies to all those who would rather read about Bass, Kotler, Hunt, Howard, Hirschman, Stern, or Brown – I shall devote my comments on self-branding via animal metaphors to . . . Morris.

I find it significant to note that virtually all of my animal-related themes – with only two or three exceptions – have appeared in single-authored articles and chapters. Apparently, this way of conceptualizing what I want to say strikes me as uniquely personal and not suited to putting somebody else's name on it. Or, perhaps more accurately, others would shy away from identifying with my own persona in this potentially embarrassing way. Indeed, many authors, reviewers, and editors appear to find the presence of animals in our literature awkward or even demeaning.

During the five years between 1991 and 1996, I presented some of my more esoteric ideas at various schools – Columbia, Stanford, Iowa State University, the University of Washington, and Edith Cowan University, among others – under the title "A Brief History of Morris the Cat: Still Crazy After All These Years." Most members of my audiences appeared to agree more with the subtitle ("Crazy") than with the main body of my text ("Morris the Cat"). Along similar lines, I recall that, when Bill Moore and I created a paper that we colloquially referred to as "designing the optimal dog" (Moore and Holbrook, 1982), reviewers rushed to reject it on the grounds that such a theme reeked of impracticality and managerial irrelevance. Clearly, this said more about the biases of our critics than it did about reality because, even then, selective breeding was widely employed to create dogs with various desirable characteristics and consequently elevated price tags. And since then – along the lines that we espoused – the world has seen a great proliferation of "designer dogs," often with provocative hybrid names such as "cockapoos" or "labradoodles." (I eagerly await the nomenclature developed to designate crossbreeding between, say, bulldogs and shih tzus.)

In general, I have found women more willing than men to write about their feelings toward animal companions. In this connection, my major collaboration on "Key Aspects of Animal Companionship" involved the participation of three female co-authors (Holbrook, Stephens, Day, Holbrook, and Strazar, 2001). And I have found – among our circle of friends – that those most dedicated to the care and protection of non-human creatures tend to be gals, not guys. One exception is Arch Woodside, with whom I co-edited a special edition of the *Journal of Business Research* (Holbrook and Woodside, 2008), which featured a beautiful photograph on the back cover taken by Ellen Day of her magnificent pet rooster (plus a smaller portrait of our beloved Rocky the Cat on the front cover).

Those Big Bad Bears

My first self-defining uses of animal metaphors drew on the imagery of Goldilocks and the Three Bears (Holbrook, 1984a, 1985, 1986f) when I likened the bears to the ugly nature of pressure toward management-oriented or consulting-based research applications at the expense of more pure or basic consumer research pursued for its own sake as an end-in-itself. In my version of the story – very troubling to those in the camp favoring managerial relevance, but indicative of my own concerns – the Three Bears, evil monsters to the core, kill Goldilocks on the spot (Holbrook, 1985).

High and Low Approaches to Beauty: Birds and Goats

About the same time, I played around with animal analogies by comparing my mentor John Howard to the pioneering jazz saxophonist Charlie Parker, who was nicknamed "Bird," allegedly because of his fondness for eating chicken (Holbrook, 1984c). Symbolically, of course, Parker's identification with avian creatures signaled his ability to soar, to take flight in solos of breathtaking freedom and beauty. In my mind, John Howard's ways of creating buyer-behavior theory bore some resemblance to this ornithology-related creative process.

Meanwhile, on the Consumer-Behavior Odyssey, I amused myself by watching a goat-judging contest at a state fair and filling my log for the day with an account of how it resembled a human beauty pageant – up to and including an explicit focus on breast sizes or what, in goats, they call udders (Holbrook, 1987b, 1991a). But this was a minor distraction from the drudgery of wandering around among the shit-kicking gun-toting redneck hillbillies (all of whom, no doubt, later voted for George W. Bush and then for Donald Trump) in the self-deluding pretense that I was somehow doing consumer research.

Self-Identification with the Consumer as a Gorilla

Far more central to my concerns as a consumer researcher, a chapter that presented "Some Radical Reflections on the Roots of Consumption" (Holbrook, 1987d) focused on Koko the Gorilla – that remarkable creature who learned to communicate in American Sign Language (ASL), who asked for a pet kitten, and who mourned inconsolably when her feline friend was accidentally killed. The point, of course, was that Koko did not rely on a rational expectancy-value model but, rather, responded to emotions in a way that also characterizes much human consumption. I called these reflections "radical" because – in the true meaning of that word – they harkened back to the "roots" of consumer behavior theory as it was first developed by economists and psychologists who were well aware that all value resides not in the product itself but rather in the experience that this product serves to provide. This point now seems obvious. But, at the time, it required considerable effort to put across. And my disquisitions on Koko helpfully provided a vivid metaphor to revive this "radical" idea.

Enter the Wolf

All this meant, of course, that I felt a strong bond with animals in general and with the nature of their consumption experiences in particular. Indeed – in conjunction with the aesthetic tastes of my wife, Sally – these tendencies conspired to fill our homes with artworks that represented various members of the animal kingdom (birds, lions, deer, zebras, penguins, and so forth). To my surprise, my friends on the CB Odyssey saw these artistic treasures as the symbolic equivalent of trophies hung on the wall – moose heads and elk antlers and stuffed owls. I was appalled by this interpretation and said so at very great length in a couple of lengthy treatises that delved deeply into my own psychoanalytic interpretations based on six years of four-times-a-week-on-the-couch Freudian analysis (Holbrook, 1988c, 1988e). Working under the title "I Am an Animal," I reported phobias connected with *Peter and the Wolf*, conjured up all sorts of associations related to early-age wolf-related castration anxieties, tied these observations to lupine material from my own psychoanalysis, and linked all this to my epiphany on viewing Karel Appel's lithograph entitled "I Am an Animal," which hangs on the wall in my study at home and which can currently be viewed online by Googling "Karel Appel 'I am an Animal.'" Based on all this, I believe that it makes sense to see our collection of artworks not as a symbolic quest to assassinate helpless creatures but rather as an attempt to provide metaphorical shelter for artistic representations of our furry and feathered friends. By the way, knowing me like a book, my psychoanalyst agrees – the ultimate "member check," beloved by CB Odyssey fans!

Turtle and Me

When signing off, at the end of my role as President of the Association for Consumer Research, I presented a brief account of my early days in high school as a very unhappy member of the football team – one more concerned, to no avail, about not freezing his hands and not getting his fingers stepped on than about fitting in with the team spirit and shining forth on the gridiron (Holbrook, 1989b). Weighing in at a pudgy 50 pounds more than my present heft, as a middle lineman, my job consisted of getting run over during team scrimmages – again and again, without surcease – by our charging fullback who almost always managed to step on me as he easily evaded my hope-lessly inept attempts to make a tackle. In self-defense, I adopted a stance in which I hunkered down close to the ground, ready to collapse into a curled-up somewhat trample-proof heap. In this unconventional position, I strongly resembled a turtle so "Turtle" became my nickname for the duration of my disastrous football career. But, on a hopeful note that in my mind was related to our role as consumer researchers, there came a day when I almost acciden-tally managed to make a very nice tackle of an opposing player running down-field. So my depressing diatribe on the dangers of football managed to end in a cheerful way. And the Turtle emerged with a smidgeon of his dignity intact.

Cats Versus Dogs: Metaphor Us All

About this time, I also developed the animal-related metaphor out of which I believe I have gotten the most mileage over the years – namely, my com-parison of marketing researchers to dogs and consumer researchers to cats (Holbrook, 1989a, 1990a, 1993b, 1995b, 1996c). The former, like our canine companions, are anxious to please their human masters (the marketing man-agers), will work for food (big consulting fees), and will fetch the evening paper or point to a bird in the bush (decision-relevant information). The latter, like our feline friends, are resolutely individualistic and curious (setting their own agendas), cannot be bribed (showing stubborn independence), and can-not be taught to "go fetch" (though they may well invent this game on their own and teach it to you). To quote myself in describing our cat Quarter:

> Briefly, dogs are obedient; they aim to please their masters; they want to do what we want them to do; they wish to follow the rules. In short, they are DOGmatic. If there were an instruction book for pets, dogs would gladly live by those guidelines.

> By contrast, cats are independent; they aim to please nobody but them-selves; they really do not care what others think; they are indifferent to the whole concept of rules and regulations. In short, from the viewpoint of the dog fancier, they are CATastrophic. If there were an instruction book for pets, cats would insist on ignoring it completely.
>
> (Holbrook, 1995c)

In other words, like dogs, marketing researchers follow the banausic path of conducting applied studies in the service of managerial relevance. By contrast, like cats, consumer researchers pursue basic knowledge for its own sake by engaging in pure rather than applied research. As I have repeated ad nauseum, I actually like dogs and have no problem with letting marketing researchers do what they do as the essence of their strongly canine beast-like nature. What I object to is the incessant pressure on the rest of us to adopt their profit-seeking proclivities in the service of applied research (say, consulting assignments or case studies) that work against the more feline curiosity-driven pursuit of knowledge for its own sake.

My own inclinations toward the latter orientation have often caused me to adopt perspectives that I identify as essentially feline in nature – as when recounting the adventures of our beloved Rocky the Cat (Holbrook, 1996d), satirizing what I believe are the excesses of some naturalistic inquiry via a parody based on the inclusion of our cat Quarter as an informant (Holbrook, 1997c), advocating the power of stereoscopic images (Holbrook, 1998d) and their ability to reveal a camouflaged snake (Holbrook, 1997b), identifying with the cat in *Breakfast at Tiffany's* (Holbrook, 1998i), or highlighting the potential ethical issues involved in an "ownership" of pets as opposed to an "involvement" with animal companions (Holbrook, 2007c, 2008d).

Other Admirable Creatures With Whom to Identify

But there are also other non-feline animal creatures that I admire greatly. These include Hoagy Carmichael and Johnny Mercer's "Skylark" as the quintessence of lyricism in ways that I associate with an openness to the study of emotions. I advocated this perspective in my presidential address at ACR (Holbrook, 1990c) – emphasizing its important link to various feminist issues – but was quite surprised when I found that some of the women in the audience were threatened by my departure from conventionally masculine-and-rational concerns. Apparently, these gals had trained themselves to think like men and did not want to revert to the more skylark-like lyrical embrace of emotions as a suitable topic for study.

Another admirable bird is the penguin featured in an old *New Yorker* cartoon. He is flying around in the air above a group of six or seven fellow penguins and is calling down: "We just weren't flapping them hard enough." I took this cartoon as my text for a commencement address that I was invited to give at Edith Cowan University in Perth, Australia (Holbrook, 1997e). The address featured comparisons between our two cultures – leading me to the subject of penguins and, from there, to the theme of flapping our wings hard enough or, in other words, trying as strenuously as we can as we go forth into the world. These were my inspirational thoughts for the graduating class.

Even more inspiring, to me, is the story of my favorite elephant – Horton, as indelibly portrayed by Dr. Seuss. When invited to speak to one of the AMA Doctoral Consortiums, I used Horton as a metaphor for qualities needed in a young faculty member conducting marketing or consumer research – namely, patience, persistence, and perseverance (Holbrook, 1990b). Horton, many readers will recall, was the noble creature who promised the Maisy Bird that he would sit on her nest and then persevered through winter storms and all sorts of other indignities until, eventually, the hatchlings resembled him more than Maisy. In other words, this fine creature represents the triumph of patience and persistence. And keeping your promises – to yourself and to others. This excellent elephant meant what he said. And he said what he meant because – in the touching evocation by Dr. Seuss – an elephant is faithful, one hundred percent. *Horton Hatches the Egg* was my favorite book as a child and still claims that honor 70-something years later (Holbrook, 1998b, 2001–2002). When we are called upon to give a baby present, we usually present the infant with *Horton*, along with an apologetic note saying that we realize it will be a few years before the child can appreciate the book fully in all its glory. But every kid should own it because it is maybe the best book ever written.

They Keep Coming

As I have ventured on, self-defining animal metaphors have continued to command my attention in more diverse ways than mentioned heretofore. Local creatures (squirrels, pigeons) occupied the landscape of my imaginary kingdom called Kroywen – New York spelled backward (Holbrook, 1998e). Digital creatures such as tamagotchis revealed charismatic charms through their display of essentially human characteristics such as Furby's facility with language (Holbrook, 2000c). Animals of all sorts populated my visit to the Phoenix Zoo, as documented in my anti-rigorous qualitative-friendly animadversions on scientism, which somehow landed me pictorially on all fours while trying to imitate a pink flamingo (Holbrook, 2006d). A gorilla reappeared – this one a nasty, dangerous, evil one – in my complaints about the problems of catering to students as customers when adopting a business model for running the university (Holbrook, 2005d). And, when attacked for the views just mentioned, I responded with complaints about the dangers of Goldilocks-inspired inclinations toward compromise (2008a). After all, that golden-haired felonious maiden – who intruded into the home of three nasty bears – was guilty of breaking and entering. And, yes, returning to earlier themes, I still believe that – when facing vicious bears or evil gorillas – there is a fatal flaw in the Goldilocks model of clinging to the middle ground. Lukewarm porridge is usually *not* "just right." (On this theme, please see Chapter 10 on "What Makes a Great Teacher?")

Winding Down

So when it came time to retire in 2009 and when I was asked to make a little speech on that occasion, I returned to my well-worn theme of cats versus dogs as metaphors for contrasting research styles. I began with some comments about why the life of a researcher in academia poses problems of discouragement bordering on despair. In that spirit, I felt obliged to offer an explanation for why I had decided to retire a bit earlier than I might have expected. I developed some new vocabulary to embrace this issue. And, seeking a cheerful denouement (veering dangerously close to Goldie herself), I found an example of a dog that I could respect – namely, a fine Golden retriever named Sebastian who lived down the hall from us in New York. I believe that – in responding to self-imposed limits so as to strike a creative balance between freedom and constraints – even a cat can learn an important lesson from Sebastian. In this, my comments went something like this.

Retirement Speech

The truth is that what we do – here, I'm talking mostly about research, teaching, and other scholarly or creative activities – is . . . quite . . . difficult. On this theme, I'm reminded of a recent true story about the great violinist Joshua Bell. This fine musician is one of the world's foremost classical violin virtuosi. A couple of years ago, somebody from the news media persuaded him to participate in a rather strange and alarming experiment. Specifically, Joshua took his two-million-dollar Stradivarius down into a Washington DC subway station at about 8:30 am, when all the local residents were rushing around trying to get to work on time. With the video cameras rolling, this world-class musical genius stood there in the public space and played his heart out, performing an excruciatingly difficult and transcendentally beautiful rendition of the "Chaconne" from the "Partitas for Solo Violin" by Johann Sebastian Bach. As documented by the news footage, later displayed on YouTube.Com, tens of thousands of people streamed by him. Two or three slowed down or stopped for a moment to listen. Maybe one person threw some pocket change into his open violin case. But, basically, nobody noticed or paid any attention at all.

Isn't what we do just like that? We knock ourselves out to create our most inspired offerings. And we are lucky if one student pays attention, if one reader notices us, or if one other author cites our latest paper. Forty years ago, Bill Moore, Gary Dodgen, Bill Havlena, and I worked long and hard – with a zillion revisions, endless trials, and countless tribulations – to publish the only paper I've ever managed to get into the excellent journal called *Marketing Science* (Holbrook, Moore, Dodgen, and Havlena, 1985). I emphasize that – like Joshua Bell playing Bach's incredibly difficult "Chaconne" in the Washington subway station – this is about the best I could ever hope to do. Yet, in the 40 years since its publication, that paper has been cited fewer than 30 times. That's less than one reference per year. Until right now, I've never even cited it myself. Go figure.

So what can we – as researchers, teachers, scholars, and thinkers – possibly do to combat the forces of darkness that surround us? In this connection, I recently learned a new word. I was reading some of the works by

Theodor Adorno – the great social commentator from the Frankfurt School who, before fleeing to the USA during the 1930s, took an intense dislike to jazz for all the wrong reasons because what he referred to as "jazz" had very little to do with Charlie Parker or Dizzy Gillespie or Miles Davis and a great deal to do with popular music from the Weimar Republic in the 1920s. (For comparison, think of mickey-mouse dance orchestras, Viennese waltzes, military marches, or polka bands, and you'll pretty much get the picture.)

In his tirades against what he incorrectly thought was "jazz," Adorno inveighs at length against something that he calls "heteronomy." But – due to some sort of shameful gap or chasmic void in my education – this was a word I had never heard of before. I got curious about how many of us actually know this word. So I sent out a little survey to a representative sample of the people invited to my retirement party. Specifically, I emailed 22 people. Among whom, 21 answered – for a response rate of over 95% – which is pretty good. And I'm relieved to report that, out of 21 replies, only 1 person – John O'Shaughnessy, whom I salute, by the way – knew the correct definition of "heteronomy." Apparently, some of the rest of us – me included – need help.

It turns out that "heteronomy" is the opposite of "autonomy." "Autonomy," of course, is a word that we do know, and it means . . . being subject to one's own self-government, being free, being independent, being directed by oneself. So "heteronomy" means just the opposite . . . namely, being subject to government by someone else, being ruled by external forces, being controlled from the outside, being directed by others.

Getting back to Theodor Adorno, in speaking of issues related to culture – usually in convoluted prose that is almost impossible to decipher intelligibly – this great thinker identifies "heteronomy" with all the evils of the capitalist system. For example, viewing 20th-century America from the perspective of someone who had fled Fascism, Adorno has very unfavorable things to say about the mass media; about art becoming commerce in the service of financial incentives; about the mass production of entertainment – including movies, radio, television, pop music, and what he misleadingly calls "jazz," all of which he thought were cranked out on a cultural assembly line according to formulas, clichés, or stereotypes intended to appeal to the lowest common denominator of uneducated tastes; about any sort of standardization in the creation of cultural offerings; about all kinds of self-abnegation in the service of money; about the dangers of losing one's individuality; about the threat of unthinking conformity; about the horrors of mindless obedience to authority; and a whole lot more.

So, among other implications, it should be clear that "heteronomy" is the number-one reason why I am retiring . . . sooner rather than later. Briefly, when I was asked to teach a standardized course aimed at a mass market of students viewed as essentially homogeneous customers and assumed to be motivated primarily by greed, I summoned all my foolish courage . . . and . . . tried very very hard to succeed. But I failed . . . very very miserably. So – in case anyone has been wondering – the resulting embarrassment, humiliation, and heartbreak explain why this strikes me as a good time to retire.

But – beyond that and far more importantly – I'm hoping . . . tonight . . . that, going forward, people will think carefully about this contrast between heteronomy and autonomy. Those of you who have been so kind about following my work will know that I tend to view this contrast in terms of a metaphor based on members of the animal kingdom – namely, an analogy drawn from the well-known differences between . . . dogs and cats.

Briefly, heteronomous researchers, teachers, and scholars seem to evince personalities that resemble the essentially canine temperament. More than anything, a dog wants to please his master. A dog will work happily at whatever task brings him a quick payoff. A dog will sit or roll over or go-fetch the evening paper or point to a bird in the bush if you reward him with a piece of candy or a milk bone or a pat on the head or a whole lot of enthusiastic praise. By retrieving knowledge in the form of your evening paper or pointing to a pheasant in a tree, a dog hopes for some sort of extrinsic reward. A dog will cheerfully, diligently, and gratefully work for food. In short, a dog is the very essence of a heteronomous creature that is governed by external forces and that exhibits unquestioning obedience to authority.

By contrast, autonomous researchers, teachers, and scholars seem to evince personalities that resemble the essentially feline temperament. More than anything, a cat insists on pleasing himself. A cat cannot be bribed to do anything that he does not want to do, no matter what kind of payoff you might offer. If a cat wants to play "go fetch," he will teach you how to play the game and then reward you by purring happily so that he trains you to do what he wants. A cat will explore tirelessly to satisfy his own curiosity. In this, a cat seeks knowledge for its own sake as an intrinsically valued end-in-itself. In short, a cat is the very essence of an autonomous creature that remains fiercely independent, stubbornly individualistic, and immovably indifferent to what others want him to do.

You may be surprised to learn that I am actually very fond of both dogs and cats – though, as someone named Morris, my sympathies naturally tend to gravitate somewhat toward the more feline side of the comparison. On the whole (sounding more like Goldilocks every minute, but insisting on the importance of the underlying tension involved), I believe that – in research, teaching, and other academic, scholarly, or creative endeavors – we benefit from a balance between the feline and canine approaches – a rapprochement between autonomy and heteronomy; a reconciliation of freedom and authority, chaos and order, the yin and the yang, non-conformity and conventionality; a dialectic in which a thesis (i.e., a structure) and an antithesis (i.e., a departure or deviation from that structure) merge to form a synthesis (i.e., a creative innovation); a process analogous to the solo by a jazz musician in which a basic pattern of restrictions (in the form of fixed chord changes) underlies purposeful violations of musical expectations (in the form of surprising melodic variations) to create a work of art (in the form of a jazz improvisation); in short, not so much thinking outside the box as thinking along the margins or at the boundaries of the box. Clearly, we need another animal metaphor to capture this point of view. And, for that purpose, I turn to my friend Sebastian.

Sebastian is a large, smart, handsome, and extremely powerful but gentle Golden Retriever who lives down the hall from us at 140 Riverside Drive in New York City. Like the quintessential dog, Sebastian is meticulously trained, faithfully obedient, and dutifully well-behaved. Sebastian loves to go for walks in the park. Of course, Sebastian's owner knows that – in New York City, by law, on such occasions – Sebastian must be at the end of a leash. So I see Sebastian walking down the hall, riding the elevator, and strolling out into Riverside Park . . . carrying his own leash in his mouth.

But, of course, Sebastian is not a cat. Typically, cats do not want to walk on a leash. Yet there is hope. Not too long ago, Sally and I were hiking up Riverside Drive on the way to School, and we passed a man with a great big fluffy cat on the sidewalk along the edge of the park with the cat happily walking on a leash.

From there, it is only one short sweet step to a vision of what I aspire to – for myself, for you, for us all – as a metaphor for how we ought to lead our lives in and out of academia . . . as researchers, as teachers, as scholars, as participants in any other kind of creative endeavor, whatever it happens to be. Combining the perspectives of Sebastian the Golden Retriever and the Anonymous Kitty in Riverside Park, I believe that we should aspire to be like a cat who carries his own leash.

Epilogue

So – to combine some self-defining animal metaphors – in my retirement speech (just quoted at some length), I poured forth my lyrical skylark song, like Bird on his saxophone or maybe more like an emotional gorilla, in ways that expressed my penguin-like struggle, my turtle-esque stubbornness, and my elephantine dedication to disciplined nonconformity for the sake of progress. Did anybody listen, hear me, and congratulate me on my inspirational message? No, No, and No. Like Joshua Bell in the subway station and like our almost-never-referenced paper in *Marketing Science*, my impassioned retirement speech fell on deaf ears and sightless eyes. Though I presented my retirement speech in 2009 to an audience of over a hundred colleagues, friends, and family members, *nobody has ever said a word to me about it*. I'm still carrying the leash, but it's getting pretty heavy.

Part II

Some Comments on the Consumption Experience

4 Essay on the Origins, Development, and Future of the Consumption Experience as a Concept in Marketing and Consumer Research

Abstract

This chapter traces the origins, development, and future of the consumption experience as a concept in marketing and consumer research. Here, the essay relies on Subjective Personal Introspection (SPI) to describe the author's contributions to the introduction and elaboration of the consumption-experience concept. The discussion shows how the concept of the consumption experience has extended to many areas of marketing and consumer research, with widespread applicability to the creation of brand-related promotional messages.

I was pleased and honored to be invited to contribute my thoughts on the origins, development, and future of the consumption experience as a concept in marketing and consumer research to a special issue of *Qualitative Market Research*. Toward that end, I adopt an approach characteristic of the self-reflective essay in the manner that I refer to as Subjective Personal Introspection (SPI). Specifically, I offer my own introspective impressions concerning ways in which the experiential view has emerged over the past 40 years. I speak from the vantage point of my own idiosyncratic perspective and report my own relevant sensibilities.

All the work to which I shall refer in the present essay grew from my early collaborations with Professor Elizabeth C. Hirschman, who cannot participate in the current writing project but whose contributions resonate throughout. As mentioned in Chapter 2, I first met Beth at an ACR conference back in 1979/1980 when I attended a session in which she held forth (Hirschman, 1980a) on the subject of the inadequacies in a paper that I had recently written with Joel Huber on the topic of affective overtones in perceptual measures (Holbrook and Huber, 1979a). This paper – like all my work up to that point – adopted a view of the consumer as a computer-like information processor who made brand choices based on a rational economic approach to purchase decisions. I had been thoroughly indoctrinated into this traditional information-processing view during years of study with my mentor John Howard at Columbia University's Graduate School of Business. In his

DOI: 10.4324/9781003560302-6

influential work with Jagdish Sheth on *The Theory of Buyer Behavior* (How-ard and Sheth, 1969), John had pursued a model of rational economic deci-sions in accord with a paradigm, traceable all the way back to the writings of Plato, that I have since labeled ICABS – that is, Information → Cognitions → Affect → Behavior → Satisfaction (Holbrook, 2001f). Very quickly, this paradigm gained ascendance in the annals of buyer behavior – as espoused by other pioneering thinkers such as Engel, Kollat, and Blackwell (1968), Franco Nicosia (1966), and Jim Bettman (1979). I had bought into this information-processing view hook-line-and-sinker, devoting my doctoral dis-sertation to an empirical demonstration of the superior appeal of advertising claims based on facts (objective denotations) as opposed to feelings (subjective connotations) (Holbrook, 1975, 1978a). During my early career on the faculty at Columbia, I continued to pursue this decision-oriented focus in work with various colleagues (Bill Havlena, Joel Huber, Mac Hulbert, Bill Moore, Mike Ryan, and others) on such manifestations of the rational economic approach as Fishbein-type multiattribute attitude models (Fishbein and Ajzen, 1975) in which preferences are formed by weighing beliefs (expectancies) by their desirabilities (values) and adding up these multiplicative expectancy-x-value scores to arrive at overall indices of likability (Holbrook and Havlena, 1988; Holbrook and Huber, 1979a, 1983; Holbrook and Hulbert, 1975; Holbrook and Moore, 1981, 1982; Holbrook, Moore, Dodgen, and Havlena, 1985; Huber and Holbrook, 1979; Ryan and Holbrook, 1982b). This work evolved in the direction of a Features-Perceptions-Affect or FPA model, inspired by Egon Brunswik (1956), which epitomized the rational but mechanical approach to the study of preference formation (Holbrook, 1981a, 1983c; Holbrook and Bertges, 1981).

Beth's presentation at ACR quite correctly criticized this rational eco-nomic decision-oriented information-processing view (embodied in my work with Joel on affective overtones, as well as in everything else I had done up to that point) as inadequate to the task of explaining the consumer's thoughts and feelings about consumption activities. As a wonderful epiphany, I found myself wholeheartedly agreeing with her critique. And, perhaps to her sur-prise, I went forward after the session and congratulated her on a job of tearing me apart that she had performed with great intelligence and insight. As we chatted, I learned that she lived two doors down from us on the Upper West Side of Manhattan (with only the apartment building that had once housed William Randolph Hearst separating our two Riverside Drive resi-dences). So, perhaps inevitably, we began to work together on the project of broadening our view of the consumer to include aspects not covered by the traditional ICABS- or FPA-type models of brand choices.

In my own defense, to repeat, I can report that – deeply influenced by the work of Phil Kotler and Sid Levy on broadening the concept of marketing (Kotler and Levy, 1969), not to mention the encouragement of my very own psychoanalyst – I had already begun to explore various nontraditional aspects of consumer behavior that included hitherto neglected offerings from the arts and entertainment. Thus, the aforementioned work by yours truly on ICABS, FPA, and multiattribute attitude formulations focused on empirical applications that covered such illustrative examples as jazz saxophonists (Holbrook and Huber, 1983, 1994); jazz-and-pop vocalists (Holbrook, 1977; Holbrook and Williams, 1978); and piano performances of a piece by J. S. Bach (Holbrook, 1981a, 1983c; Holbrook and Bertges, 1981). In short, these kinds of artistic offerings had replaced brands of toothpaste, makes of automobiles, or types of investment opportunities in my own research stream – raising concerns about the aesthetic aspects of consumer responses to the arts and entertainment (see also Holbrook, 1980b, 1981b, 1982a, 1986a, 1987e, 1993g, 1995a; Holbrook and Holloway, 1984; Holbrook and Huber, 1979b).

However, to repeat, I was still "stuck" with the traditional information-processing view as my main research paradigm (ICABS, FPA, multiattribute attitude models) and with the conventional positivistic approaches as my main methodological orientation (ANOVA tests, multiple regressions, structural equation modeling, conjoint analysis, multidimensional scaling). As I began working with Beth, we pushed beyond these ingrained and ubiquitous models and methods to recognize other less objectively utilitarian and more subjectively hedonic facets of the consumption experience. Toward this end, Beth and I began working on a large project, which rapidly grew to such daunting proportions that it ultimately emerged in 1982 as two separate articles – one, first-authored by Beth, that addressed the hedonic aspects of consumer behavior and that appeared in the *Journal of Marketing* (Hirschman and Holbrook, 1982); another, first-authored by yours truly, that focused on the consumption experience as a supplement to information-processing choice models and that was published by the *Journal of Consumer Research* (*JCR*; Holbrook and Hirschman, 1982).

In the present essay, I shall focus primarily on my side of the bifurcation, though Beth's branch has also received extensive attention from subsequent scholars. Specifically, the Holbrook-and-Hirschman piece in *JCR* contrasted an experiential view with the information-processing approach by introducing a series of comparisons based on the traditional ICABS formulation. In particular, we suggested that Information and other Inputs (I) included much more than factual details about brand features or expenditures of money – namely, symbolic meanings associated with the arts and entertainment or with other investments of time. We proposed that Cognitions (C) should be expanded to encompass not only conscious beliefs but also unconscious thoughts, mental images, free ideas, and dreams or daydreams – which, collectively, we labeled "Fantasies." We claimed that Affect (A) embraces not only brand preferences but also a wide range of emotions such as love, hate, joy, sorrow, anger, fear, disgust, curiosity, and so forth – which, we called "Feelings." And we urged that Behavior (B) refers not just to purchase choices or buying decisions but also to a wide range of playful or creative consumption activities associated with product usage – which we named "Fun." Hence, the subtitle of our article: "Consumer Fantasies, Feelings, and Fun."

At the time we wrote the "Three Fs" paper in the early 1980s, we mistakenly believed that we had invented this way of looking at consumers. Subsequently, however, we learned that the importance of consumption experiences is actually an old idea and that this idea, following a book by Stanley Lebergott (1993) called *Pursuing Happiness,* can be traced through John Maynard Keynes (1936) and Alfred Marshall (1920) all the way back to Adam Smith (1776). More recent thinkers who have stressed the importance of services performed by products to create experiences for consumers include the economist Lawrence Abbott (1955) in his work on *Quality and Competition* and Ruby Turner Norris (1941), founder of the Consumer's Union, who wrote about *The Theory of Consumer's Demand.* In marketing, emphasis on the role of consumption experiences appeared in the work by Sid Levy (1959; Boyd and Levy, 1963) on "Symbols for Sale," in the writings of Wroe Alderson (1957) on *Marketing Behavior and Executive Action,* and in the text by Alderson's disciple Walter Woods (1981) on *Consumer Behavior.* Chastened by our omission of credit(s) due to these various predecessors, we have taken pains to acknowledge their contributions in subsequent writings, wherever possible (e.g., Holbrook and Hirschman, 2015). (Notice that the same cannot be said for others, preoccupied with an emphasis on applications to marketing management, who have jumped onto the "experiential" bandwagon in recent years with no sense of where such concepts originated.)

But if we did not invent this concept of the consumption experience all by ourselves, arguably, we did shine a light on it in a way that had not been attempted previously. Specifically, it became central to our way of thinking about consumers and to the trajectory of our research that followed.

Beth took her own interests into any number of fruitful areas related to such diverse topics as innovativeness and creativity (Hirschman, 1980b), product orientation in the arts (Hirschman, 1983), experience seeking (Hirschman, 1984), humanistic inquiry (Hirschman, 1986), addiction (Hirschman, 1992), and self-oriented body images (Thompson and Hirschman, 1995). In my own case, I continued my expanded concerns with Inputs (I) that extended beyond ordinary goods and services to include music (Anand and Holbrook, 1990b; Anand, Holbrook, and Stephens, 1988; Holbrook and Anand, 1990, 1992; Holbrook, Lacher, and LaTour, 2006; Holbrook and Schindler, 1989), films (Dodds and Holbrook, 1988; Holbrook, 1988a, 1999d; Holbrook and Grayson, 1986; Wallace, Seigerman, and Holbrook, 1993), plays (Holbrook, 1988b; Holbrook, Bell, and Grayson, 1989), novels (Holbrook, 1991b, 1997f), and other types of art and entertainment (Holbrook, Greenleaf, and Schindler, 1986; Holbrook and Schindler, 1994; Holbrook and Stern, 1997, 2000; Holbrook and Zirlin, 1985; Schindler, Holbrook, and Greenleaf, 1989; Stern and Holbrook, 1994). In the area of Cognitions (C), my subsequent research began to delve into the unconscious, dream-related, fantasy-enriched, psychoanalytic aspects of consumption experiences, such as my own private and buried responses to a painting by Karel Appel called "I Am an Animal" (Holbrook, 1988c, 1988e). Under the heading of Affect

(A), my colleagues and I investigated a wide range of emotions invested in consumption experiences in general (Havlena, Holbrook, and Lehmann, 1989; Holbrook, 1986c; Holbrook and Gardner, 1993, 1998, 2000) and in the reception of advertising in particular (Batra and Holbrook, 1990; Holbrook and Batra, 1987, 1988; Holbrook and O'Shaughnessy, 1984; Holbrook and Westwood, 1989; Olney, Batra, and Holbrook, 1990; Olney, Holbrook, and Batra, 1991). In connection with Behavior (B), we explored the experience-related aspects of play, games, and leisure pursuits (Havlena and Holbrook, 1986; Holbrook, 1980a, 1987d; Holbrook, Chestnut, Oliva, and Greenleaf, 1984; Holbrook and Lehmann, 1981). And – perhaps most importantly (but not fully anticipated in the 3Fs article) – in place of the traditional focus on Satisfaction (S), my work moved toward analyzing and embracing the Concept of Consumer Value, defined as an "interactive relativistic [comparative, personal, situational] preference experience" (as explained further in Part III). In this direction, via a deep immersion in the value-related literature from axiology, I developed a typology that included eight major types of consumer value: Efficiency, Excellence, Status, Esteem, Play, Aesthetics, Ethics, and Spirituality (Holbrook, 1994a, 1994f; Holbrook and Corfman, 1985). Or – as a later, more popularized formulation entitled "The Eight Es" would have it: Efficiency, Excellence, Exhibitionism, Elitism, Entertainment, Esthetics, Ethics, and Ecstasy (Holbrook, 2012, 2014a). A thorough discussion of this value-related work (Holbrook 1999b) – with generous contributions from helpful colleagues who individually discussed each type of value – appeared in a volume I edited entitled *Consumer Value – A Framework for Analysis and Research* (Holbrook, ed. 1999; see also Holbrook, 2006f and Part III of the present volume).

I am happy to report that all of the ICABS-related extensions just reported have seen an outpouring of investigations from other interested consumer researchers who have plumbed the depths of these facets of consumption experiences . . . and more (e.g., Lanier and Rader, 2015). Any number of colleagues – especially those in Europe and the UK – have begun to explore the experiential aspects of art, entertainment, and other realms of consumer behavior (e.g., Addis and Holbrook, 2001; Batat, 2019; Bradshaw, Kerrigan, and Holbrook, 2010; Brown, ed. 2006; Brown and Patterson, ed. 2000; Carú and Cova, 2003, ed. 2007; Roederer, 2013; Roederer and Filser, 2015; please also see the special issue of the *International Journal of Arts Management* on "Forty Years of Fantasies, Feelings, and Fun" edited by Addis [2023]). Interest in psychoanalytic approaches to consumer research has grown or, perhaps I should say, re-emerged after its years of neglect in the wake of the mid-1950s retreat from Motivation Research (Cluley and Desmond, 2015; Holbrook, 2015f). Every kind of imaginable emotion has been investigated at length (Pham, 2007) – with some even arguing that, under certain circumstances, a reliance on feelings may contribute to an improvement in decision making (Pham, 2004). Studies of leisure activities – often in the context of tourism – have burgeoned and, indeed, now constitute a recognized discipline in their own right (Jackson, Morgan, and Hemmington, 2009; Tung and Ritchie, 2011). And, to my delight, investigators and collaborators (especially in Europe) have begun to address philosophical and methodological issues associated with the conceptualization and measurement of consumer value (Gallarza, Gil-Saura, and Holbrook, 2011, 2012; Sánchez-Fernández, Iniesta-Bonillo, and Holbrook, 2009).

I should also mention that Beth and I never intended that our experiential view should reject or replace the traditional focus on rational economic decision making. Rather, our original diagrammatic representation showed a contrast for each category of the ICABS formulation – that is, a series of distinctions between an information-processing side on the left and an experiential side on the right. Here, I would draw an analogy with another one of my pet themes – namely, the nature and power of stereoscopic viewing (Holbrook, 1996f, 1997g, 1997h, 1997i, 1998a, 1998d, 1998e, 1998f, 1998g, 1998i, 1999b; Holbrook and Kuwahara, 1998, 1999; Holbrook, Stephens, Day, Holbrook, and Strazar, 2001). In stereopsis, the left and right eyes see the world from slightly different vantage points. Either eye's view – left or right, considered by itself – gives an essentially flat picture. However, when the left and right images are merged by the brain into one stereoscopic impression, we see the world in three-dimensional depth – often to rather striking effect. The same logic applies in the case of our contrasts between the information-processing and experiential views of consumer behavior on the left and right sides of the distinctions shown in our diagram. Only by combining these two perspectives into one synthesized representation can we achieve a true three-dimensional in-depth understanding of the consumer.

I tried to make this point – a bit less colorfully – in a paper with John O'Shaughnessy and Stephen Bell that, after many rounds in the review process, failed to get published by the *Journal of Consumer Research*, partly on the grounds that the rational versus emotional or information-processing versus experiential views were incommensurable and could not be encompassed within the same framework (though this is exactly what we had tried to do, I believe successfully). This paper eventually appeared – thanks to the gracious editorial generosity of Beth Hirschman – in *Research in Consumer Behavior* under the title "Actions and Reactions in the Consumption Experience: The Complementary Roles of Reasons and Emotions in Consumer Behavior" (Holbrook, O'Shaughnessy, and Bell, 1990; see also, Hirschman and Holbrook, 1986). After our long and unsuccessful struggle with *JCR*, I was grateful to see it published in a good place. But I have always wondered whether the need to reconcile the decision- and experience-oriented approaches might have gained greater traction if our paper attempting to accomplish just that had appeared in a more easily accessible and widely read outlet.

Many of the avenues mentioned thus far have led in the direction of incorporating research methods new to the annals of marketing and consumer research – especially those of a nature with special interest to readers of *Qualitative Market Research*. Specifically, Beth and I soon found that exploring aspects of consumption experiences, as outlined here, required any number of approaches borrowed from the humanities and from qualitative methods in the social sciences. We discussed many of the relevant methodological issues in our treatise entitled *Postmodern Consumer Research: The Study of Consumption as Text* (Hirschman and Holbrook, 1992). In particular, after proposing our views on fantasies, feelings, and fun, we quickly found ourselves pursuing interpretive methods borrowed from semiotics, hermeneutics, literary criticism, or cultural studies (cf. Mick, 1986) and applied to the exploration of audience responses to films such as *Out of Africa* (Holbrook and Grayson, 1986) or *Gremlins* (Holbrook, 1988a), plays such as *Painting Churches* (Holbrook, 1988b) or *Coastal Disturbances* (Holbrook, Bell, and Grayson, 1989), TV dramas such as *Mrs. Cage* (Holbrook, 1996a), or novels such as *Ulysses* (Holbrook, 1991b). Between the two of us, we covered a broad spectrum of semiological research from the viewpoint of consumption experiences (Holbrook, 1987h). Ultimately, these formed the basis for our book *The Semiotics of Consumption: Interpreting Symbolic Consumer Behavior in Popular Culture and Works of Art* (Holbrook and Hirschman, 1993).

I should perhaps mention again that (as previously noted in Chapter 2) Beth and I adopted slightly different perspectives in our semiological work on consumption experiences in the arts and entertainment. Beth's viewpoint focused primarily on lessons of relevance to marketing that could be learned from the semiotic analysis of themes, characters, and plots in various motion pictures and television dramas. By contrast, my own preoccupation dwelled on what the semiology of marketing- and consumption-related imagery in artistic offerings could teach us about the meanings of those artworks. In this connection – paraphrasing John F. Kennedy – I characterized our contrasting approaches by the difference between asking "what semiotics can do for marketing" (Beth's primary focus) versus inquiring "what marketing can do for semiotics" (my own major vantage point). (For further discussion of this contrast, please see Holbrook, 2005b, 2006e.)

My tendency to pursue the latter type of orientation has won me many friends but probably even more critics among those in our discipline who show a concern for the relevance of consumer research to marketing managers. Throughout my career – from a viewpoint shared in part by Beth and by many others on the consumer-research side of things – I have tried to preserve a distinction between marketing research (aimed at serving the needs of managers in search of practical applications) and consumer research (directed toward understanding consumers and consumption as topics worthy of investigation for their own sake as an end in itself) (Holbrook, 1985, 1986e, 1986f, 1987f, 1987i, 1987j, 1993b). As discussed in Chapter 3, this contrast has led to my dogs-versus-cats analogy (Holbrook, 1989a, 1990a, 1993b, 1996c, 2014c) in which marketing researchers resemble dogs (extrinsically motivated to please their masters and to gain rewards in the form of praise or more tangible incentives), while consumer researchers resemble cats (pursuing the satisfaction of their curiosity as an intrinsically motivated end in itself to be valued for its own sake). The former "applied" researchers (imbued with a deep devotion to the pursuit of managerial relevance) regard the latter as . . . *cata*strophic; the latter "pure" researchers (dedicated to an idealistic freedom from pragmatic concerns) regard the former as . . . *dog*matic. I recognize the valuable contributions to be made from the canine side of things, but – at heart – I embrace the feline sensibility that pursues knowledge about consumers for its own sake as a self-justifying act of curiosity. As the saying goes: "Curiosity killed the cat, but satisfaction brought him back." Here's to the nine lives implicit in that sort of intellectual quest.

Throughout my career, the latter perspective – quintessentially feline – has allowed me to pursue themes and topics drawn from my vocational fascination with the arts in general, with music in particular, and with jazz most especially. As an English major in college, I developed a healthy respect for the glories of literature and the joys of consuming it deliberately (which, like a good literary critic, as noted in Part I, I do with excruciating slowness and inexhaustible patience, sometimes more approvingly referred to as "close" reading) (Holbrook, 1998b). These proclivities spilled over into my appreciation for films, plays, television dramas, and comparable text-based entertainments of all kinds. All my life, I have also loved music in many of its forms ranging from classical symphonies to popular tunes from the Great American Songbook to rock artists who blossomed during the late 1960s and then, just as quickly, disappeared (to be replaced by sonic detritus that I consider abhorrent, much of which can be gathered by streaming compressed-and-thereby-degraded MP3 files from Spotify, Pandora, YouTube, or iTunes). But – most of all – I adore jazz and especially the jazz that flowered at mid-century in performances by people like Charlie Parker, Dizzy Gillespie, Bud Powell, Thelonious Monk, Miles Davis, Clifford Brown, Horace Silver, Charles Mingus, the Modern Jazz Quartet, Chet Baker, Gerry Mulligan, Art Pepper, Stan Getz, Zoot Sims, Jimmy Giuffre, Jim Hall, Art Farmer, Oscar Peterson, Hampton Hawes, Bill Evans, Keith Jarrett, Gary Burton, and . . . .. As you can see, the list is endless. Happily for me, my position on the side of cats who advocate consumer research for its own sake allowed me to pursue these arts-, music-, and jazz-related themes wherever they might lead. As one example, I have explored the "jazz metaphor" in the context of implications for marketing managers to be gleaned from comparisons with jazz-related phenomena (Holbrook, 2003b, 2015g; please see Chapter 9). My more extended reflections on this theme appear in a monograph entitled *Playing the Changes on the Jazz Metaphor: An Expanded Conceptualization of Music-, Management-, and Marketing-Related Themes* (Holbrook, 2007e). As another example, similar preoccupations have led in the direction of research on the role of jazz in films – a topic that reflects a great deal of feline curiosity with precious little canine concern for the needs of marketing managers and that has flowered into a number of papers about meaning-enhancing jazz performances in motion pictures, as collected to constitute my book entitled *Music, Movies, Meanings, and Markets: Cinemajazzamatazz* (Holbrook, 2011).

We might conclude from everything I have said thus far that the focus on consumption experiences has treated me quite kindly. It has inspired the majority of my work for over 40 years. It has encouraged others to move in similar directions. And it promises to motivate a variety of efforts that will emerge in future years. Recently, I engaged in an email debate with my British colleague Michael Woodward that – when organized in the form of an academic paper – ultimately appeared in *Marketing Theory* under the title "Dialogue on Some Concepts, Definitions, and Issues Pertaining to 'Consumption Experiences'" (Woodward and Holbrook, 2013). At the risk of oversimplifying, I would suggest that Michael's main reservations about my views concerned my belief that *all* human experience entails consumption – that everything we do as human beings involves some sort of consumption experience. From this perspective, the study of consumption experiences is nothing less than the study of the human condition (Holbrook, 1986c, 1987d, 1987i, 2008b). Michael thought that I went a bit too far in my penchant for inclusiveness. But I'll stick with my convictions – all the more because they open the door to the pursuit of an approach that deals with the reporting of consumption experiences in the form of essays from the viewpoint of Subjective Personal Introspection (SPI).

As developed and indeed perfected by Michel de Montaigne (ed. 1993) in the 16th century, the essay (where "essai" in French means "trial" or "attempt") embodies SPI and delves into the experiences of its author as a route toward understanding the experiences of others. Beginning with what I have called my "ACR Trilogy" in the mid-1980s (Holbrook, 1986d, 1987a, 1988c), I have pursued this SPI approach in numerous places – many of them reflected and collected in my book entitled *Consumer Research: Introspective Essays on the Study of Consumption* (Holbrook, 1995b; see also Holbrook, 1994d, 1997f, 1997i, 1998d, 1998e, 1998i, 1999e, 2003e, 2005c, 2006a, 2006d). Early on, this approach won support from such consumer researchers as Steve Gould (1991, 1995). And – more recently, despite vociferous complaints by Melanie Wallendorf and Merrie Brucks (1993), along with more considered criticisms by Arch Woodside (2004, 2006) – it has won further support from distinguished scholars such as Banbury, Stinerock, and Subrahmanyan (2012); Stephen Brown (2012); Rob Kozinets (2012); Minowa, Visconti, and MacLaran (2012); Barbara Olsen (2012); John Sherry (2012); and Wohlfeil and Whelan (1012) – all represented in a special issue of the *Journal of Business Research* edited by Steve Gould (2012). The SPI approach appears frequently in fields peripherally related to marketing and consumer research (e.g., Miller, 2010, 2012). As mentioned earlier, the present essay offers one illustration of SPI and, I hope, makes a case for itself as the only reasonable way to address the issues of concern in the context of interest here.

In that spirit, I must mention my own SPI-worthy amazement at the degree to which references to consumption experiences have permeated our consumer culture in general and our world of advertising in particular. In recent years, I have amused myself by collecting examples of promotional pitches – print ads, TV commercials, sales appeals, billboards, store signs, package labels, emails, and so forth – that mention the experiential aspects of using the company's offering. I do not know to what extent – if any – these promotional claims have drawn upon the available literature in marketing and consumer research to encourage their references to the consumption experience. I do know that innumerable self-help books and motivational speeches by any number of management gurus such as Joseph Pine and James Gilmore (1999) or Bernd Schmitt (1999) have encouraged the practice of "experiential marketing" aimed at the creation of an appealing "brand experience." (For reviews of this vast and expanding literature, please see Holbrook, 2000b, 2006g, 2007f, 2007g, 2007h.) Concurrently with the appearance of such pragmatic advice, we have witnessed a great proliferation of references to "The Experience" in the various promotional media just mentioned.

So I began keeping track of these promotional appeals to consumption experiences and, very quickly, amassed a large inventory of examples that appeared in my book chapter entitled "Manufacturing Memorable Consumption Experiences from Ivy and Ivory: The Business Model, Customer Orientation, and Distortion of Academic Values in the Post-Millennial University" (Holbrook, 2009d). Since the publication of this chapter, I have continued to compile samples of ads, commercials, billboards, signs, package labels, and other promotional materials that include some mention of how the relevant product or service provides or enhances one or another sort of consumption experience. My newer file of such commercialized experiential moments has now grown to the point where it contains over 600 specific examples. A full list appears in the Appendix. A ruthlessly truncated subset of these items would include the following (where, to improve readability, I have replaced capitalized, italicized, and bold-faced type with more ordinary lettering).

Tourism

Airlines – American Airlines: "New York's Premium Travel Experience"
– Korean Air: "Experience global networking on a whole new scale"
Cruises – Celebrity X®: "Modern Luxury: Experience It"
– Cunard: "Experience it today"
– Sitmar: "The Sitmar Experience"
Automobiles – Aston Martin: "An entirely new car experience"
– Audi: "Experience the Audi A4 at your local dealer today"
– BMW: "It's a feeling you can only experience in a BMW"
– Buick Verano: "Experience Buick Lease"
– Hertz: "Elevate your next car-rental experience with the best"
Other Transportation – Holiday Bus: "Experience Excellence"
Hotels & Resorts – Baymont Inns: "Experience . . . Hometown Hospitality"
– Biltmore Hotel (Providence, RI): "Enjoy the historic experience"
– Breakers, The (Palm Beach): "Immerse yourself in a one-of-a-kind experience"

– Leela, The: "Experience the true essence of India"
– Marriott Hotels: "One Rewarding Experience Leads to Another"
– Stowe Mountain Resort: "The Experience of a Lifetime"
Travel Destinations – Canada Parks: "Expériences Inoubliables" [Unforgettable Experiences]
– Israel: "Where else can a view of the sea be a Biblical experience?"
– New York State: "Experience. Explore. Enjoy"
Travel Tours – Columbia Alumni Association: "Experience of a Lifetime by Private Jet"
– Perillo Tours: "Eight unique travel experiences"
Restaurants – Ben & Jack's Steakhouse: "A True New York Experience"
– Caribbean Xpress: "A Tasty Island Experience"
– Georgia's Café: "Experience a Taste of Europe"
– Red Lobster: "Creating an experience that's not just a meal"
– Sushi Yasaka: "Moderate price . . . Extraordinary experience"
Museums – American Museum of Natural History: "Dive in and experience the amazing underwater world of whales"
– Cooper Hewitt Smithsonian Design Museum: "Experience the New Cooper Hewitt"
– Museum of Fine Arts (Boston) – "Experience the Masterpieces"

Consumer Nondurables

Drinks – Mojito Labs (Paris): "The Mojito Experience"
Food – Seabear Wild Salmon: "Seafood Experiences to Share"
–Dorritos Tacos: "A taste experience like no other"
Health-Care Products – Glide (Dental Floss): "Experience the Glide Difference"
– Noxzema: "Experience the one and only Noxzema deep clean"
– Pine Brothers: "Not just a cough drop but an experience"
Miscellaneous – Air Wick: "A cleaner fragrance experience"

Consumer Durables

Electronics – Nook (Barnes & Noble): "The Ultimate Reading Experience™"
– Panasonic HDTV: "Experience Visual Excellence"
Cell Phones – Sony Xperia: "Experience the best in Sony smartphones"
– Sprint/Samsung: "Experience 4G"
– Vertu: "Extraordinary Experiences"
Computers – Dell: "Experience Windows 8"
– Toshiba: "Experience Windows 8"
Other Durables – Benjamin Moore (Paint): "Experience Richer Colors . . .."
– Mephisto (Footwear): "For a Comfortable and Effortless Walking Experience"
– Nespresso (Espresso Machine): "Experience the Incomparable Coffee of Nespresso"
– Rockport (Shoes): Experience the Style and Comfort of Rockport"
– Sealy (Mattresses): "An exceptional sleep experience"

Events

Broadway Shows – Jersey Boys: "Now, you can experience it for yourself"
– *Warhorse*: "Experience the wonder of *Warhorse*"
Television Shows – Awake: "Experience the Best New Show of the Season"
Films – Avatar: "The 3-D Experience comes home"
– *The Help*: "An unforgettable experience"
Jazz – Gregory Porter (Singer): "Experience the Gregory Effect now"
Classical Music and Ballet – American Ballet Theater (NYC): "Experience the Power of Dance"
– Metropolitan Opera: "Experience the Met's new *Ring* cycle"

Education

Schools – Harvard University (Planned Giving): "Donors Enrich Their Harvard Experience"
– University School of Milwaukee: "The Experience of a Lifetime"
– Third Street Music School: "A once-in-a-lifetime experience"

Housing

Homes – Atria: "Redefining Today's Senior Living Experience"
– Osborn Retirement Community, The: "Experience the Views"
– Town & Country Real Estate (East End of Long Island): "Experience Montauk"

Shopping

Stores – Brooks Brothers: "Experience the Standards of Quality and Value"
– Loewe's (Hardware): "Experience Loewe's. Let's Build Something Together"
– Ralph Lauren: "The Ultimate Experience"
– Walmart: "A pleasant shopping experience"
On-Line Shopping – BestBuy.Com: "Experience Limitless Entertainment"
– Frontgate.Com – "Experience Frontgate Quality"
– Starbucks.Com: "Experience more at Starbucks.Com"
– Stelton.Com – "We hope you enjoy your shopping experience on our website"

Services

Financial Services – Chase Bank: "Welcome to a Better Banking Experience"
– City National Bank: "Experience the Difference"
– First Republic Bank: "Banking with First Republic is a wonderful experience"
– Visa Credit Cards: "Black Card Members Experience More"
Hedonic Services – Eharmony.Com: "Experience the difference of a site that really cares about helping you find a wonderful relationship"

– Spot Experience, The (Dog Grooming): "The first luxury experience of its kind for your dog"
– Unikwax: "Feel the natural waxing experience"
Health-Care Services – United Health Care: "It's Time for a Better Health Care Experience"
Community Services – Manhattan Jewish Center: "MJE . . . Manhattan Jewish Experience"

Four persistent features – found in the preceding list – deserve brief comments before proceeding further.

First, notice the stereotyped linguistic mannerisms that advertisers and other promotional communicators have created in order to brag about the consumption experiences provided by their offerings. Some use the word "experience" as a simple noun attached to the name of their brand or company – as in "The ABC Experience," where "ABC" = Mojito, Sitmar, New York, or Manhattan Jewish Center. Others regard "experience" as a verb and urge the reader or viewer to appreciate their brand or product – as in "Experience XYZ," where "XYZ" = Glide, Noxzema, Audi, Buick, the Cooper Hewitt Museum, 4G Smart Phones, Windows 8, *Warhorse*, Gregory Porter, the *Ring* Cycle, or Montauk.

Second, observe how usage of the experiential perspective in promotional communications has become extremely widespread and cuts across the full array of product categories ranging from, say, Food to Health Care, to Tourism, to Beauty Products, to Cultural Events, to Banks or Credit Cards, to Electronic Media or Cell Phones, and to the Xmas Season. A recent holiday card offered the wish, "May you experience joy, peace and happiness this holiday season." Few, if any, product categories or services – no matter how seemingly mundane or insignificant – are immune to the claim that they provide . . . experiences. It does not surprise me when I see references to the consumption experience in the ads for, say, alcoholic beverages, food, modes of travel (airlines, cruises, cars), travel destinations (hotels, countries or states, tours), restaurants, museums, Broadway shows, TV programs, films, music (jazz, classical), bricks-and-mortar stores, online shopping, hedonic services (dating, dog grooming, waxing), or even Xmas. After all, the whole point of many such goods and services is to provide the customer with gratifyingly valuable consumption experiences. But it does surprise and, indeed, reinforce me somewhat to see similar references to consumption experiences cropping up in ads and commercials for, say, health aids (dental floss, hearing aids, skin cream, cough drops, eyeglasses), electronics (Nook, cell phones, computers), durable utilitarian products (paint, shoes, coffee machines, mattresses), education (universities, high schools, music teaching), financial services (banks, credit cards), utilitarian services (computer software, the post office), network services (phone lines, cable TV), health-care services (medical insurance), or community services (a Jewish center). Such offerings appeal mostly to rational economic motives that would traditionally have been targeted by facts-based appeals compatible with the decision-oriented information-processing view of brand choice. Nonetheless – given my belief that all human phenomena involve consumption experiences – I cannot quibble with this tendency to sell cough drops, dental floss, cell phones, banks, credit cards, health insurance, cable-TV services, and the other offerings just mentioned on the basis of their experience-enhancing virtues.

Third, notice how – in many or even most cases – the term "experience" has taken on approbative value. Apparently, businesses feel that it suffices to promise an "experience" without in any way mentioning whether that experience is a good or bad one. Rather, pleasure or happiness is assumed as part of the phenomenon of experiential consumption. Thus – without any promise that the experience will be positive – we are offered "the Mojito experience" (Alcoholic Beverage), "Seafood Experiences to Share" (Seabear Wild Salmon), an "Experience [of] the Glide Difference" (Dental Floss), "a cough drop . . . experience" (Pine Brothers), "The Sitmar Experience" (Cruise Ships), "An entirely new car experience" (Aston Martin), "a feeling you can only experience in a BMW" (Automobile), "The Experience of a Lifetime" (Stowe Mountain Resort), "a one-of-a-kind experience" (The Breakers), an "Experience [of] the true essence of India" (The Leela), "an experience that's not just a meal" (Red Lobster), an "Experience [of] the New Cooper Hewitt" (Museum), "The Ultimate Reading Experience" (Nook), "Extraordinary Experiences" (Vertu), the "Experience [of] Windows 8" (*both* Dell *and* Toshiba), "The 3-D Experience" (*Avatar*), "An unforgettable experience" (*The Help*), an "Experience [of] the Met's new *Ring* cycle" (Metropolitan Opera), the "Harvard Experience" (Education), "the Experience of a Lifetime" (University School of Milwaukee), "A once-in-a-lifetime experience" (Third Street Music School), the "Senior Living Experience" (Atria), the "Experience [of] Montauk" (Town & Country Real Estate), the "Experience [of] Loewe's" (Hardware Store), "The Ultimate Experience" (Ralph Lauren), an "Experience [of] the Difference" (City National Bank), "Your Recent Postal Experience" (US Post Office), "the natural waxing experience" (Unikwax), "the ultimate cinema experience" (Time-Warner Cable®), or the "Manhattan Jewish Experience" (Manhattan Jewish Center). Implicitly, such experiences are assumed to be good and worth pursuing – something to be desired and sought for the sake of their hedonic rewards. Nobody stops to contemplate the possibility that the drink might taste awful, that the cough drop might choke you, that the cruise ship might run aground, that the car might smell bad or pollute the atmosphere, that the ski resort might get snowed in, that the travel destination might be hot and crowded, that the lobster dinner might give you indigestion, that the museum might be boring, that the opera might drag on interminably, that the cell phone might catch on fire, that the computer operating system might be difficult to use or unreliable or both, that the college, high school, or teaching program might terrorize its students, that the senior-living accommodations might be dreary and depressing, that the seaside community might be an over-priced tourist trap, that the hardware might be dangerous to use, that the bank might screw its customers out of their life savings, that the post office might lose your package after charging you a fortune to handle it, that the wax job might be an excruciatingly painful ordeal, that the cable-TV service might offer a poor selection of pay-per-view opportunities, or that the ethnic institution might evoke shared memories of dreaded demons. Rather, an experience is, by definition, assumed to be a good thing, something worth seeking without inquiring further. This assumption obviously runs in the face of all logic or reason. To illustrate the irony implicit in this situation, recent news broadcasts reported the misadventures at a resort in the Bahamas of a ten-year-old boy who received a vicious bite on his leg when he participated in a swim with predatory members of the Chondrichthyte species. Apparently, this paradisical tourist destination refers to this dangerous recreational opportunity as "The Shark-Tank Experience."

Fourth, observe how some companies have targeted not just one but, rather, numerous promotional messages toward promising a brand-worthy experience. For example:

Time Warner Cable – "You can have a better TV experience too" and "All across America, families are coming back to Time Warner Cable for a whole new experience" and "Experience the ultimate selection of products from Time Warner Cable" and "Get the ultimate cinema experience with HD Movies on Demand"

Verizon – "Get More. Do More. Experience More . . .. A TV experience like no other . . .. Connect to a fast Internet experience" and "Switch to a better entertainment experience" and "Enjoy a bigger, better entertainment experience" and "Rev up your online experience" and "Verizon has always set out to provide you with the most powerful and reliable network experience" and "At Verizon, we strive to provide you with the best experience" and "FIOS: A Better TV Experience Is Here" and "For an entertainment experience that goes beyond cable, get FIOS TV."

My favorite illustration of a multi-pronged experiential attack came from JetBlue Airlines back in 2015. In this example, the company handed out a ticket envelope that promised, "YOUR TICKET TO A GREAT FLIGHT EXPERIENCE GOES HERE." On JetBlue, you could enjoy Wi-Fi service with the expectation that "JetBlue Fly-Fi® is real broadband Internet in the sky, delivering a robust online experience." If you needed some more room for your legs, you could pay a little extra in hopes that "When you enhance your JetBlue experience with Even More® Space, you can expect . . . Extra room to stretch out and relax." Or for a lot more money, as a "Mint" passenger, you could buy yourself reclining seats on which "The Mint experience on JetBlue gives you the flexibility to sleep, work and relax, so you can be refreshed for the day ahead." Further, "Mint" customers received a refreshment package known as the "JetBlue Birchbox" with the promise "allow us to mint you a new travel experience . . . welcome to a newly minted

experience . . . thoughtful moments throughout the experience that rejuvenate and engage a weary traveler." In sum, as part of its branding strategy,
JetBlue offered you one experience after another, escalating in price as the
experiences became increasingly exclusive and/or delicious.

All this indicates, quite clearly, that businesses have latched onto the
Concept of the Consumption Experience as a major strategic component of
attempts to promote their market offerings. It gratifies me to see this widespread embrace of the consumption experience as a means to providing value
to consumers. However, I do worry about the creeping tendency to subsume
all marketing-related activity – including consumption experiences – under
the category of "branding." It seems to me that this clouds all human experience with a slightly distasteful admixture of commerce. I don't object so
much when the "brand" in question is, say, Crest toothpaste, Coca-Cola beverages, BMW automobiles, or Apple iPads. But I do take umbrage at some
uses found for the concept of "branding" – which, based on our age-old
concept of the misleadingly puffed-up brand image, I associate with creating
an often-false impression of a product's virtues in order to gain commercial advantage in ways inspired by greed. Specifically, I object when such
applications intrude into areas that I believe should remain free from capitalistic motives – for example, universities, churches, hospitals, and prisons.
Or political candidates. Or terrorist groups. In this connection, I have been
appalled at the emergence of our former president as more a "Trump Brand"
than a dedicated public servant. And I was shocked recently to find a report
in the news media about potential damage – resulting from heinous terrorist
tactics – to the "ISIS Brand."

While I am on the subject of the Trump Brand, I should mention that
this one lone individual has done an incalculable amount of harm by almost
single-handedly dragging the concept of "Business" into the mud. Over and
over, when someone accuses Donald J. Trump of an especially egregious activity such as cheating on his taxes or overstating his wealth to secure bank loans
or diverting campaign funds for his own private gain or putting up visiting
dignitaries at his own hotels in violation of the emoluments clause or pressur-
ing government officials to falsify election results or stealing secret classified
documents or inciting an anti-democratic insurrection, DJT greets such alle-
gations by claiming that his nefarious practices are simply "Good Business."
This tends to denigrate the concept of "Business" in ways that place selfish
interests – some of them unethical or even illegal – above the consideration of
all other stakeholders (employees, suppliers, customers, society at large). The
Trumpian View of "Business" – amid alarming promises that the President
and his followers plan to run the country "like a business" – offends common
decency, ignores crucial aspects of social responsibility, and neglects issues of
ecological sustainability in ways that strike me as quite embarrassing to those
of us who have had some professional connection with a business school.
Now retired, when I go to cocktail parties and somebody asks me what I do
for a living, I say that I worked at a university where I taught . . . consumer

behavior. I don't want to use what, thanks to DJT, has become something of a sullied term – even a dirty word – namely, "Business." As DJT himself might say, in one of his obnoxious early morning tweets, "Sad!"

And – to make matters worse – something similar has happened to another important part of my own identity (lamented at great length in Chapter 12). This latter calamity surfaced recently during a broadcast on the MSNBC network of a news show called "Hardball" that featured Chris Matthews as its charmingly cantankerous host. After rattling off a long list of Donald Trump's alleged atrocities, Matthews paused as he valiantly searched his brain for a word that would encapsulate the enormity of this miscreant's transgressions. It happens that Chris Matthews, a man of enviable intelligence with a gigantic vocabulary and an impressively articulate command of the English language, never appears at a loss for words. But, this time, he struggled to find an epithet sufficiently derogatory to capture the essence of DJT's malevolent treachery. Finally, after an uncommonly awkward moment of hesitation, Chris brightened as a signal that he had at last come up with exactly the right word he had struggled to find . . . namely . . . "Marketing."

As promised, I shall return to this theme in Chapter 12. But, for now, suffice it to say that I shuddered in shame to recognize that I have long belonged to a profession that has earned such scorn – in part, I suspect, because some of our marketing comrades have chosen to take advantage of "brand experiences" (think "Shark Tank") in ways never intended by those of us who have regarded the consumption experience as an aspect of humanity that deserves study as a topic of interest in its own right for its role as a phenomenon worth studying as an end in itself.

To me, the Concept of the Consumption Experience involves a pure attempt to describe the human condition – one that should not be sullied by the commercial taint of "experiential marketing" as applied to schools or churches or medical care or prisons and one that should not be desecrated by transparently greed-serving applications to the selling of "brand experiences" that stem from activities associated with offerings ranging from dental floss to soft drinks to malevolent presidential candidates to terrorist organizations. Of course, I realize, an ancient apothegm insists that "Everything is for sale. At a price." But, surely, there must exist some place where we should draw the line. Perhaps one such place would be . . . the Human Condition.

Let me conclude, therefore, by requesting that the Concept of the Consumption Experience – which, as explained heretofore, grew from a pure curiosity about the nature of the consumer's Fantasies, Feelings, and Fun – should remain unclouded by managerially self-serving applications in the form of exercises in "experiential marketing" or appeals to the "brand experience." Such applications, true to the self-interested capitalistic spirit of the canine marketing researcher, cheapen the Concept of the Consumption Experience by trying to commercialize it. And – in my opinion, speaking as one of its original owners – we should not offer it for sale at any price.

5   Consumption Experiences in the Arts

Abstract

This chapter recalls the emergence of a focus on the experiential aspects of consumption in general and their relevance to the arts and entertainment in particular. It views a consumption experience via an extension, enlargement, and elaboration of the traditional I-C-A-B-S Model in which Information → Cognitions → Affect → Behavior → Satisfaction. In the appropriately broadened view, Information is enriched to include offerings from the arts and entertainment; Cognitions, Affect, and Behavior are expanded to embrace Fantasies, Feelings, and Fun; and Satisfaction is explained in a more nuanced representation of the different types of Consumer Value that potentially result from a consumption experience. Further exploration of the latter phenomenon appears to be a desirable objective for future research on consumption experiences in the arts.

Introduction

Beth Hirschman and I are pleased and honored to have a special issue of the *International Journal of Arts Management* (*IJAM*; Addis, 2023) devoted to the consumption experience in general and to arts-related experiences in particular. We offer our most appreciative thanks to François Colbert for initiating this project, to Michela Addis for organizing it so masterfully, to Alex Turrini and Jennifer Wiggins for all their editorial work, and to all the participants for their inspired and insightful contributions. Beth is busy doing some important work on climate change and global warming, so she has assigned me the task of providing a few words by way of introduction to the special issue. Needless to say, I owe Beth a deep debt of gratitude for our wonderful moments of collaborating over many years. In that spirit, I'll offer some comments on the development of the experiential perspective in the last four decades, beginning with the emergence and elaboration of the ideas presented in our article for the *Journal of Consumer Research* in 1982 entitled "The Experiential Aspects of Consumption: Consumer Fantasies, Feelings, and Fun."

To review some material covered in Chapter 4, back in the 1970s when we finished our doctoral programs and began our careers in teaching, the prevailing

DOI: 10.4324/9781003560302-7

view of consumer behavior subscribed to a model – introduced by John Howard and embraced by virtually every other consumer researcher (Howard and Sheth; Engel, Kollat, and Blackwell; Franco Nicosia; Alan Andreasen; Jim Bettman; Joel Cohen; many others) in which Information (from product features, advertising, word of mouth, and so forth) shaped Cognitions (beliefs about brand attributes) which led to Affect (preferences or liking for one brand vs. another) and determined Behavior (purchase decisions resulting in brand choices) leading to Satisfaction (favorable or unfavorable outcomes that fed back on earlier stages to reinforce Cognitions, Affect, and/or Behavior). This ICABS Model stood at the center of virtually every conceptualization intended to represent the behavior of consumers in the marketplace. Indeed, I used to entertain my class of MBAs in a course on consumer behavior by reviewing every single discussion of this topic from the mid-1970s that I could find and showing that, at heart, each example embodied one or another variation on ICABS.

Several aspects of the bedrock ICABS formulation circa 1975 deserve further mention as hallmarks of the way we viewed consumer behavior in those days. I shall describe these briefly before moving on to the subsequent expansion of ICABS into the experiential view.

Information

As its essential perspective, ICABS viewed the consumer or, more accurately, the buyer as an information-processing machine – something like a computer designed to incorporate incoming intel about a product or brand to generate a decision about whether or not to purchase it. The relevant products of interest were most often frequently purchased nondurables (toothpaste, soft drinks, yoghurt) or big-ticket durables (automobiles, refrigerators, furniture). Information about such products appeared in the form of various objectively verifiable design features (e.g., whitening power of a toothpaste, gas mileage of a car), clearly articulated advertising claims (vitamin content of a yoghurt, spaciousness of a refrigerator), or impressions circulated via word of mouth (thirst-quenching flavor of a soft drink, attractiveness of a leather sofa). Such information cues about tangible product offerings were assumed to shape Cognitions in the form of beliefs concerning the brand.

Cognitions

These beliefs represented perceptions of the extent to which a brand delivered various attributes – that is, the perceived likelihoods that the brand possessed various characteristics with varying degrees of desirability or importance. For example, a soft drink might be perceived as very likely to be sweet, very likely to be high in calories, moderately likely to be delicious, and extremely unlikely to be high in caffeine. Each of these beliefs (B) would then be weighted by its desirability (D) or, more problematically, by its importance (I) and then summed to create a predictive measure of Affect. A Belief-x-Desirability score

(B×D) – or, less plausibly, its Belief-×-Importance Score (B×I) – was viewed as a potential reason for preferring one brand to another, and the sum of the B×D's or B×I's across various relevant attributes was assumed to predict or to explain Affect. This Multiattribute Attitude Model thereby represented a theory of reasoned action via which a buyer processed information to make rational economic purchasing decisions.

Affect

The Affect of interest in the early days of ICABS captured an essentially uni-dimensional measure of liking for the brand. In other words, it reflected a preference hierarchy in which various offerings competed for top places in the ranking of likeability. To the extent that the proponents of ICABS dwelled on consumer emotions or feelings at all, it was this unidimensional assessment of Affect that they worried about. Such affective responses were assumed to deter-mine a buyer's Behavior toward a brand in the form of purchasing choices.

Behavior

The Behavior of interest to the early ICABS modelers concerned a buyer's pur-chase decision and the consequent expenditure of money via a choice outcome favoring the best-liked brand. Here, the ICABS researchers catered to the needs of marketing managers preoccupied with maximizing sales in ways that bol-stered the profit potential of a firm's bottom line. From this angle, the buyer was a rational economic decision maker choosing brands to purchase in ways that could be manipulated to enhance the firm's profit potential. If the resulting choice behavior provided Satisfaction to the customer, a firm might anticipate the golden prize of brand loyalty in the form of repeat-purchase behavior.

Satisfaction

Customer Satisfaction therefore represented success in the ICABS chain of events. A purchase decision deemed satisfactory by the buyer would provide information that would feed back onto earlier stages of the model so as to improve Beliefs, enhance Affect, and encourage future purchase Behavior. In other words, according to the implicit learning model, positively reinforced Behavior tended to be repeated, to solidify into Brand Loyalty, and thereby to enrich the happy producer of the goods or services in question.

Elaborations and Extensions of the ICABS Model: A Tale of Three Women

It would be hard to overestimate the number of buyer-behavior studies that flowed from the ICABS perspective just described. Eager disciples of ICABS lavished ceaseless attention on various subtleties such as the flow of effects from product features to attribute perceptions to brand affect, the comparative testing of various advertising inputs, the role of word of mouth in the adoption of innovations, the best measurement of beliefs and their proper combination with desirability (rather than importance) weights, the representation of affective responses by means of preference spaces generated by multidimensional scaling, the emergence of loyalty in the presence of brand-switching behavior, or the achievement of customer satisfaction in accord with lower versus higher expectations. Clearly, there was plenty here to occupy a host of busy marketing researchers for all their waking hours. And many a career arose from such preoccupations (mine included).

The resulting morass of ICABS-inspired empirical studies clustered around one sometimes implicit but always lurking theme – namely, a view of the consumer as a rational economic decision-making buyer who, like a computer, processed information about product features and attributes in order to make brand choices that potentially resulted in lucrative spending behavior. This perspective regarded the buyer as a cold-blooded information-processing machine rather than a warm flesh-and-blood living creature. Like so many others, I myself bought heavily into this prevalent view. My dissertation, which (after a decade's labor) saw the light of day in 1975, tried to demonstrate that facts-based advertising worked better than an alternative feelings-based approach. I was lucky enough to test this ICABS perspective for the case of automobiles, where the relevant logic seemed to apply. Following that, most of my own early research pursued various refinements and (I hope) improvements of the conventional multiattribute attitude models based on the ΣBxD formulations. Everything about these approaches, grounded in ICABS, continued to honor the prevailing rational economic view of the buyer as an information-processing reason-following computer-like machine for cranking out brand choices leading to purchase decisions.

For me personally, all that changed due to the influence of three important women in my life.

The first of these important ladies was my wife, Sally. We married in 1965. I moved from Cambridge to New York and enrolled in the MBA program at Columbia University to be with her while she finished her Master's Degree at Columbia's School of Social Work. There – along with way too much of the greed-is-good philosophy in the MBA program – I benefited from a healthy dose of concerns from the softer and more feminine side surfaced by Sally's involvement with issues related to social work and its underlying psychological assumptions. These assumptions carried Sally to further studies in psychoanalytic counseling and ultimately to a career as a psychotherapist with a PhD from New York University in clinical social work.

The clinical aspects of Sally's endeavors eventually landed both of us in extended psychoanalyses of the Freudian four-times-a-week-on-the-couch variety. And here, I encountered the influence of a second all-important female. Specifically, my psychoanalyst Dr. L*** K******** worked hard to help me understand that feelings are normal and even good – not necessarily to be degraded in comparison to facts but, rather, important aspects of the human condition and well worth reckoning with. Gradually – while engaging in a six- or seven-year analysis with, say, around 1,400 sessions in all – I opened up to a host of ideas that I would have previously regarded as childish, immature, or too irrational for serious pursuit. Freudian analysts seldom say much. But – one day, when I was rambling on about how much I enjoyed some research I was doing on preferences for jazz musicians – L. K. broke her customary silence and asked: "Why don't you do more of that?" For me, this seemingly obvious question produced an epiphany: Why not focus on consumer responses to the arts and entertainment? So . . . ultimately . . . that's what I did.

And, third, such glimmerings received further reinforcement from my new friendship in the late 1970s with Beth Hirschman, whom I met at a conference of the Association for Consumer Research but who also turned out to be my next-door neighbor in New York City, literally one block south of our home on Riverside Drive. As reported in Chapter 4, Beth and I found a deep affinity in our ideas about consumers. We began working together and continued this habit for many years until she eventually moved away from the City and ultimately ended up in rural Virginia where she now works primarily on issues related to the perils of climate change. As our first major project together, Beth and I began writing a paper about the hitherto neglected aspects of consumer behavior that we increasingly believed deserved greater recognition in our field of study. We soon realized that our collaboration had grown too lengthy for any one journal article. So we broke the work into two co-authored parts. Beth's first-authored part reflected the freewheeling nature of her adventurous spirit and emphasized the multisensory, pleasure-oriented, hedonic aspects of consumption. It appeared in the *Journal of Marketing* in 1982 under the title "Hedonic Consumption: Emerging Concepts, Methods, and Propositions." By contrast, my first-authored part – typical of my often straight-laced character – pursued a more structured approach in which I extended, enlarged, and elaborated each aspect of the ICABS formulation in a systematic some-would-say-pedantic way. The result of that approach, found in *JCR* (1982), appeared as "The Experiential Aspects of Consumption: Consumer Fantasies, Feelings, and Fun."

The Consumption Experience: Fantasies, Feelings, and Fun

The essence of our paper on the Consumption Experience was captured by a diagram showing each aspect of the ICABS approach with a left-hand side representing the prevailing conventional view and a right-hand side showing our proposed extensions, enlargements, and elaborations. Continuing the comments begun in Chapter 4, I shall discuss each of these briefly.

Information in the Experiential View

Our major extension of the prevailing traditional view entailed a recognition – encouraged by the work of Sid Levy and Phil Kotler, among others – that the conventional nondurable and durable consumer products of interest (e.g., toothpaste and automobiles) represented only the tip of the iceberg and that a host of neglected phenomena deserved attention as critical aspects of consumers' lives. These neglected aspects included various forms of entertainment, amusement, and enlightenment such as art museums, musical concerts, television shows, films, plays, novels, hobbies, sports, other leisure pursuits, and so forth – on and on in the direction of almost infinite expansion. Such activities constituted a huge proportion of human existence. And yet, they had been mostly ignored by researchers in our field of inquiry. From our perspective – friendly to the consumer viewed as a warm flesh-and-blood human being – the time had come for devoting greater attention to a much-broadened range of product categories, including those associated with the arts and entertainment.

Cognitions in the Experiential View – Fantasies

Under the heading of "Cognitions," we found an opportunity to recognize the important roles played by various types of thinking not generally recognized in the consumer-research tradition. These included daydreams, night-time dreams, unconscious ideas, and repressed thoughts of the type investigated by psychoanalytic exploration. We referred to such hidden or buried material as "Fantasies" and argued the need for expanded work devoted to their in-depth scrutiny.

Affect in the Experiential View – Feelings

Under "Affect," we reminded readers that conventional ICABS models focused only on unidimensional like-dislike representations of brand preferences but that, in actuality, a much more multifarious array of relevant emotions awaited investigation by consumer researchers. Such emotions include joy, sorrow, love, hate, fear, anger, approval, disgust, and any number of additional impulses that we summarized as "Feelings." Probably, one of the most important aspects of our broadened view was its call for more attention devoted to the role of these emotions in the lives of consumers.

Behavior in the Experiential View – Fun

Under the heading of "Behavior," we argued for the need to expand our horizons to include a host of activities not covered by the traditional prevailing focus on buyer behavior. This extended focus entailed a shift from the conventional preoccupation with the allocation of money to brand choices toward including a greatly enlarged concern for the allocation of another precious resource – namely, time. Clearly – as emphasized by the Nobel laureate Gary Becker – much consumer behavior involves choices about how we spend time in circumstances where the role of money may be more or less irrelevant. How long should I practice the piano tonight? What pieces should I play? How might I reharmonize one of these pieces to attain a more interesting chord pro-gression? Considerations like these have nothing to do with spending money. They relate instead to allocating time in ways that clearly deserve attention from consumer researchers devoted to understanding how we have "Fun" – as when we choose to view "Curb Your Enthusiasm" on HBO, to read a chap-ter from John Grisham's *The Firm*, or to attend a free concert in the park by the New York Philharmonic playing Bruckner's Seventh Symphony. All such aspects of Fun entail the allocation of time rather than merely the expenditure of $$$. I "get" that Ben Franklin proclaimed: "Time is money." But $$$ is a far more limited window from which to view the time investments that enrich the lives of consumers as part of the human condition.

Satisfaction in the Experiential View – Consumer Value

Finally, a concern that did not surface so strongly in the "Fantasies, Feelings, and Fun" paper but that came to dominate my focus in subsequent years involves the need to replace or expand our notion of "Customer Satisfaction" to include a richer and more multidimensional concept of "Consumer Value." Just as the unidimensional view of Affect failed to capture the multiplexity of relevant emotions or feelings, so too the conventional concept of Customer Satisfaction appeared rather impoverished by virtue of its inability to eluci-date the multiplicity of relevant Value-related phenomena. Thus, in work that spanned the next 40 years (further explored in Part III), I argued for a definition of Consumer Value as "an interactive relativistic preference experience." This conceptualization insisted that Value always entails an *interaction* between a subject (the consumer) and an object (a product) – as sometimes described by advocates of the Service-Dominant Logic as "the cocreation" of Value; that Value is *relativistic* in the three senses that it involves a comparison of one experience with others, that it differs from person to person, and that it varies from one situation to the next; that Value lies at the heart of consumer *prefer-ences*; and that Value always stems from a *consumption experience* rather than from the mere possession of some material object. Yes, Russ Belk (1988) has taught us that our possessions represent our extended selves; but they do not confer consumer value until they serve to provide one or another consumption experience.

As part of this preoccupation with Consumer Value, further elaborated in Part III, I developed a Value Typology that depends on three distinctions: (E) extrinsic versus (I) intrinsic value, (S) self-oriented versus (O) other-oriented value, and (A) active versus (R) reactive value. To preview briefly, combin-ing these contrasts produces eight major types of Consumer Value: Efficiency (ESA), Excellence (ESR), Status (EOA), Esteem (EOR), Play (ISA), Aesthetics (ISR), Ethics (IOA), and Spirituality (IOR). Ultimately, I would argue that any reasonable representation or analysis of the Consumption Experience requires a concern for all these various types of Consumer Value. As we shall see, an appreciation for the arts and entertainment seems particularly reso-nant with our conceptualization in this respect.

Wider Perspective, Broadened Views – The Role of the Arts

From what I have said thus far, it should be clear that we envisioned our experiential perspective – that is, our broadened view of the Consumption Experience – *not* as a way of replacing the ICABS formulation (which remains viable and valid in addressing some consumption-related issues) but *rather* as a way of shedding light on various experiential aspects that had hitherto been neglected by the prevailing ICABS tradition, thereby moving from a one-dimensional to a three-dimensional view of the consumer in depth.

In particular, our subsequent work moved in the direction of implementing the broadened perspective empirically in general and extending it in ways that embraced the arts and entertainment in particular.

Perhaps most visibly, we began to devote a great deal of attention – under the heading of Information – to products drawn from the arts and entertainment. Thus, we conducted numerous studies of consumer responses to jazz musicians, musical recordings, visual images, clothing designs, movies, plays, television shows, novels, and so forth. Many of these arts-related studies were quantitatively grounded and included approaches drawn from traditional ICABS-oriented methodologies. Others, however, tapped extended concepts of emotional responses or pursued qualitative methods to interpret symbolic meanings of consumption experiences and marketing imagery found in films (e.g., *Out of Africa*), plays (e.g., *Painting Churches*), television (e.g., *Dallas* and *Dynasty*), or novels (e.g., *Ulysses*). As noted earlier in the latter connection, paraphrasing JFK, I departed from the rationale favored by most of my colleagues to urge: "Ask not what Semiotics can do for Marketing, rather ask what Marketing can do for Semiotics."

The Cognitions of interest began to include the perception of cues fundamental to the design of artworks in various areas – for example, tempo in the case of musical stimuli or color in the case of motion pictures. Sometimes, we collected perceptual measures on a large number of beliefs that then helped to explain various artistic preferences.

Affective measures found in our work covered a very wide range of emotional responses (joy, sorrow, love, hate, fear, anger, approval, disgust, and so forth). We studied these extensively in the case of advertising effects, but I cannot think of any example in which such a breadth of feelings was addressed in our empirical work on the arts and entertainment. Clearly, this remains a compelling topic for future research.

Behavioral measures have informed studies devoted to the investment of time in various leisure pursuits. Such pursuits would include artistically creative activities associated with performances or hobbies of various kinds (e.g., singing in the church choir or watercolor painting). But this also seems to remain a topic in need of further exploration in future research.

Most importantly, the flow of studies inspired by our extended, enlarged, and elaborated conception of the Consumption Experience has included examples that explicitly acknowledge the various types of Consumer Value entailed by various experiences with the arts and entertainment. In one case (addressed further in Chapter 8), I described the multiple types of Consumer

Value enjoyed in a live performance by the great vibraphonist Gary Burton at a Manhattan nightclub (the Blue Note). The point was that Efficiency, Excellence, Status or Exhibitionism, Esteem or Elitism, Play or Entertainment, Aesthetics or Esthetics, Ethics, and Spirituality or Ecstasy all appeared in compresent abundance in this one musical moment. Here, I drew upon a purely qualitative analysis. But this value-oriented interpretation suggests the potential for quantitative exploration via the appropriate measurement techniques (discussed further in Chapter 7).

Meanwhile, I must emphasize the importance of one type of Consumer Value that finds its preeminent illustrations in the consumer's appreciation of artworks and various forms of entertainment – namely, Aesthetic Value. As studied and illuminated by innumerable philosophers of art, Aesthetic Value results from a very special kind of Consumption Experience. In my terms, as noted earlier, such an experience would be self-oriented (S) and reactive (R) in nature. Most importantly, its value must be intrinsic (I) – that is, pertaining to an appreciation or enjoyment of an object (which might be an artwork; a form of entertainment; or, indeed, some other kind of pleasurable phenomenon such as a colorful sunset or a beautiful person) where that experience is prized for its own sake as an end in itself. The moment our regard for the relevant object departs from the intrinsic and becomes extrinsic – as when a work of art is viewed as the means to some end (e.g., a sculpture used as a door stop or a painting displayed to impress the neighbors) – the experience stops being aesthetic and starts being some form of, say, efficiency or status. Only the true intrinsic value found in our appreciation of an artwork – to repeat, the experience enjoyed for its own sake as an end in itself – merits the term "aesthetic." And that possibility of aesthetic value remains an often-overlooked aspect of the human condition that invites our attention even while it challenges our understanding.

More Extensions, Enlargements, and Elaborations

So what do we mean when we use the term "Consumption Experience" and when we apply it to the consumer's appreciation of the arts and entertainment?

I believe that the answer to this question is complex because it encompasses all sorts of ways in which the traditional ICABS framework has been extended, enlarged, and elaborated to embrace an increasingly broad range of consumption-related phenomena.

Information inputs now include all sorts of product offerings that have attracted growing attention from consumer researchers in general and from those focusing on the arts and entertainment in particular. The study of perceptions arising from such offerings continues to assess brand-related beliefs but now potentially entails thoughts that arise in dreams, wishes that surface in daydreams, and even ideas that remain unconscious so as to invite psychoanalytic investigation. All such cognitions combine to generate a whole host of emotions that include brand preferences but that also comprise a broad range of feelings such as joy, sorrow, love, hate, fear, anger, approval, and disgust. Such emotions infuse behaviors that begin with purchase decisions but then branch out into all sorts of ways to invest one's time in leisure-, entertainment-, and other arts-related pursuits. Such activities and time commitments that provide consumption experiences create many different types of value (e.g., Efficiency, Excellence, Status, Esteem, Play, Aesthetic, Ethical, Spiritual), and these compresent aspects of value, in turn, serve to inform and update earlier stages of the ICABS sequence in such a way that reinforced behavior tends to be repeated in the form of brand loyalty.

All this constitutes the Consumption Experience and stands at the center of the Human Condition. The Consumption Experience pervades all aspects of our lives as consumers. And our lives as consumers capture the essence of what it means to be a human being. Consumption is what we do – all day, every day. Sleeping, eating, walking, talking, working, playing, exercising, resting, making love: They are all forms of consumption, and they completely characterize our existence as people on this planet.

Many such consumption experiences involve an exposure to and an appreciation of the arts and/or entertainment. Such aesthetic experiences and other aspects of artistic value pervade our lives and contribute to our happiness in innumerable ways that command our attention.

It should come as no surprise that something so important as the exploration of Consumption Experiences would attract the attention of management-oriented gurus concerned with offering advice to marketers – often in the form of self-help books, motivational speeches, and/or consulting contracts. Thus, a couple of decades after the appearance of our first forays into Fantasies, Feelings, Fun, a flood of literature devoted to experiential marketing began to appear. Such writing featured colorful examples, instructive illustrations, and inspirational suggestions for profitable experience-oriented sales appeals – usually with little attention to the academic background or scholarly sources where such concerns had originated. Instead of dwelling on the intellectual history of such ideas, the practitioner-oriented prophets tended to focus on ways to create experiences that would attract the greatest possible customer purchases or – in an awkward and even ugly turn of phrase – that would maximize the consumer's "spend." In this, they were devout apostles of managerial relevance – dare I say "dogs" (Chapter 3) honoring the imperatives of "greed" (Chapter 11)?

As one result of such efforts to commercialize consumption experiences, we now confront a deluge of advertising and other promotional appeals that cater to the charms envisioned by an experiential view. A couple of years ago, as previewed in Chapter 4, I spent some of my precious spare time collecting examples of experiential appeals found in print ads, TV commercials, billboards, and other signage. Admittedly, this was not a systematic effort. Rather, every time I saw an appeal to the consumption experience, I jotted it down or cut it out and tossed it into an old hat box. Pretty soon, the hat box was filled to overflowing. Without half trying, I had collected over 600 examples of experience-oriented promotional appeals (now presented in the Appendix).

As noted in Chapter 4, some of these appeals commit the fallacy of assuming that "experience" is an unequivocally approbative term. Thus, some businesses promise an "experience" without bothering to consider or to indicate whether the experience is pleasant or unpleasant. So we are promised: "Experience the Glide Difference" (Dental Floss), "The Sitmar Experience" (Cruise Ships), "The Experience of a Lifetime" (Stowe Mountain Resort), the "Harvard Experience" (Education), the "Senior Living Experience" (Atria), "The Ultimate Experience" (Ralph Lauren), or "Your Recent Postal Experience" (US Post Office). These seven illustrations are just the tip of the iceberg. Innumerable examples appear in my list of over 600 cases collected in the Appendix. Implicitly, such experiences are assumed to be good and worth pursuing. Nobody bothers to wonder about the possibility that the dental floss might make your gums bleed, that the cruise ship might run aground, that the ski resort might get snowed in at 20-below-zero, that the college might terrorize its students, that the senior-living accommodations might be dreary and depressing, that the clothing might not fit properly, or that the post office might lose your package after charging you a fortune to handle it safely. Rather, an experience is implicitly assumed to be a good thing – something pleasant, high in value, and worth seeking without asking too many questions. This assumption makes no sense and contradicts all logic or reason. I cringe every time I encounter it. And, if you don't agree, just try "The Shark-Tank Experience."

Further, to revisit a point made in Chapter 4, even the most casual inspection of my hundreds of exemplars shows the degree to which the experiential perspective in promotional communications has become so widespread as to cut across virtually every conceivable product category. These include Food, Health Care, Tourism, Beauty Products, Banks, Credit Cards, Electronic Media, and Cell Phones. Many of these make sense insofar as the main point of most goods and services is to provide the consumer with value-conferring consumption experiences. But it does seem a stretch to argue for favorable consumption experiences in cases where traditional reasons conveyed by facts-based appeals to economic rationality in decision making might actually be more persuasive. For example, Panasonic HDTV ("Experience Visual Excellence"), Sprint/ Samsung Cell Phones ("Experience 4G"), FIOS ("A Better TV Experience Is Here"), University School of Milwaukee ("The Experience of a Lifetime"), Osborn Retirement Community ("Experience the Views), Loewe's Hardware ("Experience Loewe's"), Chase Bank ("Welcome to a Better Banking Experience"), Visa Credit Cards ("Black Card Members Experience More"), US Postal Service ("Tell Us About Your Recent Postal Experience"), or United Health Care ("It's Time for a Better Health Care Experience"). I know I said that consumption experiences pervade every nook and cranny of human existence. Indeed, they do. But sometimes – especially in the case of primarily utilitarian products – it makes sense just to "give us the facts, Ma'am."

If we focus on promotional messages for offerings in the arts and entertainment, we find countless examples of appeals geared toward the heralding of artistic consumption experiences. Drawn from the aforementioned collection, a sampling of such arts-related illustrations of experiential marketing would include the following.

Museums

Bard Graduate Center (Decorative Arts, Design, History, Material Culture) – "The Interface Experience: Forty Years of Personal Computing";

Cooper Hewitt Smithsonian Design Museum – "Experience the New Cooper Hewitt";

Metropolitan Museum of Art (Membership Recruitment) – "Come for the Art. Stay for the Member Experience";

New York Historical Society – "offering a multimedia cinematic experience for museum visitors of all ages";

Whitney Museum (Calder Exhibition) – "This exhibition provides a rare opportunity to experience the works as the artist intended – in motion"

Electronics (Oriented Toward Viewing or Listening)

Acer® (Laptop Computer) – "Ultimate fun . . . Designed to maximize content enjoyment, providing the same rich multimedia, gaming and web experience you can enjoy on your home PC";

Bang & Olufsen BeoLab 11 (Subwoofer) – "Adding BeoLab 11 to your speaker set-up will greatly improve your listening and viewing experience";

BeoVision Avant HDTV – "Everyone Deserves the Bang & Olufsen Experience";

Blu-Ray Music – "Experience Jazz Classics on Blu-Ray Audio";

Bose VideoWave™ (Entertainment System) – "To be experienced by everyone and owned by a few";

Devialet (Loudspeakers) – "Are You Ready to Experience the Phantom Revolution?";

JBL – "Experience a New Standard in Wireless Headphones with the All New Everest Line-Up from JBL";

JVC (HDTVs) – "The Perfect Experience . . . JVC's HD-ILA TV is designed to fit your lifestyle – and totally change the way you experience television";

Monitor Audio (Loudspeakers) – "Experience the power and grace of Monitor Audio's Gold GX Series";

My Net™ (HD Routers) – "My Net™ . . . delivers blazing-fast HD Wi-Fi for the ultimate entertainment experience";

Nintendo (Video Games) – "Experience a New Way to Play";

Nook (Digital Books) – "The Ultimate Reading Experience™";

Panasonic (HDTVs) – "Experience Visual Excellence on a Plasma HDTV" and "Experience the Undeniable Power of Panasonic Plasma";

Playstation⁽ˣ⁾ (Video Games) – "The Ultimate Destiny Experience is on Playstation⁽ˣ⁾";

Polk (Loudspeakers) – "Connect to your TV and get the full experience of an entertainment system";

Samsung (HDTVs) – "The Complete 3D Experience" and "Enjoy a true movie experience, watching colors and details come to life";

Zenith (HDTVs) – "Zenith: Digitize the Experience"

Musical Instruments

Cannonball Saxophones – "It creates one of the most free-blowing experiences you can imagine";

Casio (Privia PX-870 Digital Piano) – "The PX-870 is the new flagship of the Privia family, designed to give you a true grand piano experience";

Dakota Saxophones – "Owning and Playing Either Model Will Be the Ultimate Reward and Experience at Any Venue";

DHR Guitar Experience – "Experience the world's finest guitars" and "Are you DHR experienced?";

Garritan/Yamaha CFX Concert Grand (Virtual Piano) – "Experience the Passion Reflected in Every Detail at Garritan.Com";

JodyJazz DV (Saxophone Mouthpiece) – "The JodyJazz DV is the best playing saxophone mouthpiece you'll ever experience";

Kawai (Novus Hybrid NV10 Digital Piano) – "Experience Evolution";

Mason & Hamlin (Pianos) – "Experience the new legendary Mason & Hamlin piano";

Yamaha (Digital Pianos) – "Experience the Nocturne Grand";

Neotech Saxophone Straps – "Experience the Innovation";

Vox (Guitar Amplifiers) – Experience the MV50";

Zildjian Cymbals – "Experience the Dark-Ride"

Broadway and Off-Broadway Shows

Beauty and the Beast (Musical) – " 'Tis the Season to Experience the Magic!";

Broadway Theater Musicians – "Live Music . . . Experience It!";

Broadway.Yahoo.Com (DVD included) – "Here's Your Ticket to the Ultimate Broadway Experience";

Cadillac/Broadway – "Cadillac Invites You to Win the Ultimate Broadway Experience";

Doubt (Play) – "An experience to last you a lifetime";

Jersey Boys (Musical) – "Now, you can experience it for yourself – *Jersey Boys*";

Memory (Play) – "A Rare Theatrical Experience to Treasure";

Once (Musical) – "Come Experience the Magic of *Once*";

Radio City Music Hall – "Experience New York like never before at 'Heart & Light'";

Roundabout Theatre – "Experience the Mystery of Edwin Drood" and "Discovered by Roundabout. Experienced by You";

Warhorse (Play) – "You only have until January 26 to experience the wonder of *Warhorse*";

Wonderland (Musical) – "Experience Alice through a Whole New Wonderland"

Television and Films

AMC Theaters – "Experience It in IMAX 3D . . . The World's Most Immersive Film Experience";

Arrival (Film) – "It's more than a film. It's an experience";

Avatar (Blue Ray DVD) – "The 3-D Experience comes home";

Awake (TV) – "Experience the Best New Show of the Season . . . *Awake*";

Bambi (Film) – "The classic childhood experience awaits";

Colbert Report (TV) – "Enhance Your Colbert Report Experience. Download the Free Zeebox App!";

Edge of Tomorrow (Film)– "Experience it on IMAX 3D June 6";

Green Hornet, The (Film) – "An Amazing 3D Experience";

Jurassic Park 3D (Film) – "You've Never Experienced Jurassic Park Like This";

Lush (Film) – "You've rarely felt more alive in a movie theater than you will experiencing *Lush*";

Magdalene Sisters, The (Film) – "Experience the Year's Most Triumphant Film";

Mao's Last Dancer (Film) – "A Magical Experience You Must Not Miss";

Monster Calls, A (Film) – "Don't miss the most spectacular motion-picture experience of the season";

National Geographic Channel (TV) – "Don't Just Watch TV. Experience It";

Netflix (Customer Service Survey) – "I am satisfied with my Netflix Customer Service experience/I am unsatisfied with my Netflix Customer Service experience";

NYTimes.Com/Experience (Videos) – "Welcome to the Experience . . . . Watch the Videos that Tell the Stories: NYTimes.Com/Experience";

Pirates of the Caribbean (Film) – "This Friday, experience the film critics are calling the perfect summer movie";

Rescue Dawn (Film) – "Experience the Incredible True Story of One Man's Journey Home";

Spider Man 2 (Film) – "Experience the Movie Event of the Summer";

Spirit (Film) – "Saddle Up and Experience the Spirit of the West!";

Suicide Squad (Film) – "Experience it on Imax";

Sundance Online Film Festival – "To experience the passion and excitement of independent film, just bring your Wi-Fi laptop";

The Help (Film) – "An unforgettable experience";

Tomb Raider – "Experience It in Imax";

Tron: The Legacy (Film) – "Now Experience the Movie 3D Was Made For";

Water for Elephants (Film) – "Experience the film that has audiences talking"

Jazz and Pop

AllanHarris.Com – "Allan Harris Experience . . . 'The headwaters of the protean talent that is Allan Harris'";

Artists Collective, The – "Experience a Jammin' Jazz Getaway";

Clef-Verve Count Basie Recordings/Mosaic Records – "Experience Why There Is No Swing Like Basie Swing";

eJazzLines.Com – "Experience the web's largest and most user-friendly catalog of jazz";

Gregory Porter (Singer) – "Experience the Gregory Effect Now";

Gretchen Parlato (Singer) – "Experience the magic";

Jazz Inside (Magazine) – "The Jazz Music Dashboard . . . Smart Listening Experiences";

JazzVoyeur.Com – "jazz voyeur . . . the visual experience";

Jean-Luc Ponty (Jazz Violinist) – "The Acatama Experience";

Jimmy Hendrix (Rock Musician) – "Are You Experienced?";

Kosa Cuba (Music Festivals) – "Are you ready for the experience of a *lifetime?*";

Litchfield Jazz Festival – "The Experience";

Mike Longo & the NY State of the Art Jazz Ensemble – "One of the Most Enjoyable Evenings of Fabulous Music You Will Ever Experience!";

New Orleans Jazz & Heritage Festival – "To everyone who experienced the healing power of music at Jazz Fest 2006 New Orleans says, 'Thank You!'";

RushRecords52@gmail.com – "Thank you for your order. We will make every effort to make sure you have a pleasant shopping experience";

Sandyland (Sandy Sasso, Singer) – "*Sandyland* Is . . . A Joyous Musical Experience";

Sheffield Jazz Recordings – "Experience the Natural Sound of Sheffield Jazz";

Southport Jazz Festival 2003 – "We Give You the Ultimate 4 Day Jazz Experience!"

Classical Music and Ballet

American Ballet Theater – "Experience the Power of Dance";

Carnegie Hall – "Dear Friend . . .. Thank you for attending Carnegie Hall's Bruckner symphony cycle. We hope you had an extraordinary experience . . .. Please help us make the Carnegie Hall experience the best it can be by answering the following question";

Chamber Music Society – "Rediscover the concert experience" and "An Unrivaled Way to Experience Unparalleled Artists";

Chase Brock (Dance) – "The Chase Brock Experience";

Lincoln Center (Great Performers Season) – "Experience one of the finest pianists and recitalists of our time . . . Richard Goode" and "Experience firsthand why tenor Mark Padmore and pianist Paul Lewis are considered one of the great musical partnerships of our time" and "Don't miss your chance to see the Los Angeles Philharmonic . . .. Experience the thrills of a Dudamel performance";

Metropolitan Opera – "Experience the Met's new *Ring* cycle";

New York Philharmonic – "Welcome to the New York Philharmonic . . . Concert Experience";

Soundspace (92nd Street Y) – "Come experience music at 92Y for yourself";

Town Hall World Cabaret Series, The – "Experience . . . the drama of German Kabarett";

Volodos (Classical Pianist) – "Experience Tchaikovsky's Piano Concerto like never before!"

Other Arts-Related Events and Offerings

Berklee College of Music – "Get the Berklee Experience";

Bodies, the Exhibition – "Real Human Bodies, Preserved Through an Innovative Process . . .. Experience the Human Body Like Never Before";

Brooklyn Expo Center, Worlds Fair Nano NY – "Experience the Future";

Dirty Dog Jazz Café – "Detroit's Best Jazz Experience";

Discover, Times Square (Interactive Attraction) – "CSI: The Experience";

Global Extremes – Mt. Everest – "Experience the Pinnacle of Live Television";

Hands On! (Music Classes for Children) – "A Musical Experience";

Jazz Times Tour – "Experience Jazz in Istanbul";

Power Within, The (Motivational Speeches by William Jefferson Clinton, Michael D. Eisner, and Lance Armstrong) – "Experience the Power Within";

Public Art Fund – "Public Art Fund invites you to experience New York City's iconic statue of Christopher Columbus as never before";

Related Urban Development – "New Yorkers dine out as an entertainment experience";

Ringling Bros. and Barnum & Bailey Circus Xtreme – "Enter a world of Xtreme and experience the highest, fastest, strongest, most daring acts on the planet . . .. Experience the amazement of seeing it live with your whole family";

Shen Yun (Performing Arts) – "Experience the divine";

Third Street Music School – "It was really a once-in-a-lifetime experience";

Walking With Dinosaurs (Presented by Immersion Edutainment) – "The Live Experience";

WSJ+ (Talks, Screenings, and Events Sponsored by the *Wall Street Journal*) – "We are delighted to welcome you to WSJ+, a whole new Wall Street Journal experience . . .. We are also continuing to expand . . . nationwide, so you can enjoy these experiences in person wherever you are";

Zarkana (Cirque de Soleil) – "Experience the Grandeur"

Electronic Access to Arts and/or Entertainment

DirectTV® – "Experience it yourself";

iO TV – "Experience DVR on every TV in the house!";

Mozilla Firefox (Web Browser) – "Firefox automatically sends some data to Mozilla so that we can improve your experience";

Optimum (Cable) – "Experience TV that goes beyond TV";

Shutterfly (Photographic Prints) – "Experience your photos like never before";

Time Warner Cable – "You can have a better TV experience too" and "Experience the ultimate selection of products from TimeWarner Cable" and "Get the ultimate cinema experience with HD Movies on Demand" and "All across America, families are coming back to Time Warner Cable for a whole new experience";

T-Mobile – "Our next-generation broadband experience";

Verizon Internet – "Rev up your online experience" and "You're invited to experience the Internet as it was meant to be" and "Verizon has always set out to provide you with the most powerful and reliable network experience" and "Get More. Do More. Experience More . . .. A TV experience like no other . . .. Connect to a fast Internet experience";

Verizon FIOS (Cable) – "FIOS: A Better TV Experience Is Here" and "Switch to a better entertainment experience" and "At Verizon, we strive to provide you with the best experience" and "Enjoy a bigger, better entertainment experience" and "For an entertainment experience that goes beyond cable, get FIOS TV"

Envoi

I hope that this list sufficiently demonstrates the fact that references to the consumption experience pervade the advertising and other messages that promote various offerings in the arts and entertainment. I also hope that these examples indicate the extent to which the use of the promise to provide "an experience" tends to remain unanalyzed and therefore vague in its implications. This shortfall reflects a tendency to ignore the different types of consumer value inherent in any given arts-related consumption experience. As mentioned earlier and as reflected in my aforementioned example of vibraphonist Gary Burton at work in the Blue Note, an artistic moment can provide Efficiency, Excellence, Status, Esteem, Play, Aesthetics, Ethics, and Spiritual Value. The point is that all these types of value deserve analysis, interpretation, and understanding. Until we explore the depths of arts-related consumption experiences in this manner, we shall remain in a state of perpetual darkness and willful confusion. Let us avoid that catastrophe and climb toward the light.

Part III

Some Theoretical and Methodological Considerations Concerning Consumer Value

6 Commentary

Consumption Experiences, Consumer Value, Subjective Personal Introspection, the Photographic Essay, and Semiological/Hermeneutic Interpretation

Abstract

This commentary revisits the author's oft-cited article published in the *Journal of Business Research*, reviews the themes contained therein, speculates on why the paper garnered more than the usual attention from marketing and consumer researchers, and offers some suggestions as to where the relevant issues and ideas might lead in the future.

Introduction: An Invitation

I received with pleasure Editor Arch Woodside's kind invitation to write a commentary on my article for the *Journal of Business Research* entitled "Consumption Experience, Customer Value, and Subjective Personal Introspection: An Illustrative Photographic Essay" (Holbrook, 2006a). Apparently, I'm proud to say, this essay has won the honor of being cited more often than most articles in *JBR* – 1,475 times, at last count on Scholar.Google.Com – so that Arch feels that something of its history and essence might be of interest to readers of the *Journal of Global Scholars of Marketing Science*. In this connection, he has asked me to "tell how/why your article achieved such high impact and tell what developments are occurring now in the topic area of your famous study."

In confronting this challenge – indeed, a daunting prospect for one who considers himself basically a shy and retiring person – I began by rereading my *JBR* essay for the first time in the past decade. In performing that task, I found myself impressed not so much by its embrace of several inter-related themes (the Consumption Experience, the nature and types of Consumer Value, the insights to be gained from Subjective Personal Introspection or SPI, the richness provided by an Illustrative Photographic Essay, and the validating evidence gleaned from a Semiological/Hermeneutic Interpretation of an informant's Written Narrative) as by my own unanticipated but nonetheless overwhelming response in the form of a wave of nostalgia that swept over me in a tsunami-like flood. After many years of neglect by its author, the essay seemed to encapsulate much if not all of what I have wanted to say about

DOI: 10.4324/9781003560302-9

consumer behavior and the study thereof. But – more importantly – it reacquainted me with the visual images and writings created by my long-deceased grandfather Arthur Tenney Holbrook (ATH) and the family setting in which I grew up, surrounded by dear ones who have since passed away but whose memory infuses the pages of my essay. I cannot expect readers from another culture at a different time to share these feelings of deep nostalgia, though I can imagine that the sincerity and authenticity that imbued my essay might have inspired others to read and to cite it.

But gaining readers requires more than just a shameless display of wallowing in one's own nostalgic emotions, so I must conclude that the essay also gained exposure by virtue of its tendency to embrace some important themes in consumer research that have emerged with increasing insistence in recent years. In what follows, I shall focus briefly on each of these themes with attention to the second of the issues posed by Arch – namely, related developments that have begun to appear.

The Consumption Experience

First, recalling Chapter 4, my essay focused on the role of the consumption experience as an expansion of our traditional view of the buyer as a computer-like information-processing decision maker concerned with making brand choices. Beth Hirschman and I had suggested this extension of the dominant paradigm in two papers that appeared in 1982 (Hirschman and Holbrook, 1982; Holbrook and Hirschman, 1982) and had followed up our initial observations in a series of studies focused on such issues as *Fantasies* (e.g., the psychoanalytic dynamics of dreams, imagination, and unconscious desires), *Feelings* (e.g., emotional responses to products and advertisements), and *Fun* (e.g., playful leisure activities or aesthetic appreciations of beauty). As noted earlier, at the time we began writing on these matters, Beth and I were blissfully unaware of previous work by economists and marketing researchers who had focused on various aspects of experiential consumption – including such distinguished contributors from marketing as Wroe Alderson (1957) and Sid Levy (1959), a long line of economists stretching back from Lawrence Abbott (1955) through John Maynard Keynes (1936) and Alfred Marshall (1920) all the way to Adam Smith (1776), plus the early consumer advocate Ruby Turner Norris (1941). (For further discussion, please see Boyd and Levy, 1963; Lebergott, 1993; Woods, 1981; Chapter 4). I managed to correct a bit for this embarrassing omission in my essay, while also complaining that more recent disciples of the experiential perspective have consistently compounded the problem by following in our footsteps and thereby failing to acknowledge the contributions of "previous thinkers who have pioneered the relevant concepts" (Holbrook 2006a, p. 715). Thus, any number of managerial self-help books have appeared – written by authors such as Arussy (2002), Pine and Gilmore (1999), Schmitt (1999), Shaw and Ivens (2002), or Smith and Wheeler (2002), to name only a few, who devote scant attention to the origins of the ideas that they espouse with such fervor. To be fair, their work seems to be aimed primarily at the instruction of marketing managers (who presumably care not about the intellectual pedigrees of the insights that they borrow), and – perhaps because of this widespread tendency to sell the concept of experiential marketing to practitioners – a recognition of the role played by the consumption experience appears to have found its way with increasing insistence into the marketing strategies of today's corporate sponsors. In this regard, as detailed in Chapters 4 and 5, I have recently amused myself by collecting rather large samples of television commercials, print ads, billboards, and other signage that tout the power of brands to deliver desirable consumption experiences (see also Holbrook, 2009d). My current collection of such examples contains over 600 items and is far too voluminous to report here. The full set appears in the Appendix to this volume and contains such newly added specimens as the following.

Consumer Nondurables

Drinks

LavAzza (Italian Coffee) – "Experience an Italian Classic Since 1895";
Smartwater Sparkling (Bottled Water) – "Elevate Your Experience";

Food

Dorritos Tacos – "A taste experience like no other";
Lindt (Lindor Chocolate) – "Like nothing you have ever experienced";

Miscellaneous Nondurables

Glide (Dental Floss) – "Experience the Glide Difference";
Pine Brothers – "Not just a cough drop but an experience";

Tourism

Airlines

Alaska Air Line – "An Entirely New Flight Experience";
American Airlines – "New York's Premium Travel Experience . . . Our premium travel experience gives you the luxury and convenience you expect";

Cruises

Crystal Cruises – "Start with your personal Crystal Experience" and "Collect the Kind of Experiences that Add to the Narrative of Your Life";
Sitmar Cruises – "The Sitmar Experience";

Automobiles

Buick – "Experience . . . Buick";
Toyota – "A carefree driving experience";

Other Transportation

Bay Bus Service – "Experience the Difference";
Taxi Entertainment Network – "Making your taxi experience better";

Hotels and Resorts

Baymont Inns – "Experience . . . Hometown Hospitality";
Mar-a-Lago Club – "An Experience Rich in History";

Travel Destinations

New Hampshire – "Live Free and Experience";
New York – "Welcome to New York . . .. Experience . . . Explore . . . Enjoy";

Travel Tours

Hop-On Hop-Off Sightseeing Tours – "Experience Washington DC in Full Bloom";
Perillo Tours – "Eight unique travel experiences";

Travel Books

Must Do (Magazine) – "Experience the top 10 . . . Beautiful Beaches . . . Unique Shopping";
Tripadvisor – "Every experience counts";

Restaurants

Empire Steak House – "Experience the Taste";
Red Lobster – "Creating an Experience that's not just a meal";

Consumer Durables

Electronics

Intel® – "Experience what's inside";
Nook (Barnes & Noble) – "The Ultimate Reading Experience™";

Other Durables

Mephisto (Footwear) – "For a Comfortable and Effortless Walking Experience";
Rockport (Shoes) – "Experience the Style and Comfort of Rockport";

Events

Broadway and Off-Broadway Shows

Jersey Boys – "Now, you can experience it for yourself – *Jersey Boys*";
Once – "Come Experience the Magic of *Once*";

TV Shows and Films

Arrival – "It's more than a film. It's an experience";
Pirates of the Caribbean – "This Friday, experience . . . the perfect summer
    movie";

Jazz and Pop

Gregory Porter (Singer) – "Experience the Gregory Effect Now";
Sandyland (Sandy Sasso, Singer) – "*Sandyland* Is . . . A Joyous Musical
    Experience";

Classical Music and Ballet

American Ballet Theater – "Experience the Power of Dance";
Chamber Music Society – "An Unrivaled Way to Experience Unparalleled
    Artists" and "Rediscover the concert experience";

Museums

Intrepid Sea, Air, & Space Museum – "Inspiring experiences for all ages";
Metropolitan Museum – "Come for the Art. Stay for the Member Experience";

Other Events

New York City Marathon – "Experience the mania";
Zarkana (Cirque de Soleil) – "Experience the Grandeur";

Education

Columbia Business School – "Experience the Joys (visit the site)";
University School of Milwaukee – "The Experience of a Lifetime"

Housing

Atria – "Redefining Today's Senior Living Experience";
Town & Country Real Estate (East End of Long Island) – "Experience
    Montauk";

Shopping

Bricks-and Mortar Stores

Art of Shaving, The – "Experience the Perfect Shave";
Ralph Lauren – "The Ultimate Experience";

Online Shopping

BestBuy.Com – "Experience Limitless Entertainment";
Zabar's.Com – "Ship a N.Y.C. Experience";

Other Shopping

Premiere Caterers – "Experience the Difference";
US Outdoor Sports Center – "Experience Patagonia";

Financial Services

Banks

Chase – "Welcome to a Better Banking Experience";
City National Bank – "Experience the Difference";

Credit Cards

Chase Freedom® Credit Card – "Experience Chase Freedom®";
Mastercard® – "Mastercard® is reserving priceless . . . experiences just
   for you";

Other Financial Services

Quicken Loans – "For a mortgage experience that's engineered to amaze";
TIAA (Retirement Investments) – "Shorter name. New experience";

Miscellaneous Services

Utilitarian Services

Microsoft Windows – "One experience for everything in your life";
United States Postal Service – "Tell Us about Your Recent Postal Experience
   at PostalExperience.Com/Pos";

Hedonic Services

Exhale® Mind-Body Spa – "Experiences";

Spa at the Providence Biltmore Hotel – "Experience the very best in massage, skin care, nail treatments";

Health-Care Services

United Health Care – "It's Time for a Better Health Care Experience";
Weill Cornell Medicine/New York Presbyterian Hospital – "Experience the Difference a World-Class ENT Physician Can Make";

Other Services

Jewish Center, The – "MJE . . . Manhattan Jewish Experience";
Spot (Dog Grooming & Daycare) – "The Spot Experience is the first luxury experience of its kind for your dog"

A couple of persistent features – found in the preceding list – deserve brief reminders before proceeding further.

First, notice again how usage of the experiential perspective in promotional communications has become extremely widespread and cuts across the full array of product categories ranging from, say, Food or Drinks to Household Products, to Tourism, to Electronics, to Cultural Events, to Education, to Housing, to Shops and Websites, to Banks or Credit Cards or Other Financial Services, and to Cable TV or Beauty Spas or Health-Care Services or Pet Grooming. Few, if any, goods or services seem to be excluded from the presumed benefits of claiming that they provide . . . experiences.

Second, notice once more how – in many or even most cases – the term "experience" has taken on approbative value. Apparently, businesses feel that it suffices to promise an "experience" without in any way mentioning whether the experience is a good or bad one. Rather, pleasure or happiness is assumed as part of the phenomenon of experiential consumption. Thus – without promising that the experience will be positive – we are offered "a taste experience like no other" (Dorritos Tacos), "An Entirely New Flight Experience" (Alaska Air Line), "The Sitmar Experience" (Sitmar Cruises), the "New York . . . Experience" (New York), "Eight unique travel experiences" (Perillo Tours), "an experience that's not just a meal" (Red Lobster), "the concert experience" (Chamber Music Society), "the Member Experience" (Metropolitan Museum), "the experience of a lifetime" (University School), "a N.Y.C. Experience" (Zabar's.Com), or just "Experiences" (Exhale® Spa). Implicitly, such experiences are assumed to be good and worth pursuing – something to be sought for their own sake as ends in themselves. If we are lucky, we can "Experience an Italian Classic" (LavAzza), "Experience the Glide Difference," "Experience . . . Buick," "Experience the Difference" (Bay Bus Service), "Experience Washington DC," "Experience the Taste" (Empire Steak House), "Experience what's inside" (Intel®), "Experience Montauk," "Experience Patagonia," or (again) "Experience the

Difference" (City National Bank). Neither the sender nor the receiver of the relevant promotional message stops to contemplate the possibility that the coffee might taste bitter, that the dental floss might hurt your gums, that the car might handle poorly on the turns, that the bus service might run on unreliable schedules, that the nation's capital might be full of corrupt politicians, that the steaks might be tough and overcooked, that the computers might crash at every opportunity, that Montauk might be crowded with loud-and-obnoxious party-crazed greed-chasing millennial hedge-fund managers from Wall Street, that the sports clothing might shrink in the wash, or that the bank might impose usurious mortgage rates. Rather, an "experience," by definition, implies a good thing, something worth seeking without inquiring further. By contrast, my own somewhat jaded view is that, all too often, the experience provided by (say) a bank, an insurance company, a car, or a computer is rather undesirable or even painful. Please, Dear Reader, contemplate again the dangers of "The Shark-Tank Experience." All of this brings us to the second major topic covered by my *JBR* essay.

Consumer Value

As implied by my preceding comments and with the shining exception of LaSalle and Britton (2003), many or even most of the marketing gurus who wax eloquent on the subject of consumption experiences ignore the even more important point that these experiences matter because they potentially provide a foundation for the attainment of Consumer Value – defined in my *JBR* essay and elsewhere as an "*interactive relativistic preference experience*" (Holbrook, 2006a, p. 715). In the essay, I confined myself to the derivation and illustration of four main types of Consumer Value – Economic, Social, Hedonic, and Altruistic. These four types of value result from the services that products or events perform in providing consumption experiences and – in ways frequently neglected by the aforementioned authors of managerial self-help books – embody the essence of why we care about consumption experiences in the first place. One implication of my view is that *all* products are *services* in the sense that they provide the experiences that result in consumer value. Based on that recognition, I have devoted considerable attention over the years to analyzing the nature and types of Consumer Value (Holbrook, 1994f, 1999a, 1999c), and my *JBR* essay presents one example of that quest. However, with one exception (Holbrook and Corfman, 1985), my own value-related research has tended to pursue conceptual insights rather than empirical tests. Perhaps my *JBR* essay could (charitably) be viewed as an attempt at empirical validation (albeit of a highly qualitative kind), but – more importantly – a number of researchers (e.g., Gallarza, Arteaga, Del Chiappa, Gil-Saura, and Holbrook, 2017; Gallarza, Gil-Saura, and Holbrook, 2011, 2012; Sánchez-Fernández and Iniesta-Bonillo, 2006; Sánchez-Fernández, Iniesta-Bonillo, and Holbrook, 2009) have now begun to seek methods for quantifying and measuring the various types of consumer value that potentially lead to purchase satisfaction and, ultimately, to brand loyalty. I take little credit for this expansion of interest among consumer researchers in measuring the relevant aspects of consumer value, but I feel encouraged that this sort of work has begun to proceed apace.

Subjective Personal Introspection

Rather than using quantitative measurement-oriented methods, my approach to studying consumer value has most frequently followed a more qualitative path that I refer to as Subjective Personal Introspection (SPI), that I first developed during the mid-1980s in a series of articles that I call my "ACR Trilogy" (Holbrook, 1986d, 1987a, 1988c), and that received further scholarly elaboration in two important pieces for the *Journal of Consumer Research* by Steve Gould (1991, 1995). As briefly described in my *JBR* essay, via SPI "the consumer researcher engages in a sort of participant observation of his or her own consumption experiences . . . what a cultural anthropologist or SPI-friendly apologist might call *autoethnography* . . . leading to its justification as a form of observant participation in one's own life" (Holbrook, 2006a, p. 716; see also Miller, 2010, 2012). SPI harkens back to the invention of the personal essay by Michel de Montaigne (1533–1592), who argued – rather persuasively – that, as a human, he was uniquely qualified to write about the human condition. Obviously, such an approach bears more resemblance to the humanities (philosophy, history, literary criticism, cultural studies) than to the physical sciences (chemistry, geology, astronomy) or the social sciences (conventional sociology or mainstream psychology). For that reason, SPI has drawn its fair share of criticism from neopositivistically inclined commentators – as in the rather strident attack on the work of Gould by Professors Wallendorf and Brucks (1993). More empathetic critiques have come from Arch Woodside (2004, 2006). And, as Editor of *JBR*, Arch has demonstrated his admirable open-mindedness by publishing at least three of my own SPI-oriented ramblings (Holbrook 2005c, 2006a, 2008d) and by opening the pages of *JBR* to a special issue on SPI edited by Steve Gould (2012), with SPI-oriented contributions from such distinguished consumer researchers as (among several others) Stephen Brown (2012); Barbara Olsen (2012); John Sherry (2012); Robert Kozinets (2012); Minowa, Visconti, and Maclaran (2012); and Banbury, Stinerock, and Subrahmanyan (2012). So, in writings by these and other brave souls, the pursuit of SPI has continued – especially in the work by Markus Wohlfeil and Susan Whelan, who have shined the light of SPI on topics such as the researchers' own personal appreciation of films by the actress Jenna Malone (Wohlfeil and Whelan, 2012), the marketing of events (Wohlfeil and Whelan, 2006), and the role of branding (Whelan and Wohlfeil, 2006). But – despite its emphasis on subjective personal introspective revelations and like all other bases for claims of truthfulness – SPI benefits from whatever corroborating evidence we can muster to support our essentially impressionistic assertions. In my *JBR* article, the search for such corroboration led in two directions – an illustrative photographic essay and a semiotic/hermeneutic interpretation of narrative writings.

The Illustrative Photographic Essay

To support my analysis of Consumer Value derived from Consumption Experiences, I focused my SPI-directed comments on a set of 35-mm Kodachrome slides taken by my grandfather Arthur Tenney Holbrook (ATH) at the Brule River in Northern Wisconsin during the 1940s and 1950s. These photographs – which had languished away in my parents' basement for roughly 50 years until I inherited them when my father passed away – served to illustrate the relevant types of consumer value and, in my view, brought an immediacy to the analysis that would have been lacking without visual images to support it. In many previous studies, I had used my own photographs (e.g., Holbrook, 1997i, 1998e) or photographs taken by informants (e.g., Holbrook, 2005g; Holbrook and Kuwahara, 1998) to suggest or to support key conclusions. And, of course, others have pursued similar research strategies to telling effect (e.g., Heisley and Levy, 1991). I have continued – as have many others – to play with photographs in my more recent work (e.g., Holbrook, 2006d, 2017). But I believe that the photos taken by (or, in some cases, of) ATH brought a special resonance to the themes of interest in my *JBR* essay – all the more because, when visiting the *JBR* archives online – the images appear in glorious color, proving once again (if anybody needed further demonstrations) that Kodachrome embodied a film technology richly deserving its immortalization in the famous song by Paul Simon.

The Semiological/Hermeneutic Interpretation of a Written Narrative

My second strategy for bolstering the analysis of experience-dependent consumer value in my *JBR* essay drew upon written evidence provided by ATH himself in the form of an autobiographical book entitled *From the Log of a Trout Fisherman* (A. T. Holbrook, 1949). In drawing on these north-woods stories, I extended a semiotic approach introduced into consumer research by the influential work of David Mick (1986), who had been rubbing elbows with folks from the Research Center for Language and Semiotic Studies at Indiana University. My own efforts in this direction had focused on the interpretation of consumption symbolism in films (e.g., Holbrook and Grayson, 1986), plays (e.g., Holbrook, 1988b), television dramas (e.g., Holbrook, 1996a), and novels (e.g., Holbrook, 1991b, 1997f). In these efforts, I was again joined by Beth Hirschman. Together, we published a book entitled *The Semiotics of Consumption: Interpreting Symbolic Consumer Behavior in Popular Culture and Works of Art* (Holbrook and Hirschman, 1993). We have both continued these semiological/hermeneutic interpretations in more recent years (e.g., Hirschman, 2000; Hirschman and

Holbrook, 2011; Holbrook, 2011) – as have many others too numerous
to mention. However, beyond such arts- or entertainment-oriented applications, I believe that the narrative written by ATH bolstered the arguments
in my *JBR* essay with special force and to an unusual degree – due entirely
to the rather prodigious facility with which the man wielded what was
in those days literally a fountain pen. Examples abound in my *JBR* essay
and – in my view – reinforce the claims made by my interpretations with
a forcefulness and clarity seldom encountered in the verbal responses of a
more traditional informant. I do not know how ATH came to achieve this
sort of narrative finesse. Ostensibly, he was a perfectly ordinary physician
in Milwaukee with no particular reason to possess any literary skills. True,
he had studied at Harvard with William James, which might have tuned up
his facility with phenomenological introspections. But I do not recall ever
seeing him reading (say) a novel by William's brother Henry, a screed by H.
L. Mencken, or an essay by E. B. White (whose writing style that of ATH
resembles to a noticeable degree). Let us just imagine that ATH was born
with a gift for self-expression and that I managed to take advantage of that
gift in finding written passages from his *Trout Fisherman* book to illustrate
my points concerning the types of consumer value. I would like to think
that the eloquence of these passages – as illuminated, I hope, by my own
semiological/hermeneutic interpretations – have appealed to readers in ways
that would not have resulted from a more traditional exegesis. Indeed, when
I recently re-read my quotations from ATH, I found myself in tears – not
quite sure of why I was weeping, but nonetheless certain that it had less to
do with the substance of what ATH was saying and far more to do with the
manner in which he was saying it. One example among many concerns his
deep love for his wife, Bertha, who had recently passed away, and his recol-
lection of the ceremonial significance with which the couple always paused
en route upstream to drink from a spring using two silver cups that they had
received as a wedding gift many decades earlier and that today sit in a place
of honor on a shelf in my study:

> As we come to The Spring and sing together the words of "Little
> Brown Jug," Ed [the Chippewa guide] slows down and sweeps under
> the overhanging cedars, for he knows from a hundred such trips that
> from the basket will come the leather case that carries the two silver
> traveling cups, which were a wedding gift, and which first went up the
> Brule River on the honeymoon, nearly fifty years ago. There is not a
> spring from the Blue Springs at Stone's to the Co-op Park, where these
> beloved cups have not been filled, and although they have been around
> the world, and have been filled in the Arctic Circle and in the Cape
> of Good Hope in southernmost Africa, and have crossed the Atlantic
> twenty times – their first trip was to Gitche Gumee [the family's lodge],
> and it is the springs along the Brule that they know best.
>
> (p. 166)

Pathetic fallacy? You bet. But, in my *JBR* essay, I offered this passage as an illustration of spiritual value. I am well aware of the sacred meanings associated with ritualistically drinking pure water from silver cups. But I do not think that any sanctimonious sermon could have captured this essence as powerfully as the reflections by ATH about The Spring on the Brule River. More recently, in my own work, I have tried to emulate the penetrating sincerity with which ATH reported the most seemingly ordinary occurrences of everyday life. For example, in an effort at autobiography (Holbrook, 2017; please see Chapter 2), I have tried to attain a tone something like that which ATH achieved with such apparent effortlessness. Trust me: Such an accomplishment is difficult if not impossible. But, hey, it's worth a try.

Conclusions

I conclude that whatever merits my *JBR* essay possessed, whatever aspects sparked the interest of more than a few readers, and whatever impacts it might have on present and future research in consumer behavior stem from what was, for me, an atypical success in combining five key themes that resonate and work together in what I hope has been a convincing way:

The Consumption Experience
The Concept of Consumer Value (CCV)
Subjective Personal Introspection (SPI)
The Illustrative Photographic Essay
The Semiological/Hermeneutic Interpretation of a Written Narrative

Each of these themes has appeared ubiquitously in our literature. But – to the best of my knowledge – there are few, if any, cases where all five have appeared together and have reinforced each other in ways that I hope to have provided in my *JBR* essay. I am grateful to have been allowed the opportunity to produce such an essay and thank the Editor Arch Woodside for making this possible.

7 The Concept of Consumer Value (CCV)

Its Development, Implications, and Trajectory

Abstract

This subjective personal introspective essay – an impressionistic autobiographical SPI review – traces the development of the author's own particular Concept of Consumer Value (CCV); positions CCV as an extension of earlier work on the Consumption Experience; mentions various aspects of CCV that are often debated, misunderstood, or ignored; and refers briefly to those on the international scene who have addressed conceptual refinements and measurement-related empirical issues in ways that, despite the author's own participation, strike him as still embryonic and in need of further development.

In this subjective personal introspective essay, I shall pursue an impressionistic autobiographical SPI approach to trace the development of my own particular Concept of Consumer Value (CCV); to position CCV as an extension of the earlier work on the Consumption Experience; to mention various aspects of CCV that are often debated, misunderstood, or ignored; and to refer briefly to those on the international scene who have addressed conceptual refinements and measurement-related empirical issues in ways that, despite my own participation, I believe are still embryonic and in need of further development.

So let us start at what was, for me, the beginning. When I arrived on the scene as an MBA candidate at Columbia University's Graduate School of Business in 1965, I enjoyed the privilege of joining the intellectual ferment that surrounded the proliferation of new attempts to construct theories of buyer behavior that embraced the sorts of boxes-and-arrows models introduced by the Nobel-Prize winner Herbert Simon and his colleagues. Writers like John Howard (1963); Franco Nicosia (1966); Engel, Kollat, and Blackwell (1968); and (later) Jim Bettman (1979) were beginning to formulate models of the buyer as a rational information-processing brand-choosing decision maker. And such emerging approaches reached their full flower right under my nose as a student in John Howard's buyer-behavior class at Columbia. Together with Jagdish Sheth, John's former PhD student at the University of Pittsburgh, Howard was immersed in the creative throes of building the conceptual structure that ultimately blossomed as their monumentally influential *Theory of Buyer Behavior* (Howard and Sheth, 1969). In

DOI: 10.4324/9781003560302-10

class, John invited us students to extend, question, debate, and even attack his ideas. And I found this process of discovery thrilling. In short, I became addicted to the then-nascent study of buyer behavior, started on research to seek empirical support for the Howard-Sheth Theory, wrote my dissertation on aspects of advertising illustrative of the Howard-Sheth approach, and embarked upon a career as a consumer researcher with a strong bias toward the sorts of rational information-processing decision-oriented views espoused by Howard and Sheth and by the other buyer-behavior gurus of the time. (For reviews, please see Holbrook, 1995b, 2001f; Chapters 2 and 4.)

In writings akin to those presented in previous chapters, I have documented the undeniable fact that these and other models of buyer behavior all tended to follow the same sort of logical progression – traceable all the way back to Plato – in which Information (from brand features, advertising, word of mouth, and so forth) builds Cognitions (beliefs about the relevant brands) that combine to create Affect (preferences in the form of liking or disliking the available offerings) that encourage Behavior (an actual purchase decision that produces a brand choice) that leads to Satisfaction (a favorable or unfavorable post-purchase evaluation that does or doesn't reinforce learning to buy the brand repeatedly). As noted in earlier chapters, this ICABS model held sway in the voluminous amount of empirical work produced by Howard and his colleagues at Columbia (Farley, Howard, and Ring, ed. 1974; Farley and Ring, 1970; Holbrook, 1974) and, for example, by those working on Fishbein- or Rosenberg-type multiattribute attitude models (Fishbein and Ajzen, 1975; Rosenberg, 1956) (for reviews and extensions, please see Holbrook, 1977a, 1981a; Ryan and Holbrook, 1982b). These theoretical approaches did a rather nice job of explaining brand choices in the area of mostly functional utilitarian products such as, say, toothpaste or laundry detergent or lawn mowers or insurance policies. But the ICABS formulations failed to plumb the depths of consumer responses to more hedonic emotionally connected offerings such as, say, perfume or jewelry or luxury cruises or rock concerts.

I had felt a creeping awareness of this problem as an MBA student when I had questioned Professor Howard himself about why automobile advertisements showed beautiful scantily clad women draped across the hoods of luxury cars and so forth. But he had convinced me that the important criteria hinged on such economically rational performance specifications as horsepower, miles per gallon, and speed of accelerating from 0 to 60 miles per hour. So – though I was a willing convert – it took the catalytic force of Beth Hirschman to wake me from my theoretical slumbers. Thus, when I first met Beth at an ACR Conference in 1979/1980, I found her embarked on a program of research that, under an umbrella that could be broadly characterized as hedonic consumption, openly embraced emotions, irrationality, aesthetic responses, and many other phenomena not comfortably accommodated by the traditional ICABS formulations. To this task, Beth brought an explosive onslaught of intellectual energy and penetrating insight that I have not seen equaled, before or since. Being a nearby neighbor on Riverside Drive in New York City, I was able to work closely with Beth to unleash some relevant conceptual analyses that took the form of one article on hedonic consumption first-authored by Beth (Hirschman and Holbrook, 1982) and another on the Consumption Experience first-authored by yours truly (Holbrook and Hirschman, 1982). Together, these two publications signaled our awareness of the need to expand beyond the confines of the traditional decision-oriented ICABS formulation to include additional experiential aspects of each component that embraced (I) aesthetic offerings such as music, movies, television programs, and visual arts; (C) unconscious thoughts, dreams, and daydreams; (A) emotional responses that went well beyond brand preferences to include love, hate, joy, sorrow, fear, anger, lust, disgust, and so forth; (B) pre- and post-purchase activities that extended into areas of play and leisure pursuits; and (S) satisfaction as a rich pattern of desire-fulfilling enjoyment (Holbrook and Hirschman, 1982). In this (sometimes in ways that we did not fully recognize at the time but have since taken pains to acknowledge wherever possible), we built upon the earlier work of marketing researchers (Alderson, 1957; Boyd and Levy, 1963; Kotler and Levy, 1969; Levy, 1959; Woods, 1981), economists (Abbott, 1955; Keynes, 1936; Marshall, 1920), and consumer advocates (Norris, 1941). Indeed, Stanley Lebergott (1993) has traced the importance of the consumption experience backward through John Maynard Keynes (1936) to Alfred Marshall (1920) and all the way to Adam Smith (1776). (For a review, please see Holbrook, 1994b.) For short, we referred to the central C-A-B portion of our elaborations as Fantasies, Feelings, and Fun (the Three F's.)

This focus on an expanded concept of the Consumption Experience spilled over into all aspects of my own work dealing with entertainment and the arts, emotional responses to products and advertisements, leisure pursuits, and consumer esthetics – producing a stream of research too voluminous to cite here but covered at some length in a recent autobiographical essay (Holbrook, 2017; Chapter 2). These new directions of inquiry into the Three F's expanded my consciousness in many ways, but this expanded consciousness did not yet include a fully elaborated view of the last element in the ICABS chain – namely, (S) Satisfaction. Howard and Sheth and others had tended to view Satisfaction as an outcome of post-purchase evaluation that, if positive, reinforced repeat-purchase tendencies in ways that elevated the strength of brand loyalty. Writers like Rich Oliver (1980, 1997; Mano and Oliver, 1993) had made a career out of studying Satisfaction and explaining how it reflected the degrees to which Performances (Ps) exceeded Expectations (Es) on a number of relevant evaluative criteria (somewhat confusingly referred to as "disconfirmation," which sounds bad but, if Ps > Es, is actually good). This fruitful and widely accepted view did much to orient marketing strategists in a direction useful to building repeat-purchase behavior by raising Ps to ensure that Ps > Es on a variety of key evaluative criteria. (Or – conversely, I've always thought – lowering Es without improving Ps to keep Ps > Es according to the logic that if your expectations are low, you won't be disappointed.)

But I gradually came to realize that this traditional view of Ps > Es as the key to post-purchase Satisfaction did not fully capture the complex nature of the value that results from a consumption experience. This realization dawned on me with some force as the result of a couple of coincidentally related events in (roughly) 1983. First, for Xmas, my Aunt Kitty and Uncle Harry gave me a copy of Robert Pirsig's *Zen and the Art of Motorcycle Maintenance: An Inquiry into Values* (Pirsig, 1974). I fell in love with this book, pondered its deeply philosophical implications, and – pursuing one of its main themes – came away with an interest in the whole problem of defining "Quality." Second, down at New York University (Columbia's sister school to the south), Jack Jacoby (NYU) and Jerry Olson (then at Penn State) organized a conference on "Quality" and invited me to submit a paper and to make a presentation on that theme. Toward that end, I elicited the participation of Kim Corfman, a Columbia PhD student at the time and now a professor at NYU in her own right.

My work on this project happened to coincide with the first sabbatical that I enjoyed after receiving tenure – a moment of newly liberated energies and broadened horizons. So I had a bit of extra time to reflect, ponder, and extrapolate conceptual conclusions. Kim took charge of the data-gathering phase and produced some nice empirical results that I'll mention again later (but that lie outside my main focus at the moment), while I buried myself in my office and agonized over the meaning of "Quality" in ways reminiscent of the self-absorbed reflections reported by Pirsig (1974) in connection with an alter-ego whom (harkening back to Plato) he called Phaedrus – hence, the subtitle of the ultimate chapter by Holbrook and Corfman (1985): "Phaedrus Rides Again."

To further this rather abstruse or even esoteric inquiry into the meaning of "Quality," I turned to literature from the branch of philosophy known as "Axiology." Not to be misdirected by good-natured jokes from Hal Kassarjian concerning the undersides of automobiles, Axiology involves the philosophical study of value in general or, in my case, the Concept of Consumer Value (CCV) in particular. Toward the end of gaining insights into CCV, I visited the stacks at Columbia University's Butler Library for probably the only time that I have penetrated those hallowed halls during my 50-plus years at the school and found myself confronted by a long shelf of books on this recondite topic. Many of these volumes came from the personal collection of that grand old Columbia professor John Dewey. In those days, library books had small pouches in the back with cards indicating relevant information about the dates when people had borrowed them from the library. But this evidence indicated that – with the possible exception of Professor Dewey himself – these books had never been checked out or read by anybody whomsoever. In short, I realized that I was exploring virgin territory – albeit territory that, over the years, had suffered from immense buildups of mold and mildew and other evil-smelling substances that afflict books if you let them sit on a humid shelf without touching them for half a century. I selected a huge armful of volumes with likely sounding titles and carried them back to my office. But – because I suffer from rampant allergies and occasional attacks of asthma – I could not think of reading these tomes until I had donned a surgical mask and, sometimes gasping for air, Xeroxed every page of every book – a large labor of love, not to mention an exorbitant expenditure on copier costs, to put it mildly. I then returned the fetid axiology books to Butler Library (where they undoubtedly languish to this day, growing more putrid by the minute) and began the task of reading my odorless Xerox copies of the collective wisdom on the philosophy of value.

In my reading, I found much to contemplate among many helpful contributions from bygone philosophers with names like Mortimer Adler (1981), Monroe Beardsley (1967), E. J. Bond (1983), William Frankena (1973), Risieri Frondizi (1971), Everett Hall (1961), Robert Hartman (1967), A. L. Hilliard (1950), Johan Huizinga (1938), W. D. Lamont (1955), C. I. Lewis (1946), L. M. Loring (1966), George Herbert Mead (1938), Charles Morris (1956), Radhakamal Mukerjee (1964), Harold Osborne (1933), Dewitt Parker (1957), Stephen Pepper (1958), Ralph Barton Perry (1954), Eli Siegel (1981), Paul Taylor (1961), and Georg Henrik Von Wright (1963). The accumulated insights of these brave axiologists gradually coalesced into my emerging views on the Concept of Consumer Value – that is, the nature and types of value derived by consumers from consumption experiences. This investigation of CCV suggested the following conclusions concerning (1) the nature and (2) the types of consumer value.

First, regarding the *Nature of Consumer Value*, I defined value as *an interactive relativistic preference experience*.

Consumer Value is *interactive* insofar as it depends on a relationship between a Subject (the consumer) and an Object (the relevant product or event). Value cannot exist without a value-producing Object of some kind (meaning, for example, that beauty is *not* only in the eye of the beholder). Nor can it exist without a Subject to appreciate it (meaning, for example, that a work of art cannot have value apart from those who admire it . . . or pay for it). Rather, Consumer Value entails a subject-object interaction in which the consumption experience resulting from a product or event appeals to one or another individual. This aspect of consumer value has inspired disciples of the Service-Dominant Logic (SDL, Vargo and Lusch, 2004) or the managerial gurus who espouse experiential marketing (Prahalad and Ramaswamy, 2004) to celebrate the *co-creation* of value (Arnould, 2007; Cova, Dalli, and Zwick, 2011; Sorensen, Andrews, and Drennan, 2017), thereby overlapping with the Concept of Consumer Value (CCV) in ways that I shall mention later and that exhibit a considerable degree of refined analysis but that do confuse the picture somewhat in their tendency to use the term "interaction" to refer to interpersonal relations between customers and service providers ("direct interaction") as opposed to a broader relation ("indirect interaction") between a product or event (Object) and a consumer (Subject) (Grönroos, 2011, 2012; Grönroos and Ravald, 2001; Grönroos and Voima, 2013; Sorensen, Andrews, and Drennan, 2017). In other words, those with a service-marketing orientation tend to use the term "interaction" to refer to interpersonal communications or joint activities between customers and service personnel, whereas my concept of the subject-object interaction encompasses a much broader inclusion of inter-relationships between products or events (objects) and consumers (subjects). Hence, joint co-creation activities as envisioned by theorists such as Grönroos (2011, 2012) are only part – indeed, an important but a small part – of the story as I see it.

Consumer Value is *relativistic* in at least three senses. Specifically, it is *comparative, personal,* and *situational*.

Value is *comparative* insofar as we can state the value of one object only in reference to that of one or more other objects as evaluated by the same individual. Thus, legitimate value judgments involve relative preferences among objects for a given person rather than illegitimate utility comparisons among people. Put differently, there is no valid absolute measure of consumer value that can be applied across individuals – that is, no valid measure of what the economists call "Cardinal Utility." This means that – common measurement practices notwithstanding – I cannot validly claim that I like vanilla ice cream at a level of 9 on a 10-point scale of absolute value. Rather, I can validly claim only that I like vanilla ice cream better than I like, say, chocolate ice cream (perhaps with some sort of calibration to assess how much better). For this reason, as economists have long insisted, *interpersonal* utility comparisons of the form "I like vanilla ice cream better than my wife Sally likes vanilla ice cream" are *illegitimate*. Rather, I can *legitimately* claim only that "I like vanilla ice cream better than chocolate, whereas Sally likes chocolate better than vanilla," which involves only comparisons made at the *intrapersonal* level. Notice that this issue concerning the invalidity of interpersonal utility comparisons bedeviled the early research on multiattribute attitude models. Researchers were in the habit of collecting belief and affect scores across a sample of respondents for one or another object (say, a political candidate or a make of automobile), forming sums of beliefs multiplied times desirability weights for each respondent, and then using these summative scores to predict or explain overall affect toward the brand across respondents. Unfortunately, such procedures involved interpersonal utility comparisons that negated their validity (Bass and Wilkie, 1973). The word began to circulate informally that – realizing this – Frank Bass, then editor of the *Journal of Marketing Research*, would no longer accept attitude-measurement papers that transgressed by correlating the components of attitude models across people. This inspired many of us to conduct research according to what Jaccard and Wood (1986) called an "idiothetic" approach in which comparisons were made and correlations run across a number of objects within each respondent at the intrapersonal level (e.g., Holbrook, 1977a, 1981a). This within-individuals across-objects approach avoids the fallacy of interpersonal utility comparisons and carries implications for the future of value-related research to be discussed later.

Consumer Value is *personal* insofar as it differs among people. To repeat, I like vanilla better than chocolate, Sally likes chocolate better than vanilla, and never the twain shall meet. The realization that different people have different preference functions relating features (vanilla/chocolate) to beliefs (delicious/disgusting) to evaluations (more/less favorable) is, of course, the basis for market segmentation and, therefore, the foundation for much or even most marketing strategy. Any self-respecting axiologist could have figured out the essence of marketing long before that field of study was invented.

Consumer Value is *situational* in that it varies from one context to the next. For example, suppose that, when eating a strawberry sundae, I prefer vanilla to chocolate ice cream but that, when eating a hot fudge sundae, I prefer chocolate to vanilla. Here appears a shining example of the well-known and highly publicized fact that a (comparative personal) value judgment (preferring vanilla/chocolate ice cream) depends on the context in which the evaluation is made (strawberry/hot fudge sundae). This realization implies the need to include the relevant situation(s) in any market-segmentation scheme. Russ Belk (1975) investigated this theme thoroughly in the case of such offerings as beverages, snack foods, or leisure activities; and I later extended this perspective to the case of situation-specific ideal points in preference functions for radio stations when listening at home, at work, or in the car (Holbrook, 1984b). For example, at home, I might prefer a station that plays refined classical music; at work, I might calm my nerves by listening to smooth jazz; whereas, in the car, I might seek out a 24-hour news station. Analogous context-dependent applications are ubiquitous throughout the world of marketing research.

Clearly and as implied in everything said thus far, Consumer Value pertains to a *preference* among alternative experience-producing objects or events – vanilla versus chocolate, strawberry, salty caramel, mint chip, rum raisin, pistachio, peppermint, cookie dough, rocky road, moose tracks, bear claw, and so forth. Here, it is important to distinguish between "Valu*e*" (singular) and "Valu*es*" (plural). The latter, of great interest to sociologists such as Rokeach (1968, 1973), concern the criteria used to determine an evaluation – as when, for example, my values suggest that I prefer a politician who is honest; smart; competent; in favor of free speech, racial equality, and women's rights; peace-loving; concerned about climate change, global warming, and protecting the environment; not corrupted by personal business interests; not compromised by ties to unfriendly foreign powers such as Russia; not inclined to appoint family members to high government positions; and not likely to spend way too much time on the golf course. Based on the criteria determined by these valu*es* (plural), I can evaluate any number of candidates to reach summary judgments of valu*e* (singular) for each and can then (comparatively, personally, and situationally) conclude that I prefer Candidate KDH to Candidate DJT.

Finally, most important and consistent with the work that Beth and I had done on the aforementioned experiential view of consumer behavior, Consumer Value can result *only* from a consumption *experience*. By itself, an object (product or event) has no value. As implied by the need for an object-subject interaction, value results only when that object performs the service of providing an experience that comparatively, personally, and situationally produces a preference in the form of a favorable evaluation. From this, it follows that the distinction between goods and services is more or less meaningless in the sense that, essentially, *any* offering (whether labeled a "good" or a "service") performs the *service* of providing a value-producing consumption experience. Thus, a lollipop (traditionally regarded as a "good") performs a hunger-reducing and taste-satisfying service just as much as a bank teller (traditionally regarded as a "service") performs a check-cashing and money-handling service. So, conceptually, the distinction between the two becomes rather pointless (all the more if the teller hands out free lollipops). What matters is the nature of the experience provided by the service-performing object (product, event, or whatever) – often enhanced, by the way, via some degree of *self*-service on the part of the customer (Grönroos, 2011).

All of that falls under the heading of the *Nature of Consumer Value* viewed as an *interactive relativistic (comparative, personal, situational) preference experience*. But, second, the next key question concerns an identification of the various *Types of Consumer Value*.

All during my years of post-graduate education and after, I have been a big fan of building typologies based on a series of two or more dichotomous distinctions. For example, in one of my proudest moments, this approach – based on distinctions between (1) Verbal/Visual Modalities and (2) Inputs/Outputs – led me to discover the existence of a fourth monkey to accompany Hear-No-Evil, See-No-Evil, and Speak-No-Evil, as follows:

	Verbal Modality	*Visual Modality*
Inputs	Hear-No-Evil	See-No-Evil
Outputs	Speak-No-Evil	?????

We find the fourth monkey (?????) lurking around the playground during recess, wearing a trench coat, and terrifying the children who stray too far from the jungle gym. His name is "Show-No-Evil." Obviously, with the availability of a method like that for isolating key types of one or another phenomenon, I could not resist applying the 2×2×2 approach to an identification of the different *Types of Consumer Value*.

(Please note that, here and in what follows, I shall treat the three key distinctions of interest as dichotomies even though they could more defensibly be viewed as continua ranging from one extreme to the other. The reader should keep in mind that the typology I propose could be represented more accurately by a multidimensional space in which continuous dimensions replace the simplified dichotomies that I shall discuss here.)

The first distinction commands almost universal recognition among the various axiologists and concerns the difference between Extrinsic and Intrinsic Value. *Extrinsic Value* refers to the case in which a product or event serves as the *means to some end*, as when my bat hits a ball over the fence in left field for a home run, wherein the extrinsic value of my bat-wielding experience lies in its goal-achieving run-producing efficacy. By contrast, *Intrinsic Value* refers to the case in which the experience of a product or event is prized *as an end in itself*, as when I appreciate hearing the sonorous tonalities and majestic themes in a performance of Bruckner's Seventh Symphony as a listening experience valued for its own sake. It happened that, at the time of developing the value typology, I resonated to the Extrinsic/Intrinsic distinction with special force because I was simultaneously involved in working with Bob Zirlin – a real PhD in Philosophy from Johns Hopkins – to write a review of the aesthetic aspects of consumer behavior, where the aesthetic aspects of art and entertainment are characterized by the intrinsic nature of the value they provide (Holbrook and Zirlin, 1985). Finding the same Extrinsic/Intrinsic distinction rampant in the writings of age-old axiologists gave me confidence that this is indeed a key dichotomy or dimension on which to focus.

Second, I found widespread support for another key distinction based on the difference between Self-Oriented and Other-Oriented Value. *Self-Oriented Value* depends on how I respond to some consumption experience or on how it affects me. By contrast, *Other-Oriented Value* depends on how some consumption experience affects others or on how they respond to it. Here, I intend "Other" to encompass a broad spectrum that ranges from the Deity to the Cosmos, to Mother Nature, to the Planet, to the Country, to one's Town or Community, to one's circle of Friends and Acquaintances, to one's Family and Loved Ones, and even to potentially difficult-to-access Subcomponents of One's Own Personality. Clearly, at one level, this distinction refers to the conventional contrast between self-oriented individual interests compared with the other-oriented social aspects of value creation. And, just as clearly, sometimes the lines tend to get a bit blurred. One example of such blurring occurs in various Eastern religions that posit a sort of internal "other" with which the "self" needs to get in touch in order to experience some kind of epiphany. Something similar might be said for the kind of internal quest that occurs in various forms of psychoanalysis. In what follows, I shall include these kinds of internal explorations under the heading of "other-oriented" even though the "other" in question lies within the "self" as conventionally conceived.

Third, hints appear to support a contrast between Active and Reactive Value. *Active Value* refers to a manipulation of some product- or event-produced experience in order to reap the relevant type of reward by virtue of *the effect I have on it*. By contrast, *Reactive Value* stems from my responding to some product- or event-produced experience to appreciate its value by virtue of *the effect it has on me*. Pounding a nail with a hammer clearly exhibits active value. Conversely, my enjoyment of a massage in which the masseuse pounds my back with her fists exhibits reactive value.

Putting these distinctions together, Holbrook and Corfman (1985) produced the following 2×2×2 or eight-fold *Typology of Consumer Value* with value types shown in CAPITAL LETTERS (and major examples shown parenthetically).

		Extrinsic	*Intrinsic*
Self-Oriented	*Active*	EFFICIENCY (Convenience)	PLAY (Fun)
	Passive	EXCELLENCE (Quality)	ESTHETICS (Beauty)
Other-Oriented	*Active*	POLITICS (Success)	MORALITY (Virtue)
	Passive	ESTEEM (Reputation)	RELIGION (Faith)

In subsequent writings, much of this terminology has been refined and, I believe, improved in clarity. Specifically, as already indicated, what we then called "Passive Value" I now call "Reactive Value" (Holbrook, 1999a, 1999c). "Politics" is now identified as "Status (Success, Impression Management)." "Esteem" now includes "(Reputation, Materialism, Possessions)." "Morality (Virtue)" has been replaced by "Ethics (Virtue, Justice, Morality)." And "Religion (Faith)" has become "Spirituality (Faith, Ecstasy, Sacredness, Magic)." However – because they are based on the same three underlying dimensions, distinctions, or dichotomies – the types themselves have remained virtually unchanged over the years (Holbrook, 1999a, 1999c).

		Extrinsic	*Intrinsic*
Self-Oriented	*Active*	EFFICIENCY (O/I or O-I, Convenience)	PLAY (Fun)
	Reactive	EXCELLENCE (Quality)	AESTHETICS (Beauty)
Other-Oriented	*Active*	STATUS (Success, Impression Management)	ETHICS (Virtue, Justice, Morality)
	Reactive	ESTEEM (Reputation, Materialism, Possessions)	SPIRITUALITY (Faith, Ecstasy, Sacredness, Magic)

Efficiency refers to the active manipulation of some experience produced by a product or an event as a means to some self-oriented end – as when I push on the gas pedal to increase the speed of the car or strike a match to produce the flame for lighting a candle. Very often, Efficiency is measured as the ratio or difference between an Output (O) and an Input (I) – as when I assess my car's performance in terms of miles per gallon (O/I) or evaluate the benefits-less-costs of a mutual fund according to its returns-minus-fees (O-I). In the case of Convenience, one special kind of Efficiency, the Input

(I) of interest is time – as when I measure my car's performance by clocking miles per hour or judge the value of a doctor's visit according to how long I am kept waiting. Thus, the whole value of a "convenience" store such as, say, Seven-Eleven lies not in the quality of its merchandise or the attentiveness of its staff or the breadth of its selection but, rather, in the timeliness of its availability when you are driving down the highway late at night looking for a place to stock up on corn puffs. As I'll mention later, a great deal of the value-related literature – such as the work on SERVQUAL (Parasuraman, Zeithaml, and Berry, 1988; Zeithaml, 1988) – focuses on this O/I or O-I logic to construct get-versus-give- or benefits-versus-sacrifices-based measures of value-for-the-money or other indices that essentially capture what I am calling Efficiency (sometimes at the expense of neglecting other major types of value).

Excellence represents the reactive side of Efficiency wherein I appreciate some product or event for its capacity to serve as the means to a self-oriented end but without actually needing to use it for that purpose. Ascendant among the various aspects of Excellence, we find the notion of Quality. This refers to my admiration for the degree to which some product or event could accomplish some task to satisfy a self-oriented goal without my necessarily putting that ability into practice. For example, my knife made from Damascus steel (an ancient gift from my grandfather) may be sharp enough to cut in half your dropped silk scarf from Hermès, but I can admire this excellent quality without actually needing to destroy your hideously expensive garment. Or, as another example, the excellence of my Ferrari might allow it to roar down the highway at 120 mph, but I can appreciate this unexcelled quality without actually taking my chances on getting a speeding ticket. This definition of Quality as an extrinsic self-oriented reactive type of consumer value proceeds directly from our attempt to address the questions posed by Jack Jacoby's and Jerry Olson's "Perceived Quality" conference at NYU and reflects the view that I absorbed from the axiological literature that any given type of value (in this case Quality) can be understood only by virtue of interpreting its relationships with other types of value. In this case, Quality is a sub-species of Excellence as distinct from the other seven types of value identified by the eight-fold typology.

Status refers to the case in which I actively manipulate some consumption experience as a means to the end of producing a desired response in others. Examples would include various aspects of Impression Management – as when I don an elegant long-sleeved striped shirt from Ralph Lauren, a snappy tie from Brooks Brothers, and a preppy jacket from J. Press in order to Dress for Success. Notice that status entails the conscious management of my own consumption with an eye to how others respond to it.

By contrast, *Esteem* involves my reactive appreciation of the way(s) in which others might potentially respond to my own consumption as a means of producing an effect on them. For example, I could contemplate how one or another of my Possessions might potentially enhance my Reputation with admiring friends and neighbors without actually showing them the relevant object(s) or overtly seeking their approval. As a personality characteristic, Materialism has a bit of this esteem-oriented flavor. Yielding to my own occasionally materialistic impulses, I have a closet full of over-priced neckties – mostly gifts from extravagant friends and family members – that I would probably never wear in public but that I keep just for the satisfaction of knowing that they would be there if I needed them.

Turning to the intrinsic side of the typology, *Play* refers to consumption experiences actively pursued for the self-oriented satisfaction of the effect they have on me when enjoyed for their own sake as ends in themselves. The nature of leisure activities – indeed, the essence of Fun – is that the relevant consumption experiences serve as their own rewards and provide me with pleasures that achieve no other purpose. The moment that such an event is treated as the means to some self-oriented end – say, the accomplishment of a money-earning task – it stops being leisure and starts being work. Rather, purely purposeless playful activities enjoyed for their own sake are the province of children and some liberated adults – especially those with an inclination toward creativity. My friends from a jazz-ensemble class (how to play nicely with others) do not understand why I do not want to pursue gigs that would involve getting paid (a very small amount) to perform in public. The answer lies in the difference between Play and Efficiency (plus the fact that such jobs do not pay well enough to inspire me to sacrifice my lofty principles).

The reactive side of play is *Aesthetics* or *Esthetics*. Either spelling is correct, and I cannot make up my mind which I prefer – Greek or British. So I have used both. (A)esthetics refers to the intrinsic self-oriented value attained through my response to a consumption experience appreciated as an end in itself. Indeed, this aspect of enjoying an experience for its own sake is the hallmark of philosophical definitions of Aesthetics (Holbrook and Zirlin, 1985) and the essence of evaluations that fall under the heading of "Beauty" and that bolster the part of the cliché that can be considered valid when claiming that "beauty is in the eye of the beholder." (As previously mentioned, Beauty also requires the existence of some sort of object, a product or event, to behold as part of the subject-object interaction.) Beauty implies the appreciation of an experience valued intrinsically for its own sake. So the minute I stop admiring my sculpture by Hans Arp for its graceful lines, delicate balance, and gleaming finish and start appreciating its ability to serve as a doorstop, the relevant type of value shifts from Beauty to Quality. (It's a really excellent doorstop, but that has nothing to do with its aesthetic appeal.)

Ethics concerns the active manipulation of a consumption experience intrinsically appreciated for its own sake by virtue of the way it affects others or how others respond to it. For example, I might donate money to a charity so as to experience the feeling of helping other people. Or I might endeavor to be honest and tell the truth for the sake of avoiding the harm that would otherwise befall others. Sub-species of Ethics such as Virtue, Justice, and

Morality have received little attention from consumer researchers and – in my view, from the macromarketing side of things – deserve far more energetic investigation by the members of our discipline (Cooper-Martin and Holbrook, 1993; Holbrook, 1994c; Murphy and Laczniak, 2012; Smith and Quelch, 1992).

Finally, *Spirituality* refers to the sort of experience in which I feel that my Self has achieved some sort of communion with an Other in a way that I value intrinsically for its own sake as an end in itself. Thus, axiologists see Ecstasy as involving an intrinsically rewarding disappearance of the Self/Other dichotomy – as when, in a state of rapture, I feel myself merging with some sort of greater power. As mentioned earlier, the Other in question could be the Deity, the Cosmos, Mother Nature, my community, my friends and family, or even some hitherto unapproachable part of myself with which I have found a way to communicate. Thus, this type of value involves aspects of Faith, Sacredness, or Magic and inspires one or another sort of religious or quasi-religious experience.

As part of our NYU offering, Kim and I presented the Concept of Consumer Value (CCV) as just described and then reported the results of a small experimental study in which – by manipulating various aspects of a musical consumption experience – we showed that Overall Preference depended on perceptions of Beauty, Quality, and Fun. However, the conference organizers – Jack Jacoby and Jerry Olson – felt that our paper was much too long to be included in the conference-based book on *Perceived Quality*; so, in the end, we cut back greatly on the philosophical material related to CCV and focused instead on the more collaborative empirical section (Holbrook and Corfman, 1985). I suspect that Jack and Jerry were somewhat disappointed by this strategy for shortening the paper; but, in the co-authored chapter, I wanted to emphasize the part of the work in which Kim had played the greater role and to save the more esoteric stuff for pursuing on my own at a later date.

This "later date" turned out to be a bit slow in coming. Specifically, after much additional labor, I managed to crank out a lengthy philosophically oriented paper addressing the Concept of Consumer Value. But I could not bear to submit this work on CCV to the journal that should have served as its logical target publication – namely, the *Journal of Consumer Research*. Having endured *JCR*'s review process countless times, I knew that – even if I received an invitation to revise-and-resubmit – by the time the editors and reviewers had finished with my CCV paper it would have retained little resemblance to what I truly wanted to say. And, caring as I did about the value-related topic, I could not stand to let this happen. (For an illustration of the way[s] in which my CCV lends itself to misunderstanding, misinterpretation, and misrepresentation, please see Woodruff [1997, p. 141].)

I did manage to insert intimations of CCV into various projects devoted to broader issues. For example in a chapter entitled "Expanding the Ontology and Methodology of Research on the Consumption Experience" for a book edited by Dave Brinberg and Rich Lutz, Beth and I built upon our earlier treatment of Fantasies, Feelings, and Fun to extend the ICABS formulation in ways that included expanded aspects of the Situation, Inputs, Thoughts, Emotions, Activities, and Value or STEAV (Hirschman and Holbrook, 1986). A bit later, in an article entitled "Actions and Reactions in the Consumption Experience: The Complementary Roles of Reasons and Emotions in Consumer Behavior," John O'Shaughnessy, Stephen Bell, and I tried to achieve an integrated view of consumer behavior that sought a rapprochement of the decision-oriented approach with the experiential or hedonic perspective and that took Value (as opposed to Satisfaction) as its main output variable of interest. We tried very hard to publish this paper in *JCR*, but a rather persistently resistant reviewer convinced the editors to reject our work on the rather absurd grounds that reasons and emotions are, in principle, "incommensurable." With generous help from Beth Hirschman as editor, we managed to publish the piece in *Research in Consumer Behavior* (Holbrook, O'Shaughnessy, and Bell, 1990). But I have often suspected that, if the article had appeared in *JCR*, it would have attracted a wider audience, would have saved the world quite a bit of needless bickering about the relative importance of Thoughts and Emotions, and would have established Consumer Value as the key output of primary importance.

Meanwhile, I waited. And waited. And, during the time that I waited, I took my Concept of Consumer Value on the road and presented it at a large number of schools, conferences, and other venues – including (by the time I was finished) the University of Utah, the University of Michigan, Ohio State University, the University of Quebec in Montreal, Dartmouth's Tuck School, the University of Illinois, McGill University in Montreal, the University of Pennsylvania's Wharton School (twice), the University of California in Los Angeles, the University of British Columbia, Rutgers University in New Brunswick, the University of Arizona, Iowa State University, the City University of New York's Baruch College, Edith Cowan University in Perth (Australia), the University of Texas in Austin, Diamond Inc. in Tokyo, Hakuhodo Inc. in Tokyo, the Japanese Marketing Association in Tokyo, the University of Miami (AMA Doctoral Consortium), the Society for Marketing Advances (St. Pete Beach, FL), and – of course, my home turf – Columbia University itself (at least a couple of times in special seminars and many times in my class on Consumer Behavior). So it seems fair to say that, while I withheld my major work on CCV from submission to a journal, I took it around the world and exposed it, via formal presentations, to virtually every marketing scholar residing in the USA, Canada, Australia, and Japan. (True, Europe did not appear on my road-show itinerary – which seems ironic given that this is where my work on consumer value has ultimately had its greatest impact.)

Finally, I got a chance to publish my treatise on the Concept of Consumer Value in the form that I intended. Specifically, in the book they edited on *Service Quality*, Roland Rust and Rich Oliver were so kind as to include my lengthy CCV paper under the title "The Nature of Customer

Value: An Axiology of Services in the Consumption Experience" (Holbrook, 1994f). According to Scholar.Google.Com, this chapter has become my fifth-most-cited publication with 3,274 references. About the same time, in a volume edited by Marilyn Revell DeLong and Ann Marie Fiore on *Aesthetics of Textiles and Clothing*, a popularized version of my thoughts about CCV appeared as "Axiology, Aesthetics, and Apparel: Some Reflections on the Old School Tie" (Holbrook, 1994a).

Then – in 1996, at the conference of the Association for Consumer Research – I organized a Special Session on CCV that featured a brief introduction by me and mini-presentations by eight experts on the eight main types of Consumer Value (Holbrook, 1996e). According to the conference chairpeople, Kim Corfman and John Lynch, this was the best-attended session at an ACR conference up to that moment in time. Encouraged by this populous response, I persuaded all but one of the session participants to collaborate with me on a book for Routledge on the theme of *Consumer Value: A Framework for Analysis and Research* (Holbrook, ed. 1999). This volume has gone on to become my fourth-most-cited publication with 5,161 references. Herein, after an Introduction by yours truly (Holbrook, 1999c), eight chapters cover the eight major types of Consumer Value, as follows: Efficiency (France Leclerc and Bernd Schmitt), Excellence (Rich Oliver), Status (Mike Solomon), Esteem (Marsha Richins), Play (Kent Grayson), Aesthetics (Janet Wagner), Ethics (Craig Smith), and Spirituality (Stephen Brown). The collective wisdom of these authors persuaded me to change the title of the book from *Customer Value* to *Consumer Value*. This distinction deserves a few words of commentary before proceeding further.

Specifically, I should pause to clarify the terminological distinction between "Customer Value" and "Consumer Value." When I first began worrying about the nature of value in general and quality in particular, as part of our contribution to the Jacoby-and-Olson conference at NYU, I adopted a perspective oriented toward the concerns of marketing managers wishing to provide value to the buyer in ways that would contribute to satisfaction and thereby encourage brand loyalty so as to achieve high rates of repeat-purchasing behavior. In short, this focus dwelled on market-embedded buying decisions and the benefits derived therefrom in pursuit of outcomes favorable to the firm's bottom line. The target of such efforts was the buyer or customer – hence, the term "Customer Value" (Holbrook, 1994a, 1994f; Holbrook and Corfman, 1985). Over time, however, I had adopted a vantage point that focused more broadly on all aspects of the consumption experience – including, of course, those aspects that manifested themselves in market-related buying behavior but also embracing aspects of the human condition that did not necessarily involve profit-oriented cash-based market transactions and that would more appropriately be termed "Consumer Value." Increasingly, I viewed consumer research as concerning itself with all forms of consumption experiences without restrictions as to whether these experiences stemmed from purchase decisions or from some other sort of offering or event. In this, I regarded *Customer Value* as the province of *marketing research* and *Consumer Value* as the proper focus of *consumer research*. Hence, the friends and colleagues who participated in the afore-mentioned collection of value-related essays easily convinced me to title the book in ways that reflected my own expanded interests in the consumption experience considered broadly – *Consumer Value: A Framework for Analysis and Research* (Holbrook, ed. 1999). In line with this distinction between Customer Value and Consumer Value and my own gravitation toward the latter direction of inquiry, I now use the latter term in most situations where the need for such terminology appears.

Meanwhile, I have continued to write the occasional essay on the subject of Consumer Value. Two of these appeared as articles for the *Journal of Business Research* – namely, "Customer Value and Autoethnography: Subjective Personal Introspection and the Meanings of a Photograph Collection" (Holbrook, 2005c) and "Consumption Experience, Customer Value, and Subjective Personal Introspection: An Illustrative Photographic Essay" (Holbrook, 2006a). Both studies make use of a collection of photos inherited from my grandfather to illustrate the different types of Consumer Value. In this sense, the articles are quite similar so I find it interesting if confusing to speculate on how they managed to appear in the same journal only a few months apart. (For further details, please see Chapter 6.) In the second study for *JBR*, I collapsed the distinction between active and reactive value to focus on just four major types, as follows:

	Extrinsic	*Intrinsic*
Self-Oriented	Economic	Hedonic
Other-Oriented	Social	Altruistic

This reduction of the eight types of value to just four major types – Economic, Social, Hedonic, and Altruistic – allows for more expedient discussion and has also proven useful in the classroom (where I have found that time-pressed, career-oriented, sometimes anti-intellectual MBAs really do not care about enriching their understanding of Consumer Value to include eight as opposed to four major types). While in this simplification-oriented mood, I also tried to persuade advocates of the Service-Dominant Logic (SDL) that their rather complex list of relevant considerations could be easily encapsulated under the rubric of the Concept of Consumer Value (CCV). Bob Lusch and Steve Vargo were so kind as to include my reflections in this direction as part of their book on the SDL theme, and I believe that when it benefits from careful scrutiny, my title says it all: "ROSE-PEKICECIVECI versus CCV – The Resource-Operant, Skills-Exchanging, Performance-Experiencing, Knowledge-Informed, Competence-Enacting, Coproducer-Involved, Value-Emerging, Customer-Interactive View of Marketing Versus the Concept of Customer Value: 'I Can Get It For You Wholesale'"

(Holbrook, 2006f). A final simplification for the sake of difficult-to-elicit popularization appeared in two more recent book chapters. The first, for a book on *Marketing Management* edited by Lisa Peñaloza, Nil Toulouse, and Luca Massimiliano Visconti, discussed (not optimistically) the kinds of consumer value contributed by academic institutions under the heading "Catering to Consumers or Consuming the Caterers: A Bridge Too Far . . ., Way Too Far" (Holbrook, 2012). The second, on a happier theme for *The Routledge Companion to Arts Marketing* edited by Daragh O'Reilly, Ruth Rentschker, and Theresa A. Kirchner, reviewed the value-related aspects of artistic offerings in general and provided a detailed illustration based on performances by the great vibraphonist Gary Burton in a chapter entitled "Consumption Criteria in Arts Marketing" (Holbrook, 2014a; please see Chapter 8). In both cases, I offered a Typology of Consumer Value with categories renamed so that, for ease of memorization, they all begin with the letter "E":

		Extrinsic	*Intrinsic*
Self-Oriented	Active	EFFICIENCY (O/I, O-I)	ENTERTAINMENT (Play, Fun)
	Reactive	EXCELLENCE (Quality)	ESTHETICS (Beauty)
Other-Oriented	Active	EXHIBITIONISM (Status, Impression Management)	ETHICS (Justice, Virtue, Morality)
	Reactive	ELITISM (Esteem, Materialism)	ECSTASY (Spirituality, Rapture)

As the reader may have gathered from my enthusiasm about the Three F's, I like typologies with category names that all begin with the same letter. Hence, I am happy with my Eight E's scheme and consider this to be a strong argument in favor of spelling "Esthetics" with an "E" instead of an "AE."

The Gary Burton example just mentioned leads us toward a short discussion of special problems and issues raised by the Concept of Consumer Value. Almost as soon as I finish explaining everything that I have said so far about CCV, someone invariably raises a hand and asks, "But isn't it possible for some consumption experience to offer more than one type of value?" The answer is, of course, "Absolutely, Yes!" Indeed, the axiologists amused themselves by coining a term for this – namely, "Compresence." According to this notion of Compresence, any value-creating experience may partake of one, two, three, more, or even all of the various types of value at any one time (though, most often, a smaller number are more prominent than others). Over the years, I have repeatedly illustrated this point with examples based on my Columbia Business School necktie (Holbrook,

1994a), my grandfather's enjoyment of trips to the Brule River in Northern Wisconsin (Holbrook, 2005c, 2006a), the satisfactions provided by a vibraphone (Holbrook, 2006f), the educational experience at an academic institution (Holbrook, 2012), and – as just mentioned – performances by the great vibraphonist Gary Burton (Holbrook, 2014a). (Yes, I have vibraphones on my mind, and they are indeed a copious source of different types of value in my life as a consumer.) I hope the reader will agree that it makes perfect sense for multiple types of value to appear simultaneously and that the word "Compresence" describes this situation perfectly.

Another sometimes troubling issue relates to the reason why, in the afore-mentioned article (Holbrook, 2006a), I collapsed the Active/Reactive distinction, thereby condensing the typology to just four major types of value (Economic, Social, Hedonic, and Altruistic). Specifically, over the years, I have found that people seem to have some trouble identifying the difference between active and reactive value. As mentioned earlier, this distinction hinges on whether I actively manipulate some object so as to create an effect on it that results in a value-laden experience or, rather, reactively appreciate and respond to an object because of the effect it has on me by virtue of its capacity to perform in some way. Thus, in the case of Ethics, I act for the benefit of one or more Other(s). By contrast, in the case of Spirituality or Ecstasy, my Self responds to some Other(s), often in a way that involves a disappearance of the Self/Other dichotomy. I feel as if I have become one with the Deity or the Cosmos or Mother Nature or some hitherto inaccessible part of my Own Being. To me, this Active/Reactive distinction seems fairly straightforward; yet many people do not "get" it. Similarly, the contrast between Status or Exhibitionism and Esteem or Elitism hinges on whether I manipulate my consumption actively as a means to producing some response in others (as in the case of Impression Management) or reactively appreciate the capacity of one or another product or event (such as my Possessions) potentially to produce a favorable response from others (as in the case of Materialism). Again, this contrast strikes me as fairly clear; yet Marsha Richins complained about its obscurity in her chapter on Esteem for the aforementioned book on *Consumer Value* (Holbrook, ed. 1999). Hence, especially when teaching, I have sometimes dropped the third active-reactive distinction and relied on the four-fold typology mentioned earlier: Economic, Social, Hedonic, and Altruistic (Holbrook, 2006a).

By the way, the day after I wrote the last paragraph, I passed a Beauty Parlor called the "Concept Salon" on 2nd Avenue at 58th Street in New York City with a sign in the window that said, "Style is not a display of wealth, But an expression of imagination." Though worded a bit clumsily, this slogan seems to compare Status or Exhibitionism (dressing or coiffing in a way that impresses others with its expensiveness) with Esteem or Elitism (imaginatively contemplating an awareness of one's own good taste in clothes and beauty-related products). Patrons of the Concept Salon apparently understand the difference, implicitly if not explicitly.

Also, one might wonder whether there might exist some additional distinction(s) not covered in the present CCV but leading to eight or more additional types of Consumer Value with which to grapple. In reading the axiologists, I tried to make sure that I included what I deemed to be the most important and oft-mentioned distinctions (Extrinsic/Intrinsic, Self-Oriented/Other-Oriented, Active/Reactive). But I cannot guarantee that someone might not eventually come up with one or more additional contrasts that might multiply the relevant number of value types by two or more. Not so secretly, I hope that this will not happen because I do not think I could gracefully cope with 16 or more value types. Eight seems like more than enough to keep us busy.

Another issue concerns the somewhat careless use in our discipline of the term "Customer Value" or "Consumer Value" itself. When I originally began the series of investigations reported in this essay, I envisioned Customer Value as the key output from any analysis of consumer behavior. According to my interpretation, Consumer Value emerges from the relevant Fantasies, Feelings, and Fun or from the chain of effects moving from the Situation to Thoughts to Emotions to Activities to Value – which, in turn, serves as the major determinant of Brand Loyalty (every marketing manager's profit-maximizing dream). And – quite obviously, but just to be clear – by CCV, I meant the *Value OF the Firm's Offering TO the Consumer*. But the time came in 2006 when two of my more brilliant colleagues – Sunil Gupta and Don Lehmann (2006), exploring the sources of a firm's profitability attributable to buyer loyalty in the form of repeat-purchase behavior – came up with the term "Customer Lifetime Value (CLV)," by which they meant the *Value OF the Customer TO the Firm*. Sunil and Don's article was part of an entire issue of the *Journal of Relationship Marketing* devoted to CLV. Due to the eminence and prestige of these and other colleagues who have latched onto the CLV terminology, I fear that – as implied by Woodruff (1997) – the rather oppositional meanings embodied by CCV and CLV have caused confusion among readers and researchers alike. Not so secretly, given that my CCV came first and had been well-publicized over the years, I wish that my colleagues would drop CLV and adopt another term such as, say, "Long-Term Customer Profitability (LTCP)." But, considering the well-respected importance of their contributions, I fear that CLV will continue to co-exist with CCV, causing confusion and perhaps even frustration among students, teachers, and people who write essays about marketing-related topics such as value.

On the whole, along similar lines and despite my self-promoting efforts reported in the present essay, I feel that the Concept of Consumer Value has received something less than the attention it deserves from members of our discipline in general and from the advocates of Consumer Culture Theory (CCT) in particular. Apparently, I am regarded as one of the original progenitors of CCT (Arnould and Thompson, 2005; Askegaard and Scott, 2013) – sometimes with good-natured descriptions of my work as "wild," "wacky," or "weird" (Bode and Østergaard, 2013). Yet after listing me (plus many others) in that capacity, those who promote the "CCT Brand" (Arnould and Thompson, 2007) typically go on to imply, by the omission of references to my more recent work, that I stopped creating anything worthwhile after a couple of frequently cited articles from the early 1980s. As an example, consider the chapter by Eric Arnould (2007) in celebration of CCT in which he argues that many of the insights provided by the Service-Dominant Logic (SDL) overlap and cohere with perspectives friendly to the CCT viewpoint. Because I am regarded as a CCT-friendly author and because Eric explicitly refers to the SDL-oriented volume that contains my aforementioned chapter suggesting that CCV encompasses most or even all of the issues raised by SDL (Holbrook, 2006f), I might have hoped for a bit of recognition that CCV has already contributed to many of the insights claimed by Eric for CCT as a supplement or replacement for SDL. But – even though my chapter is sitting there and staring him in the face, with me sometimes seen as an early proponent of CCT – Eric makes no mention of Morris. In proposing a CCT-based lexicon, Eric does emphasize the "experience"- and "value"-related aspects of interest, but without acknowledging the sources for these concepts (p. 68). Thus, as topics worthy of further research, he asks, "Where does 'value' come from and what makes that 'value' worth coproducing?" (p. 71) without noticing that some of us have been wrestling with those issues for decades. In a more recent article (Arnould, 2013), Eric continues in a similar vein. Here, he does acknowledge my work on consumer value (Holbrook, 1994f, 1999c), but he describes my approach as "limited" to "the kind of exchange that predominates in capitalist market economies" (p. 131) and complains that I "fetishize the quest for the unified sense of being capitalism sunders" (p. 132). Not thinking of myself as limited to "fetishizing" and being unacquainted with the more advanced aspects of the CCT jargon, I have no idea what Eric means by these characterizations of CCV, but I gather that his appraisals somehow reflect an energetic advocacy for the CCT Brand (Arnould and Thompson, 2007). All this tends to make me feel a bit frustrated and causes me to worry that the Concept of Consumer Value receives more than its fair share of neglect or misrepresentation from the gurus who move and shake our consumer-research community.

Further neglect is ubiquitous in writings by the numerous business experts who have created managerial self-help books on what is sometimes called "Experiential Marketing" or the "Brand Experience." I have not read all such works, but in multiple book reviews (Holbrook, 2000b, 2006g, 2007f, 2007g, 2007h), I have covered experientially oriented publications by a number of authors such as Arussy (2002), Carbone (2004), LaSalle and Britton (2003), Milligan and Smith (ed. 2002), Pine and Gilmore (1998, 1999), Samuel (2003), Schmitt (1999, 2003, 2007, 2012), Schmitt, Rogers, and Vrotsos (2003), Schmitt and Simonson (1997), Shaw and Ivens (2002), and Smith and Wheeler (2002). Most of these writers, intent on popularization, show little concern for or awareness of the research on the Consumption Experience that has been contributed by those with a somewhat more scholarly bent, and virtually nobody among the experiential gurus pursues the role of consumption experiences in the direction of examining their relevance to the creation of Consumer Value. If they mention my work at all, they cite one of the early articles with Beth on hedonic consumption (Hirschman and Holbrook, 1982) or the experiential view (Holbrook and Hirschman, 1982) and let it go at that, never mentioning the rather voluminous amount of subsequent follow-up work on Fantasies, Feelings, and Fun or Thoughts, Emotions, Activities, and Value that stemmed therefrom and never noticing the emergence of a more important and fundamental focus on Consumer Value. The one exception I have found to this mostly anti-intellectual approach to the proliferation of managerial self-help books on experiential marketing and the brand experience appears in an excellent volume by LaSalle and Britton (2003) – two authors who do recognize the role of consumption experiences in providing the bases for consumer value. To anyone interested in pursuing the conventional wisdom on the marketing of value-creating experiences, I recommend LaSalle and Britton's helpful guide.

As mentioned earlier, I carried my value-centric message to all parts of the USA, to Canada, to Australia, and to Japan and was a bit surprised but greatly reassured to discover that the Concept of Consumer Value seems to resonate with ideas and beliefs found in different cultures worldwide. For example, members of my Japanese audiences graciously approached me and told me that they had found my ideas about the nature and types of consumer value useful in structuring market analyses for their local companies. Indeed, they gave me various handsomely produced corporate documents that featured representations of my Typology of Consumer Value. Unfortunately for me, I do not read Japanese and was not able to plumb the depths of their discoveries, but I felt reassured to know that some of the ideas reported herein have found their way to acceptance and application at the global level.

As mentioned earlier, major places that I did *not* visit to preach my value-oriented ideas about consumers were Western Europe and the UK. Yet, somewhat paradoxically, Europe in general and Spain in particular turn out to be the locales where my work seems to have attracted its most enthusiastic following. Besides the USA, contributions referenced in the present essay have come from (alphabetically) Australia, Belgium, Canada, China, Denmark, Finland, France, Italy, Spain, and the UK. Early in the present millennium, I began email correspondences with two Spanish professors – Raquel Sánchez-Fernández and Martina González-Gallarza Granizo – who did not know each other but who, by coincidence and without any mutual awareness, had begun to work on issues related to consumer value in the tourist- and hospitality-services industries. So their research covered closely related themes. And both had long Spanish names with several components that, to an ignorant American, seemed somewhat indistinguishable. So – for a while, being in the foolish habit of carelessly clicking on "Reply to Sender" when responding to emails (without paying proper attention to the full name of the person to whom I am replying) – I actually thought that they were the same person. Eventually, emerging from my dim-witted slumbers, I figured out their separate identities. And, in time, both traveled to New York as visiting scholars at Columbia so that I could have the pleasure of working with them. Operating separately from each other but sometimes with me and other coauthors, Martina and Raquel have contributed definitive reviews of the literature on the Concept of Consumer Value (Gallarza, Arteaga, Del Chiappo, Gil-Saura, and Holbrook, 2017; Gallarza, Gil-Saura, and Holbrook, 2011, 2012; Sánchez-Fernández and Iniesta-Bonillo, 2006; Sánchez-Fernández, Iniesta-Bonillo, and Holbrook, 2009). Their work has helped to arouse and to reinforce the value-related interests of other European colleagues. So, if I wanted to receive a warm reception of my value-related ideas, I could probably skip Chicago or Boston or Palo Alto and head directly to Spain and surrounding countries where, I feel pretty sure, there exists an emerging community of scholars with a strong interest in CCV (not to mention an inviting climate, friendly people, beautiful scenery, fantastic food, and a vibrant cultural reverence for the arts).

A problem area closely related to that of conceptualization concerns the whole issue of measurement and empirical testing. In that connection, we observe a long line of data-driven studies with relevance to the various types of consumer value discussed herein. Some have focused on just one major type of value, as in the tradeoff-oriented, get-versus-give, benefits-versus-sacrifices, or quality-versus-price formulations championed by Dodds and Monroe (1985; Dodds, Monroe, and Grewal, 1991) or by Zeithaml (1988) and related to the aspects of Quality assessed via the SERVQUAL index developed by Pasuraman, Zeithaml, and Berry (1988) to represent what I have called "Excellence" in service industries. Others have addressed just two major types of value, as in the work by Batra and Ahtola (1991), by Mano and Oliver (1993), and by Babin, Darden, and Griffin (1994) on developing measures for the Utilitarian versus Hedonic aspects of Consumer Value. Still others have pursued broader approaches to multiple types of value, as in studies such as that on the PERVAL Scale by Sweeney and Soutar (2001) and by Wang, Lo, Chi, and Yang (2004), who have attempted with mixed success to operationalize the list of categories of value proposed by Sheth, Newman, and Gross (1991) – namely, Functional Value, Social Value, Emotional Value, Epistemic Value, and Conditional Value. And some brave souls – again, with mixed success – have sought support for subsets of my own eight-fold value types using either qualitative interpretive analyses (Bevan and Murphy, 2001; Kim, 2002) or quantitative empirical approaches (Bourdeau, Chebat, and Counturier, 2002; Leroi-Werelds, Streukens, Brady, and Swinnen, 2014; Mathwick, Malhotra, and Rigdon, 2001, 2002). In my own work, I have used the eight-fold typology of value as an interpretive lens through which to understand the different types of value lurking in photographs taken by my grandfather (Holbrook, 2005c, 2006a) and present in situations involving clothes (Holbrook, 1994a), musical instruments (Holbrook, 2006f), academic institutions (Holbrook, 2012), or musicians (Holbrook, 2014a). I cannot come close to claiming an in-depth familiarity with all of the innumerable relevant empirical applications. However, excellent accounts of the empirical work appear in the reviews by Raquel (Sánchez-Fernández and Iniesta-Bonillo, 2007) and by Martina (Gallarza and Gil-Saura, 2008). And both these researchers have worked with various coauthors (including yours truly) to begin the process of developing reliable and valid measures for the types of consumer value distinguished by my eight-fold typology, often with a focus on tourism (Gallarza and Gil-Saura, 2008) or hospitality services (Gallarza, Arteaga, Del Chiappa, Gil-Saura, and Holbrook, 2017; Sánchez-Fernández, Iniesta-Bonillo, and Holbrook, 2009) and with expanded implications concerning the relationship of value types to links in the chain of effects involving overall value, satisfaction, and loyalty (Gallarza and Gil-Saura, 2006; Gallarza, Gil-Saura, and Arteaga Moreno, 2013). As an indication of the international scope of such research, in the case of Gallarza, Arteaga, Del Chiappa, Gil-Saura, and Holbrook (2017), I am the fifth co-author of a paper with colleagues whose affiliations reach from Spain to Italy and even to South Africa.

That said, I must confess that the empirical applications I have seen thus far – including those in which I myself have participated – tend to fall short of certain measurement-related ideals that I alluded to earlier when describing the relativistic aspects of consumer value. Specifically, at the risk of excessive generalization, it seems to me that most if not all of the empirical value-oriented research has worded questions in ways that pertain to just one consumption experience (such as dining in a restaurant or staying in a hotel), rather than seeking a more universal set of indices that can be applied across a wide range of consumption situations, has ignored the economist's persuasive strictures against interpersonal utility comparisons, has compiled measurement scales that encourage various methods artifacts, and has too often demonstrated statistical reliability without showing validity in the form of predicting a key outcome variable such as Brand Loyalty. In these connections, I worry especially about the ways in which the relevant scales are typically constructed and the ways in which they are usually tested across people (inter-individually) rather than across experiences (intra-individually). Too often, the multiple items generated to form an index of each value type are all worded in the same positive direction. This encourages yay- or nay-saying biases in which assessments of index reliability merely reflect the fact that different people tend to mark different ends of the relevant scales. In my opinion, future research should work toward wording a random half of the various scales in the reverse directions so as to minimize these yay- and nay-saying biases. Further, scales are often grouped into sub-sections of a questionnaire in such a way that all the items pertaining to a particular type of value appear together. This encourages another type of methods artifact in which respondents fall into a pattern of answering and stick with it until they encounter a new sub-section, thereby enhancing apparent index reliability for reasons that are largely spurious. Clearly, it would be far preferable to present the various scale items in a random order to discourage such response-set biases. The threats to reliability and validity introduced by these two habits of questionnaire construction seem bad enough, but their damaging impact is greatly intensified by the common (I believe, virtually universal) practice of designing the various measures for applicability to just one sort of consumption experience evaluated by a large sample of respondents with the relevant tests run across people, thereby committing the sin of making interpersonal utility comparisons. It would be far more sound methodologically to ask each respondent to evaluate a sizable set of consumption experiences on generally applicable value scales, to standardize or normalize these value scores within individuals, and then to run the relevant correlations and other analyses across experiences (within individuals) rather than across people (for one experience at a time). Yes, I realize that such an approach places a much greater burden on the time and effort of respondents. We shall need, say, $8 \times 10 = 80$ vignettes describing different consumption experiences; $4 \times 8 = 32$ value scales (16 reverse-worded and all 32 scrambled randomly); and a set of patient respondents to provide the various ratings of each experience on each value scale ($80 \times 32 = 2,560$ ratings in all). The bad news is that the task will take a long time to complete and that these respondents will have to be rewarded generously for their demanding participation. The good news is that we can regard these respondents as content-analytic judges and can probably get by with as few as 10 or 12 of these judges. I have never tried this approach with value-related scales for vignettes describing consumption experiences. But, as noted earlier, I pursued a comparable approach in much of my work on multiattribute attitude models (e.g., among many examples, Holbrook, 1977a, 1981a); also, Bill Havlena did something similar for his dissertation on "The Varieties of Consumption Experience" (e.g., Havlena and Holbrook, 1986); and Rajeev Batra, T. J. Olney, and I used essentially the same approach in obtaining measures of emotional responses to TV commercials (e.g., Batra and Holbrook, 1990; Holbrook and Batra, 1987; Olney, Holbrook, and Batra, 1991). (Please note that sometimes the relevant scores are standardized within individuals across objects, aggregated across individuals for each object, and then analyzed across objects. This preserves the essence of a within-individual across-objects approach and allows for testing the homogeneity of value judgments via assessments of inter-judge reliability.) Based on these earlier studies, I have every confidence that – using items worded to apply across a broad range of consumption experiences – a within-individual across-objects approach will lend itself to the development of reliable general-purpose indices for measuring the eight types of consumer value in ways that validly predict an outcome variable such as brand loyalty. And when the day arrives on which we successfully develop General Purpose Indices of Consumer Value, it will indeed be a happy day.

O, Happy Day – with a clear blue sky, the sun shining, birds singing, the leaves rustling to make a soothing sound, and the sweet smell of magnolias or maybe Valencia oranges wafting in the breeze. On this happy day, our more refined ways of measuring consumer value will contribute to the fulfillment of all eight relevant value types – Efficiency (pursuing a timely and low-cost path to new knowledge), Excellence (enjoying our contemplation of a high-quality set of value measures), Status or Exhibitionism (impressing the world with our new discoveries in ways that might earn some young professor a well-deserved promotion), Esteem or Elitism (appreciating the refinement that, if paraded in public, would win widespread respect for our methods), Play or Entertainment (thrilling to the fun of making new discoveries that satisfy our curiosity), Aesthetics or Esthetics (admiring the beauty of our conceptual scheme and its operationalization in the form of reliable and valid measures), Ethics (planning to use our approach to help marketers better serve their customers and society), and Spirituality or Ecstasy (feeling a sense of rapture over epiphanies that we seem to share with the rest of Humanity and maybe even with the larger forces of the Cosmos). The nice thing about working on the Concept of Consumer Value is that it enables us to conjure up such enticing dreams. As I said, "O, Happy Day! O, Happy, *Happy* Day!!"

8 Consumption Criteria in Arts Marketing

Abstract

This chapter applies the Concept of Consumer Value (CCV) to the case of arts marketing. A typology distinguishes eight major types of consumer value (Efficiency, Excellence, Exhibitionism, Elitism, Entertainment, Esthetics, Ethics, and Ecstasy). Taking the jazz vibraphonist Gary Burton as an illustration, the chapter argues that all eight types of value may coexist in any one consumption experience. Thus, for example, multiple market segments may respond favorably and profitably to a brand in general or to the Gary Burton offering in particular.

Fundamentally, the job of the arts marketer seems pretty simple: Find out what criteria guide the choices of audience members or arts patrons in the relevant segments of consumers, design an offering that appeals to those criteria, and communicate the nature and availability of this offering to the potentially relevant customers. Yet even this simple characterization of the arts-marketing job embodies at least one source of conflict that has troubled the area of arts marketing in ways similar, say, to the areas of education, religion, medicine, or jurisprudence. Specifically and increasingly, the arts institution – like the university, the church, the hospital, or the court system – tends to assume that its offering should reflect the criteria brought to bear by relevant customers, whereas the actual producer of the offerings in question – the professor, the preacher, the doctor, the judge, or the artist – may well feel that standards of excellence unique to the relevant profession should guide the design of product offerings and other elements in the marketing mix.

In this sense, true artists do behave in a way that is profoundly customer-oriented, but only insofar as the artists themselves play the role of the key customers for their own artistic products. Often stubbornly, they see their task as that of pleasing themselves. The fact that this vanishingly small and inveterately egocentric customer segment typically honors criteria of excellence very different from those of ordinary audience members or arts patrons serves to drive a wedge between the viewpoints of artists and arts administrators. Unfortunately, this inherent conflict is so fundamental to the artistic enterprise that it should probably be regarded as inevitable and unavoidable in nature.

DOI: 10.4324/9781003560302-11

A second related but conceptually distinct tension in the artistic community refers to the distinction between High Art (with a capital "A") and popular culture (with a small "c") or entertainment (with a small "e"). The former (High Art) reflects the highest standards of creative integrity and artistic sophistication; it appeals primarily to those with well-educated artistic tastes; it therefore attracts only a small audience of the most elite arts patrons. The latter (pop culture or entertainment) – whether purposely or inadvertently – dumbs down its offerings to make them more accessible to the mass audience; it thereby appeals to larger numbers of ordinary audience members with uneducated artistic tastes; it therefore attracts a larger audience of naïve or unsophisticated fans. Almost everybody – especially anybody with a background in sociology – feels some degree of discomfort in recognizing, let alone talking about, this tension between "class" and "mass." The fact is that taste does mirror differences in social status (partly due to differences in education and partly due to the use by higher-status groups of artistic preferences as ways of marking their elevated social standing). But, whether we like it or not, the fact is that there is a difference between Glenn Gould playing Bach and Paul McCartney singing Rock. And that difference – primarily a difference in ease of apprehension – renders the audience for the former small and that for the latter enormous.

Putting these two contrasts together, it seems fair to suggest that all arts administrators wish the artists they manage would cleave closer to the popular end of the cultural continuum, would appeal more to larger if less cultivated groups of customers, and would behave more like Paul and less like Glenn. True artists, of course, take just the opposite stance – maintaining elevated standards of excellence, pursuing the highest levels of creative integrity, and pleasing themselves above all others. These irreconcilable differences lead toward a marketing strategy that Ted Levitt characterized as the "selling orientation." That is, manufacture the product (say, an uncompromisingly challenging jazz performance, a painting that comprises nothing but squiggles and erasure marks, an art film with unknown actors and no discernible plot, or an atonal concerto for unaccompanied nose flute); find out that, oops, nobody wants it (precisely because it appeals to such refined tastes that few people alive possess the requisite degree of sophistication); and, then (having ignored the tastes of the audience when creating the product), go out and promote the living daylights out of it (half-price tickets, student discounts, senior citizen passes, membership series, fund drives, free cocktails at the bar of the cabaret-style venue). All too often, this is exactly what we see when a theater series packages a group of three or four unintelligible plays by Harold Pinter and his friends. Or when a fine art museum recruits busloads of school children to attend the Salvador Dali exposition. Or when the films of Andy Warhol appear uninterrupted in a three-day outdoor festival at the open-air band shell near you. Or when your favorite NPR FM station or PBS TV channel bores you to tears with non-stop fund-raising or membership-drive marathons featuring Jack Jones and his cohorts.

We might wonder how this immutable tension can reach any sort of resolution in the world of arts marketing. My perhaps overly sanguine answer lies in the hope that an artistic creation adhering to the highest standards of aesthetic excellence (thereby pleasing the artist) can at the same time attract multiple modest-sized customer segments (so as to appeal to an overall audience large enough to please the arts administrator). The secret to achieving this outcome, I believe, is to recognize that any given artistic offering potentially delivers multiple types of consumer value; that different customer segments seek different types of value; that these value types are in no way mutually contradictory; but, rather, that they tend to coexist in any arts-related consumption experience; and, therefore, that a given artistic offering can be positioned in ways that cater to multiple value segments simultaneously.

To develop this point further, I draw on the field of *axiology* in general and on the *theory of consumer value* in particular. In various works over the past 40 years, as limned in earlier chapters, I have developed a definition of Consumer Value as an *interactive relativistic preference experience*. By this – to review quickly – I mean, first, that Consumer Value is *interactive* in the sense that it involves a relationship between some subject (the consumer) and some object (the offering). Value depends on a match between the two that some refer to as the "co-creation" of value. Second, Consumer Value is *relativistic* in the sense that it is *comparative* (where some offering can attain value only by contrast with some other offering and not in any absolute sense, as when vanilla ice cream is good compared to chocolate ice cream but chocolate is good compared to rum raisin), *personal* (where value differs from one individual to the next, just as surely as you prefer chocolate and I prefer vanilla), and *situational* (where value depends on the context in which the evaluation occurs, as when cold ice cream tastes great in the summer but hot cocoa tastes better in the winter). Third, Consumer Value manifests itself in a *preference* wherein *value* (singular) refers to an individual's liking of one offering better than another in a particular situation and wherein *values* (plural) refer to the criteria on which that preference is based. And, fourth, Consumer Value inheres in a *consumption experience* in such a way that a product (conventionally conceived) performs services that bring about desirable experiential events. In this sense, by the way, *all* goods perform services, and the distinction between the two becomes meaningless.

Given this definition, I have gone on to develop a *Typology of Consumer Value* based on three key dimensions or distinctions. First, Consumer Value may be *extrinsic* (insofar as it refers to an offering prized for its ability to serve as a means to some desirable end) or *intrinsic* (insofar as it refers to an experience appreciated as a self-justifying end-in-itself). Second, Consumer Value may be *self-oriented* (insofar as it relates to something that I prize for my own sake, for how I respond to it, or for the effect that it has on me) or *other-oriented* (insofar as it relates to something that I appreciate for the sake of others, for how they respond to it, or for the effect that it has on them). Third, Consumer Value may be *active* (resulting from my manipulation of the relevant offering in the sense that I act on it) or *reactive* (reflecting my response to the relevant offering in the sense that it acts on me).

Combining these three distinctions results in my *Typology of Consumer Value*. Over the years, I have refined and tweaked this typology in various ways that have now culminated in a version that I refer to as the "Eight E's" – meaning that each of the relevant value types (in CAPITAL LETTERS) begins with the letter "E" (with examples shown parenthetically in Small Letters).

Typology of Consumer Value: The Eight E's

		Extrinsic	*Intrinsic*
Self-Oriented	*Active*	EFFICIENCY (O/I Ratio; EVC; Convenience)	ENTERTAINMENT (Play; Fun; Leisure Activities)
	Reactive	EXCELLENCE (Quality)	ESTHETICS (Beauty)
Other-Oriented	*Active*	EXHIBITIONISM (Social Status; Impression Management)	ETHICS (Justice; Virtue; Morality)
	Reactive	ELITISM (Esteem; Self-Esteem; Materialism)	ECSTASY (Spirituality; Rapture; Exultation)

To summarize briefly:

1. EFFICIENCY refers to the active manipulation of my own consumption as an extrinsic means to achieving some self-oriented end. This is the one type of value that explicitly takes into account the trade-off between "getting" and "giving" – that is, the contrast between what I acquire and what I sacrifice. Colloquially, we sometimes speak of "value for the money," as when we make a particularly frugal purchase at a price-discount store. More formally, efficiency is often measured as an O/I Ratio (i.e., a ratio of outputs to inputs) or as Economic Value to the Customer (EVC, computed as the net present value of benefits minus costs). Efficiency most often captures our attention when evaluating such highly functional products as automobiles (miles per gallon). Further, we often focus on a special type of efficiency in which the primary input is time – miles per hour in the case of a car or, more generally, Convenience as in the case of a "convenience" store that offers a maximum number of items purchased per minute despite an absence of other discernible benefits (poor selection, high prices, indifferent service, unpleasant atmosphere, and so forth).
2. EXCELLENCE refers to the reactive appreciation of some offering as a potential extrinsic means toward some self-oriented end. Here, the key point is that we admire the product for its capacity to perform well in serving a particular function without necessarily using it for that purpose. A clear example appears in the case of Quality – where we prize the functional capabilities of some product without necessarily engaging in its active use for those purposes. Thus, the quality of my knife lies in the sharpness of its blade (without my actually using it to cut you). The

quality of my $1.4-million 6.0-liter V12 700HP Aston Martin One-77 entails its ability to cruise at 220 mph (without my actually breaking the law by shattering the speed limits on Route 80).

3. EXHIBITIONISM refers to the active manipulation of my consumption as an extrinsic means of attaining some other-oriented goal such as enhancing my Social Status or achieving favorable Impression Management in a job interview. Thus, I might conspicuously park the aforementioned Aston Martin in the driveway of my lavish house overlooking the Pacific Ocean, knowing that my neighbors will be powerfully impressed by this high-status spectacle – all the more because of the exclusiveness implied by the fact that the One-77 is sold to only 77 other discerning-not-to-mention-wealthy individuals.

4. ELITISM refers to my reactive appreciation of my own consumption as the potential extrinsic means to attaining some desired response from others such as Esteem or even Self-Esteem (if I regard my "self" as an identifiable "other" whom I am eager to impress). Again – as in the contrast between efficiency and excellence – the difference between Exhibitionism and Esteem is that, in the latter case, I need only appreciate the potential use of my consumption habits without necessarily flaunting them in the manner that would produce the relevant response from others. Thus, a high level of Materialism implies that I take great satisfaction in owning nice things without necessarily displaying them in public. My potentially enviable "possessions" might even include such intangibles as unique knowledge, skill, or expertise. For example, I might derive some elitist satisfaction from privately enjoying my own automotive know-how when replacing the platinum spark plugs in my Aston Martin One-77. Please note that, here, I use the term "elitism" in a judgmentally neutral sense and not in the pejorative manner in which it is so commonly employed. Under the thrall of political correctness, there is probably no word in our vocabulary that carries such opprobrium as describing someone as "elitist." The term – as too often used – implies snobbery, self-satisfaction, and a profound lack of empathy for just plain ordinary folks. But, here, I simply wish to refer to the private delight – the boost in potential esteem or actual self-esteem – that a person might feel as the result of a "job well done" or, in this case, a consumption task performed in a way that others would implicitly approve or envy.

5. ENTERTAINMENT refers to the active manipulation of my own self-oriented consumption experience in a way that I enjoy intrinsically for its own sake as an end-in-itself. This definition captures the essence of Play, Fun, or Leisure Activities – namely, that they serve no ulterior purpose but are pleasing in and of themselves. Otherwise, they would become "work" (i.e., an activity pursued for reasons of efficiency or exhibitionism). Hey, my Aston Martin One-77 is just so much fun to drive. I feel the sun on my elbow, the wind in my hair, the throb of the throaty roar from the 700 HP engine. What a ball, getting my kicks on Route 66. (By the way, did you know that the composer of that famous song, Bobby Troup, was a Wharton graduate? Just like Donald Trump.)

6. ESTHETICS refers to my reactive appreciation of my own self-oriented consumption as an experience intrinsically valued for its own sake as an end-in-itself. Thus, I derive esthetic value from Beauty experienced in the world around me – in scenes from nature, in paintings by Matisse, in Bruckner's Seventh Symphony, in Julianne Moore. It goes without saying that my Aston Martin One-77 is the veritable epitome, the nonpareil paragon, of beauty on wheels. Just look at those sleek lines, those graceful curves, that scintillating silver color, that toothy front grill, those recessed headlights – indeed, the whole awe-inspiring aerodynamic design. All things considered, my Aston Martin One-77 is so beautiful that I hardly dare drive it for fear of a disfiguring scratch, dent, or bird dropping.

7. ETHICS refers to the active manipulation of my consumption experiences for the sake of the intrinsically valued benefits that they have for others – as when I pursue Justice by paying my taxes so as to fund steadily declining education in the public schools and ever-diminishing service on the local buses, when I seek Virtue by avoiding the temptation of my favorite candy bars and vanilla frozen custard, or when I honor Morality by steering clear of the "F" word and those alluring porn sites. It goes without saying that my purchase and ownership of an Aston Martin One-77 attains key aspects of ethical value – as when it guarantees jobs for at least six otherwise unemployed British factory workers at the company's plant in Gaydon (Warwickshire, UK); when it subsidizes the fortunes of shareholders in Exxon-Mobile, thanks to the car's rather thirsty 11-miles-per-gallon gasoline habit; or when I avoid polluting the atmosphere with fumes from its astonishingly noisy engine by not really driving it very much. Indeed, this whole story carries some important honesty-related ethical implications insofar as – truth be told – I do not actually own an Aston Martin One-77 (in case you were wondering). Rather, it is a pure figment of my febrile imagination, which leads us to . . .

8. ECSTASY refers to my reactive appreciation of consumption experiences valued intrinsically for aspects that involve a disappearance of the self-other dichotomy – as when I feel a sense of Ecstasy, Rapture, or Exultation. Obviously, such transcendent moments may occur at the heights of religious experience, during Stendahl-like encounters with magnificent works of art, or at the peak of imaginative fantasies involving extravagantly appealing but realistically unattainable sports cars. Thus, the ecstasy-rapture-exultation responses associated with my imaginary Aston Martin One-77 entail a merging of the self with the other at a level that transcends mere reality and enters the realm of pure fantasy. As John Keats reminded us in his "Ode on a Grecian Urn," "Heard melodies are sweet, but those unheard/Are sweeter."

As the sensitive reader will no doubt have noticed and as I have tirelessly insisted on any number of occasions, *all eight* of the aforementioned types of consumer value are likely to coexist in *any* or even in *every* consumption experience – albeit in varying degrees, depending on the product, the consumer, the context, and various other circumstances. In the words of the philosopher, all eight value types tend to be *compresent* – that is, to occur simultaneously – in virtually any case of consumer behavior. I have illustrated this phenomenon of *compresence* in the case of an automobile – my imaginary Aston Martin One-77 – but, needless to say, exactly the same argument pertains to the case of a painting, a sculpture, a symphonic composition, a television show, an artist, a performer, a film, a play, a concert, a musical recording, a gallery, a museum, and indeed *any* aspect of the High Arts or pop culture of interest to the arts administrator or entertainment marketer.

Thus, the main point of the present essay is that – without compromising the artistic integrity inherent in a given artistic offering – opportunities exist to broaden its audience by virtue of appealing to at least eight different types of consumer value, some of which are more/less important to one/another segment of consumers. By making each market segment aware of benefits suited to its own distinct value-oriented proclivities, arts marketers can achieve far greater market penetration than would be possible by catering to just one or a few customer segments pursuing just one or a few types of value.

All this hinges on the aforementioned compresence of at least eight value types in virtually any arts-related consumption experience. To illustrate this point, as anticipated in Chapter 5, let us consider the example of the New Gary Burton Quartet – which, before the leader's more recent retirement, appeared on the night of Wednesday September 21, 2011, at the Blue Note jazz club in New York City's Greenwich Village (Gary Burton on vibraphone, Julian Lage on guitar, Scott Colley on bass, and Antonio Sanchez on drums). Careful introspection suggests that, for me, the appearance by this jazz quartet provided all eight types of consumer value in abundant quantity, as follows.

Efficiency. The cost per person of an evening at the Blue Note to see Gary Burton's group play an 80-minute set was at least $40 – that is, a $35 cover charge plus a $5 minimum from the restaurant/bar (though the latter can add up to a lot more than that if you happen to be hungry or thirsty). It happens that Burton had developed perhaps the most blazing instrumental technique of any living jazz musician. Using his own innovative four-mallet approach, he poured out more notes at a higher volume than virtually any vibes player whom one might have recruited to challenge his supremacy on the instrument. This means that, in terms of his O/I ratio (measured in notes per second or decibels per minute), Gary reigned supreme. (Somewhat surprisingly, having twice sat literally under Burton's vibes on the stage above me, I can vouch for the fact that, in his hands, the vibraphone was an amazingly loud instrument. I own four vibraphones and thought I was familiar with their capabilities, but I was astonished to discover what happens if you sit underneath one of those things.) Further, in terms of Economic Value to the Customer (EVC, measured as the present value of benefits minus the $40 out-of-pocket cost), Burton-at-the-Blue-Note clearly dominated the various

$200-a-seat Broadway shows that offer significantly less artistry or entertainment at considerably greater expense. For somebody visiting New York on a budget, such considerations can matter greatly and suggest the advantages of marketing Burton and other artists appearing at the Blue Note or comparable jazz clubs as providing a "good value for your money," an impressive "bang for your buck." The folks sitting next to us at the Blue Note were from Orlando and, especially compared to Disney World, seemed thrilled by the under-$50 economics of the Gary Burton Show.

Excellence. An appreciation of the excellence in Gary Burton's playing stemmed especially from an admiration for those moments in which he held his potential virtuosity in check and delivered some kind of soulful bluesy phrasing or some sort of soft tender balladry. Here, the secret to quality lies in a reactive response to the subtlety of power held in abeyance. Such an appreciation of quality affects my own response to Gary's restrained performance (with guitarist Lage) of "Gorgeous" by Mitchell Forman on Burton's album for Concord Jazz entitled *Generations*. I once put my CD player on "repeat" and listened to that track over and over for a couple of hours. Here, the effect resembles the serenity of the One-77 taking a turn gracefully at, say, a quiet 30 mph instead of a noisy 220 miles per hour. We know that it could go faster or get louder, but we admire its quality more for its potential than for its actual speed and sound.

Exhibitionism. For purposes of exhibitionism, located in the heart of New York's Greenwich Village – the quintessence of hipness in many people's minds – the Blue Note is a propitious place to be seen, displaying one's sophisticated jazz tastes in a chic atmosphere that makes a favorable impression on, say, a date or a business associate. Compared to a proposition such as "Let's grab a beer-and-burger at the Olive Garden," an offer of "Let's take in a set at the Blue Note" conveys some sort of status in the City's artistic community. I, personally, would never dream of frequenting a nightclub just for the sake of appearing cool. But I have every confidence that the idea has crossed the mind of many a status seeker wanting to impress a friend or colleague.

Elitism. I myself am more guilty of succumbing to the reactive side of exhibitionism – namely, elitism – in which my self-esteem hinges on knowing things or owning things that fall beyond the purview of most ordinary folks. For example, though I would not succumb to the temptation of bragging about my record collection in public, I take a sort of quiet satisfaction from my secret awareness that I own 22 LPs and 41 CDs by Gary Burton – probably more than most dedicated jazz fans (which, now that I think about it, is not much of a secret anymore). Beyond these materialistic concerns, I also take some pride in having acquired enough background knowledge to follow along mentally as Gary negotiated various tricky chord progressions or to recognize obscure tunes that he performed without announcing their names. At the Blue Note, for example, he played "I Hear a Rhapsody" (by George Fragos, Jack Baker, and Dick Gasparre) and "Bag's Groove" (by Milt

Jackson) unannounced. I derived some clandestine pleasure from recognizing these tunes without help from the performers. I felt no need to share this information with those sitting near me in the audience – not even the lady from Orlando. It's more a question of below-the-radar self-esteem.

Entertainment. Gary Burton provides a good example of a musician who was not afraid to cater to the tastes of audience members coming to his music from the side of pop culture. Back in his early days, circa 1960, he embraced country music and made an album for Columbia called *Jazz Winds from a New Direction* with the great country guitarist Hank Garland – later followed up by *Tennessee Firebird* under Gary's own name on RCA. After stints with the very popular groups led by George Shearing and Stan Getz, during the mid-1960s, Burton grew his hair long, sported a mustache, wore trendy Beatles-type clothing, and fronted a quartet that included the rock-tinged guitarist Larry Coryell (e.g., *Lofty Fake Anagram* on RCA/BMG). Other crowd-pleasing habits have included tributes to the familiar music of various swing-era masters such as Red Norvo and Lionel Hampton (*For Hamp, Red, Bags, and Cal* on Concord Jazz) or Benny Goodman (*Benny Rides Again* with clarinetist Eddie Daniels on GRP Records). Then there are the multiple tributes to the tango king Astor Piazzolla (e.g., *Astor Piazzolla Reunion* and *Libertango* on Concord Jazz or *The New Tango* on Atlantic Jazz), not to mention the revival of classical treasures by Ravel, Rachmaninoff, Scarlatti, and Brahms (*Virtuosi* with pianist Makoto Ozone on Concord Jazz). I could go on, but the point is that Gary Burton has happily made his music accessible – playful, fun to listen to, and a prime example of leisure-as-opposed-to-work in what can otherwise be the challenging art form of jazz. Before Gary's retirement, all this and more appeared with impressively vivid clarity on his self-promoting website at www.garyburton.com (now no longer online). To some extent, this is art-for-mart's sake.

Esthetics. By contrast, for jazz purists, Gary Burton has provided unmatched esthetic moments of the highest possible artistic integrity – that is, the purest form of art-for-art's sake. Nowhere was the beauty of his conception more apparent than in his solo performances – strongly influenced by the harmonic innovations of Bill Evans on piano – in which he did things with four mallets that most pianists would struggle to duplicate with ten fingers and that were as technically brilliant as they were sonically delicious. Favorite examples would include "Chega De Saudade (No More Blues)" (*Alone at Last*, Atlantic Jazz) and "My Foolish Heart" (*Live in Cannes*, Jazz World). Appreciated as ends-in-themselves – that is, as experiences treasured for their own sake – the beauty of these creations attains a profound level of esthetic magnificence.

Ethics. Gary Burton has evinced a highly developed sense of ethics more conspicuous than that found among many members of the jazz community. First, until his retirement in 2003, Burton served for 33 years on the faculty of the Berklee College of Music in Boston, ultimately rising to a top position of leadership and administrative responsibility at the school (first Dean of

Curriculum, then Executive Vice President). Obviously, his work as a teacher served to bolster the careers of many young aspiring students of jazz. When hearing Gary perform at the Blue Note, I noticed a definite tendency for him to announce tunes in ways that were instructive as well as entertaining – mentioning the composer, the title, and important details about each composition to be played. Apparently, the sharing of knowledge and wisdom has been an ingrained part of his nature. Second, in a similar manner, Burton has served as a mentor to fledgling musicians on their way up. He recruited promising youngsters as members of his band and gave them a chance to shine. At the Blue Note, his band featured three young fellows whom he introduced with great respect and whose compositions he played at length – namely, "Never the Same Way" (by bassist Scott Colley), "Etude" (by guitarist Julian Lage), and "Common Ground" (by drummer Antonio Sanchez). Another repertoire choice entitled "Last Snow" was written by a former youthful member of a Burton group (Ukrainian pianist Vadim Neselovskyi). In watching the Burton Quartet at the Blue Note, I was struck by the extent to which he seemed to support these younger musicians. Most conspicuously, Gary announced that he had been playing with the guitarist Lage since Julian was 12 years old. They first recorded together when Julian was 15, then again at age 17. Third, Gary has displayed considerable sensitivity to social concerns in his handling of issues pertaining to the place of homosexuality in the jazz world. In this connection, at the Village Vanguard during the late 1990s, I heard him speak at a panel discussion on the experiences of gay jazz musicians. Here, again, Gary has served as something of a role model for others. Apparently, after a couple of failed marriages to women, Burton found that he liked men and embarked upon a long-term relationship that, because of its public nature, required him to come "out of the closet." In sharing his experiences with others, he has adopted an ethically enlightened stance. Paradoxically, he appeared confused and even disappointed that no jazz critics or commentators had bothered to comment on any potential aspects of his musical persona that might have reflected his evolving sexual preferences. At the Blue Note, I could detect nothing in his music or demeanor that would relate to his love life – one way or the other.

Ecstasy. There have been times in Gary Burton's playing when he – taking the listener with him – has appeared to achieve a nearly miraculous rapport with his instrument, a merging of musician (self) and vibraphone (other) that works toward also drawing the listener (self) into the music (other). The apparent merging of self and other in a musical performance is a rare event in my experience. (For an especially impressive example, see the performance by Keith Jarrett of "Solar" from his *Solo Tribute* concert in Japan, available on YouTube.Com.) The merging of self and other in the listening experience seems comparably rare and leads, as a form of spirituality, to what can only be described as ecstatic feelings of rapture and exultation. Watching Gary Burton – body swaying, arms flailing, wrists snapping – attain one-ness with his vibraphone contributed greatly to this sort of rapturous exultation.

Further, the instrument itself evokes a sort of spiritual essence with its clear bell-like tones and inherent purity of sound. In a sense, a three-octave vibraphone is "nothing but" a set of 37 perfectly adjusted tuning forks. More than virtually any other instrument, its sound has a pristine, ethereal, heavenly quality. (For another rapture-inducing example of the vibraphone playing a celestial role, try Milt Jackson's solo on the Modern Jazz Quartet's recording of "Over the Rainbow" from the *Fontessa* album on Atlantic Jazz, also available on YouTube.Com.)

The bottom line from all this is that a performance by Gary Burton – like virtually any other artistic offering – appealed to all eight basic types of consumer value: efficiency, excellence, exhibitionism, elitism, entertainment, esthetics, ethics, and ecstasy. Obviously, different market segments adopt consumption criteria that reflect more or less of these eight different value types. The trick to successful arts marketing, I believe, is to appeal to all these value types simultaneously, remembering that they are in no way mutually contradictory and, indeed, that they are all potentially compresent in any consumption experience. We might ask whether the Blue Note succeeded in doing this in the brochure that we found on our table at the jazz club. Amidst voluminous announcements of coming events, a full page of this pamphlet is devoted to the Gary Burton New Quartet (featuring the other musicians mentioned earlier). Having read this promotional write-up only **after** writing the preceding comments, I feel somewhat vindicated to note that all of our eight types of consumer value are included, as follows:

Efficiency – the cover charge of "$35 @ TABLE/$20 @ BAR"

Excellence – "incredible musicianship . . . incredible improvisation in a group setting"

Exhibitionism – "the No. 1 spot on Billboard magazine's jazz chart . . . the Sixth Grammy for Burton at the 2009 Grammy Awards"

Elitism – "an honorary doctorate of music from [Berklee] college"

Entertainment – "compositions that drew from all over the map . . . collaborations with old friends and new, including tours and recordings with Chick Corea, Pat Metheny, Makoto Ozone, Spanish pianist and composer Polo Orti, and French accordionist Richard Galliano"

Esthetics – "Alone at Last, a solo vibraphone concert"

Ethics – "discovering more than a few youngsters who later became legends . . . in the '70s, Burton began his music education career at the Berklee College of Music in Boston . . . he was named Dean of Curriculum in 1985 . . . and in 1996, he was appointed Executive Vice President"

Ecstasy – "smashed conventions and blew audiences away"

It appears that Gary Burton's publicists (Ted Kurland Associates) – doubtless with help from the man himself – have done a good job of reflecting on ways in which this stellar musician has contributed to attaining all eight types of consumer value described herein. Anyone reading the Blue Note write-up or countless other promotional materials available online and else-where – not to mention the cover story on Gary's quartet in the October 2011 issue of *DownBeat* magazine – cannot help but conclude that, in his market-ing efforts as in his musical accomplishments, Gary Burton offered all eight types of customer value to which different market segments might aspire in varying degrees. In retrospect, his success seems assured from the start.

Additional Listening

Besides the various LPs, CDs, and DVDs mentioned in this essay, the inter-ested reader/listener will find numerous vivid examples available on You-Tube.Com. To find excellent illustrations of the work by Gary Burton and others, I highly recommend visiting that website and searching for the fol-lowing keyword combinations (listed alphabetically): "Gary Burton Chega De Saudade," "Gary Burton Larry Coryell Berlin," "Gary Burton Makoto Ozone Scarlatti," "Gary Burton Pat Metheny Umbria," "Gary Burton Piaz-zolla Reunion Libertango," "Keith Jarrett Solar Japan," "Modern Jazz Quartet Over The Rainbow," "New Gary Burton Quartet Bag's Groove," "New Gary Burton Quartet Common Ground," "New Gary Burton Quartet Vienna Afro Blue," and (especially) "Gary Burton Gorgeous."

Part IV

Some Perspectives From Jazz

9   The Marketing Manager as a Jazz Musician

Abstract

Recently, organizational theorists and business thinkers have discovered the jazz metaphor and have employed this trope as an analogy to infer and describe best practices in the areas of organizational innovation and business strategy. The present chapter extends and amplifies this insight in the area of marketing practice and compares the marketing manager to the jazz musician with special attention to the problem of introducing new offerings during the mature stage of the product life cycle – namely, the strategic issue that concerns most marketing managers most of the time.

Introduction: The Jazz Metaphor

In recent years, writers on organization theory and business strategy have devoted considerable attention to the development of a *jazz metaphor* based on analogies between improvisational music and creativity in general (Holbrook, 1995b), the development of marketing theory in particular (Holbrook, 1984c), or managerial practice as a special case (Weick, 1998). Widespread attention to this topic emerged at a symposium sponsored by the Academy of Management and represented by a special issue of *Organization Science* featuring a collection of papers by distinguished jazz musicians and organizational researchers (Meyer, Frost, and Weick, 1998). Subsequent work along these lines has concerned issues related to innovation (Moorman and Miner, 1998a, 1998b), leadership (Hasse, 2004; Newton, 2004), teamwork (Dolata and Schwabe, 2014; Jennings, 2007; Waltzer and Salcher, 2003), leading creative or entrepreneurial teams (Humphreys, Ucbasaran, and Lockett, 2011; Ucbasaran, Lockett, and Humphreys, 2011), negotiated collaborative coordination (Faulkner and Becker, 2009; Holbrook, 2010), organizational change (Leybourne, 2006), project management (Leybourne, 2009), strategic planning (Cunha, Clegg, and Kamoche, 2012), competitive advantage (Bingham and Eisenhardt, 2011), institutional adaptability (Hatch, 1998, 1999), networking (Pavlovich, 2003), empowerment as the freedom to be spontaneous within certain constraints or limitations (Oakes, 2009), marketing strategy

DOI: 10.4324/9781003560302-13

(Dennis and Macaulay, 2003, 2007), new product development (Kamoche and Cunha, 2001; Kyriakopoulos, 2011), service performances (John, Grove, and Fisk, 2006), complexity theory (Holbrook, 2003b), the ethics of organizational leadership (Sorensen, 2013), teaching economics (Tinari and Khandke, 2000), teaching an integrated capstone strategic management course (Mills, 2009), teaching a marketing-research course (Mills, 2010), management education (Meyer and Shambu, 2010), executive education (Gold and Hirshfeld, 2005), collaborative management research (Börjesson and Fredberg, 2004), and a variety of related topics of interest to organizational researchers and business scholars as encompassed by various collections (Kamoche, Cunha, and Cunha, 2003, ed. 2002), special issues (Leybourne, Lynn, and Vendelø, 2014), reviews (Hadida and Tarvainen, 2014; Holbrook, 2007e), and calls for papers (Oakes, Brownlie, and Dennis, 2011).

The present essay pursues this theme in connection with one particular aspect of *marketing strategy* – namely, the design and introduction of *new offerings* during the *mature phase* of the *product life cycle*. Much of the previous literature related to the jazz metaphor has emphasized its obvious relevance to problems of leadership (listening responsively, achieving coordination, motivating others, and so forth) and to aspects of innovation (creativity as a departure or deviation that fits a broader set of requirements, out-of-the-box or on-the-boundaries thinking, freedom subject to constraints, and so forth). Such analogies with jazz improvisation – especially in connection with issues related to new product design – appear particularly apt when filtered through the sensibilities of performing jazz artists (e.g., Berliner, 1994). Further, they seem especially relevant when applied to the less glamorous but potentially more pervasive problem of introducing a modified or repositioned offering during the mature phase of the product life cycle.

Marketing Management as a Constant Vigil

Introduction

We might regard the period of *introduction* as the most glamorous and exciting phase of the product life cycle. Here, the innovative firm produces something completely new – something never seen before that plunges consumers into extensive problem solving with the aid of information acquired through effortful search activities (word of mouth, self-exposure to promotional communications, rational decision making, and so forth). But – glamorous and exciting though it may be – the introductory phase involves just one firm in any given case and therefore does not concern most marketers most of the time.

Rapid Growth

By contrast, the period of *rapid growth* involves many firms rushing to compete in the expanding market for the new product by producing their own versions of the novel offering. But – though many firms are involved – these copy-cat activities last only a relatively short time before the market reaches a plateau and begins to stabilize so that, during the rapid-growth phase, many participate but only briefly.

Maturity

This leaves the period of *maturity* as the phase of the product life cycle that concerns most marketing managers most of the time. During the mature phase, the market has stopped growing. By now, the only way to increase sales (every marketing manager's number-one priority) is to increase market share. And the only way to increase market share (the holy grail) is to steal customers away from competitors. And the only way to steal customers (the guiding imperative) is to create a differential advantage wherein some segment of customers whose needs are not being fully met by available offerings can better satisfy those needs with your brand than with competing versions.

The Differential Advantage

All this means that the creation of a differentiated offering that appeals to one or more particular segment(s) in ways not available elsewhere – thereby attaining a competitive advantage – becomes the *sine qua non* of effective marketing strategy. This pursuit of a differential advantage, in short, is why the world needs new Diet Coke without Caffeine. Or a new five-ounce size of Coca-Cola. Or new Zero-Calorie Coke (with all the taste of regular Coke). Or a new "healthy" version of Coca-Cola (with various vitamins added). Or Coke in a new all-aluminum can. Or Heaven knows whatever other imaginative version of fizzy brown sugar water the marketing geniuses at Coca-Cola can dream up next.

The Constant Vigil

But the moment one of these new entries becomes successful by attaining a true differential advantage – say, Coke in an All-Aluminum Can – what happens next? Answer: Just as ineluctably as Spring follows Winter, we get a brand-new version of (you guessed it) Pepsi in an All-Aluminum Can. In other words, though I can't recall exactly who said it (probably Ted Levitt in one of his many inspired moments), successfully differentiated offerings lead immediately to "imitation as the sincerest form of competition." In practice, this means that the marketing manager's life becomes a *constant vigil* – first, achieving a differential advantage via the introduction of some successfully targeted offering; next, watching this achievement shamelessly copied by competitors; then, inevitably, returning to the problem of seeking a new differential advantage. And so on. Ad infinitum.

The Jazz Metaphor: Two Songs by David Frishberg

Clearly, the situation just described shows striking parallels with the problems faced by a creative artist in general or by a jazz musician in particular. The relevant analogy appears conspicuously in two apposite songs by the great jazz pianist, lyricist, and composer Dave Frishberg – namely, "Another Song About Paris" and "Zoot Walks In" – which, by coincidence, are alphabetically the first and last entries in his long list of over 40 titles (Frishberg, undated). Curious listeners will find these songs on Frishberg's recordings entitled *Where You At?* (1991) and *Can't Take You Nowhere* (1987), respectively. The first vividly raises the relevant problem. The second suggests the jazz-related solution.

The Problem: "Another Song About Paris"

In his tribute to the art of writing Parisian *chansons*, Frishberg agonizes over the issue of how to avoid repeating all the old familiar clichés that earlier songwriters have endlessly reiterated in every tune previously written on the subject. Of course – in a minor masterpiece of reflexive self-parody – in mentioning these clichés, he himself recirculates them yet another time. So he reminds us of the flowers in the stalls and the small romantic cafés and pigeons under glass and the mysteries of Notre Dame and all the rest while asking plaintively how he can write one more song about Paris without repeating everything that has been said before – the point being, of course, that he cannot. Ultimately, "café au lait" always rhymes with "Rue de la Paix" and "Champs Elysees" and "Maurice Chevalier" and, indeed, "a cliché" so that every song about Paris sounds "exactly the same." Faced with this sort of quandary – endlessly familiar to every marketing manager in the shape of the parity products that proliferate during the mature phase of the product life cycle – the solution, for a songwriter such as Frishberg, appears in the form of the true jazz improviser.

The Solution: "Zoot Walks In"

During much of his early career in New York in the 1950s and 1960s, Frishberg – an excellent jazz pianist, as both soloist and accompanist – served as a member of the house rhythm section for the old Half Note Café at the intersection of Spring and Hudson Streets down in the West Village. In that capacity, he had frequent occasion to play with many of the great jazz artists who wandered through town – people like Al Cohn, Phil Woods, Clark Terry, Bob Brookmeyer, Jimmy Rushing, and (perhaps most notably) Zoot Sims. Frishberg's musical hero and sometime "boss," Zoot was the supreme master of loosely flowing, effortlessly melodic, brilliantly articulated improvisations on the tenor saxophone. He was the consummate swinger, the ultimate originator, the greatest of improvisers. So how did he do it? Frishberg answers this question by pointing out that not every saxophonist has his "own sound" but that, when "Zoot Walks In," you will know it is "totally him you're hearing." In other words, his tone is "all his own" – mostly "happy," but with just the right touches of "sadness" and even "madness." As a result, when Zoot appears, "every tenor man in the joint starts cheering." In short, like the astute marketing manager in pursuit of a differential advantage, Zoot produced a quintessentially unique offering that nonetheless fit the needs of the relevant target segment in ways that provided maximum consumer value.

The Marketing Analogy

The aforementioned pairing of songs by Frishberg (1987, 1991, undated) thus highlights the relevant analogies between jazz improvisation and the problems faced or solutions attempted by the typical marketing manager during the mature phase of the product life cycle. (Here, I refer to the "marketing manager," but the relevant unit of observation could of course be a "marketing team" or even an entire "market-oriented organization" [Hadida and Tarvainen, 2014].)

The Jazz Dialectic

Jazz improvisation follows a sort of *dialectic* that proceeds from *structure* (thesis) to *departure* (antithesis) to *reconciliation* (synthesis) (Holbrook, 1984c, 1995b, 2003b, 2007e).

Structure (Thesis). The jazz musician begins with a pre-existing structure – say, a familiar tune with well-known chord changes ("I Got Rhythm" or "Indiana" or "Show Me the Way to Go Home" or whatever). Both the melody and the harmonic progression – having been repeated ceaselessly for countless decades – are instantly recognizable and perhaps even trite, dull, or boring to those who hear or play them.

Departure (Antithesis). But the specialty of the jazz musician is to depart from this familiar structure by introducing variations and deviations that break free from the established pattern to pursue new melodic inventions of a unique and personal nature. These deviations from or variations of the melody embody significant departures that violate expectations – hence, *New Yorker* writer Whitney Balliett's famous characterization of jazz as *The Sound of Surprise* (Balliett, 1959).

Reconciliation (Synthesis). Yet these deviations from or violations of expectations are resolved in ways that achieve reconciliation with the underlying structure; that fit the larger unfolding pattern; and, indeed, that create a new structure to serve as the basis for subsequent departures and reconciliations. Meyer (1956, 1967) describes this process of establishing, violating, and rebuilding expectations as the basis for *Emotion and Meaning in Music* (Meyer, 1956). For the jazz musician, the nature of this dialectic process implies that improvisatory variations must fit the harmonic progression in ways that maintain the precarious balance between chaos and control, disorder and order, randomness and pattern, and freedom and restrictions. Indeed, this delicate balance – this precarious integration of opposites – lies at the heart of successful jazz improvisation (Holbrook, 1984c, 1995b, 2003b, 2007e).

The Marketing Dialectic

Notice how the marketing manager – during the mature phase of the product life cycle – follows a process strongly reminiscent of the jazz musician's improvisatory dialectic.

Structure (Thesis). Deep into the mature phase – enmeshed in the status quo – the product has become something of a commodity with parity versions vying for patronage on the basis of only the most trivial differences. One brand of cola looks, smells, and tastes a lot like the next (Coke, Pepsi). One make of menthol filter cigarette closely resembles the others (Newport, Salem, Kool). Every toothpaste offering seems pretty much the same (Crest, Colgate, Aim, Gleem). Each recordable CD-R seems like a clone of the competitor's version (TDK, Sony, Memorex, Verbatim). And one company's gas guzzles just about as well as another's (Exxon, Shell, Gulf, Hess, Mobil, Texaco).

Departure (Antithesis). The marketing manager therefore faces the challenge of finding some variation of or deviation from the norm – some new twist to differentiate the firm's offering from those of competitors in some significant way – cola in an all-aluminum can; a longer or shorter or square-shaped or green-colored menthol-filter cigarette; mint-flavored toothpaste gel with tartar control, whitening power, and red-white-and-blue stripes; gold-plated recordable CD-Rs; gasoline that smells like maple syrup.

Reconciliation (Synthesis). Such inspired departures from the norm remain meaningless, however, unless they fit the needs of customers so as to achieve reconciliation in the form of enhanced consumer value. In short, for at least one market segment, the new offering must offer value not obtainable elsewhere – a match between the differentiated product and hitherto unsatisfied consumer needs or wants. The differentiated offering achieves success only if target customers in sufficient numbers actually prefer aluminum-clad cola, square cigarettes, striped toothpaste, golden CDs, or maple-scented motor fuel.

Finale

Ultimately, we are struck by the rather profound ways in which – true to the jazz metaphor – the marketing manager during the mature phase of the product life cycle resembles an improvising musician.

Both begin with a clearly established structure – a melody and chord pattern in the case of the jazz musician, a set of commodity-like competing parity brands in the case of the marketing manager.

Both respond by introducing deviations or departures from the existing structure – novel melodic variations in the case of the jazz improviser, a differentiated offering in the case of the marketer.

And both achieve success only if the deviations or departures fit the demands of the relevant structure – the underlying chord pattern in the case of the jazz performer, the criteria for consumer value in the case of the marketing strategist.

For both the jazz musician and the marketing manager, success means finding a meaningful deviation from the norm that nonetheless fits the requirements of the relevant situation. When the jazz improviser gets it right, the music is . . . *beautiful*. When the marketing manager attains analogous success, the product is . . . *profitable*.

Coda

Roughly 20 years ago, while walking through the lobby of Columbia University's Graduate School of Business *en route* to my trip home on the subway, I felt a tap on my shoulder and turned around to encounter a 30-ish young man who quickly explained: "I *had* you." By this, he meant that he had taken my course on Consumer Behavior – in which, comparable to my approach in the present essay, I used numerous songs by David Frishberg to illustrate various consumer- and marketing-related concepts. It turned out that, after graduation, this former student had moved to England and had taken a job with a music-management firm that assigned him to cover the British singer/pianist Jamie Cullum as his primary client. It turned out that Cullum was a big fan of music by such American singer/songwriters as Bob Dorough and Dave Frishberg (who had collaborated on the jazz classic "I'm Hip," one of the tunes that I had used for illustrative purposes in class). And, apparently, the only thing that Cullum and my former student had in common – the key to their working relationship – was their mutual appreciation of and admiration for the work of Frishberg. Somehow, anecdotally, it seems significant that one of my few achievements in advancing the career of an MBA student stemmed from the benefits of his familiarity with the work of the marvelous tunesmith whose creations serve as a touchstone for our consideration of the marketing manager as a jazz musician.

10 Reflections on Jazz Training and Marketing Education

What Makes a Great Teacher?

Abstract

In recent years, numerous marketing and organizational theorists have called attention to the analogy between jazz and management strategy. From the perspective of this jazz metaphor, key questions concern the implications of jazz training for marketing education. Too often – say, in motion pictures or television dramas – jazz is portrayed as an innocent folk music whose performance requires more feeling than knowledge. This inaccurate stereotype colors the treatment of music instruction found in the film *Mr. Holland's Opus* (1995). A contrasting view of jazz as a technically demanding art form appears in the movie *Whiplash* (2014). These two films also represent diametrically opposed teaching styles – the first nurturing and *customer-oriented*, the second sadistic and *product-oriented*. A third motion picture, entitled *Keep On Keepin'* On (2014), presents a resolution of this dialectic in the form of a *marketing-oriented* instructor whose method of teaching combines kindness (the customer-oriented thesis) with rigor (the product-oriented antithesis) to achieve a balanced reconciliation (the marketing-oriented synthesis). From this perspective, like jazz training, marketing education is itself embarked on a marketing project that benefits from a rapprochement of customer-oriented and product-oriented impulses to attain a marketing-oriented synthesis. Thus, insights about jazz training become relevant to the challenges of marketing education – as illustrated by various examples from the author's own experiences.

Introduction: The Jazz Metaphor

In previous work, I have argued strenuously for the proposition that the job of the marketing manager noticeably resembles that of the jazz musician (Holbrook, 2003b, 2015g; Chapter 9). In general, this comparison of marketing managers with jazz musicians stems from a long line of research on organization theory and business strategy in which management- or marketing-oriented writers have devoted considerable attention to the development of a *jazz metaphor* based on analogies between improvisational music and creativity in general (Holbrook, 1995b), the development of

DOI: 10.4324/9781003560302-14

marketing theory in particular (Holbrook, 1984c), or managerial practice as a special case (Weick, 1998). (For reviews and collections, please see Hadida and Tarvainen, 2014; Holbrook, 2007e, 2015g; Kamoche, Cunha, and Cunha, 2003, ed. 2002; Leybourne, Lynn, and Vendelø, 2014; Meyer, Frost, and Weick, 1998; Chapter 9.)

The Case of Teaching

The present essay emphasizes that the analogy between jazz and marketing pertains with special force to the case of teaching. In this connection, Holbrook and Day (1994) applied the jazz metaphor to issues involved in the contrast between pandering to students by pursuing a customer-oriented approach and giving those students-as-consumers what they want, as opposed to preserving one's intellectual integrity by adopting a more product-oriented approach to education based on a dedication to academic discipline and a faithfulness to scholarly rigor. In other words, the familiar contrast between customer orientation and product orientation for the arts in general and for jazz in particular appears in the case of teaching in ways that suggest the importance of achieving a workable balance or rapprochement between the two. (For a general discussion of this theme, please see Hirschman, 1983.)

Consider, for example, the case of a marketing professor who worries about the potentially negative effects of business practices on the environment but who faces a classroom full of students concerned primarily with pointers on how to pursue a successful career. Here – as in many other comparable cases – intellectual integrity in teaching (like artistic integrity in music) demands an adherence to one's vision of the truth (like the jazz performer's reliance on a personal style) and a refusal to pander to the ill-considered preferences of students (like the musician's rejection of cheap effects that cater to the tastes of uninformed audience members). In short, teachers face an obligation to offer their own insights and to honor a commitment to the protection of divergent thinking, even where such material may run against the grain of popular appeal to students. This ethos should characterize the university's mindset and should set an academic program in marketing education apart from what one would expect in an executive-training course or a trade school. As participants in the educational process, we would not want it any other way.

The lesson seems fairly clear. Specifically, marketing professors face problems similar to those of the jazz musician – namely, the question of how to balance one's commitment to pursue one's intellectual convictions at any cost with the student's demand for accessible career-advancing knowledge that is more entertaining than challenging (Holbrook and Day, 1994, p. 142).

Jazz . . . Jazz training . . . Marketing . . . Marketing Education

This, then, establishes the conceptual connections between jazz musicianship, jazz training, marketing management in general, and marketing education in particular. Indeed, marketing education is itself embarked on a marketing project in which the challenge involves a process of positioning the educational offering in ways such that certain key ideas, concepts, techniques, and methods (e.g., multivariate statistics, multidimensional scaling, structural equation models, game theory, data-mining techniques, consumer value, consumption experiences, the service-dominant logic, social responsibility, and so forth) become appealing or at least acceptable within the intellectual repertoire and work ethic of the target audience of students. Toward this end, the student's skills require rigorous training. But that training can move forward only if it is offered in a manner that is empathetic, considerate, respectful, and caring.

The Cinematic Misrepresentation of Jazz Training

From the preceding discussion, it follows that the successful teaching of skills in jazz improvisation and expertise in marketing management might share much common ground. Indeed, one might imagine that techniques useful in coaching the aspiring jazz musician – that is, implications of the jazz metaphor in music training – might find helpful applications in marketing education. But, unfortunately, such progress is hindered by our widespread shared misunderstanding of what the performance of jazz requires from the committed artist.

Such a misunderstanding has appeared ubiquitously in all sorts of public displays of ignorance on the subject of the requirements for learning to play jazz. One gleaming example showed up in *The Benny Goodman Story* (1956, directed by Valentine Davies). In this film, young Benny has studied classical clarinet but hankers to try his hand at jazz. With absolutely no prior knowledge of the latter type of music, he joins the great New Orleans trombonist Kid Ory on the bandstand and, within two minutes of his initiation, has mastered every nuance of the relevant requirements for playing masterful jazz solos and for executing impossibly intricate musical passages in unison without benefit of previous rehearsal. Clearly, this scene is rather insulting to New Orleans musicians such as Ory who have spent lifetimes mastering this incredibly complex art form. Further, the same sort of ridiculous misrepresentation reappears in the film when Goodman & Co. jam with Lionel Hampton in ways that grotesquely understate the amount of hard work needed to prepare for such a performance. Their on-screen impromptu rendition of "Avalon" features an absurdly complicated riff that should have required hours of practice to master, again propounding the rather insulting view of jazz musicians as spontaneous musical naifs who somehow rely on sheer intuition to play together with flawless precision (Holbrook, 2011, pp. 300, 331).

We might imagine that such misconceptions on the part of filmmakers would have gone the way of the dodo bird. But, alas, the misunderstanding of what it takes to play jazz continues to rear its ugly head wherever artistic license gives it a chance to shine. One example appears in an episode of the television drama *Forever* entitled "6 A.M." (which aired on Tuesday November 18, 2014, on the ABC TV network). In this series, Dr. Henry Morgan (played by Ioan Gruffudd) – who is 200 years old, never ages, and cannot be killed – works as a medical examiner for New York City. His son Abe (played by Judd Hirsch) – who is quite a bit older than Henry looks (because Henry never ages) – runs an antique shop and likes to listen to old recordings by Charlie Parker and similar jazz heroes. Like Abe (a jazz musician), Henry plays the piano (but is more of a classicist).

During the episode in question, in a flashback to 1956, we see how Abe learns to play jazz. Specifically, as a boy, Abe devotes many hours to struggling with classical pieces on the piano. His father Henry tries to show him how to play Chopin's Nocturne in E-Flat Major. Then a hip African American neighbor drops by one day, agrees with Abe that Chopin is boring, and asks the boy if he's ever tried to play jazz. Abe says that he doesn't have the sheet music. But the neighbor replies that the beautiful thing about jazz is that you don't need sheet music. You just take the music by that old fuddy-duddy Chopin and make it your own.

In another flashback to 1956, Henry further recalls Abe's first attempt to learn to play jazz. In this scene, the same neighbor plays a little boogie-woogie on the ivories and then teaches young Abe how to improvise by telling him to forget about the sheet music and just to play what he feels. Within moments of his first attempt at improvisation – armed with no jazz-oriented knowledge beyond his untutored feelings – while the neighbor lays down a boogie pattern in the bass, little Abe immediately begins to play blues licks that would put Meade Lux Lewis to shame.

A similar scene repeats itself at the end of the program. We find Abe sitting around and listening to Chopin's nocturne. Henry enters and, in a conciliatory mood, says that he has developed a new appreciation for jazz and that maybe some of it has some merit. Abe replies that, hey, it's more fun to play. And, surprisingly, Henry asks Abe to show him how. They sit down at the piano with Abe on the bass notes and Henry on the treble. Abe offers the sum total of his instructive message – namely, that playing jazz is all about feeling. Abe begins a boogie pattern in the bass, while Henry – relying on nothing but his knowledge-free emotional impulses – proceeds to play inspired blues choruses at a level of excellence that compares favorably with the most accomplished jazz professional. Henry concludes that, in Abe, he has an excellent teacher. Professor Longhair and Dr. John, beware.

The Relevance of Jazz Training to Marketing Education

Given the aforementioned affinities between marketing and jazz, it should come as no surprise that aspects of jazz training also show parallels to important considerations involved in marketing education. But, before we can make any progress in relating the exigencies of jazz training to those of marketing education, we must bypass the sorts of misbegotten clichés that appear in *The BG Story* or *Forever* and come to terms with the fact that the jazz musician requires a repertoire of skills that exceed even those commonly associated with the classical artist.

True, classical musicians can read and perform the most complex musical compositions on their instruments. But the best-trained jazz musicians have achieved comparable levels of reading and performing written music. Beyond that – in ways seldom tapped by young classical trainees – jazz musicians require advanced knowledge of chords, scales, modes, harmonic progressions, tunes of every kind, ear training, the ability to improvise under intense time pressure at tempos ranging from the slowest to the most rapid humanly possible, and the skills to do all this on all tunes from an immense repertoire when played in all 12 keys. To put it mildly, such expertise entails countless hours of daily practice, a depth of musical knowledge seldom possessed by even the best-trained classical artists, and – above all – an ability to compose complex music in real time at breakneck speeds.

By analogy, as students, marketing managers also require in-depth training. They must perfect the science of market analysis. They must gain a profound knowledge of complex multivariate statistical techniques, multidimensional scaling, structural equation models, game theory, data-mining procedures, financial models, strategic thinking, consumer behavior, behavioral economics, issues of social responsibility, and much more. In short, the demanding skills needed to equip the marketing manager for the aforementioned tasks parallel in difficulty those required of the jazz artist. Like jazz training, marketing education requires long hard years of dedicated study, diligent effort, and unflagging perseverance.

So all this raises the question of how such expertise might best be taught to the aspiring jazz musician and – by extension – to the fledgling marketing manager. To repeat, this educational project is itself a marketing endeavor that involves a positioning problem in which certain key ideas, concepts, techniques, and methods (whether musical or managerial) are introduced into the student's repertoire of skills in such a way that they become acceptable or even appealing, while motivating the student to invest the considerable effort and hard work needed to master the relevant skill set. Toward this end, the student's "chops" require rigorous training that can move forward only if it is offered in a manner that gains the student's trust and respect. The term "chops" comes from the jazz lexicon and referred originally to the mouth of a horn player or, in other words, to that performer's embouchure. Brass or reed players with a virtuosic command over their instruments are said to possess good "chops." So – by extension – other instrumentalists such as piano, guitar, or bass players with superlative techniques are also said to have great "chops." Whether in jazz or in marketing, indoctrination into the relevant skill set – that is, building the student's "chops" – becomes the primary objective. The key question concerns how to accomplish this objective in the most effective way.

As potential answers to that question, in the case of jazz, we encounter three motion pictures, each of which has something to say about one or another style of teaching music, with potential relevance to aspects of marketing education. Here, I refer to *Mr. Holland's Opus* (1995), *Whiplash* (2014), and *Keep On Keepin' On* (2014). In what follows, I shall argue that these three films pursue a Fichtean-Hegelian *dialectic* (thesis, antithesis, and synthesis) in which a *thesis* (customer orientation in *Mr. Holland*) is challenged by its *antithesis* (product orientation in *Whiplash*) in ways that lead toward a *synthesis* (marketing orientation in *Keepin' On*).

Thesis – Customer Orientation: *Mr. Holland's Opus* (1995)

I have previously expounded at length on the topic of *Mr. Holland's Opus* (1995) – a film directed by Stephen Herek in which Richard Dreyfuss won an Oscar Award for portraying a dedicated music teacher named Glenn Holland who panders to his class of young students by charming them into becoming surprisingly appreciative audience members and amazingly competent musicians (Holbrook, 1998h). Still viewing music instruction in general and jazz training in particular in the simplistic terms found in *The BG Story* or *Forever*, the story has a sort of warm gooey niceness about it. The teacher cares deeply about his students, treats them with the utmost kindness, and sacrifices himself for their benefit. In short, he displays an extreme degree of customer orientation.

It is a sweet film. When it appeared, it won enormous audience popularity, was adopted as a rallying call by the community of music teachers, and garnered strong praise from most of the difficult-to-please movie critics. To this day, it enjoys a 6.8/10 rating from critics on Rottentomatoes.Com and a 7.3/10 rating from viewers on IMDB.Com.

With a strong emphasis on Glenn Holland's love of jazz, while perpetuating the aforementioned inaccurate view of jazz as a sort of naïve folk music, the film attempts to offer insights into the process of education in general and musical instruction in particular. Yet, despite such good intentions, the image of education that emerges strikes me as misguided at best and, at worst, as downright perverse. Specifically, Mr. Holland approaches the challenge of musical instruction as a confirmed populist who eschews any sort of elite critical standards in the teaching of music. Rather than encourage distinctions between good and bad music, the essence of music appreciation, he reveals a non-discriminating tendency to like *all* music – Bach, Beethoven, the Beatles, the Gershwins, Miles, Trane, John Philip Sousa, . . . whatever. It's all the same to Mr. Holland – all fine and dandy if it appeals to even the most uneducated popular tastes. This sort of unqualified admiration for everything stifles all critical judgment by pandering to the tastes of even the most ill-informed students. By claiming to love *all* music, he fails to show artistic selectivity, aesthetic discernment, or discrimination between good and bad – thereby betraying an inherent lack of true respect for *any* music.

Most lamentably, this populist attitude spills over into Mr. Holland's approach to teaching. Faced with students who show little interest in learning about music, he proceeds to pander to their low-brow tastes. He tells them that they already like the music of J. S. Bach because, hey, Bach's "Minuet in G" is just like a tune called "Lover's Concerto" performed by a pathetic rock group named "The Toys." This pattern of watering down each teaching moment by shamelessly appealing to the lowest common denominator reappears again and again as Mr. Holland shows a tone-deaf wrestler how to beat a bass drum on one and three in the school's marching band; helps a promising young singer to dumb down "Someone To Watch Over Me" to a simplified set of three or four chord changes; and convinces a woefully inept clarinet player that she already knows the piece she is unsuccessfully trying to play and that all will be well if she forgets about the sheet music, closes her eyes, and tries to sound like the sunset.

In sum, throughout and with implications that subvert the essence of effective teaching, Mr. Holland pursues an extreme form of customer orientation by catering to the ill-informed bad taste and ingrained ineptitude of his student-consumers in ways that obliterate any possibility of teaching them anything important about music appreciation or musical performance. He charms them by implying that they already know everything important and that they need only reach deep within themselves to liberate that innate understanding so that facile intuition can take the place of hard work. Moreover, he conveys that all tastes are equally legitimate and that all artistic offerings are equally excellent. Indeed, Mr. Holland's absurd slogan that his lackluster student should just imitate the sunset, in its complete lack of musical validity, matches the aforementioned mantra from *Forever* that one should just play what one feels. In reality, no student instructed in this manner will achieve anything beyond pitiful ineptitude.

But where, we might wonder, does Mr. Holland's extreme form of customer orientation find its parallel in marketing education? The simple answer is: Anywhere that the need to inform, challenge, and instruct students in the demanding skill set of marketing concepts and techniques takes a back seat to the desire to please them in return for higher course evaluations or, in other words, better customer-satisfaction scores. One example of this wayward impetus appears in the increasing tendency for marketing instructors to rely on the Case Method in business education. I fully recognize that Harvard cases and the like win the hearts if not the minds of MBA students, helping to bolster the popularity of teachers who use them to excess. But, essentially, classroom cases represent an inherently dangerous con game. They pose as real-life situations pregnant with implications that inspire penetrating insights from those who study them. Yet they contain highly fictionalized accounts full of doctored data, distorted details, and convenient oversimplifications. Further, students are manipulated into arriving at the conclusions suggested by teaching notes or instruction manuals, whereby professors know exactly what the blackboard should look like at the end of the class meeting and extract all-over-the-map responses from the participants until some of these have finally, if accidentally, provided the answers they seek. No fundamental concepts or techniques tend to emerge from such discussions. Rather, students are flattered into believing that they already know everything needed to solve the case and that their own powers of deduction have somehow led them in the direction of real-world truths about managerial practice more profound than anything available in merely theoretical perspectives. Indeed, for such students, the word "theory" tends to carry negative connotations as something inferior to "practice." Thus does this whole charade elevate intuitive habits above critical analysis in ways that reward students for their own self-congratulatory intellectual vacuity.

Antithesis – Product Orientation: *Whiplash* (2014)

The inadequacies of *Mr. Holland's Opus* as a model for teaching music, marketing, or anything else are so spectacular as to make us wonder how such a film could ever have been imagined, let alone produced. But, more recently, we have confronted another music-education film – one that was honored with five Oscar nominations, that has won a long string of awards (Oscar, Golden Globe, BAFTA, Screen Actors Guild, National Society of Film Critics, New York Film Critics, and many others) for best supporting actor (J. K. Simmons), that has achieved an audience rating of 8.6/10.0 on IMDB.Com and a critics rating of 8.6/10.0 on Rottentomatoes.Com, but that adopts an antithetical yet equally absurd perspective on the requisites of good teaching – namely, extreme product orientation. Specifically, in *Whiplash* (2014, written and directed by Damien Chazelle), a young drummer named Andrew Neiman (played by Miles Teller) enrolls at the Shaffer Conservatory of Music (described as the foremost music school in the USA) where he encounters the pedagogical methods of a technique-driven classroom sadist named Terence Fletcher (J. K. Simmons). The latter instructs his students in ways intended to build their musical "chops" by terrorizing them in a manner that far exceeds the point of mental cruelty. Indeed – formerly known as a journeyman actor who has played relatively non-demanding parts as Police Chief Will Pope on Kyra Sedgwick's TNT series entitled *The Closer* and as the kindly salesman in television commercials for Farmers Insurance – J. K. Simmons (who has a college degree in music and who, in one crucial scene, actually plays some admirably straightforward jazz piano) seems to have found his inner monster just in time to unleash this beast in the form of the world's nastiest teacher.

Terence Fletcher challenges his students by forcing them to play impossibly difficult charts at outrageously brisk tempos. For example, the title tune "Whiplash" is in 14/8 or 7/4 at a very rapid pace, which involves a complex metric structure that runs counter to anything normally familiar in Western music and imposes huge demands on all concerned – including the drummer. With that as a foundation, in a big-band rehearsal, Fletcher viciously berates his victim Andrew for rushing, . . . then for dragging, . . . then for rushing, . . . and so forth – relying on fine tempo-related distinctions that elude detection by even the most savvy cinematic viewer. Finally, Fletcher throws a chair at Andrew's head and, working himself up into a high dudgeon, threatens him with words deemed too foul to appear in a linguistically respectable publication.

But all this pedagogic torture only spurs young Andrew to greater heights of masochistic self-punishment, involving self-destructive practice sessions during which his hands bleed profusely and splatter blood all over his drum kit until, after unsuccessfully applying layers of Band Aids, he plunges them into a bucket of ice that promptly turns bright red.

Some of Terence Fletcher's sadistic tirades are so over the top that they become almost comical. Consider, for example, the virtuosically gutter-mouthed harangue in which he offers his student big band his own personal brand of encouragement before they take the stage at the Overbrook Jazz Competition – beginning with an onslaught of insults to their masculinity, casting aspersions on their musical competence, and ending with a masterpiece of irony in which he promises that in the future he will stop being so polite.

But Andrew perseveres in his obsessively compulsive way – aiming at musical greatness, no matter what the cost. Indeed, the cost becomes pretty huge as Andrew travels to the Dunellen Competition. *En route*, a truck crashes into his car. He crawls from the wreckage – covered with blood – runs the rest of the way to the concert stage and, after further cruel treatment by Fletcher, attacks his professor physically. This results in his expulsion from the Shaffer Conservatory. And – when questioned by a member of the school's administration – he talks about Fletcher's misbehavior in ways that get the teacher dismissed as well.

Andrew gives up the drums and works behind the counter at a delicatessen. But, pretty soon, he stumbles into a jazz club called Nowells where Terence Fletcher performs with a trio (with J. K. Simmons himself expertly playing the piano part). Fletcher invites Andrew to have a drink and spills his guts on the theme of his dismissal from the school and his philosophy of teaching – which boils down to a quintessentially product-oriented insistence on excellence, no matter what price must be paid in terms of human relationships.

In this scene, apparently voicing the film's central meaning, Fletcher articulates his pedagogic philosophy – namely, that jazz performance requires super-human musical skills that can only be learned/taught by driving one-self/others to their ultimate limits. As a justification for this teaching method, Fletcher cites a famous incident in which, to express his disapproval, the Kansas City drummer Jo Jones threw a cymbal at the young Charlie Parker – potentially injuring the fledgling alto player, humiliating him mercilessly, but inspiring him to practice night and day until he became the genius improviser known as "Bird" (Russell, 1973). Specifically, Bird conducted these rigorous practice sessions while gigging at a resort in the Ozark Mountains – figuratively, in a "woodshed," which may be where the term "woodshedding" comes from. In this connection, note that the term "wood-shedding" and its association with the tendency of jazz musicians to refer to their instruments as their "axes" – which are often involved in "cutting" contests – may also carry some resonance in the jazz lexicon with the word "chops" (as discussed earlier) in the sense that "axes" are good for "chopping" logs in the "woodshed," with all this lumberjack imagery suggestive of a jazz musician's technical mastery of his or her instrument. Indeed, wood-shedding is this film's central premise – all the more when the Oscar-winning hero of *Whiplash* behaves like the intellectual equivalent of an axe murderer. In a pivotal speech, Fletcher recounts how Parker was embarrassed by the cymbal-throwing incident, but how it fueled his desire to improve and how – inspired by his determination – he practiced-practiced-practiced until he did indeed become the greatest alto saxophonist who ever lived. Because of his intentions to achieve comparable results with his students, though fired from his teaching position at Schaffer, Fletcher refuses to apologize for his product-oriented teaching style.

If Terence Fletcher represents an extreme level of product orientation – that is, an unapologetically technique- or proficiency-driven approach – we might wonder how such proclivities would manifest themselves in the sphere of marketing education. In all honesty, I must admit that I have never encountered a marketing professor who rose – or sank – to Fletcher's level of sadism. But the same cannot be said for members of the closely related Discipline Y. In the latter connection, please allow me to describe an academic example that demonstrated the Fletcherian product-oriented tendencies in full flower.

The teacher in question – let us call him Professor X – ran a required course on Discipline Y for doctoral students during my graduate program in Marketing. Clearly, the material he covered and the techniques he wanted to impart represented key aspects of the skill set demanded of an aspiring marketing academic. The only problem was that – with any semblance of human civility appearing to lie far outside his powers of social interaction – his chosen approach to conveying the desired concepts and methods relied primarily on terrorist tactics of the Fletcherian variety. All this came to a head for me personally in conjunction with a term project designed to familiarize the class with various relevant procedures related to Method Z. These Z-related techniques were of undeniable importance to our academic training and included material essential to the "chops" of a doctoral student in Marketing. But, unfortunately for me, the due date for this term project coincided closely with the birth of our son via a medically complicated delivery that put my wife Sally back in the hospital for another ten days and left me at home at age 25 with a screaming baby to care for and with no pediatric skills to do the job properly. Obviously, this was a moment of crisis for me, and it moved me (for the first time in my life) to request an "incomplete" grade in Professor X's class with an extension so that I could do a proper job on the Method Z project after Sally returned from her prolonged hospitalization. The response of Professor X was that he would not allow such a postponement because he would then have no way of knowing that I would complete the assignment and, besides, because "everybody has some sort of a problem." Terence Fletcher could not have put it better himself. Suffice it to say that members of our class felt that they had learned nothing from Professor X. To repeat, it was clear that Method Z was an important research tool. I did learn about Z at a later date and have used it many times in my own work. But I did not learn it from Professor X and have trouble imagining that I could learn anything from that individual.

Beyond the extreme excesses of Terence Fletcher and Professor X, a less sadistic but nonetheless ineffective approach to product-oriented marketing education involves the use of standardized courses that – in their quest for efficiencies and cost reductions – produce one version of a syllabus and class materials intended to be taught by all professors. Sort of like Henry Ford's Model Ts. True, professors save time and effort by using a common set of teaching notes and/or PowerPoint slides provided by the textbook publisher. But standardization deprives the students of any choice among teaching styles and thereby stifles all semblance of intellectual integrity. A move in this direction at my own school proved disastrous to my ability to teach and precipitated my early retirement (as described in Chapter 3).

The Teaching Dialectic

Presumably, the truth about what makes for great teaching lies somewhere other than the two poles represented by *Mr. Holland's Opus* at one extreme (the sweet and loving mentor who is concerned mostly about support or even flattery but who cares very little about skill development, appreciative discrimination, or critical judgment) and *Whiplash* at the other (the sadistic tormentor who sacrifices all semblance of humanity in pursuit of the most rigorous standards of self-discipline in the service of musical excellence). Considering these two extremes – serenely mimicking the sunset versus sadomasochistically struggling with impossibly fast tempos in 7/4 – one might too readily anticipate that surely the optimal approach (the real path to pedagogic success) must lie somewhere in the middle. Yet I am on record as opposing the mollifying comforts of compromise (Holbrook, 2008a). Such a Goldilocks solution – not too hot, not too cold, but just right – seems destined to produce nothing better than lukewarm porridge. That is, tepid pabulum fit for a baby or bland gruel suitable for the innocent heroine of a fairy tale. Indeed, in this light, I could not defend the recommendation of a severe-but-laid-back teaching style that emphasizes learning whatever-one-can-manage-without-trying-very-hard. Such a wishy-washy middle-of-the-road approach seems guaranteed to produce a middling result. Or, less politely, it seems sure to achieve nothing better than . . . mediocrity.

What we need then is not a compromise between Mr. Holland and Terence Fletcher but rather a synthesis of the thesis and antithesis represented by these two opposing forces – that is, an integration that resolves the tension between them in ways that contribute to the advancement of learning. Viewing education as essentially a marketing project, we need a balanced approach that reconciles the customer orientation (sensitive to external opportunities in general and student tastes in particular) with the product orientation (sensitive to internal pressures in general and technical excellence in particular) in a way that achieves a true marketing orientation (involving a balanced rapprochement between the two counterposed tendencies). Such a resolution of the dialectic would involve a teacher who displays the humanity of Mr. Holland (generous, loving, concerned for his students' well-being) with the commitment to excellence of Terence Fletcher (rigorous, demanding, dedicated to the perfection of technical expertise). In other words, such a teacher would motivate with kindness but elevate with disciplined training.

A schematic diagram of the proposed marketing-oriented teaching dialectic appears in Figure 10.1. Here, the horizontal axis represents the contrast between a Kind/Generous/Loving teaching style at one extreme and a Nasty/Brutal/Sadistic orientation at the other. Meanwhile, the vertical axis captures the contrast between a Pandering/Uncritical/Intuitive approach and a Demanding/Rigorous/Disciplined commitment. As the *thesis*, Glenn Holland (Richard Dreyfuss) occupies the upper right-hand territory – a kind-generous-loving teacher who panders to his students in an uncritical and intuitive manner (extreme customer orientation). By contrast – as the

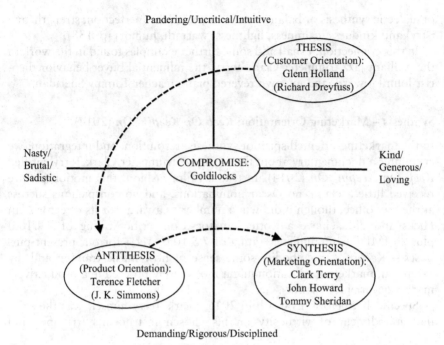

Pandering/Uncritical/Intuitive

THESIS
(Customer Orientation):
Glenn Holland
(Richard Dreyfuss)

Nasty/
Brutal/
Sadistic

COMPROMISE:
Goldilocks

Kind/
Generous/
Loving

ANTITHESIS
(Product Orientation):
Terence Fletcher
(J. K. Simmons)

SYNTHESIS
(Marketing Orientation):
Clark Terry
John Howard
Tommy Sheridan

Demanding/Rigorous/Disciplined

Figure 10.1 Schematic Diagram of the Teaching Dialectic

antithesis, found in the lower left-hand corner of the diagram – Terence Fletcher (J. K. Simmons) pursues a demanding-rigorous-disciplined approach in a manner that is nasty, brutal, and sadistic (extreme product orientation). One option – which I reject – would favor a Goldilocks-like middle-of-the-road compromise in which a teacher shows lukewarm concern for the happiness of students while offering them a moderate level of instructional rigor in ways that I believe are guaranteed to produce mediocrity. Rather, I wish to argue for the merits of a *synthesis* – that is, a resolution or integration – of the two positive poles, as found in the lower right-hand corner of the diagram, which recommends a kind-generous-loving approach to demanding-rigorous-disciplined instruction (marketing orientation).

Embryonic arguments on behalf of such a synthesis appeared in an issue of *DownBeat* with a section devoted to jazz training. Here, a tribute to the late Steve Zegree – Professor of Music at Indiana University – makes it clear that this champion of vocal jazz combined the dialectic qualities just described by being both demanding (placing high expectations on his students) and compassionate (with a disarming sense of humor) (*DownBeat*, 2015, p. 102). Another article in the same issue honored the contributions of the late Rayburn Wright, Professor at the Eastman School of Music (Garcia and Hunsberger, 2015). An especially telling comment came from the noted jazz composer-arranger Maria Schneider, who again referred to the same sort of dialectic synthesis or balance between excellence (perfection, strength, artistry) and kindness (calmness, lightness, warmth, humor) (p. 138).

In this connection, I shall add some further examples found in the work of the brilliant jazz trumpeter Clark Terry, the influential buyer-behavior theorist John Howard, and my own revered piano teacher Tommy Sheridan.

Synthesis – Marketing Orientation: *Keep On Keepin' On* (2014)

In the marketing-oriented spirit of synthesis, resolution, and integration, we encounter a documentary about the great jazz trumpeter Clark Terry entitled *Keep On Keepin' On* (2014). In true art-film fashion, this motion picture received little acclaim, no Oscar nominations, and no conspicuous success at the box office, though it did win a number of awards for its director Alan Hicks and did achieve a Rottentomatoes.Com critics rating of 7.4/10.0 plus an IMDB.Com audience rating of 7.5/10.0. Yet – for our present purposes – *Keepin' On* embodies some sense of how music training and, by extension, marketing education might most wisely proceed in a productively marketing-oriented manner.

Specifically, before his death in 2015, Clark Terry himself was the shining embodiment of virtuosity on his chosen instruments (trumpet and

Figure 10.2 Clark Terry at Microphone on Flugelhorn – NYC

flugelhorn). He played with both the Count Basie and the Duke Ellington bands before embarking on a distinguished career as a studio-session man (e.g., *The Tonight Show*), leader of his own groups (e.g., the Bob Brookmeyer – Clark Terry Quintet), master of trumpet-related technical wizardry (e.g., circular breathing via which he could sustain a constant flow of notes without pausing for air), leader or featured artist on over 370 jazz recordings, and acclaimed instructor (The University of New Hampshire, William Patterson College in New Jersey, The University of Arkansas, and many other schools). Clearly, with "chops" to spare, he drew on a vast accumulation of jazz-related knowledge (harmony, melodic improvisation, tunes in the repertoire, trumpet technique, and so forth). The documentary shows Clark Terry (CT) – at an advanced age, ranging from 89 to 93, having lost his eyesight and much of his ability to play – imparting this knowledge to a young blind pianist Justin Kauflin, whom he has taken under his pedagogic wing.

Here, I use the term "wing" advisedly because CT's treatment of his youthful student puts one in mind of something that T. S. Eliot might have dreamed up – that is, a nurturing protectiveness within the scope of a spiritual center. Fundamentally, Terry had a wealth of expertise and chops-building know-how to impart, and the documentary shows how he did this in a way that was as supportive as it was demanding of excellence.

Many details of CT's life, career, and passion for teaching appear in his autobiography entitled *Clark: The Autobiography of Clark Terry* (Terry and Terry, 2011). In an "Introduction," David Demsey of William Patterson University refers to CT as "one of the original creators of jazz education" (p. xv). Indeed, Terry mentored thousands of young musicians – many of whom went on to become first-rank jazz artists (Byron Stripling, Conrad Herwig, Branford Marsalis, Ryan Kisor, and many others) – teaching at numerous universities, receiving countless honorary degrees, winning innumerable awards, and sharing his knowledge of jazz with anyone and everyone who cared to ask. For example, the *Autobiography* reports how – in Seattle, after late nights of playing at a gig – Terry arises at 6:00 am to give lessons to a young Quincy Jones (who never forgets CT's generosity) (p. 121).

Clark makes it clear that, in his teaching, he endeavors to combine discipline with kindness. Reminiscent of the punch line to that old joke about how to get to Carnegie Hall, he tells his students that they must practice-practice-practice by playing each passage over and over and over until they achieve perfection (pp. 196, 213).

In the documentary, Justin Kauflin meets CT when the latter is teaching at William Paterson University in New Jersey. Partly because of their mutual eyesight problems, the two hit it off famously, and Clark proceeds to offer Justin dedicated instruction. We see them practicing finger exercises together, conducting ear-training lessons, learning new and unfamiliar tunes from the repertoire, and discussing the merits of songs like Duke's "Sophisticated Lady." Throughout, CT emphasizes the seriousness of the jazz-training process while simultaneously conveying a joyful exuberance – even while blind, breathing oxygen, and ultimately bed-ridden – that inspires the young pianist to greater heights.

When Justin asks CT what is the difference between an amateur and a master, Clark – in the gentlest possible way, while affectionately patting Justin's seeing-eye dog Candy – stresses the desire to excel, to play the best, to know your shortcomings, and to work on fixing them. Thus does Clark Terry extol the chops-building virtues of rigorous training, constant effort, steady practicing, and a solid work ethic. He appreciates Justin because Justin displays these qualities, and he voices these demands as a taskmaster with a loving generosity that supports Justin every step of the way.

So, when Justin experiences extreme stage fright before performing at the Thelonious Monk competition, Clark comforts him with the most supportive message imaginable, telling Justin that challenges come with the territory and that he understands his stage fright but that Justin must reach deep within himself and do his best. Justin does not win the Monk contest, nor even rank among the top three contestants; but, with determination, he vows to put in extra hours of practicing – a goal that CT strongly endorses.

Meanwhile, Terry's health continues to fail. But, even while acknowledging that he is in terrible pain, he has uplifting advice to offer Justin on the theme of working hard and doing it the right way rather than the easy way. These are, of course, the words that Clark Terry himself has lived by, to the everlasting glory of his own fabulous musical performances. Justin follows this advice. And, pretty soon, he finds himself on a world tour with Quincy Jones. While appearing at the Montreux Jazz Festival, Justin receives another message from CT extolling the importance of cultivating positive thoughts and ending with a profound expression of love.

This emphasis on positivity shines throughout the playing and teaching of Clark Terry. In one powerful scene, we find him lying in the hospital – in obvious physical discomfort, with an oxygen tube in his nose, IVs connected to various limbs, and monitors blinking and beeping in the background – happily singing a tune he likes called "Breeze" in an effort to teach it to Justin and smiling as if this music has transported him beyond all worldly cares in ways suggesting that the effort and sacrifice are worth every moment. A person who exudes this sort of joy in the making and teaching of music will inevitably exert a strong impact on those privileged to learn from his wisdom. This ability to inspire receives fitting tributes from two star witnesses – speaking on-camera – the great jazz singer Diane Reeves (who wanted to live up to CT's demanding standards) and the legendary composer/arranger/bandleader Quincy Jones (who cannot forget CT's mentoring and encouragement).

So Clark Terry's success as a teacher stems from the rejection of compromise. Rather, it reflects a dialectic reconciliation of rigorous demands on one hand and supportive love on the other. Via this resolution of the thesis (Mr. Holland's customer-oriented humanity) with the antithesis (Terence Fletcher's product-oriented discipline), Clark Terry achieves pedagogic success that transcends anything possible without the sort of dialectic (marketing-oriented) synthesis that he embodies so conspicuously.

Tommy Sheridan (Music) and John Howard (Marketing)

I believe that the example of Clark Terry and Justin Kauflin argues powerfully in favor of the proposed marketing-oriented synthesis of student-friendly caring (Glenn Holland's customer orientation) and strict discipline (Terence Fletcher's product orientation).

Thus, sympathetic to the strict-but-loving approach of Clark Terry, I have celebrated the miraculous powers of my own piano teacher Tommy Sheridan, a wonderful jazz pianist in Milwaukee, who resembled CT far more than either Mr. Holland or Terence Fletcher. In short, Tommy conveyed an appreciation of the music and a love for his students that inspired his protégés in general and yours truly in particular to strive for greater musical insight and knowledge of jazz. The work was difficult, but the rewards were enormous – all the more because they received Tommy's loving support.

Along similar lines, John Howard at Columbia University did something comparable in the case of marketing education in general and buyer-behavior theory in particular. He maintained the highest standards of academic integrity and scholarly discipline – pushing himself as hard as he pushed his students and junior colleagues. He very seldom talked or thought about anything other than buyer-behavior theory – of which, arguably, he was the father and which he approached with a reverential, nearly religious attention to the perfection of his conceptual scheme. He expected and won the same level of devotion from his students and younger colleagues. But – combined with this – he mentored, guided, and watched over us at every step of the way with the greatest kindness and generosity. Those of us who showed a dedication to building our mastery of marketing and buyer-behavior concepts and methods received his unqualified support. My own career, for example, would have gone absolutely nowhere without John Howard as a mentor. As with Clark Terry's emphasis on his students' needs to be true to themselves, John Howard's support extended to an encouragement of the student's need to take risks, to endure the uncertainty of challenging conventional thought, and to construct new theoretical paradigms and methodological approaches that pushed the conceptual and technical boundaries beyond their previous comfort zones (cf. Holbrook, 1997a). And this was true, by the way, even when I was busy with iconoclastic efforts to subvert the theoretical edifice – the decision-oriented information-based rational economic model – that he himself had so patiently built. In this, Howard's range of tolerance encouraged what Earl and Potts (2013) call "edgy" approaches – that is, those that pushed the envelope beyond the "mainstream" (the conventional wisdom represented by his own work) without becoming overly "experimental" (overshooting the mark by creating an over-the-top offering in the *avant-garde* realm of ideas-for-ideas'-sake) (p. 165).

I was blessed to encounter these two great teachers – neither of whom had a pandering or sadomasochistic bone in his body – at critical formative moments of my own development. In the area of marketing education, I have been privileged to acknowledge the nurturing influence of my beneficent teacher John Howard on various occasions (Holbrook, 1998c, 2001f, videotape 1989) and dedicated my most important book to this great man: "*For John A. Howard – Teacher, Mentor, Colleague, Friend – An Inspiration in Every Way*" (Holbrook, 1995b). Indeed, I have suggested that – as a marketing theorist – John Howard was to our academic discipline what Charlie Parker was to jazz (Holbrook, 1984c). And that is the biggest tribute I know how to offer.

So – to elaborate a bit further on the characteristics of a great teacher – I might end this essay on the connection between jazz training and marketing education by quoting a letter that I wrote to my jazz-piano instructor Tommy Sheridan near the end of his teaching career, referring to a book that Beth Hirschman and I had edited (Hirschman and Holbrook, ed. 1981).

Dear Tom,

Last spring, a friend of mine at NYU (Beth Hirschman) and I organized a conference on what I like to call "Consumer Esthetics." When the time came to collect the conference papers into a book, we decided to dedicate the volume to the teacher(s) that each of us felt had done the most for us. In my case, it was very easy to decide who that person is: You! (See page iv.)

I have attended some pretty fancy schools. But, of all the professors I studied with in my 14 years at Country Day and 4 years at Harvard and 10 years at Columbia, none ever taught me half as much as you did in the years that you worked with me. You gave me a gift that I shall cherish always. You taught me the joy of music and showed me that, if it *sounds* right, it *is* right. From you, I learned things about creativity and artistic sensitivity that cannot be found in any book. And I shall always be profoundly grateful.

You are a magic person and have brought happiness to everyone who has ever known you. I don't know if you realize how many people you have filled with delight through your abounding talent and how many you have touched with your generous humanity. If you do, you must be very proud. I hope you are – because you deserve it.

Thank you so much.

With Love and Appreciation
From Morris

I received a most gracious reply to this letter from Tommy. Even 40-plus years later, I feel a sense of joy when I read his kind words: "Let me tell you, Morris, I have never been so thrilled in my life as I was when I read your beautiful letter." It strikes me very powerfully how much just a few simple words of thanks can mean to a teacher in general and to one as special as Tommy in particular: "I just can't put the words together to tell you how deeply I was touched . . .. These are the kindest and most beautiful words anyone has ever said to me." Tommy went on to mention that he was having the letter framed for his studio, and I took great pleasure from imagining it on the wall above the piano where I had spent so many happy hours.

There is a moral here. Dear Reader, if you have ever been blessed by having a great teacher who – like Clark Terry or John Howard or Tommy Sheridan – combined strict discipline with loving support in ways that elevated your own powers to a level otherwise impossible to attain, don't wait around to express your gratitude. ***Thank your teacher now! Today! This minute!*** You may be surprised to discover how much it means to him or her to know that you took the time to acknowledge that his or her efforts have been truly appreciated. And you'll be glad you did.

Part V

Some Criticisms, Cavils, Complaints, and Controversies

11 The Greedy Bastard's Guide to Business

Abstract

Greedy Bastards, eager to achieve success in the business world, need helpful advice on steps toward climbing to the top. Drawing on the author's 35-plus years of experience in teaching MBAs, the present satirical treatise offers tips in the form of a self-help tutorial that parodies an inspirational guide. In that ironic spirit, the discussion covers pertinent aspects of business education; impression management (Dre$$ for $ucce$$); tips from travel services; ethics; borderline-legal corruption; and unintended benefits such as obesity, traffic, cell phones, or impacts on popular culture – culminating in a Greedy Bastard's Honor Roll of Civic Achievements.

Introduction: Calling All Greedy Bastards

Face it: In the world we inhabit today, we find ourselves surrounded by Greedy Bastards in virtually every walk of life. Just pause for a moment to contemplate the sheer enormity of the greedy-bastard population in the present times, and you will find yourself amazed at their undeniable and unstoppable ubiquity:

- Chief executive officers at mammoth banks and giant financial institutions – who pilfer money from their hapless and helpless clients, drive their companies into hopeless debt, accept generous government bailouts, and then reward themselves with multi-million-dollar year-end bonuses
- Corrupt politicians who line their own pockets with under-the-table donations while voting for socially disastrous legislation in support of every sort of self-serving special interest from tax cuts for the wealthy, to spending cuts in entitlements for the less fortunate, to cuts in the enforcement of gun controls, to cuts in the accessibility of voting rights, to cuts in the representativeness of election districts
- Clergymen who live a well-supported life of comfort in the bosom of the Church while engaging in pedophilia, homoerotic dalliances, and all sorts of other forbidden but enjoyable indiscretions

DOI: 10.4324/9781003560302-16

- Jewel-bedecked drug dealers who lurk outside high schools to sell cocaine to teen-aged crack addicts
- Crime lords who tour the streets in fancy BMWs and armored Mercedes limousines collecting payoffs from otherwise respectable restaurants and dry-cleaning establishments
- Sports heroes who pump themselves full of steroids in the service of commanding gigantic paychecks that reflect their bulked-up homer-hitting, quarterback-sacking, or bicycle-riding skills
- Entertainers who sell out their artistic abilities for the sake of creating a commercially successful pop album, a runaway best-seller, a chance to win a dance contest, or a spot as guest host on late-night TV
- Teachers who compromise their calling by writing self-help guides that cater to Greedy Bastards

Yes, the list seems endless. And, of course, I find myself ensconced thereon along with all the other self-aggrandizing characters to whom I have just referred and to whom I address the present tutorial. Until my retirement, 15 years ago, I pulled down a fairly hefty salary as a chaired professor at a major graduate school of business. My unofficial job description involved teaching Greedy Bastards like you and me how to be even greedier and more bastardly in their dealings with their fellow human creatures. Clearly, my experience in this milieu has prepared me uniquely to handle the demands of the present literary project.

And you, Dear Reader, by consulting my guide have revealed yourself to be nothing other than a potential Greedy Bastard seeking instruction and enlightenment of the kind that I – by virtue of long experience and deep immersion – can promise to provide. I truly hope that you will deploy these resources in an enormously greedy future to become the truly selfish bastard that you long to be. I applaud your wisdom in turning to me for help because I plan to give you exactly what you deserve as you read on and lick your chops.

I might mention, with respect to the issue of politically correct gender neutrality, that – as an enthusiastic advocate of equal opportunities for all – I intend the term "Greedy Bastard" to refer to both male and female members of the business community. However, I shall often use masculine pronouns – "he," "him," "his" – in situations where it appears to me that men greatly outnumber women in their propensities toward bastardly greed.

Also, please note that – in this guide – I shall focus primarily on Greedy Bastards in the United States of America. I realize that many other countries – like Russia and China – have recently embraced capitalist ideals in ways that have led them to emulate the shining example of the USA. Nevertheless – if, among nations, America ranks 24th in life expectancy; 72nd in health care; 39th in environmental performance; 23rd in quality of transportation infrastructure; and 33rd, 27th, and 22nd in reading, math, and science, respectively (www.photius.com) – it surely ranks first in bastardly greed. I plan to celebrate this enviable achievement in the present treatise.

So please read on – for your enlightenment and edification – with hopes that, by the end of only a few hours or even (if you are a speed reader) a few minutes, you too will earn the right to claim ascension to the ranks of the Greedy Bastards that surround us on all sides.

Getting Started – Business Education

Obviously, preparation for your role as a Greedy Bastard will require some specialized education. For a start, a college degree with a business major will provide some help in pointing you in the right direction. (Just look at what Wharton did for Donald J. Trump.) Surely, it would be a terrible mistake to waste a college education on something useless like English literature, something irrelevant like philosophy, or something with no practical application like mathematics. One can only pity those misguided college kids who major in English, philosophy, math, or similarly esoteric branches of the liberal arts. These pointless fields of study neither reflect the real world nor offer any assistance on the path to gainful employment in the job of your choice.

Nonetheless, once you graduate with a BA in Business (say, finance, accounting, management, marketing, or some other worthwhile specialty), you will find yourself in the company of a zillion other folks your own age who have also just emerged with a business degree as good or better than yours. They, too, are beating down the doors of prospective employers, hoping to be hired in exactly the same positions to which you also aspire. If you are a true Greedy Bastard, you will surmise that there must be some easier way to climb the ladder of success. At which point, you will no doubt realize that what you need is more business education beyond the BA degree. In other words, a business degree at the graduate level. That is, a Master of Business Administration or an MBA.

Empirical studies have shown that an MBA degree adds considerably to the expected lifetime income of the happy student who receives it. For this reason, potential Greedy Bastards flock to our nation's graduate business schools in hopes of enjoying the salary bump that the MBA brings to their financial welfare.

I should emphasize that one does not enroll in an MBA program for the purpose of learning anything beyond what one could absorb from reading the *Wall Street Journal* or the Business Section of the *New York Times*. Certainly, one does not aspire to gaining, say, a working knowledge of Accounting, an understanding of Statistics, or a command of sophisticated Marketing-Research techniques. One knows that – in any corporate job worthy of the name – one would simply delegate all such responsibilities to unfortunate nerd-like underlings who have not been blessed with an MBA degree. So there's just no point in learning this useless stuff. Rather, one attends a graduate school of business primarily for the privilege of networking with other like-minded Greedy Bastards.

Foremost among our country's schools of business, we find the Harvard Business School – pioneer of the famous Case Method wherein HBS students study "real-world" business situations for the insights that they provide into how best to manage a company. By the time they graduate, HBS students have tackled over 500 such case examples and are thus qualified to deal with at least 500 possible "real-world" situations, should they happen to encounter one of these on the job. This case-oriented approach (supplemented by various other kinds of "immersion experiences" in the field) frees HBS from the need to preach any sort of pie-in-the-sky ivory-tower overly theoretical concepts and liberates the school from all temptations to bother itself with anything smacking of impractical intellectualism.

Thus, HBS professors spend most of their time writing cases and seldom engage in meaninglessly theoretical research of the type that one might find at less-enlightened schools. HBS administrators ensure the maximum efficiency of its job-recruiting process. HBS students industriously occupy themselves with their responsibilities for memorizing the intricate details of carefully prepared cases while avoiding any temptation to look for underlying concepts or theoretical principles of the sort that, as HBS teaches, lack managerial relevance or on-the-job applicability.

For all these reasons, the Harvard Business School has achieved a ranking at the top of America's graduate schools of business that is unexcelled in its well-earned reputation for anti-intellectualism in the service of self-interest. This place in the rankings, with Harvard at the top and everybody else struggling to catch up, plays a crucial role in the School's success in recruiting the greediest of students and placing them in the most bastardly of jobs. Such rankings appear each year in publications like *Business Week* and *US News & World Report*. School administrators wait eagerly for the results and cringe when their own schools fare less well than they think they deserve. Of course, every school thinks that it should appear in the top five. One of my old deans used to joke that our own institution was one of the 20 schools in the top ten. Wishful thinking, perhaps, because – for many years – our school did not do as well as it probably deserved . . . on paper.

Specifically, if you took the various indicators used to compute rankings for the various schools, our school looked as if it should do quite well. But, year after year, it ranked lower in the *Business Week* polls than it appeared to merit. After careful study, I demonstrated empirically that this poor showing in the *BW* polls resulted from a phenomenon that I labeled "ingratitude." Specifically if inexplicably, our students took delight in giving our school poor ratings in the *BW* survey of student satisfaction. One might think that undeniably intelligent and commendably greedy students would hesitate before shooting themselves in the foot by giving their own school poor evaluations in ways that would drag down its reputation in the polls that job recruiters consult to figure out whether or not they went to a good school. But, apparently, our students were not quite smart and selfish enough to figure this out. Also, coming mostly from large cities on the East Coast, it may be that they displayed some sort of in-bred, culture-entrenched, and therefore uncontrollable degree of cynicism, petulance, animosity, and . . . ingratitude.

In teaching the crop of MBA students at our school, I came to comprehend the fundamental nature of the GB Ethos as it emerges in the MBA classroom. At bottom, the MBA Mind views classes or coursework as an unwelcome distraction from its main preoccupation with networking among fellow MBA students. After all, the main reason for attending an MBA program is to make friends with like-minded Greedy Bastards who can aid one's career at some point down the road. Recognizing this, my school groups class members into clusters of 60 or so students who take all their required core courses together. This ensures that people who otherwise might never make any sort of friends are practically compelled to form friendships with the 59 other cluster members who attend their 10 required classes in the core curriculum. By the end of two years – after sitting next to the same person in ten classes for an hour-and-a-half, twice a week, for 12 weeks – this $10 \times 1.5 \times 2 \times 12 = 360$-hour barrage of face-to-face contact almost guarantees that mere exposure will encourage the formation of friendships that will prove lucrative going forward. Or so goes the hope – bravely flying in the face of the old adage that familiarity breeds contempt.

I have seen this friendliness phenomenon at work in ways that I find truly inspiring. Classroom neighbors will happily copy each other's answers to homework problems. During class, a bored student will generously share the pleasures of surfing the Web with the occupant of a nearby seat. After the session, small cliques will gather spontaneously to discuss with delight the many inadequacies of the professor, all the more if the professor has foolishly attempted to teach them anything that they perceive as "too theoretical."

Beyond doubt, the most effective way to win the hearts of such students is to teach them something truly practical that they can use on day one of their first job. The promise of an immediate payback elevates the appeal of any reading, lecture, exercise, or case – all the more if the teacher can somehow convey that his small group of 60 cluster buddies are the only ones out there who will enjoy the advantage thus conveyed.

Occasionally, I used to ponder the expediency of offering my MBA students advice that really would prove undeniably useful to them – such as, say, a mini-course in basic manners, help on grammar mistakes to avoid, or coaching in how to hide their greed behind a veil of pretenses that falsely implied a caring for others. Specifically, I considered adding to my curriculum such items as the following:

- *Interviewing Skills.* Practice a handshake that is neither too firm nor too limp. Do not grab the other participant's fingers with yours. No sweaty palms, please.
- *Classroom Participation.* Do not sit in the first row during class while simultaneously text-messaging on your iPhone, surfing the Web on your iPad, or auditioning the MP3 files on your iPod. If you plan to participate in such time-honored classroom activities, slink to the rear of the room and lurk in the back row. But be sure not to cry out in glee when executing an especially fortuitous deal on E*Trade.
- *Basic Grammar.* Try not to begin a sentence with "Me and my friend." Also try not to say "Between you and I." Of course, both these phrases sound great to you and to all those with whom you hang, but an overly zealous stickler might point out that, technically, they are not quite as correct as you might think. Also, please avoid using "data" as a single rather

than plural noun. And try not to deploy a verb as a noun; rather, please practice "the resist." Above all, do not refer to a consumer's expenditures for your product offering as "the spend."

- *Simple Etiquette*. Unless invited, do not call a professor old enough to be your grandfather by his first name, as in "Yo, Morris . . . ." Remember that "Professor Morris" is especially awkward in this respect.
- *Common Decency*. Do not stand at one end of the lobby and shout to your buddy at the other end in a declamation that includes liberal usage of words such as "Fuck" and "Shit."
- *Tricky Maneuvers*. Try to resist the temptation to slither like a snake through a door that is closing rather than holding it open for the person behind you – especially if that person is a professor carrying a heavy box full of teaching materials on his way to class.
- *Cell Phones*. Do not come to your professor's office hours if you plan to receive more than, say, five or six cell-phone calls during your visit.

But, ultimately, I realized that self-respecting MBA candidates would take offense at any implication that they were not already perfect or that the whole point of bringing them into the classroom was anything other than allowing them a chance to display their already-perfect wisdom to each other in a fully public forum.

One aspect of this perfect wisdom manifests itself when a classroom full of Greedy Bastards fills out course evaluations at the end of the term. This exercise gives every student the welcome opportunity to register anonymous complaints about his or her teacher and to punish the offending individual by giving low ratings on the various evaluation scales. To make this expression of student dissatisfaction even more interesting, the teacher has no idea which student(s) assigned which rating(s). Did the smartest guy or gal in the class think you were terrific, while the dumbest thought you were terrible? Or was it the other way around? Because you have no idea which is which, you have little incentive to make changes in your teaching style in response to this anonymous advice – which, by virtue of its anonymity, is all the more vitriolic. (As an analogous strategy, I once proposed that students receive their grades in a manner that did not report which grade came from which course, but this proposal did not gain much traction among those empowered to vote for it.)

In an example of the course evaluations in action, my favorite student comment of all time came from a dissatisfied MBA candidate who complained about the fact that I had prepared a schedule of topics and assignments so that my syllabus gave some indication of having been planned in advance, leaving no room to make changes in response to her own helpful inputs. Specifically (paraphrasing, but with a fair degree of accuracy), she said, "I knew I would hate this class from day one when I looked at the course outline, saw that the topics and readings had already been selected, and realized that there would be no opportunity for me to shape the material in accord with my own needs and wants." Though probably written by a woman (to judge from the handwriting), this sort of comment epitomizes an attitude worthy of every

MBA candidate. That female GB tells it like it is. What self-confidence! What chutzpah! One day, she will make some fortunate male GB a wonderful wife. But heaven help him if he makes plans – say, a reservation for dinner at a restaurant – without first consulting her.

Impression Management – Dre$$ for $ucce$$

We all know that clothes make the (wo)man. And in your case – Dear Reader – as a typical upwardly mobile Greedy Bastard, clutching a newly minted MBA diploma, clothes may represent pretty much the sum total of what you have to offer. So you should make damn sure that your style of dress gets the job done. As they say, you never get a second chance to make a first impression. In your case, that first impression had better imply that you possess estimable qualities that, in truth, you totally lack. (Here, I'll focus primarily on the case of male GBs, emphasizing that analogous arguments apply to female members of the species.)

Given the urgent importance of effective impression management, sagacious Greedy Bastards understand that their sartorial choices constitute one arena of competition in which their customary stinginess must take a back seat to their need to shine. In short, if you want to win the game of Dre$$ing for $ucce$$, you had better open your high-priced and well-stocked wallet and spend lavishly on threads that will command attention and respect from all who observe them – the folks conducting the job interview, your boss, your co-workers, your clients, and even members of your own family (who need to respect you in order to obey you without question in the manner that you so richly deserve).

This means that you should compute whatever figure you might normally want to spend on, say, an overcoat and then quadruple it. Happy with a Madison Golden Fleece® suit off the rack at Brooks Brothers for $395? Multiply that by six and head to Giorgio Armani for a little nicer outfit at around $2,395. Accustomed to forking over $990 for a pair of Gucci loafers? Lose that idea and try out the $1,390 Ferragamo wing tips that feel so soft you barely know you've got them on. And don't forget the $295 Zegna necktie, the $326 Dunhill belt, and the Oxford dress shirt from Ralph Lauren for $390.

Then realize that you can't just have one of each of these items. Rather, you need a different one for each day of the week – or, better yet, each day of the month. These will hang in the spacious walk-in closet that you'll need to add to your master bedroom – even if it means sacrificing what would otherwise have been one of the kids' rooms. (Adjust your family-size plans accordingly.)

But don't stop there. Realize that semi-formal attire only meets your needs for the Monday-to-Friday eight-to-midnight portion of your work week. For the weekends – company picnics, golf games at the club, cocktails on the executive yacht – you'll need a full array of informal and sports clothes. If possible – because more people, including managers' spouses, will see you – your casual dress should be even more extravagantly elegant than what you normally wear in the workplace. Probably somebody makes a $1,200 pair of running shoes, and you should make sure that you find and buy them. Think cashmere. Think silk. Think platinum. Think alligator. Think shark-skin. Think ivory. (Sure, some of these are illegal due to endangered-species restrictions, but you don't care.) Don't stop until you know for certain that the wife of every one of your business associates will compare him to you, find him wanting, and file you away in the back of her mind as someone on the rise. Maybe you'll even get a chance to cash in on that later in some intimate bedroom-eyes sort of way – one of the many perks of being a self-celebrating Greedy Bastard. Just make sure that she too is a Greedy Bastard with enough brains to keep her big fat GB mouth shut.

Understand that the aforementioned sartorial choices represent only one small facet of your dedicated commitment to effective impression management, a concept that extends way beyond mere clothing. Indeed, as anticipated so brilliantly by Thorstein Veblen (1899) in his book *The Theory of the Leisure Class*, you should regard everything you wear or carry or use and, beyond that, everything you own as an aspect of your ceaseless quest to gain social status by impressing others with the most exhibitionistic types of conspicuous consumption.

Let's start with your body. Plan to work on it at the gym for at least 20 hours per week, no fewer than half of which you should spend networking in the sauna or steam room. Be sure that this gym reeks of prestige, with an annual membership fee of no less than 12,000 dollars. Keep in mind that this membership fee means a lot more than the actual shape of your torso itself (which, as we shall see later, you may have reason to push in the direction of corpulence). And be sure that you adorn yourself from head to toe with the finest of Rolex watches, the most elegant of Montecristi hats, and the most fragrant of Clive Christian colognes. Plus the $660 plaid scarf from Burberry, the $365 deerskin gloves from Bergdorf Goodman, the $180 snakeskin wallet from Aspinal of London, and the $1,895 Ghurka briefcase.

But there's more. When you drink, insist on The Macallan 25-year Highland at $2,600 per liter or, if possible, an even more esoteric and costly single-malt Scotch. Dine only at, say, Per Se. And, when you do, go ahead and order the 1990 Krug "Clos du Mesnil" at $2,678 for the table. Ride home in your chauffeur-driven Bentley Continental GT ($229,558). Or perhaps you'd prefer a sportier Aston Martin Roadster ($453,936). Live lavishly in the most upper-crust bedroom community you can find (Scarsdale, Darien, Menlo Park, Wilmette, the Main Line, . . .). Send your kids to Groton so that – like you – they can get accepted at Princeton, Brown, or Williams. Summer in the Hamptons or on the Cape. Winter in Sun Valley or Vail. Recreate at the MOMA, the Metropolitan Opera, David Geffen Hall, and Yankee Stadium in the box seats right behind home plate at $5,000 a pop. Be among the first to procure first-row tickets to see Taylor Swift at a mere $64,388 or so.

Remember, too, that even the most seemingly inconsequential detail of your personal and household consumption habits may carry important implications for your social standing. Take, for example, the family pet. If you must own a cat, make sure it's a Bengal. But, far better, get a much more visible high-priced dog. Forget the idea of owning a lowly Cocker Spaniel or a humble Golden Retriever. Rather, when you walk your pooch, you want to create an impressive display that will convince every observant neighbor of your superior status. Insist on one of those elegant designer breeds that bespeak your refinement and taste – perhaps a Cockapoo or a Labradoodle. Wait eagerly for the day when some enterprising breeder mates a Pekingese with a Poodle and you can buy a Peekapoo. Or better yet, following the eventual conjugal coupling of a Bull Dog and a Shih Tzu, ...

Take Some Tips From Travel Services

To maximize the speed of your progress on the Greedy Bastard's path to business success, whenever possible, drag yourself to the nearest airport and take a trip on a plane. True, you will endure many hours of miserable discomfort mixed with apprehension on the brink of terror. These afflictions have escalated at an astonishingly rapid rate over the past couple of decades.

On an airline, the conventional rules of civility and sociability are suspended and replaced by planespeak and aerologic. From the moment you enter the airport, you are treated like an alien enemy. You wait in an endless succession of slow-moving lines (checking in at the ticket counter, passing through the security station, boarding the plane, waiting on the runway for take-off, leaving the plane, looking for your luggage in the baggage-claim area, joining the three-mile queue at the taxi stand). You hear dire warnings (proper procedures in the event that the air supply is cut off and you need to breathe through a tube or what to do if the aircraft drops into the sea and you must escape through one of the window exits conveniently located toward the front and rear of the plane). You experience inexplicable discomforts (plunged into darkness and forced to read with the help of a dim light pointed somewhere other than the book in your lap). You resist countless intrusive temptations to spend money (the gift catalog that clutters up the pouch on the back of the seat in front of you or the menu of all-too-expensive sandwiches that you can buy at exorbitant prices if you feel in danger of starving). You fight for your right to exit the plane (when hundreds of formerly comatose bodies spring to life and fill the aisles while shrieking amplified voices proclaim the dire consequences that will occur if people do not remain comfortably seated until the aircraft has reached a complete stop at the passenger terminal and the captain has extinguished the seat-belt sign). Amid these grim pronouncements of aerologic and these irritating eruptions of planespeak, you thank your lucky stars if you manage to escape from the flying engine of death in which you have taken this soul-wrenching trip (somewhere between a roller-coaster ride and a concentration camp). And you pray for enough stamina and fortitude to retrieve your luggage and to find a cab at the taxi stand (for an automotive ride that, according to well-publicized statistics, is even more dangerous than the one on the plane that you have just barely survived).

So, in sum, flying on an airplane may be one of the most unpleasant of common and ordinary consumption experiences. Nonetheless, I find two reasons why self-subjection to the dreaded dangers and drastic discomforts of air travel may reward Greedy Bastards with helpful insights that will prove useful toward advancing their careers in the business world.

First, a visit to the airport bookshop will present an enormous array of managerial self-help books written by any number of financial wizards, marketing geniuses, and other business gurus who, for a few bucks, will gladly dispense actionable advice that will enhance your business acumen while expanding your hands-on opportunities and shaping your on-the-job experience. The present guide pales in comparison with the many invaluable-not-to-mention-inspirational repositories of wisdom that will grease your path toward higher earnings and promote your ascension on the professional ladder. These tutorials provide the wind beneath your wings. Twice as cheap at half the price, they carry such provocative titles as:

- *The Experience! How to Wow Your Customers and Create a Passionate Workplace* (Arussy, 2002)
- *Clued In: How to Keep Customers Coming Back Again and Again* (Carbone, 2004)
- *The Experience Economy: Work Is Theatre & Every Business a Stage* (Pine and Gilmore, 1999)
- *The Trend Commandments™: Turning Cultural Fluency into Marketing Opportunity* (Samuel, 2003)
- *Chocolates on the Pillow Aren't Enough: Reinventing the Customer Experience* (Tisch and Weber, 2007)

My point is that, after procuring one of these repositories of business advice at the airport bookshop, you will find yourself with plenty of time – while waiting endlessly at the gate and then sitting for a couple of hours on the tarmac behind 30 or so other planes ahead of yours in line for take-off – to read one or two of these invaluable sources of business wisdom. After the much-delayed and insufferably lengthy trip to your final destination – during which you will have skipped the invariably inane child-oriented G-rated film that you could have watched if only your seat had had a functioning TV screen and your earphones had worked properly – you will have acquired much invaluable expert knowledge on how to conquer the challenges of the business environment so as to prosper as a Greedy Bastard in today's remunerative marketplace.

But – second, as if the benefits just described were not enough to motivate your next flying experience – travel by airplane also affords the aspiring Greedy Bastard a unique opportunity to observe the marketing strategy practiced by members of an industry that remains unexcelled in its ability to take merciless advantage of every customer who crosses its path, surely an opportunity for close-up hands-on inspection of business acumen that we should consider worth several times its price of admission. Here, the most basic lesson to be learned and marveled at with wonder is as follows: *Screw the customers in general and, wherever possible, charge them outrageous fees for services that they would normally expect to receive free of charge.*

In the case of the airlines, such strategies for capitalizing on the imprisoned status of the customer-as-captive-market would include:

- A $13.40 tax for landing at an airport in the USA
- A $100 fee for checking a bag through to the final destination
- An extra $200 fee for checking an additional bag
- A $6 charge for a beer bought on the plane (wholesale price = 35 cents)
- A $10 charge for a sandwich bought on the plane (wholesale price = $2.75, true value = 59 cents)
- A prohibition against bringing food or drinks through the security checkpoint, coupled with a $7 surcharge for any drinkable or edible item bought in the waiting area and carried onto the plane
- A $5 charge for renting headphones that don't work properly to watch a movie that sucks, that is aimed at the sophistication level of a seven-year-old, and that can't be seen clearly on your malfunctioning TV monitor
- A $29 extra fee for occupying a seat next to a window or on an aisle
- Variable prices for purchasing things from the gift catalog that clutters up every seat-back pocket, with those prices invariably set at three or four times the market value of the crappy merchandise contained therein
- Exorbitant captive-audience rates for rental cars at the airport terminals (Hertz, Avis, Alamo, Enterprise, Budget, and the rest)
- A hefty monetary penalty for returning one of these cars at a different airport (implying a missed flying opportunity)

These helpful tips for scamming the customer represent only a few of the zillion ways in which examples offered by the airlines can improve your business savvy and inspire your opportunistic marketing efforts. But – lest the lesson be lost on those Greedy Bastards too busy, tired, or otherwise preoccupied to extrapolate airline practices to implications for implementation at their own companies – let us end this section by offering a few potential applications to your own organization:

- Charge every client a $40 parking fee collected at the gate of your firm's parking lot
- Collect a chair-rental fee of $10 for each seat in the waiting room, with a surcharge of $3 for each additional hour of waiting (because, after all, they don't call it a "waiting" room for nothing and you need to capitalize on that)
- Install a coin-operated toll system at each elevator with graduated rates of $5 up-front plus $1 per floor so that riders to, say, the 23rd floor will pay $5.00 + $23.00 = $28.00 in pocket change to take the lift

- For those unwilling to pay, provide fire stairs for a fixed charge of just $10 – setting the elevator-versus-stairs breakeven fee at $10 for five floors – but increase this levy to $25 in case of an actual fire
- Put a credit-card scanner on the lock of every men's and ladies' room ($5.00 charge), with additional devices on every stall ($3.00), urinal ($2.00), and washbasin ($1.00)
- Charge a nickel for every paper hand towel and a dime for every squirt of liquid soap
- On every floor install Purell dispensers that read fingerprints and automatically debit the client's bank account 25 cents for every dollop of sanitizer (making sure that your place of business is filthy enough to guarantee a robust demand for such hand cleansers)

Of course, these sorts of suggestions touch only on the fringe activities of your company. Obviously, in themselves, these ancillary sources of revenue embody a gratifying level of pure profit potential. But, far more importantly, scrutinize the fee structure for all the core services or manufactured goods that you offer. Multiply each of these by three and reprint your offer sheet or catalog accordingly. In the case of a captive market truly dependent on a necessary offering (say, a dialysis machine or a life-saving drug), multiply by six or seven (or more if you are smart enough to do mathematics with such big numbers). Do this ASAP. You'll be glad you did. And you can thank me later.

Forget Ethics

As any self-respecting Greedy Bastard will immediately realize, ethical issues can erect unwelcome but nonetheless formidable roadblocks on the path to business success. Many an otherwise admirable business plan has gone off the tracks because some overly scrupulous manager has paused to entertain doubts based on moral or religious concerns. Too often, businesspeople sacrifice enticingly remunerative outcomes due to silly preoccupations with needlessly cumbersome questions of justice, social welfare, or the common good. Obviously, aspiring Greedy Bastards must resist any such weakness or frailty. Their tough moral fiber must ensure their ability to withstand any foolish or overly romantic impetus toward caring about unproductive aspects of virtue, goodness, or character. In short, every Greedy Bastard needs an ethical code by which he or she can fruitfully live while relentlessly pursuing his or her immutable goals of career advancement and material wealth.

Many otherwise well-intentioned philosophers have unsuccessfully tried to formulate such an all-purpose Code of Ethics suitable for guiding our behavior in the modern world. But, through no fault of their own, earnest thinkers such as, say, Socrates, Plato, Aristotle, Epicurus, Descartes, Hobbes, Locke, Spinoza, Bentham, Mill, Russell, and Colbert have proven inadequate to the task. Foremost among these failures, Immanuel Kant proposed a Categorical Imperative that deserves brief consideration due to its seductive tendency to lead us to stray from the righteous path of bastardly greed.

Specifically, Kant's Categorical Imperative requires that we *act in such a way that we would want the principle that guides our action to be the guiding principle for all actions by all people.* Or something like that. Obviously, this maxim bears a strong resemblance to what Christians refer to as the Golden Rule: *Do unto others as you would have others do unto you.* Various commentators – including Kant himself – have endeavored to "splain" this Categorical Imperative by translating it into other terms that they regard as more or less synonymous with its implications. One example proposes: *Always treat every other person as an end and never as a means.* But this interpretation makes it abundantly clear that, obviously, Kant got it wrong. Way wrong.

Indeed, from the inherently righteous perspective of the Greedy Bastard, Kant actually got it backward. The Kantian philosophy of ethics runs in exactly the opposite direction from everything that the Greedy Bastard holds sacred. Specifically, the Greedy Bastard subscribes to a diametrically opposed maxim: *Always treat every other person as a means to your own selfish and egocentric ends.* As a direct corollary, the fundamental proposition that *greed is good* puts its emphasis on a principle that every self-centered, egomaniacal, and quintessentially greedy bastard will applaud – namely, *look out for number one* (yourself); *ignore any fallout that potentially damages others* (sometimes referred to as "externalities"); or – better yet – *treat others as the means to your own self-interested ends* (such that the ends justify the means). Thus, as a Rule of Thumb, when a person says that he feels "used," we infer that he has probably engaged in a transaction that has benefited some commendably Greedy Bastard.

Clearly, this GB Imperative provides a ringing endorsement for the many otherwise problematic things that a Greedy Bastard must do to get ahead in the world of business. For example, on their climbs to the top, Greedy Bastards must step rather heavily on a great number of less fortunate souls who do not rise upward with a comparably unscrupulous degree of unremorseful celerity. Someone – Walter Winchell? Wilson Mizner? Jimmy Durante? Yogi Berra? – has unwisely said, "Be nice to people on the way up because you'll pass them again on the way down." But the foolish folks who say that sort of thing do not sufficiently appreciate that the truly successful Greedy Bastard never does "come down." As high as one might climb on the corporate ladder, there always remain more people to step on so as to climb even higher – all the way to becoming the President, the Pope, the Monarch, the Network News Tycoon, or Donald Trump. Never fear: The GB Imperative serves as an infallible guide to power, to wealth, and therefore to happiness.

It might prove propaedeutic to offer an example of the GB Imperative in action as it has influenced thinking at one of our top business schools. In this connection, when I first arrived as an MBA candidate at a major Graduate School of Business in 1965, I noticed a message engraved on the outside wall slightly to the left of the front entrance. It was a quote from the illustrious American philosopher Alfred North Whitehead: "A great society is a society in which its men of business think greatly of their functions." Clearly, with that slogan, ANW would not win many fans among the feminists. But to me at the time, in my pre-GB days, this quotation symbolized the ethos of an upward-aspiring business community aimed at providing benefits to society at large in ways that would make the world a better place. Indeed, something like that sort of socially responsible impetus seemed to characterize the episteme of the Graduate Business School back in those halcyon pre-GB days. True, we had the Vietnam War to worry about – plus a few other noticeable manifestations of what Ike Eisenhower had famously called the "military-industrial complex" – not to mention cars that were unsafe at any speed, poor who paid more, and a glamorous cover girl for Ivory Snow who doubled as a porn star in movies like *Behind the Green Door* and who later served as a two-time candidate for vice-president of the USA. But, basically, the business-school community had its heart in what it mistakenly believed was the right place.

Little did the administration, faculty, and students at the Graduate Business School realize, back then, how tectonically the terrain must shift to drag this particular academic community – kicking and screaming – into the light of a new millennium. The change toward a firm embrace of the GB Imperative emerged slowly, over a period of 50 years, in a series of sometimes painful quakes and tremors. Successive deans deemphasized the role of scholarly research (pie-in-the-sky thinking or ivory-tower irrelevance), upgraded the importance of executive education (teaching Greedy Bastards to embrace the GB Imperative even more enthusiastically), rededicated the School to pursuing a Business Model (aimed at the maximization of revenues through the delivery of maximal customer satisfaction), and orchestrated a revised curriculum that catered or indeed pandered to the whims of the School's essential customers (the students who sought their MBAs primarily as a pathway to networking with other like-minded GBs *en route* to career advancement in the direction of ratcheting up their already elevated incomes).

Because serving corporate recruiters in ways that bolstered student careers became the School's number-one priority, the old entranceway fell to the wrecking ball in order to erect bigger and better job-interview rooms. Of course, the now-obsolete (male chauvinist) or even offensive (non-GB) quotation from A. N. Whitehead disappeared, along with the outside wall that had once enshrined his anachronistic words of wisdom. Ultimately, just before I retired in 2009, I entered the building one day and found – emblazoned across the front vestibule – a huge banner, probably 20 feet in length, that proclaimed the essence of the School's newly adopted Honor Code: *I will not lie, cheat, steal, or tolerate those who do.*

What a perfect encapsulation of what I have called the GB Imperative!!! If we follow other philosophical commentators by interpreting this motto to surface its true underlying meaning, I believe it reduces to: *Do whatever you want as long as it's legal or you don't get caught.* Hence, compared with the aspirations of A. N. Whitehead, it symbolizes an appropriate lowering of the ethical bar to the most downward possible level, where it so clearly belongs. Gone are any foolish concerns about the welfare of society. Vanished are all those silly preoccupations with benefits to one's fellow humans. Just don't break the law. Or – if you do – get the job done in a way that is not noticed and is therefore tolerated by others.

It happened that, on the day I first encountered this tribute to the GB Imperative in the front hall of my own beloved Alma Mater, the School's Dean was standing in the lobby, right below the sign in question. I eagerly approached him and enthusiastically congratulated him on having erected a signal that eloquently proclaimed the School's embrace of an ethical code aspiring to the lowest possible level of morality and virtue. In response, he expressed some personal doubts about the adequacy of this particular representation of the GB Ethos but assured me that the sign would remain in place for the duration of the academic year because, as the all-important criterion, this was what the students wanted. The students, of course, were justifiably proud of having hit the proverbial nail on the head with their new Honor Code. To repeat, the ethical message is so simple and powerful that any aspiring Greedy Bastard can master it with ease: *Don't lie, cheat, or steal; or, if you do, don't get caught.*

The Greedy Bastard Award for Borderline-Legal Corruption

The present section follows up on the educational and ethical issues raised thus far by honoring the spirit of those who inhabit the veritable home – the Temple, the Shrine, the Mecca – for the quintessential Ethos of Greedy Bastards in the world today. I refer, of course, to the Harvard Business School and its tireless advocacy of the Case Method as a route to enlightened business education in general and academic advances in the service of greed in particular. No self-help guide aimed at Greedy Bastards could claim completeness without at least one case history designed to illustrate the potential opportunities enjoyed by adherents to the GB Philosophy. In that spirit, I offer the Greedy Bastard Award for Borderline-Legal Corruption – the GBABLC – to recognize the achievements of a firm that has excelled in pursuing the GB Imperative explained in the previous section on ethics – namely, *I shall not lie, cheat, steal, or tolerate those who do.* Or, in other words, *I shall pursue my own greedy self-interest up to the point of my ability to get away with it under the law.*

In bestowing the prestigious Greedy Bastard Award for Borderline-Legal Corruption, I have searched high and low among truly exemplary cases from which to choose. Few will find it surprising that the GBABLC goes to Verizon in general and to that company's long-distance telephone service in particular. The details of the Verizon Case – the specific achievement for which the firm receives its honors in the present report – pertain to its fees for long-distance calls and to the manner in which these were presented to potential customers when I enrolled in Verizon's long-distance service in October of 2010.

As of 10/20/2010, the price for the particular plan to which I subscribed – that is, the so-called "Talk Time^{sm} 30 Plan" – appeared both in a mail brochure and on the company's website as $6.50 per month for the first 30 minutes plus 10 cents for each additional minute. However, there was another deemphasized component of the fee structure – namely, a minimum charge of $9.99. As far as I am concerned, this is equivalent to a monthly fee of $9.99 for the first 64.9 minutes plus 10 cents for each additional minute. This amounts to a true fee that starts at $9.99/$6.50 = 153.69% of that claimed – a sleight-of-hand price inflation that will move Greedy Bastards to lick their chops in glee.

Foolishly and ungratefully, I went so far as to complain about this misleading fee structure to both the Federal Trade Commission (FTC Complaint #28163192) and the Federal Communications Commission (FCC Complaint #10-C00261421–1). The exact wording of my official complaint was as follows:

> Verizon offered me a monthly long-distance rate of $6.50 [for 30 minutes] plus 10 cents for each additional minute. However, they impose a "minimum monthly charge" of $9.99 – which means that the true rate is $9.99 for 64.9 minutes plus 10 cents for each additional minute. This manner of stating their rate for promotional purposes is clearly a form of deceptive advertising, misrepresentation, fraud, or whatever you want to call it. Their true rate is $9.99 for 64.9 minutes plus 10 cents for each additional minute (not the $6.50 for 30 minutes implied by their so-called "Talk Time 30 Plan"). I believe that Verizon should be required to charge the rate of $6.50 offered by their Talk-Time-30-Plan and that this should be the actual minimum rate charged. I also believe that this should apply to the millions of customers who may have been misled by Verizon's deceptive practices.

Of the two federal agencies, I received only a half-hearted response from the FTC (suggesting that they would file my complaint and make it available to other interested parties), but the FCC went so far as to contact Verizon and ask for an explanation. This request yielded a response from Verizon to the FCC on January 4, 2011, in which Verizon thanked the FCC for calling my complaint to their attention; reported that the company had contacted me to explain that the $9.99 in question represents "the minimum spend level charge"; promised that they had offered to switch me to a different plan but that I had declined; announced that they had closed the complaint as "resolved"; and urged the FCC to do the same.

Surely, we must admire Verizon's stubborn insistence that an actual minimum fee of $9.99 for 64.9 minutes is equivalent to an advertised fee of $6.50 for 30 minutes. Quite reasonably, the FCC was more than satisfied with this convincing explanation and contacted me on 01/05/2011 to report that the FCC had received a message from the company addressing my concerns; that the FCC was therefore closing my case; that, if not satisfied, I could convert my "informal" complaint to a "formal" complaint; but that, in that case, I would need to follow "certain procedural and evidentiary rules" and would be required to pay "a filing fee" (set at $200, according to www.fcc.gov).

Notice the brilliant way in which Verizon and the FCC have cooperated so as to turn this potential threat into an opportunity. Obviously, it's a win-win situation – the proverbial making of lemonade from lemons. Verizon gets to ignore anybody who objects to the misrepresentation of its fee structure, while the FCC gains a chance to collect a filing fee of $200 from anybody dumb enough to pursue the matter in a formal complaint. I am not quite that stupid. But – impressed though I was with the Verizon-FCC one-two punch – I did persist long enough to share the following thoughts with the FCC's Consumer Inquiries & Complaints Division on January 10, 2011:

A couple of days ago, I received a copy of the [letter] written by [Verizon] and sent to the FCC.

The circumlocutions in this letter concerning a "minimum spend charge" and a "shortfall charge" do not disguise the fact that the **real** rate is $9.99 (not $6.50 as claimed by the "Talktime 30 Plan"). There is no way to dispute the fact that the company has misrepresented its rate structure.

Equally frustrating, the agent who contacted me offered a more expensive plan (which, of course, I declined) and then asked if the matter had been "resolved." I very clearly indicated that the matter *has not* been "resolved" and *will not* be "resolved" until the company ceases and desists from this and other false advertising.

You might wonder why I am getting so hot and bothered about a $3.49 difference in the claimed-versus-actual rate. Note that this $3.49 difference applies for 12 months a year. That's $41.99. Then suppose that I keep the service for 5 years. That's $209.40. Then assume that the same misrepresentation applies to the phone accounts of (say) a hundred million customers. . . . That's 2.094 billion dollars. In other words, Verizon's deceptive practices amount to a very large amount of money gained via fraud and misrepresentation. . . . I believe that the FCC should do something about this.

Needless to say, the FCC did *nothing* about this, and I *never heard from them again*. It does happen that – as of April 1, 2013, April Fool's Day, on www.buyverizon.com/verizon-long-distance.aspx – Verizon now accurately listed its TalkTime 30 Plan at $9.99 per month, as follows:

VERIZON TalkTime 30
Your first 30 minutes of domestic direct-dialed long distance calls are covered for only $9.99/mo. Additional minutes cost only 10¢/min; intrastate minutes cost 12¢/min.[†]

One might infer that Verizon honored my foolish concerns, caved in to my silly demands, and took steps to correct the false impression conveyed by its misleading advertising (though please note that now you got only 30 minutes, instead of 64.9 minutes, for $9.99). However, the same website also featured a Verizon Timeless Bundle Plan[sm] for only $5.00 per month, as follows:

VERIZON TIMELESS BUNDLE PLAN[SM]
   Go classic with Verizon and pay just 10¢ a minute and $5.00 a month for this long distance plan.[†]

The company also listed a Verizon Five Cents Standalone Plan[sm] for only $6.00 per month as follows:

VERIZON FIVE CENTS STANDALONE PLAN [SM]
   Pay only $6.00 a month and 5¢ a minute for your long distance calls. Take advantage of this very popular long distance plan.[†]

Only when you pursue that little insignia – "†" – that appears right after "plan" and read the very tiny print at or below the bottom of your computer screen, do you learn that

   † The Verizon Five Cents Standalone Plan, Timeless Bundle Plan and Talk-Time30 plans have a monthly Minimum Spend Level (MSL) of $9.99/mo. The monthly fee contributes toward the MSL.

So Verizon had indeed found an inspired solution to any inconvenience that might have been imposed due to the FCC inquiry prompted by my letter. Verizon could truthfully tell the FCC or prospective customers that it had corrected the way that the company stated its fee structure for the Talk Time 30 Plan[sm]. Perhaps the FCC or prospective customers would not notice that the exact same inaccuracy that I had foolishly complained about now appeared in their claims for the Timeless Bundle Plan[sm] and the Five Cents Standalone Plan[sm]. In short, my impression is that – no matter how quickly the FCC might respond to relevant customer complaints – Verizon will move just a little bit faster to stay ahead of any potential impediments to its imaginative pricing strategies. We can only applaud such resourcefulness and creativity in the service of bilking the customer for every available dime.

Unintended Benefits One: Obesity

The growing prevalence and dominion of Greedy Bastards in the world today has brought with it several unintended consequences that happen to qualify as benefits – meaning, as far as typical Greedy Bastards are concerned, that any beneficial effects for others stem entirely from the accidental results of their otherwise selfish enterprises. This tendency for sheer greed inadvertently to produce societal good has attracted the attention of every smart thinker from Adam Smith (in praise of the invisible hand that steers self-interested free enterprise in the direction of economic prosperity) to Ayn Rand (in celebration of self-serving actions that contribute to the happiness of all). Teachings of the former have served as an intellectual foundation for the profit-oriented capitalist system of which we are all such enthusiastic members, while those of the latter have inspired the political agendas of congressmen and other leaders whose efforts have moved America and especially its right-wing Republicans in the direction of ever more righteous legislative and executive wisdom.

So it should surprise no one that – however inadvertently, haphazardly, or unintentionally – the activities of Greedy Bastards have enriched the world with blessings almost too numerous to encompass in such a short work as the present treatise. With regrets at omitting so many of these unintended benefits, in this and the following three sections I shall confine myself to describing four major focal points for the salubrious fallout – the fortuitous externalities, the advantageous third-party impacts, the salutary side effects – gained from bastardly greed: (1) Obesity, (2) Traffic, (3) Cell Phones, and (4) Dumbed-Down Popular Culture.

Let us begin, in the present section, with the most conspicuous outgrowth of the Greedy Bastard Ethos – namely, obesity. All observers agree that the America of this New Millennium has achieved an unprecedented level of adiposity in its population. Over two-thirds of our citizens are overweight, and over half of those are classified as obese (www.cdc.gov).

True, uninformed do-gooders have too often stood in the way of this ponderous progress. The Mayor of New York once tried to ban the sales of soda pop in larger-than-16-ounce cups – apparently not recognizing that a large thirst needs a 64-ounce Double Big Gulp with which to quench it and that the ability to quaff huge quantities of soft drinks without limit stands as a fundamental constitutional right, second only to that of carrying an AR-15. Busy-body administrators of school cafeterias – unconscionably insensitive to the gustatory cravings of their students – have tried to foist salads instead of pizzas, whole-wheat toast instead of cupcakes, and milk instead of Coke on the hungry children who crowd the lunch rooms and beg to be fed with junk food. Incompetent managers have carelessly and tragically pursued the closing of Hostess Brands and the removal of Twinkies from the supermarket shelves.

But such reactionary and recalcitrant radicals ignore the emerging evidence – both scientific and anecdotal – that obesity is a good thing that brings many desirable blessings. Studies have shown that overweight people live longer. If illness strikes, they have a larger reserve of blubber to carry them through difficult times. Also, fatter people are happier or even – according to a stereotype so entrenched that it must be true – downright jolly. They fill themselves full of delicious victuals. They avoid the pain of self-restraint and shun the discomfort of excessive exercise – which can prove tedious, uncomfortable, or even potentially dangerous if you happen to slide or to trip-and-fall on the slippery treadmill. Beyond that, as part of the economic system, fatsos consume far more than their share of expensive things to eat and drink, thereby helping to create employment for butchers, bakers, waiters, waitresses, short-order cooks, chefs, cashier operators, and especially garbage men. In short, the benefits of obesity to society are damn near incalculable. Those properly attuned to externalities or third-party effects must find themselves speechless with wonder and gratitude.

But we must pause to inquire about the root causes of obesity in today's USA. What irresistible force has promoted the apparently inexorable rise in the portliness of our populace? What spark has fueled the flames of fatness? What hidden impetus has driven the widespread increase in corporeal bulk? Whence stems the trend from thin to plump, from fit to fat, from lean to stout, from skinny to chubby, from slender to pudgy, from slim to paunchy, from trim to zaftig?

The answer, seldom if ever adequately recognized in the literature on this topic, is that credit for this salubrious shift in the shape of our society belongs to those brave individuals who, here as elsewhere, deserve nothing but praise for their thoughts and deeds – namely, Greedy Bastards. It might not appear obvious to the casual reader that Greedy Bastards deserve full credit for the nation's burgeoning level of obesity, but a little reflection should make the truth of this proposition apparent to every concerned citizen. And not necessarily for the mundane reasons that might immediately leap to mind.

I am, of course, aware that the GBs who run large food corporations spend zillions of dollars on R&D to develop offerings loaded with chemical additives that make them habit forming to the point of addiction. Eat one foul-tasting Pringle, and you can't resist finishing the whole canister (920 calories). Take one sip of sugar-infused Coca-Cola, and you'll want to finish the whole 34-ounce bottle (400 calories). Many people blame America's high-and-rising obesity level on this engineering of addictive junk food. But I don't believe a word of it.

Clearly, people do not grow fat merely because of a desire to eat more of the available chemically enhanced calorie-laden nutrient-deprived offerings. Rather, even after the money-hungry food manufacturers have worked their seductive magic, viands such as a Big Mac with Bacon, a Double Whopper with Cheese, a Taco Bell Burrito, a Krispy Kreme Cruller, a Dunkin' Donuts Frappe, or a Starbucks Cinnamon Dolce Latte are so fundamentally disgusting that no one would willingly eat them did they not efficiently contribute to a more worthy end-in-view. That end, put simply, is to become large – to grow in size, to swell in proportions, to occupy more territory – a concept that appeals with great force to the mindset of the typical Greedy Bastard.

In essence, Greedy Bastards view every aspect of life as a contest in which they struggle to gain more for themselves at the expense of others, who deserve and get less. The most familiar examples pertain to money and wealth, success on the job, club memberships, and sailboats. But the case relevant to obesity pertains to physical space. Like everything else on the Planet Earth, Greedy Bastards want more of it – more room for themselves, more degrees of freedom in which to navigate, more opportunity to stretch out, more area in which to circulate, more scope for spreading out their corporeal bulk. In short, the stampede toward obesity – reminiscent of the rush toward California two centuries ago (but without the gold) – is nothing more nor less than a real-estate grab. But, this time, it's not just the Native Americans who are at risk. Rather, in today's far-flung feeding frenzy, one grows fat as a means to the end of occupying more space at the expense of everybody else.

I should mention, in passing, that I think of yours truly – the greediest of bastards – as a fat person trapped in a thin person's body, longing to escape. As a child, I was quite overweight, to the point at which friends, relatives, and even parents would constantly berate the visible evidence of my ravenous eating habits. I weighed about 50 pounds more than I do now – a greater-than-33% difference. Indeed, consciously, I still crave cookies, cake, ice cream, and pie. But at the unconscious level – being a GB – I no doubt desire more space for myself so that others will have to move aside to make room for me when I enter a room or walk down the street or take over a bench on the subway.

Just take a look around you. We find Big Fat Greedy Bastards everywhere – filling the best seats in the movie theater, hogging the sidewalk, monopolizing the park bench, blocking the aisle at the supermarket. Observe the humongous individual riding on the subway with thighs so enormous that he cannot squeeze them together into a space that occupies less than the width of three seats – his and the ones on either side. Don't bother trying to sit next to him because he will give you a dirty look reminiscent of a mother bear defending her cubs. And, of course, he's a lot bigger than you are. Hey, he's a Big Fat Greedy Bastard with a shape to prove it, and he feels entitled to three times the normal allotment of acreage on a subway car, with zero left over for you and your companion.

If a cynic – according to Oscar Wilde – is someone who knows the price of everything and the value of nothing at all, being cynical, we might inquire what price society places on the fat person's quest to appropriate the real estate of others. The answer, of course, is that – because we basically approve of Greedy Bastards and wish them well in their self-interested endeavors – we attach a very low cost to the acquisition of terrain at the expense of everybody else. Thus, when you board an airplane, you can safely bet that the odds favor your sharing a large portion of your very expensive airline seat with an overweight Greedy Bastard who plops down next to you, raises the armrest, and intrudes onto your lap with his chubby elbow. Indeed, if you are stuck in the middle of a row, the laws of probability suggest a $2/3 \times 2/3 = 4/9$ or 44.4% likelihood that you will be hemmed in or, more accurately, smothered on both sides. The price to your two ponderous seat mates is zero; the cost to you is a miserable trip on a plane that is already a source of agony (as described in the earlier section on that theme). Your only defense, as an aspiring GB is: Don't get mad; get even. In other words, get equally fat yourself. The sooner, the better.

Admittedly, some airlines have toyed with the idea of charging overweight folks an additional tariff for the extra room they consume. But don't worry; these people couldn't care less. The pleasures of colonizing the space around them so far outweigh any potential monetary penalties that they remain insatiable. If you are what you eat, true to the GB Ethos, Greedy Bastards are fundamentally gastronomic territorial expansionists.

Meanwhile – at a more macroscopic level – because the American judicial system regards a corporation as more-or-less equivalent to a person, it makes sense to regard mergers and acquisitions (M&As) as one more example of the Greedy Bastard's tendency toward growing larger in size, in this case toward the end of taking up so much economic space as to become "too big to fail." Just as individual GBs enlarge themselves for the sake of occupying more physical space, the GB-inspired post-M&A corporation grows in size for the sake of claiming more of everyone else's tax dollars when the inevitable bailout becomes necessary. That said, I shall leave the elaboration of the manifest connections between GBs, obesity, and M&As as a homework exercise for the attentive reader.

Unintended Benefits Two: Traffic

As everyone knows, we live in a world that has grown far too fast-paced to prove conducive to the mental health of our citizens. This daily whirlwind of activity contributes malevolently to our elevated levels of psychologically and physically unhealthy stress. Experts advise that, to combat all this dangerous tension, one should moderate one's activation level by learning to stop and smell the roses. Clearly, no better place exists for purposes of stopping and smelling than the typical freeway at rush hour. Many of us spend at least two or three hours of our day paused in such immobile and odoriferous surroundings. For example, the Long Island Expressway at 6:00 pm has been described by knowledgeable participants as a "longitudinal parking lot." And, for this, we must thank our burgeoning population of Greedy Bastards, who deserve our traffic-related encomiums for two major reasons.

First, if you look around you on the crowded highway, you will discover that you are surrounded by hundreds if not thousands of massive semi-trailer trucks. If you peer inside these behemoths or simply read the signage on the vehicles' exteriors, you will see that they mostly pursue the task of hauling farm equipment, home appliances, potatoes, vegetables, fruit, chickens, livestock, and other food-related stuff from the farmer or manufacturer to the warehouse, retailer, or customer. In other words, they transport the provisions needed to guarantee the growth of every Greedy Bastard to his most gigantic possible girth (as described in the previous section). In this, they work tirelessly toward keeping the nation as portly as we might wish. Without the Greedy Bastard's quest for the greatest possible physical size so as to occupy the largest possible amount of real estate, supermarkets would not sell staggering amounts of junk food, consumers would not devour gargantuan helpings of Stouffer's Frozen Lasagna and Kraft Cool Whip, and the circumferences of waistlines would not expand toward their most voluminous possible proportions. So it boils down to ravenous eating by Greedy Bastards as the first main cause of our endlessly pleasing highway congestion. We can only marvel with gratitude over their contribution to stalled traffic.

Second, we must consider the vehicles driven by the Greedy Bastards themselves because these, too, reflect the GB's desire for a bigger footprint on American soil. Specifically and understandably, every Greedy Bastard wants to put his big fat ass behind the wheel of a big fat Sports Utility Vehicle (after sliding his seat far enough back to crush the legs of anyone so unfortunate as to be sitting in the rear). In this, the SUV – or, better yet, the pickup truck – becomes an extension of the Greedy Bastard's body in such a way that it occupies space on the roadway at the expense of smaller cars, vans, or station wagons. The relevant homology appears crystal clear:

SUV : Car :: Obese : Thin :: Greedy Bastard : Ordinary Loser.

In other words, the same impulse to occupy space at the expense of others that renders Greedy Bastards obese also motivates them to annex territory on the highway by crowding out those unfortunate and improvident drivers foolish enough to ride in a Mini-Cooper, a Volkswagen, or a Prius.

Speaking of the pointlessly abstemious Prius owner, it goes without saying that Greedy Bastards and their SUVs guzzle gas at a rate commensurate with the GB's consumption of all other heft-related products. This, of course, bestows incalculable benefits on the nation's economy and helps to ensure that the military-industrial complex, in its constant quest for access to oil, will continue to find reasons to promote warfare in the Middle East for decades to come.

The laudable capacity of the SUV to colonize the space around it does not cease at the end of the Greedy Bastard's motor trip. Instead, it represents the gift that keeps on giving when the Greedy Bastard parks his over-sized vehicle in a way that occupies two spaces at the suburban shopping mall or in a manner that takes up half a city block in the downtown metropolitan area. When it comes to parking, the rule of thumb for a Greedy Bastard is to make sure that his enormous SUV straddles at least one white line. I have even observed cases of double straddling where, through an inspired degree of diagonalization, three entire parking spaces have been rendered useless to others. Surely, this rates as a consummation devoutly to be wished.

No matter what make or model of SUV the Greedy Bastard chooses to drive, one facet of the vehicle's performance will remain constant from owner to owner – namely, the installation and activation of a stupendously loud alarm system that will set itself off every few hours, especially in the middle of the night, with relentless wailing, honking, and the flashing of lights so as to let everyone in the neighborhood know that a successful SUV-owning Greedy Bastard is in their midst. For those occasions when the Greedy Bastard is actually inside the SUV, the alarm makes less sense and is replaced by a loud beeping sound that fills the air whenever he puts the vehicle into reverse. Needless to say, the GB will derive considerable joy from backing down a narrow city street at 3:00 am in front of a large apartment building.

One must, of course, display extreme caution when driving anywhere near a Greedy Bastard in his SUV. If he is in front of you, prepare for him to straddle a line so as to occupy two lanes. If you are passing him, expect him to change lanes, sideswiping you without warning. If you are in front of him, count on merciless tailgating and a chorus of blows from his horn, followed by the screeching of tires as he veers around you.

And, if you are a pedestrian, remember that Greedy Bastards always know that they have the right of way. Do not carelessly assume that a stop sign, a red light, the walk signal, or a cross-walk has any meaning to a Greedy Bastard. As I recall, I once crossed West End Avenue at 79th Street in the cross-walk with the light and headed directly toward a sign that read "No Honking; Fine $200." Directly under the sign, a policeman stood and watched as a Greedy Bastard in his SUV careened around the corner and leaned on his horn to frighten me out of the pedestrian crossing at my earliest opportunity. Foolishly thinking of my own needs, I attracted the attention of the policeman and pointed to the sign directly above his head. Quite appropriately, *he* became angry with *me* and chewed me out for being an inconsiderate pedestrian. I count myself lucky that he did not give me a well-deserved ticket for blocking traffic or a citation for annoying an SUV-driving GB.

Unintended Benefits Three: Cell Phones

I am the only person I know who does not carry a cell phone. I carry no iPhone, no Palm Pilot, no BlackBerry, no Smart Phone. No Nokia, no Motorola, no Panasonic, no Apple. No AT&T, no Sprint, no Verizon, no T-Mobile. I can go wherever I want – into the subway, down the street, through the park, on a sailboat, in a canoe, to a restaurant, to a movie, to a square dance – knowing that my phone won't ring because I don't have one with me. To some extent, this gives me a bit of freedom. But that freedom comes with a cost almost too heavy to bear – especially when its weight is amplified by the intimidating gravitas of the cell-phone usage displayed by Greedy Bastards everywhere.

The number-one impulse that accounts for the larger-than-life behavior of Greedy Bastards in their consumption of cell phones bears a close resemblance to the eating habits responsible for their obesity and the driving-and-parking routines associated with their traffic-clogging motor vehicles. Specifically, they want more of something than others have at their disposal. And the "something" that they want to have more of than anybody else is, in this case, the airwaves.

Once upon a time, back in the old days when dinosaurs roamed the earth, the world was a pretty quiet place. Very few sounds filled the air beyond the occasional cries of a Tyrannosaurus Rex chasing a Protoceratops. Frankly, it was spooky enough to creep out even the most stalwart participant. Certainly not a place that you or I would want to inhabit. Just look at what happened to the dinosaurs.

But then, thank heavens, God put people on the planet. And people built motorcycles, boom-box radios, power lawnmowers, car alarms, and leaf blowers. Pretty soon, the planet became a reassuringly noisy place. Today, we find ourselves surrounded by a refreshingly obstreperous onslaught of cacophony. And contributing powerfully to that clamorous din – indeed, at the center of its sonorous impact where it fills every possible crevice of the airwaves with its ceaseless racket – we find the hubbub of cell-phone conversations between Greedy Bastards.

We see them all around us – obliviously parading down the street while talking, texting, or taking selfies and bumping into passing strangers. If you find yourself playing the role of such a pedestrian who has just been trampled by a careless Greedy Bastard wielding an iPhone, you had better say, "Excuse me" pronto because, as covered in the last couple of sections, he or she is way bigger than you are. This necessity for all Greedy Bastards to talk and text continuously on cell phones carries a deep meaning as a form of symbolic consumption. Specifically, it proclaims that they are more important than you are – so important that they must remain in touch with those who need them 24/7/365 (366 during leap years).

For this reason, our sonic surroundings are now completely saturated with the sounds of Greedy Bastards talking on their cell phones and clicking at their text-messaging keypads. If you want a spectacular example of this, try riding the Long Island Railroad on a late Friday afternoon headed from Pennsylvania Station to East Hampton. All the Wall Street financial wizards – that is, the most greedy of bastards – have climbed aboard, traveling to their weekend retreats. During such an experience, you will gain a true appreciation for what the Tower of Babel would sound like if everyone were speaking the same language (businessese or financespeak).

Another place to enjoy the cell-phone palaver of Greedy Bastards is an airplane. I once sat on the tarmac for two hours while my neighbor brayed into a cell phone held approximately two inches from my ear. At the end of this formidable intrusion into my own personal air space – when the plane finally moved toward taxiing for take-off – the cell-phone caller in the next seat said "Well, Goodbye" and, to my surprise, waved his hand in the air. Two rows ahead of us in the cabin, a hand shot up and waved back. The Greedy Bastard next to me had been talking for two hours with another Greedy Bastard less than ten feet away on the same plane.

Of course, the airborne cell phone lends itself to many other worthwhile uses – playing solitaire or cribbage or chess, watching teeny-tiny videos, listening to music via MP3 files so degraded in fidelity that they all pretty much sound the same, surfing the Web, looking up names and addresses, keeping one's appointment calendar, taking crappy-looking selfies, and so on. For many of these apps, Greedy Bastards wear earbuds, diverting them from fulfilling their righteous obligation to saturate the airwaves with their personal sounds. Just before take-off, announcements come over the PA system asking all the Greedy Bastards to comply with FAA requirements by turning off their cell phones and other devices. But they don't hear the announcements because they are listening to Lady Gaga or One Direction or Taylor Swift on their MP3 players. Or watching *Transformers* on their miniature video screens. Or talking to their bosses about their success in running the hedge funds that they manage. So, oblivious to FAA requirements of any kind, the Greedy Bastards continue to play with their cell phones throughout the flight. And, the minute the plane touches down, they call everyone they know – which is a lot of people because, hey, they are Really Important Greedy Bastards – to tell all these folks that they have landed safely and will be home soon, "home" being a euphemism for "the office."

Cell phones have grown so important to the lives of Greedy Bastards and, therefore, to the episteme of our society that their implications now permeate virtually every corner of entertainment and the arts. At the theater, many a plot twist turns on the implications of an adventitious cell-phone call. In movies, the hero and heroine keep in constant touch via cell-phone communications. In a TV sitcom, the cell phone rings at the drop of a hat to initiate the next awkward moment. And in a detective novel, the police trace the whereabouts of criminals by the use of cell-phone tracking devices. If you are a murderer or a bank robber on the run, it pays to use a "burner phone." One wonders what we ever did without cell phones. How did we get along in the world?

Beyond the cultural fallout just described, Greedy Bastards creatively orchestrate their own show-and-tell spectacles with the help of their cell-phone technologies. As a way of riveting the attention of others to themselves, they take photos with their cell phones and then show these photos to groups of people in such a way that the cell phone must be passed from hand to hand, taking up the maximum amount of everybody else's time with the minimum amount of pictorial payback. Never mind that these pictures – captured by a cheap plastic lens with the lowest possible resolution – depart dramatically from the antiquated photographic standards for clarity and vividness. Greedy Bastards love their cell-phone photos. So much so that this ranks as the number one reason why Kodak has stopped making real cameras. (At the time of this writing, a 60-second television commercial proclaims that, every day, more photographs are taken with iPhones than with any other camera. Take that, Nikon. Live with it, Pentax. Screw you, Leica. Significantly, the iPhone ad features shots of people in a restaurant taking pictures of their food to share with their friends. Apparently, Greedy Bastards love to see photos of what other Greedy Bastards are eating.)

Of course, in a manner typical of the Greedy Bastard's characteristic posture, less fortunate members of society must suffer because of all this – especially children and dogs. Children in baby strollers now have no one to talk to because the person pushing the carriage (often into the legs of other pedestrians) busily chats on a cell phone (holding the stroller in one hand and the phone in the other) and completely ignores the child (who will probably grow up with some sort of learning disability or cognitive impairment due to the resulting lapses in mental development).

But at least the neglected child can take a nap while being pushed around. Dogs have it far worse. Once accustomed to playing with their owners and enjoying the reassuring patter of human contact while walking around the neighborhood, the dog now leads a lonely life of smelling fire hydrants and peeing on lamp posts while its human companion uses the thumbs on both hands to work the text-messaging keypad. One can only guess what damaging effects on the psyches of dogs must result from this intrusion of cell phones into their once-happy lives.

The moral, of course, is that the cell phone provides one efficient tool to ensure the Greedy Bastards' (GBs') dominion over those around them – that is, all small and vulnerable two- and four-legged creatures, indeed everyone within earshot of the GBs' loud conversations. By monopolizing the airwaves, the Greedy Bastard whips all potential competitors into shape.

Unintended Benefits Four: Dumbed-Down Popular Culture

When appraising the current state of our media and popular culture, way too many critics and commentators have focused on such inherently meaningless criteria as intellectual content, educational value, artistic integrity, and aesthetic excellence. Clearly, such essentially elitist concerns emphasize aspects of art and entertainment that win little respect from the vast majority of audience members who, in general, favor cultural events that pander to the lowest common denominator of intelligence and taste. Ever so fortuitously for the psychic health of our society, we can thank Greedy Bastards for ensuring that we benefit as a nation from a popular culture that is as dumbed-down as we might wish.

The Greedy Bastards who run our media – television, radio, motion pictures, theaters, newspapers, books, recordings – know that profits depend on sales; that sales depend on catering to the largest possible audience; that the largest possible audience includes masses of people who are, as a statistical truism, below average in refinement and intelligence; and that the way to please those below-average tastes – in other words, the way to appeal to the Lowest Common Denominator – is to offer pure dumbed-down crap in place of anything remotely connected with artistic quality or aesthetic value. Thus, in the media just mentioned, we get: (1) *American Idol*, (2) Top-40

Programming, (3) *Dumb and Dumber*, (4) *The Lion King*, (5) *USA Today*, (6) *Secret Storm* by Amelia James, and (6) "Viva La Vida" by Coldplay.

Back in the day, tiny children used to drive their parents crazy by going to an unused and invariably out-of-tune piano and playing the chord changes to "Heart and Soul" – namely, C-Am-Dm-G, repeated over and over . . . ad nauseum. If we reverse the order of these chords – namely, Dm-G-C-Am – and transpose this progression down a third to A-Flat Major, we get "Viva La Vida" in the form of four chords – namely, Bbm-Eb-Ab-Fm, repeated . . . *ad nauseum in extremis* . . . for about 5:25 minutes (in the live version at YouTube.Com). We must applaud the blandness thus achieved by Coldplay. The Greedy Bastards who build gigantic media empires – folks who aspire to emulate people like, say, Rupert Murdoch – know that audience members shy away from thoughts too deep, emotions too complex, words too big, or music too challenging. Hence, the triumph of cultural populism. Hey, Baby, just chill and remember: "Hakuna Matata."

Indeed, beyond their role as media moguls and advocates for cultural populism, one cannot praise too much the pervasive impact that Greedy Bastards have exerted on the development and growth of popular culture in America today. Most obviously, GBs have appeared ubiquitously as heroes and heroines in movies, plays, and TV shows dedicated to glorifying their exploits. Recall, for example, the adventures of Gordon Gekko, played by Michael Douglas, who proclaimed that greed is good in the film *Wall Street*. Consider the machinations of brothers and sisters eager to collect their share of the family inheritance in Horton Foote's play entitled *Dividing the Estate*. Admire Larry Hagman's embodiment of self-interest as J. R. Ewing on the TV drama *Dallas*.

Wherever we look – screen, stage, Samsung – we encounter greedy folks going about their greedy lives with obsessively greedy concerns for their own fortunes and precious little regard for the welfare of others. In a hegemonic cultural world – where rich capitalists sponsor and control the very media that proclaim the sanctity of the profit-centered market-driven system on which they themselves thrive – we should expect no less. Fortunately, smart people – scholars like Frederich August Hayek or Milton Friedman, who have held distinguished professorships and have won Nobel Prizes – have justified the merits of this natural order by proclaiming the beneficence of free enterprise. And less smart but even more outspoken writers – say, Ayn Rand – have pressed the case for selfish individualism at great length, much to the delight of politicians such as Paul Ryan, Ron Paul, Rand Paul, and other masterminds of the Republican Right.

I could wax more and more enthusiastic about the innumerable ways in which our contemporary media devote their storylines and shape their characters to capture the sensibilities of Greedy Bastards. However, I wish to return to a theme raised earlier – namely, the demonstrable connection between bastardly greed and rampant obesity. As we have seen, Greedy

Bastards lead the race toward bigger and bigger bodies not as much because the food they eat is irresistibly delicious as because they seek, perhaps below the level of consciousness, to occupy more space on the Planet Earth, to grab some extra real estate for themselves, to enlarge their formidable footprints. (If you are overweight and are reading this and are not aware of any such motivations, please remember that I admit they may be unconscious.) From this, it follows that the huge audience of Greedy Bastards will respond with special enthusiasm and even reverence to stories and programs that feature fat folks.

Because of this link between Greedy Bastards and widespread obesity, our airwaves have exploded with TV shows about people of gigantic proportions. For example, one of the earliest television shows that I can recall – *The Honeymooners* – featured the adventures of an overweight bus driver (Ralph Cramden, played by the incomparable Jackie Gleason) and his slim-and-pretty wife (Alice, played by Audrey Meadows). Subsequent sitcoms have followed a similar formula – as in the case of *The King of Queens* with its chubby hero Doug Heffernan (Kevin James) and his skinny spouse Carrie (Leah Remini) or *According To Jim* with the paunchy Jim (Jim Belushi) and his gorgeous partner Cheryl (Courtney Thorne-Smith). Then there was *Roseanne*, with a husband played by John Goodman. More recently, two strikingly overweight actors – Billy Gardell as Officer Michael Biggs and Melissa McCarthy as Molly Flynn-Biggs – have struck award-winning pay dirt as the lovable couple on *Mike and Molly*. The trend should be clear.

But these examples pale in comparison with the ultimate obesity parade found on the hit program *The Biggest Loser*, which has been so success-ful that it has commanded two hours of weeknight primetime on NBC. To appeal with maximum force to its audience of Greedy Bastards, contestants on this reality show win prize money if they successfully lose their target weights and thereby avoid getting voted off the team. The climactic peak of excitement arrives when one or another massive 425-pound guy strips off all of his clothing except a little bikini swimsuit, reveals gigantic rolls of jiggling flab cascading down his torso, and steps upon an enormous scale, whose dial begins to spin as stirring music rises in the background. Just as his success or failure to achieve his targeted weight loss is about to be revealed, the show breaks for commercials, and we must wait for several minutes to reach the resolution of our suspense.

Obviously, this show has appealed with irresistible attraction to Big Fat Greedy Bastards. The brilliant marketing strategy behind its inspired pro-gramming appears to capitalize on the fact that BFGBs constitute proba-bly the largest subcultural market segment in our society. Larger than, say, innocent schoolchildren, horny adolescents, young married couples, His-panic adults, Black males, Jewish women, dedicated Democrats, or even bit-ter Republicans. In short, larger – in both numbers and suit sizes – than any other demographic or socioeconomic group you could define. Thus, the immensity of the chubby-and-selfish greedy-bastard market segment ensures strong audience ratings for a program such as *The Biggest Loser* or any of the many fat-flaunting TV sitcoms and has led to their resounding success.

The Greedy Bastard's Honor Roll of Civic Achievements

In addition to the major social benefits described in the last four sections, Greedy Bastards must take justifiable pride in various achievements for which they seldom receive the credit that they so richly deserve. Fully aware that they are too numerous to describe in their entirety, I shall settle for providing just a brief list of these accomplishments under the heading The Greedy Bastard's Honor Role of Civic Achievements. As usual with such communications, a series of bullet points promises to do the job nicely.

- *Pollution.* With enormous motor vehicles consuming humongous tanks of gasoline and belching forth massive clouds of black soot; with huge houses soaking up electricity for air-conditioning, fuel oil for immense furnaces, and natural gas for restaurant-sized ovens; with business interests that include the burning of coal to provide energy for manufacturing plentiful goods and providing multitudinous services that consumers want but do not need; and with no detectable concern for the ecological impact of all this, Greedy Bastards do far more than their share in contributing to the pollution of our environment.
- *Global Warming.* The ecological contributions just mentioned do much to ensure that the dangerous trend toward global warming will continue apace. Soon, the polar ice caps will have melted completely, and much of the East Coast will be under water. The Greedy Bastards who manage insurance companies have already laid plans to deny claims for flood damage, while those who run construction businesses look forward to rebuilding lost sea-level houses at higher elevations. Lucrative opportunities await GBs poised to construct Atlantic-Ocean beach-front condos in Vermont, Pennsylvania, West Virginia, Kentucky, and Tennessee.
- *Crime and Litter.* Much of the charm of the tourist attractions in our major metropolitan areas stems from their unique combination of crime and litter. Clearly, the two go together. As Malcolm Gladwell (2000) explains in *The Tipping Point*, the "broken window" phenomenon indicates that even something as seemingly innocent as a broken window, left unrepaired, can prompt a surge in litterbugs and felons. People see a cracked pane of glass, conclude that nobody cares, and surrender to the irresistible urge to snatch a purse or dump their trash. Obviously, Greedy Bastards contribute powerfully to this cause. By virtue of their unrestrained consumption, they generate far more disposable garbage than anyone else. And they carry around huge Coach briefcases and gigantic Louis Vuitton purses that beg to be snatched. Without their efforts, litter and crime might disappear completely.

- *The Proliferation of Firearms.* The trend toward increased crime and littering – so ably abetted by the efforts of Greedy Bastards – also calls forth an increase in our need to carry weapons. Hence, Greedy Bastards have moved to the forefront in demanding their inalienable constitutional right to bear arms. They have effectively fought all gun-control legislation, largely through their efforts in supporting such lobby groups as the National Rifle Association. Scandalously, contributions to the NRA are not tax deductible. (At least, not yet.) But, as conceded by Warren Buffett, Greedy Bastards generally avoid this problem by paying lower tax rates than their secretaries.

- *Inequitable Distribution of Income.* Speaking of income-tax rates, all available data indicate that Greedy Bastards collect far more than their fair share of income in the USA. Specifically, the income for the wealthiest 10% is about 12.63 times that for the lowest 10% (Census.Gov). Greedy Bastards gladly fulfill their duty to see that this inequitable distribution remains in place by taking such extreme measures as voting, first, for George W. Bush; later, for Mitt Romney or John McCain; and eventually, for Donald Trump. Fully responsive to the GB Ethos, such candidates favor reductions in funds aimed at propping up unjustified "entitlement" programs such as, say, Social Security or Medicare, with concomitant decreases in the unfair burdens of taxes levied against the super-rich.

- *Downsizing Companies and Exporting Jobs.* Such GB-friendly policies ensure – in the words of those old songs – that, as predicted by Whiting-Kahn-and-Egan in "Ain't We Got Fun," the rich become richer and the poor grow poorer or that, as explained by Billie Holiday in "God Bless the Child," people who have wealth will get more of it while those who don't will get less. This outcome follows from the Marxian Law of Increasing Poverty and echoes no less an authority than the *Holy Bible*: "For whosoever hath, to him shall be given, and he shall have more abundance: but whosoever hath not, from him shall be taken away even that he hath" (Matthew 13:12). Such hardships among the middle class reduce the demand for consumer goods and services. This leads to the downsizing of company payrolls. That prompts even less demand, losses of profits, and the shipping of jobs overseas (where one can pay some impoverished Asian worker a few cents a day to do a job that would have earned an American quite a few dollars). Greedy Bastards find this trade-off quite satisfactory and do not want to be told how they might contrive to do things differently.

- *The Disappearance of Retail Stores.* Most of the commercial properties in metropolitan areas like New York City are owned by Greedy Bastards whose main concern in life centers on the maximization of the rents that they charge their retail tenants. From this, it follows that, every time a lease expires, the landlord jacks up the rent to a point at which the retailer can no longer afford to do business there. The store closes, and the space sits empty – sometimes for quite a few years. The happy Greedy Bastards who have engineered this situation can congratulate themselves on the high rents that they would be charging if only prospective tenants could afford to occupy these over-priced retail spaces. Thanks to the GB Ethos, pedestrians find many fewer temptations to shop as they wander down the forlorn streets of the barren city gazing at "Store For Rent" signs.

- *Obeisance to College Sports.* We cannot help but notice the major scandal that occurred recently at Pennsylvania State University when a renowned football coach allegedly molested numerous children in the school's locker room and when the response of his superiors allegedly involved a rather far-reaching cover-up. But, amidst their outrage, few commentators gave sufficient credit to the behind-the-scenes influence of Greedy Bastards and their GB Ethos in ways that made such outcomes virtually inevitable. Face it, college sports in general and football in particular are big money makers on campuses across the land. Huge revenues accrue to ticket sales, television rights, and alumni donations – all of which reflect the extent to which a school's team manages to put together a winning season. Hence, a successful coach is worth his weight in gold and is typically compensated at a level that greatly exceeds that of the university president. In this context, it goes without saying that anything potentially injurious to the health of the football or basketball team will get rejected, avoided, ignored, shunned, or – in short – covered up. The issues obscured in this way include the sports program's obvious lack of relevance to any aspect of education or academic values. Intent on maximizing their school's cash flow, the Greedy Bastards who run the place could not care less about scholarly pursuits. They care only about winning games and thereby ensuring the biggest possible revenues from tickets, television, and donations. What happened at Penn State is simply the tip of a Gigantic GB Iceberg – symptomatic of a ubiquitous situation that pervades all college campuses. And, once again, we must thank our Greedy Bastards for their contributions in that direction.
- *The Triumph of Self-Interest.* Let us close with one more tribute to the list of Greedy Bastards with which we began – reworded in the light of all that we have learned in the intervening pages:

  - CEOs on Wall Street who scam money from their clients at one end while they reward themselves with enormous bonuses at the other
  - Corrupt politicians whose support is for hire by every sort of self-interested lobby group
  - Clergymen who preach sanctity while molesting children
  - Drug dealers whose lifestyles feed directly on the debasement of young addicts
  - Crime lords who enact a philosophy reminiscent of Tony Soprano
  - The sports hero whose remunerative performance on the field amounts to nothing more than a steroid-hyped hoax

- Entertainers who shamelessly pander to the lowest common denominator of bad taste
- Teachers who compromise their true beliefs in order to sell books

Thus, we complete our Greedy Bastard's Honor Roll of Civic Achievements. Please do not feel disappointed if your own favorite examples of the GB Ethos do not appear on this list. There are simply too many available illustrations to do them all justice in one treatise because – to paraphrase the old saying – every time God closes down one Greedy Bastard, a new one opens for business. Indeed, "Business" is the Greedy Bastard's middle name. And, in that spirit, we now conclude *The Greedy Bastard's Guide to Business*.

Postscript

I hope that, in these pages, aspiring Greedy Bastards have found inspiration to speed their progress toward righteous fulfillment as well as explanations for some otherwise puzzling social phenomena. With luck, I have offered persuasive reasons for why greed is good; have encouraged the pursuit of an ethically justified ethos of selfishness; have shown the connection between bastardly greed and other salubrious social trends – such as obesity, traffic, cell phones, and dumbed-down popular culture – and have clarified the links between the ascendancy of Greedy Bastards and various related cultural phenomena.

In conclusion, Dear Reader, I wish you success, happiness, and the unimpeded pursuit of your own self-interest, wherever this path may lead you. Always be proud to number yourself among the ranks of those who follow *The Greedy Bastard's Guide to Business*.

12 What for Art Thou, Marketing?

Abstract

Like it or not, the term *marketing* has come to evoke negative connotations similar to those that have long afflicted the term *selling*. This development raises doubts about whether *marketing* can be rehabilitated so as to regain whatever luster and respectability it might once have possessed. This chapter casts doubt on such a possibility and cautions those who operate under the *marketing* banner to carefully consider the problem of how to introduce themselves at cocktail parties.

A few years ago (as mentioned briefly in Chapter 4), with absorbed fascination but disturbing alarm, I watched on television as Chris Matthews – one of the smartest and most articulate MSNBC news anchors – listed a long line of atrocities committed by Donald Trump. After running through a lengthy recitation of one contemptible act of corruption after another, Matthews paused, poised to summarize his tirade with the one word that would encapsulate the enormity of this political miscreant's parade of egregious malfeasances. This accomplished news reporter was and is a man of great learning with a huge vocabulary and profound insights on any number of topics. I once saw Matthews perform as a celebrity contestant on the quiz program *Jeopardy!* where he effortlessly stole the show from the other participants, clearly demonstrating his intellectual gifts and the breadth of his knowledge. If any human being could produce the *mot juste* to capture the magnitude of the offending scumbag's transgressions, it would be Chris Matthews. But Matthews stopped. Seemingly nonplussed, he pondered. He searched his extensive memory bank for the most appropriate word to describe the horrific litany of infractions that he had so vividly compiled. And finally, he announced his choice for the most fitting epithet to encompass DJT's crimes and misdemeanors: *Marketing*.

This sorry episode led me to realize that the word *marketing*, as used colloquially, has almost imperceptibly slid uncomfortably far in the direction of acquiring negative, unfavorable, and even derogatory connotations as it is commonly used by members of our culture in our current climate of public opinion. This untoward downward spiral carries significant implications for a person such as myself or perhaps yourself who has spent his

DOI: 10.4324/9781003560302-17

entire career – roughly 60 years – teaching themes and researching topics that fall under the rubric of *Marketing*. During that time, with fierce dedication, I have tried to treat marketing as an exemplary activity fully capable of doing good in the world. I have entertained MBA students with a view of the firm as a Dynamic Open Complex Adaptive System (DOCAS) that must fit into its proper ecological niche in a way that responds to pressures from a number of stakeholders and environmental participants (customers, employees, suppliers, regulatory agencies, investors, meteorologists, and so on) in a manner that aims at and with luck achieves survival. In that spirit, I have advocated the Marketing Concept as a potential force toward guiding and fulfilling the goals of well-being, health, prosperity, and happiness in the lives of our planet's citizens. Yet – increasingly, with a little help from social critics such as Chris Matthews – I have come to realize that many or even most people in our society tend more and more to regard *marketing* as a synonym for dishonesty, misrepresentation, false claims, deceitful advertising, greedy selfishness, corruption, and any number of other grievances that one might care to condemn and to castigate vociferously. So, when I go to a cocktail party and some new acquaintance asks me what I do for a living, I no longer reply, "I'm a retired Professor of Marketing in an MBA program." Rather, I give some sort of evasive answer such as, "I study consumer behavior and have taught courses on the culture of consumption." I realize that the word *consumption* itself has a few connotational problems. But, if given the chance, I happily explain to inquisitors that this term encapsulates the essence of the human condition. And, to most, this appears to seem like a reasonable and worthwhile subject for investigation.

Meanwhile, government officials and news commentators have continued to push our conception of *marketing* in the general direction of ever-mounting scorn or even loathing. Still speaking of Donald J. Trump, as denounced earlier by Chris Matthews, I recently saw an interview on MSNBC's *Saturday Show with Jonathan Capehart* in which Claire McCaskill, a former Democratic US senator from Missouri, voiced her harshly disapproving assessment of the oft-indicted alleged felon as follows:

> Yeah, listen, this guy is a marketer. . . . His integrity is rock-bottom. His character is laughable. But he is a marketer. That's all he's ever been in his life: A huckster and a marketer and a con man.

Here, quite repetitively (three times if we are counting), McCaskill uses *marketer* as a synonym for a person of low integrity, an individual of poor character, a swindler, and somebody likely to perpetrate a scam. If we start with the well-founded assumption that the wayward politico is all these things and more, we understand that the implications for *marketing* are indeed incriminating, condemnatory, and damning.

Such opprobrium used to be reserved for just one salient but only partial aspect of marketing – namely, *selling*. As preached by thinkers such as the influentially hypermetropic Ted Levitt, the verb *to sell* acquired derogatory meanings or "demeanings" that became accepted and even embraced in our language. Thus, if we consult the definition of *to sell* in the *Merriam-Webster Unabridged Dictionary* via the apposite entry found on Google.Com, we find the following (in the order shown):

- "to deliver or give up in violation of duty, trust, or loyalty"
- "BETRAY – often used with *out*"
- "to give up in return for something else especially foolishly or dishonorably"
- "to deliver into slavery for money"
- "to give into the power of another [as in] *sold* his soul to the devil"
- "to dispose of or manage for profit instead of in accordance with conscience, justice, or duty"
- "to impose on: CHEAT"
- "a deliberate deception: HOAX"
- "to betray the faith of"
- "to fail to value properly: UNDERESTIMATE"

Here, *market* is given as a synonym – thereby anticipating the encroaching sorry state of this broader term in today's evolving vernacular. Oh, sure, we find some comparatively harmless aspects of the verb *to sell*, such as "to exchange in return for money or something else of value"; "to develop a belief in the truth, value, or desirability of"; or "to persuade or influence to a course of action or to the acceptance of something." But, despite these occasional concessions in the direction of neutrality, I think it is fair or even generous to say that the prevailing sense attributed to the word *sell* is that it stinks. Such degrading associations help to explain the title of Nicholas O'Shaughnessy's insightful book about Nazi propaganda: *Selling Hitler* (2021).

So, in sum, it appears that meanings of the term *marketing* currently plunge downward in a sort of free fall toward the level of disapprobation long endured by the word *sell*. And, at the current rate of decline, it won't be long until we feel downright ashamed to have anything to do with the field of study whose title now appears above our names in our school's course catalog.

Now, the reader may be thinking that "a rose by any other name would smell as sweet" or, conversely, that a skunk otherwise designated would discharge just as bad a stench. The word *marketing* seems to have gravitated in the direction of the latter mephitic category. Recall the TV commercial for an odor-elimination product called Pooph: "If it's not Pooph, it stinks." It appears that the term *marketing* now heads toward a semiotic signification where, metaphorically, it will find itself badly in need of the proverbial Pooph application.

Of course, I am aware of the various spokespeople and organizations that have done everything they can to salvage the *marketing* brand. Perhaps most conspicuously, the American Marketing Association (AMA) – clearly, a group that should know all about the relevant quagmire of ethical and ecological issues – adopts a suitably sunny view of its eponymous focus and defines *marketing* as "the activity, set of institutions, and processes for creating, communicating, delivering, and exchanging offerings that have value for customers, clients, partners, and society at large (Approved 2017)." I am especially happy to see that this self-justifying definition stresses the importance of creating consumer value, but I must nevertheless object that the AMA's propitiatory brand-positioning strategy appears to gloss over various problems that combine to tarnish the image of *marketing* in our everyday parlance.

In 2013, I addressed some of these issues in an article for the *Journal of Macromarketing* entitled "The Greedy Bastard's Guide to Business" (please see Chapter 11). My approach in that particular screed probably came across as a bit melodramatic, perhaps overly ironic, or even outlandishly sarcastic. But, after all, please recall that I was something of a tormented soul who could not attend even a friendly cocktail party without straining to invent some non-marketing way to portray myself. *Consumer Research? Culture of Consumption?* Whatever might avoid the stigma of a link with the much-despised, -discredited, and -deprecated *Marketing*.

More systematic onslaughts directed toward attacks on *marketing* have appeared elsewhere. I shall briefly celebrate two of these – the first for its broad sphere of influence, the second for its impressive scholarship.

First, Steven H. Star (1989) published a paper in the widely circulated *Harvard Business Review* entitled "Marketing and Its Discontents," in which he offered some telling criticisms of *marketing* in ways that worked toward further corroding its already tarnished brand image. Star distinguished between two major types of problems – those stemming from excesses and those related to expertness. Under the former category, he included the sorts of things that bothered Claire McCaskill in the aforementioned political example – namely, shoddy products, deceptive advertising, misleading packages, selling scams, and appeals to false values. But Star gave only brief attention to these hallmark concerns of the consumerist movement in favor of dwelling on the latter category of problems that arise because of poor fits between customer segments and the available means for reaching those target markets. These slippages cause distractions or frustrations and thereby evoke criticism or blame. But they are an inevitable part of marketing systems that, innocently if unsuccessfully, strive to overcome them. So, implicitly, we can forgive marketing for many if not most of its shortcomings. Probably, that's about as much of a critique as we should expect from a business-oriented article published in *HBR*.

Second, in a recent issue of the *International Journal of Social Ecology and Sustainable Development*, Pratap Chandra Mandal (2023) presents a scholarly review entitled "Social Implications and Criticisms of Marketing," which indicates how things have changed in the meanings buried among the connotations of *marketing* as we have come to view it and talk about it today. Here, we find a panoply of complaints that in their way are as complete as anything imagined by Chris Matthews or Claire McCaskill in their televised rants against their least favorite politician. Mandal's list of 73 references is admirably thorough and current with only four citations dated prior to 2009 and none older than 2000. Specifically, Mandal points to such grounds for the condemnation of *marketing* as

- Excessive prices
- Deceitful advertising

- Deceptive packages
- High-pressure sales tactics
- Dangerous or shoddy products
- Planned obsolescence
- Discrimination against disadvantaged consumers
- Misleading celebrity endorsements
- Encouragement of materialistic values
- Lack of social responsibility
- Dumbing down of the consumer culture
- Anti-competitive practices

Clearly, Mandal presents a long list of anti-marketing animadversions. And he does so with enough passion to adumbrate the path where the debate seems to be headed – namely, toward a progressive derogation of *marketing* causing considerable damage to what a reflexively inclined commentator might call its *brand image*. Those of us who labor in the fields of marketing-related teaching, research, and writing have reason to shrink with dread and alarm from the degradation of our specialty, especially when we must identify ourselves and our professions in public.

So, Dear Reader, what are we to do about this discrediting of the term that characterizes the gist of our professional and academic lives? One approach – metaphorically akin to the application of a smell eliminator such as Pooph – might focus on rehabilitating the brand image of the field in which we work. For example, we might attempt a resurrection and reaffirmation of the Marketing Concept in ways that really do pay attention to its potential role in the improvement of social welfare. As one avenue in this direction, mentioned earlier, we might more vigorously accept and promote a view of the firm as a Dynamic Open Complex Adaptive System (DOCAS) struggling to survive in a suitable and sustainable ecological niche.

But, much as I like that potential approach or some similar way of sanitizing and refurbishing the image and connotations of *marketing* as that term is deployed in our current vernacular and colloquial conversations, I fear that damage to this linguistic item has gone too far to permit resuscitating or reviving it in ways that might cleanse it of unsavory associations. In short (still speaking metaphorically), meanings of the term *marketing* that stink to High Heaven have grown too ubiquitous and too smelly to be saved by a puff of Pooph. Rather, given the aforementioned predicament of one who must identify at public gatherings with a field that has fallen into widespread disrepute, I can think of only one admittedly inconvenient solution, one possible cure for the problem at hand: Go to fewer cocktail parties.

13 A Subjective Personal Introspective Essay on the Evolution of Business Schools, the Fate of Marketing Education, and Aspirations Toward a Great Society

Abstract

This essay pursues the subjective personal introspective approach to comment on the author's own impressions concerning his experiences over the past 60 years at one of our leading graduate schools of business. Herein, the essay traces the author's progress from MBA candidate to doctoral student to faculty member to retiree by suggesting ways in which – from his admittedly idiosyncratic perspective – business education has devolved toward a lower level of academic excellence; an abandonment of scholarly values; an unfortunate anti-intellectualism; a neglect of its commitment to the advancement of business-, marketing-, or consumer-related knowledge for its own sake; and a betrayal of its responsibility to work toward the protection of social welfare. Though the situation seems a bit hopeless, the chapter offers a few modest suggestions for possible improvement.

I am pleased and honored to receive an invitation to contribute my comments to a special issue of the *Australasian Marketing Journal* (*AMJ*) on Marketing Education. Toward that end, I shall pursue an approach that I refer to as Subjective Personal Introspection (SPI) so as to report my private impressions concerning the ways in which the practice, habits, values, and goals of marketing-related MBA education have changed and – in my opinion – declined over the past half-century during which I have participated in the business-school scene. I hope that my long involvement in the world of business teaching and marketing instruction qualifies me to offer my reflections in ways that might be of interest to readers of *AMJ*.

Before continuing further, I should point out that I love my school – Columbia University in general and its Graduate School of Business in particular. For over 50 years, I have been fortunate, privileged, and indeed blessed to attend and serve this great institution – as an MBA candidate, a doctoral student, a junior faculty member, a senior professor, and an emeritus retiree. Throughout, the school has treated me with kindness and generosity, for which I am truly grateful. But – despite or, actually, because of all this – Columbia is the school I know best and, therefore, the one I must often use as an example to illustrate what I perceive as difficulties in our educational system that will

DOI: 10.4324/9781003560302-18

concern me in what follows. I mean no disrespect to the fine institution where I have studied and taught for most of my life. Rather, I see it as my duty to share my observations in ways that might conceivably encourage others to make much-needed improvements to benefit us all.

To start at the beginning, when I completed my undergraduate years as an English major at Harvard in 1965, I realized that I would need to find some profession more lucrative than writing poetry in order to support myself in the manner to which I hoped to become accustomed. This implied an imperative for me to seek some sort of career-enhancing program of graduate study. I thought about continuing in English literature or switching to my other avocation, music, but the courses I had taken in these subjects during my crushingly difficult college years had seized upon things that I had once loved – books and musical performances – and, through an excess of mind-numbing pedantry, had spoiled them for me. Fortunately, my love of books and music eventually reawakened in the fullness of time. But meanwhile, to prevent such spoilage in the future, I decided to find an area of study devoted to a topic that could not be ruined for me because I already hated it. This quest led me straight to the field of Business.

Despite my inveterate distaste for the capitalist ethos, I understood that I needed to work at something, that the reason they call it work is that you don't enjoy it, and that business was as far from something I might enjoy as I could imagine. So I applied to the Harvard Business School (HBS, right across the Charles River and visible from my window in Dunster House), Columbia University's Graduate School of Business (CUGSB), and another couple of schools just for the fun of it. My beloved bride-to-be Sally had already spent one year in Columbia's Master of Social Work program. And we were scheduled to be married on August 14, 1965 (one week before the fateful deadline that Lynden Johnson later set for marriage-related draft exemptions). So we made a deal that – in retrospect, from a feminist viewpoint – seems rather preposterous. Specifically, we agreed that, if I was accepted at HBS, Sally would move with me to Boston, whereas, if I was accepted at CUGSB but not HBS, I would move to New York City to be with Sally at Columbia.

Foolishly, I felt fairly confident of being accepted at HBS because my grades at Harvard College – the ironic product of a tortured academic existence – had been pretty good. But my alma mater's business school quickly disabused me of any such unwarranted optimism by rejecting my application on the grounds that I lacked real-world experience, with the recommendation that I could gain the required maturity by joining the US Army. This helpful advice descended upon me in the spring of 1965 at the time of the military buildup in Vietnam, and I greeted it with a lack of appreciation that I still feel to the present day. Suffice it to say that this episode left me with a hearty dislike for real-world experience and, I must confess, a deep-seated hatred of the Harvard Business School. I shall pursue this theme again later when I discuss my opinions concerning the deficiencies of the much-touted but woefully over-rated Harvard Case Method.

So I entered the MBA program at what we then called Columbia University's Graduate School of Business (CUGSB) and, somewhat to my surprise, found it to be a warm and caring place. The administrators were nurturing; the professors were accessible and supportive; and my fellow MBA candidates were friendly, thoughtful, and intellectually curious. We wore coats and ties to class, and we treated our professors with the respect they deserved. I could not have imagined calling a professor by his first name. Nor could I have imagined coming to class in a tank top, blue jeans, and sandals. And, yes, the clearly masculine references in the last couple of sentences are intentional and even politically correct because – in those days, not counting secretaries and a few administrative staff members – there was not one single woman to be found within the walls of Uris Hall where CUGSB had its home. There were also no people of color, no Latinos, and no international students to speak of. In short, the place – like many or most other American business schools at the time – was as homogeneous in terms of gender and ethnicity as you might imagine. (I do not have statistics to support this assertion, but that's how I remember it from the vantage point of SPI, and I do not fear that the detailed data would contradict me.)

All this changed, of course, over time. Soon after I arrived, the school hired its first female professor – Margaret Chandler, a distinguished sociologist with a specialty in union-related issues and a very nice lady. And, today, the school prides itself on its inclusiveness in recruiting and admitting women, members of all ethnic groups, and a huge diversity of students from all around the world. But, in 1965, it was just us white guys.

To my delight, the courses I encountered when I arrived at Columbia – when compared to my ordeal as an undergraduate in English at Harvard – seemed interesting, full of new information, and (surprisingly) not too difficult. Our professors showed concerns with issues of real intellectual import, and I was constantly challenged to think about questions and problems that had never crossed my mind. Indeed, I found myself in a climate of real scholarly excitement about the study of business, and I began to regard this study as an academic endeavor worth pursuing for its own sake. In that light, I found a special resonance in a passage from Alfred North Whitehead (already mentioned in Chapter 11) that was engraved on the wall of Uris Hall just outside its main entrance: "A Great Society is a Society in which its Men of Business Think Greatly of their Functions." This slogan implied a vision of CUGSB's purpose as one of contributing to social welfare in ways that would benefit a wide variety of stakeholders – owners, managers, employees, suppliers, customers, other members of the surrounding community, and the environment at large. I eagerly bought into that kind of idealism in ways that, to my dismay, would be challenged in the years to come.

Best of all, I decided to concentrate in the area of Marketing and very quickly encountered some marvelous teachers in that field of study – Al Oxenfeldt (a well-trained economist with a delightfully acerbic sense of humor), Abe Shuchman (a master of statistical analysis with a deep irreverence toward excessive pedantry), Charles Ramond (a psychologist who served with distinction as Editor of the *Journal of Advertising Research*), and especially . . . John A. Howard. Working with his former doctoral student at the University of Pittsburgh – Jagdish Sheth, now a young faculty member at Columbia – Professor Howard taught the course on buyer behavior, while he and Sheth worked feverishly to complete the creation of their masterpiece on that topic (*The Theory of Buyer Behavior*, Howard and Sheth, 1969). John (whom I did not call by his first name for another 25 years or so) would walk into every class meeting with his arms full of mimeographed copies of their latest chapter (this being before the days of Xerox machines). We the students would devour these stimulating documents and would then participate in rivetingly intense discussions about various subtleties of interest. (For example, does Confidence mediate the effect of Affect on Purchase Intention or does C moderate the relationship between A and PI? John believed the former, I the latter. And we never could agree about that. As late as 1994, when I helped with revisions to John's textbook, we were still debating this point.) As a teacher, no one could have been more open to the ideas of others than John. Indeed, in my own case, he generously went far beyond the call of duty – hiring me as a research assistant for two summers; after I received my MBA, shepherding me into the PhD program where I studied with him for another eight years; and, ultimately, giving me a job on the CUGSB faculty in 1975, where I remained until I retired in 2009, almost 35 years later.

I indelibly remember the phone call I got from John right after my first year in the MBA program at CUGSB. I was indolently lounging on the beach at a lake near Charlottesville, Virginia. John somehow got wind of the sad fact that I did not have a summer job. So, via persistent calls to my parents in Milwaukee, he managed to track me down in the wilderness and offered me a position as his research assistant on what became the famous Post Instant Breakfast study. These acts of kindness, generosity, and even mercy continued for the rest of our time together, up until he passed away in 1999, three and a half decades after we had first met (Holbrook, videotape 1989, 1998c, 2001f, 2016; for further details, please see Chapter 10).

It should be clear from what I have said thus far that my CUGSB professors in general and John Howard in particular were, in every sense, "full service" education providers. They felt excited about the intellectual content of business and marketing studies, they regarded their areas of expertise as real academic specialties, and they encouraged the efforts of any student who shared their interest in research-related methods and topics. They preached and practiced the virtues of scholarly investigation, and they supported the efforts of those who, like yours truly, wanted to follow in their footsteps.

During my first few years on the CUGSB faculty, starting in 1975, I keenly felt the oft-acknowledged pressure to "publish or perish." But the School facilitated my task by letting me teach the same course over and over – the Introduction to Marketing Strategy (which I taught four times a year for 17 years) – so as to save preparation time and thereby maximize my opportunities for engaging in research. Very often, in those days, my MBA students took an interest in my research and wished to pursue independent studies – which I sponsored quite eagerly, in many cases getting publishable joint-authored papers as the rewards for my efforts. The topics of these articles included (among others) the multidimensional scaling of preferences toward jazz singers with Rebecca Williams (Holbrook and Williams, 1978); a structured projective technique for assessing product images with Neville Hughes (Holbrook and Hughes, 1978); an information-display board suitable for use in a mail questionnaire with Karl Maier (Holbrook and Maier, 1978) and then, again, with David Velez and Gerard Tabouret (Holbrook, Velez, and Tabouret, 1981); a Features-Perceptions-Affect model of responses toward performances of a piece by J. S. Bach as played by Stephen Bertges (Holbrook and Bertges, 1981); studies of the spatial representations of preferences toward jazz musicians with Doug Holloway (Holbrook and Holloway, 1984) and with Glenn Dixon (Holbrook and Dixon, 1985); a philosophical analysis of aesthetic value with Bob Zirlin (Holbrook and Zirlin, 1985); an interpretive study of consumption symbolism found in the film *Out of Africa* with Mark Grayson (Holbrook and Grayson,1986); a multidimensional representation of features determining preferences toward different versions of a pop song by Gary Dodgen (Holbrook, Moore, Dodgen, and Havlena, 1985); estimating the financial rewards from winning Oscars in various categories with John Dodds (Dodds and Holbrook, 1988); assessing the financial returns from including one or another star in a motion picture with Tim Wallace and Alan Seigerman (Wallace, Seigerman, and Holbrook, 1993); and a technique for measuring price differentials related to brand equity with David Bello (Bello and Holbrook, 1995). Clearly, the list of genuinely committed and appreciative MBA students who wanted to study with me and who did excellent work in that direction, leading in many cases to successful publications, is a long one. And please notice that these were MBA students and not PhD students. (I enjoyed the help of quite a few doctoral students, as well, but here we are focusing on the MBA program.) So, yes, the level of intellectual involvement among the MBAs as part of our community of scholars excelled in those days – during the 1970s, 1980s, and into the early 1990s – but, unfortunately, all this would change in ways that now command our attention.

As we entered the 1990s, the MBA students in my marketing-strategy classes at Columbia still retained quite a bit of the old scholarly spark and inquisitive curiosity that had endeared this group to me so strongly over the years. My enthusiasm as a teacher in this inviting climate reached its zenith during the early 1990s, about the time when I accepted an invitation to visit my friends and colleagues at Edith Cowan University (ECU) in Perth, Australia, in March 1996. My duties as an official ECU visitor included presenting a couple of talks about my research; making a short documentary film about my work; and delivering the commencement address at the graduation ceremony of ECU's Business School. The latter assignment strayed far beyond the ambit of anything that I had ever attempted before (or since) and filled me with so much anxiety that I spent months – probably more time than I had ever invested in any publication for even the most prestigious marketing journal – preparing what turned out to be a ten-minute speech. Into that oration, I wove all sorts of references to things Australian – kangaroos, wallabies, koalas, wombats, dingoes, platypuses, echidnas, crocodiles, emus, black swans, and kookaburras; trees that drop their bark; Rupert Murdoch, "Banjo" Paterson, Paul Hogan, Mel Gibson, and Evonne Goolagong; Vegemite; brollies, tellies, jaffles, and yabbies; "Waltizng Matilda"; and – most of all – penguins. My main thrust focused on the most obvious and hackneyed of themes – namely, that life is tough but we must try as hard as we can. Or – as Donald Trump recently put it in his commencement address at Liberty University in Lynchburg, Virginia – "Nothing worth doing ever, ever, ever came easy." To pursue this trite but nonetheless sincere attempt at an inspirational message in a way that I hoped would resonate with Australian sensibilities, I conjured up 12 admirable characteristics of penguins, truly exceptional creatures whom we would do well to emulate, recommended that we should all aspire to the display of comparable virtues, and concluded with the following homespun story (Holbrook, 1997e).

> On this theme, I wish to conclude by reporting a related insight that recently appeared in the literature on penguins. It comes from that great American fountain of knowledge about business, namely *The New Yorker* magazine, as found last September in a somewhat corny but nonetheless relevant cartoon by S. Gross.
>
> In this drawing, nine penguins stand on the edge of an iceberg, surrounded by a dark and choppy sea below, gazing up at the tenth penguin who hovers overhead with his wings extended and calls out, "We just haven't been flapping them hard enough."
>
> I have mentioned this cartoon to quite a few people and have found that hardly anybody ever laughs. Frankly, most people just don't seem to think it's all that funny. At first, I wondered why nobody laughs. But, lately, I have concluded that the cartoon fails to amuse partly because it appears to express something so profound about the human condition in general and about life as a businessperson in particular.
>
> In this spirit, I regard this cartoon as a metaphor that encapsulates almost everything I have said and almost everything we need to know about the achievement of success and about the related goals for education in the world of business.
>
> The truth is that, however hard business graduates may have worked on their studies in the past, they will now have to work even harder, the only difference being that, in the future, they will get paid for it. The truth is that the world of business can often provide painful options about as attractive as the choice between standing on an iceberg or plunging into the cold sea.
>
> Figuratively speaking, the truth is that, however hard we may have been flapping our wings until now, we probably have not been flapping them hard enough. And, I'm afraid, the truth is also that, flap though we might, we are often going to flop.

In truth, like real-life penguins, as opposed to cartoon characters, we shall never actually manage to fly, no matter how hard we flap our wings. But that expenditure of effort on striving to achieve something inherently unattainable can still make us strong.

And pursuing this sort of strength can bring us one blessing that we might share with the flying penguin in the otherwise corny cartoon by Gross: Nobody will laugh.

Optimistic as this vignette might sound, I dimly recognized as early as the mid-1990s that the tide had begun to turn against the sort of committed intellectual curiosity and dedicated scholarly inquisitiveness that I had so much enjoyed while working in the academic community that had existed at CUGSB during the 1960s, 1970s, and 1980s. In my opinion, the first symptom of trouble began when Columbia – like so many other schools – introduced its program of student-centered course evaluations. The manner in which these student-satisfaction surveys were and are conducted was and is so misguided that I must regard them as a cynical attempt to cater – even to pander – to students regarded as customers with course offerings regarded as products provided by the professors who teach them. The underlying logic regards the school as a business dedicated to maximizing the customer satisfaction of its students in ways that they will recognize and appreciate because they respond favorably to the flattery of being asked to register their often ill-conceived opinions. Of course, I realize that some sort of feedback from students can improve and strengthen a professor's design and delivery of course materials. To me, this sort of helpful feedback arrived most conspicuously when students used their body language (yawning, dozing, staring out the window) or their interpersonal-communication skills (dropping by to complain or to ask questions after class) to signal their approval or disdain. And, of course, I also recognize that a formal set of course evaluations must reach the professor only after the grades have been turned in so as to avoid any retaliatory biases that might otherwise exist. However, those who have planned the course-evaluation systems at my school and elsewhere have made the colossal mistake of thinking that these evaluations should be anonymous (presumably to ensure the freedom of students to respond as irresponsibly as they might wish without fear of being detected). (By the way, this reminds me of the misbegotten logic that argues for the anonymity of those who participate in a journal's review process. But my strong animadversions to the system of reviewing submissions to our major journals stray a bit too far from the present topic and will not entertain us further in the present essay.)

To my amazement, many or even most people with whom I have spoken do not immediately recognize the profound absurdity of a course-evaluation system based on anonymous responses. So please permit me to offer what I hope is an instructive analogy. Imagine that, at the end of every term, each student received a list of his or her grades in the five courses that he or she had been taking – say, an A, two Bs, one C, and an F. Further suppose that no attempt was made to identify which grade pertained to which course so that the student was powerless to ascertain which grade belonged to, say, accounting and which to, say, marketing. Obviously, the students affected by this ridiculous policy would riot or, in today's culture of political correctness, would vociferously present their discomfort with what they saw as an inappropriate grading system through the intervention of their class representatives. They would demand the right to know which professor had given them which grade. And, of course, their objections would carry the force of unassailable rectitude. Yet, please notice, the typical system of anonymous course evaluations proceeds in a manner fully as preposterous as that of the anonymous grading system just imagined. For a professor who gets a negative response in the course evaluations, it makes all the difference in the world whether that response has emanated from the brightest and most dedicated student in the class or from some slacker who never attended class meetings, never did the assignments, did not understand the material, and – during those few moments when he did show up – spent his time playing with his iPhone or making E*Trade deals on his laptop. As the recipient of student-satisfaction results, I felt that it was my right (after turning in the grades) to know which student provided which evaluation. For a while, based on suitably persuasive explanations, I succeeded in convincing most members of my classes to sign their reviews. (These I read with care while ignoring the rest.) But – over time, with the increasing surge of student entitlement that accompanied the school's posture of running itself like a business and treating its MBAs as customers – students felt no need to comply with my wishes and, indeed, began to voice their dissent (punishingly but, of course, anonymously). So I gave up. And, in my opinion, the still-anonymous student-satisfaction course-evaluation system is the worse for it.

This trend toward running the school like a business and pandering to students by embracing a system of anonymous customer-satisfaction surveys gained momentum when CUGSB hired a new dean in the early 1990s. I should preface my related comments by gratefully acknowledging that this new dean was exceedingly nice to me – kind, generous, and supportive in ways that inspire my most sincere gratitude. But he bolstered his new position by launching two initiatives that – albeit unintentionally – proved damaging (in my opinion) to the intellectual climate of the school.

First – recognizing that Columbia has the advantage of its location in the world's financial capital, New York City (along with New York University's Stern School and City University's Baruch School, both of which are even closer to Wall Street) – our new dean proclaimed his intention of making CUGSB a more finance-oriented educational institution. This meant elevating the position of the Finance-and-Economics Division (which, after considerable enlargement, came to be known as the "Mega-Division") and, conversely, diminishing the footprint of the Marketing Division (which gradually began to sink toward a lower level of course offerings and related resources). Feeling their oats, members of the Finance-and-Economics Division began insisting on a posture that was caricatured in the movie *Wall Street* by Michael Douglas as Gordon Gekko with his slogan claiming that

"Greed Is Good." Or – put more politely – the school's guiding philosophy gravitated toward a finance-friendly emphasis on the mandate to "Maximize Shareholder Equity." This, of course, implies ignoring other stakeholders that used to be of real concern to business-oriented academics – managers, employees, suppliers, customers, and other external participants. For years, to my marketing-strategy students, I had been preaching a gospel of regarding the firm as a Dynamic Open Complex Adaptive System (DOCAS) trying to survive in a potentially threatening environment – which implied a purposeful sensitivity to sustainability within a reciprocally interconnected ecology (Holbrook, 2003c). This focus on DOCAS, to my mind, had resonated with the aforementioned words of Alfred North Whitehead – carved on the wall at the entrance to our building – advocating the need to "think greatly" of our business function (please see Chapter 11). But those words had disappeared a few years earlier when the school covered over the wall in the process of adding more rooms to house student-employer job interviews. And now, with the intensified finance-inspired mantra of maximizing shareholder equity, the former concerns for social welfare and ecological responsibility had vanished along with ANW's memorable exhortation.

Second, though the new dean came from a background in marketing, he had apparently forgotten or chose to ignore the first lesson taught in Marketing Strategy 101. Virtually every marketing educator would agree that the key to gaining a competitive advantage entails differentiating one's offering in a way that shields it from competition. Conversely, the biggest mistake a marketing manager can make is to try to appeal to the average consumer via a mass-marketing approach with a one-size-fits-all offering. Yet, ironically enough, the imitation of other schools in ways that offered standardized core courses to students regarded as a mass market was exactly the direction in which our new dean chose to move. Specifically, he had noticed that some other schools – Wharton, Columbia's number-one competitor, rumored to be among them (though further rumors suggested that Wharton had experienced disappointing results with this strategy) – had begun to cluster students into groups that took all their required core courses together. Allegedly, students loved this clustering approach because it gave them a chance to make a few friends among the never-changing set of people with whom they constantly mingled in all their basic courses, hour after hour, day after day. However, this networking-oriented clustering plan for required core courses necessitated that each core course be standardized so that students could feel that they were all offered exactly the same thing by whichever professor was assigned to teach their particular section. Formerly, students had been given the chance to take different versions of the basic marketing-strategy course taught by professors with different styles in ways that covered somewhat differing points of view. Each student had enjoyed the opportunity to choose the version of the course that best fit his or her needs and wants. In other words, the student market had effectively been treated as self-selected segments with differing preferences. The system had worked pretty well, and some students had ended up in my sections because they actually valued my somewhat unconventional style of teaching marketing strategy (involving, as previously mentioned, DOCAS and all that). Those self-selected students were relatively happy, whereas other students (e.g., those obsessed with maximizing shareholder equity) would have been miserable if forced to take my sections of the marketing-strategy course. But the clustering-oriented mandate to standardize the course changed all that. Now, to ensure that all sections were as identical as possible so as to avoid potential complaints about a lack of equality ("equality" being more important than "quality" in this regime), each instructor was required to teach the same material, with the same textbooks, with the same lecture notes, with the same PowerPoint displays, with the same cases, with the same problem sets, and even with the same predigested jokes and stories. One belabored argument in support of this disastrous idea was based on the efficiency entailed by such a scheme. Specifically – because every professor would teach the exact same version of the course – if there were (say) five professors leading sections of a given core course in a particular term, each would need to prepare only one-fifth of the material, using that prepared by the other four faculty members for the remaining classes. Then they could pass their course materials to those teaching during the next term for even greater savings in labor. Efficient? Yes. Intellectually honest? Not so much. So, when the plan was brought to a vote at one of our faculty meetings, I rose for perhaps the only time that I ever spoke in one of these convocations, wrote "McCourse" on the blackboard (echoing some of the famous arguments offered by George Ritzer [1993] along similar lines), and proceeded to explain why I thought and still think that standardized course offerings represent a truly terrible idea. After my heartfelt speech, our inexplicably complacent faculty members voted to approve the cluster-based standardized core-course offerings by a unanimous show of hands, mine being the only hand conspicuously not raised in support (though one compatriot spirit did come forth surreptitiously after the meeting to say that she secretly agreed with me). So, with spectacular irony, my acquiescent colleagues ratified the design and implementation of an introductory marketing-strategy course that thoroughly embodied and vividly exemplified the single greatest marketing fallacy that it is possible to commit – namely, a ruinous mass-marketing initiative based on the much-discredited premise that one-size-fits-all.

Predictably and for very good reasons, the MBA students who attended CUGSB at the time hated the new standardized core course. In preparing the homogenized classes, any shred of individual initiative, personal investment, or intellectual endeavor had left the building. And it was obvious to our then-current crop of MBAs that their opportunities for a stimulating educational experience had also flown the coop. But ask yourself, Dear Reader, what happens when such a relentlessly ill-advised clusterfuck is put into practice and stubbornly retained despite the cries of outrage coming from its intended victims. The answer is that – gradually, over time – the new curriculum begins to attract applications from the kinds of students who like to have their marketing lessons and other course materials spooned out to them like pabulum in homogenized and predigested form. So the students with stubbornly original and restlessly creative minds, whom I had liked so much and with whom (as listed earlier) I had rejoiced in working on collaborative research, began to disappear from the school to be replaced by those who, with networking always foremost on their minds, preferred to march in lock-step through the corridors of learning to achieve an elevated level of conformity as duped disciples of identical standardized lesson plans. (Alarmingly, one self-satisfied MBA candidate even confessed, in a *New York Times* interview, that he had come to Columbia for its networking opportunities and did not care a hoot about anything his professors might have to offer.)

I anticipated all this and – despite the much-touted advantages of efficiency – begged to be excused from teaching the standardized McCourse on Marketing Strategy in the future. I paid a heavy price for this resistance because, to replace my marketing-strategy core-course assignments, I then needed to prepare two entirely new courses – namely, Consumer Behavior and Commercial Communication in the Culture of Consumption. The first was a fairly traditional CB course – albeit with my own peculiar slants, biases, and preoccupations. The second was a rather innovative seminar that borrowed from the emerging postmodern perspectives to examine ways of understanding audiences for the arts, entertainment, and advertising. Both courses started out strongly in terms of enrollments and reception. But – as the years went by and greater numbers of sheep-like, profit-oriented, finance-minded, networking-inclined, job-seeking automatons populated the school's class rosters – fewer and fewer students showed up to take my two courses. Eventually, only six or seven seemingly inquisitive and appreciative MBAs would appear in my classes. Some additional seats were filled by students from other parts of the university – Teacher's College, the School of International and Public Affairs, Barnard College, Columbia College, the Behavioral Sciences, Journalism, Law, Medicine, Social Work, and so forth. I enjoyed this diverse group of students. And cross-registrations such as these struck me as part of the essence of what a great university has to offer. But, unfortunately, such cross-registrants did not pay tuition directly to CUGSB in ways that pleased the school's administration. So – in due course, during the first few years of the new millennium – the chairman of my division told me that I must go back to teaching the required now-standardized core course on marketing strategy to three clusters totaling roughly 200 networking-obsessed learning-averse MBA candidates.

Anticipating trouble, never in my life have I worked so hard to succeed on any assignment. Yet never have I failed so miserably. (There were two separate terms during two different periods of time covered by the present narrative. I am collapsing these into one account for the sake of verbal economy.) For starters, the course itself – as designed by a committee of my colleagues – struck me as a pedagogical disaster. To prepare, I attended a section taught by one of our most talented and esteemed faculty members. But I discerned no clear structure in the course outline. The material struck me as dumbed down in ways aimed at the lowest common denominator. The shared PowerPoint presentations seemed poorly constructed and amateurish. The readings were haphazard and unconvincing. And – worst of all but true to the tendency to copy competitors – the course made extensive use of Harvard Business School cases – a teaching style that, for good reasons, I deplore.

O, Harvard Case Method. How do I despise thee? Let me count the ways.

I despise thee though I realize, of course, that HBS cases are tremendously popular with MBA students and teachers alike. They give the students a feeling that they are participating in a hands-on experience that reflects the real world in ways not available when taking courses from those misguided professors who (like yours truly) rely on arcane concepts and abstract theory found in scholarly books and journal articles. Far better, these students believe, to delve into the nitty-gritty of real business practicalities, as represented by the HBS cases. But, unfortunately, these cases and the ways in which they are taught embody a carefully engineered, collectively condoned, and fundamentally phony teaching scheme that, when carefully considered, qualifies as nothing more than a Gigantic Hoax.

These aspects of collusive misdirection arise in at least three ways related to the three key participants – the case writers, the students, and the teachers.

First, the cases are designed to appear like veridical accounts of facts and figures that represent true real-world business problems tackled by actual business organizations. However, close inspection suggests that – in an attempt to create a streamlined teaching vehicle that does not embarrass its protagonists – the case-based narrative fictionalizes many aspects of the situation in question. Various issues are collapsed, glossed over, or rearranged in order to meet the relevant teaching objectives. Key data that must remain proprietary are omitted or disguised in ways that preserve secrecy. Complexities are disregarded or dumbed down so as to serve pedagogical purposes. In short, in my opinion, anyone who really wanted to gain real-world knowledge of one or another business organization would do better by reading its annual report, by studying relevant stories in the *Wall Street Journal*, or by watching shows such as those hosted by Jim Cramer on CNBC and Maria Bartiromo on Fox Business News.

Second, the prescribed technique for teaching a case hoodwinks students into believing that – by putting their ill-informed minds together for an hour or two – they can successfully grope their way to the solution of a challenging business problem that has confounded real-life managers for months or years. Unequipped with relevant concepts or pertinent theories, these students approach the case with little more than their common sense and popular misconceptions to rely on. Almost at random or (more politely) by trial and error, they voice disconnected opinions and offer scattered observations that would amount to nothing were they not winnowed and collated by an essentially manipulative teaching strategy.

Specifically, third and most appallingly, the discussion leader pretends that the solution to the case emerges from the insightful colloquy among members of the MBA class. In truth, after carefully studying the helpful instructor's manual that conveniently accompanies every case and perhaps even reading the case itself, the teacher knows in advance what solution he or she is looking for, guides the discussion in that direction, selectively latches onto whatever haphazard student comments happen accidentally to fit the lesson plan, writes them on the board, and in this way steers the group toward arriving at precisely the solution that the case writer intended to encourage all along. At the end of the class, the blackboard looks exactly like the creators of the case planned it. Yet the students incorrectly believe that they have worked together to arrive at an inspired solution. In truth, they have been outrageously scammed and don't even know it.

I should mention that I wrote the preceding paragraphs before reading the excellent book by Duff McDonald entitled *The Golden Passport: Harvard Business School, the Limits of Capitalism, and the Moral Failure of the MBA Elite* (McDonald, 2017). Drawing on work by scholars such as Henry Mintzberg (2009) and Contardo and Wensley (2004), McDonald (2017) excoriates the Harvard Business School in ways that gladden my heart – especially when he incisively attacks the lamentable excesses of the HBS Case Method. I might add that McDonald & Friends expose the dim-witted insistence with which HBS disciples celebrate their ingrained obeisance to real-life practicalities at the expense of potentially insightful theories. I regret to say that my own school has partially succumbed to this managerially pleasing practice-worshipping litany. For example, I recently participated in writing a chapter on marketing for a book commemorating CUGSB's 100th anniversary (Holbrook, Lehmann, and Schmitt, 2016). While reading the finished volume and being strongly impressed by the admirable achievements of my esteemed Columbia colleagues, I was powerfully struck by the frequency with which the carefully edited authors of various chapters harped on the practice-based justification for the school's curriculum and research initiatives. Without half trying, in 242 pages, I found over 50 such often formulaic and sometimes far-fetched appeals to the practitioner-oriented ethos.

For all these reasons I view the Case Method as an inherently anti-intellectual activity – one that arouses my distaste but that appeals irresistibly to the minds and egos of the sorts of MBA students who want to take a required standardized course taught in lockstep by members in a committee of professors who teach from the same set of lecture notes, reading assignments, problems sets, exam questions, and PowerPoint displays. I am too much of a nonconformist to participate cheerfully in that kind of intellectual dishonesty.

But, albeit with feelings of dread, I tried. Indeed, as previously mentioned, I worked harder to prepare for that course than I have worked on any other undertaking in my life. I struggled to make the prescribed course content fit with my own beliefs about what students should learn. I strived to include all the talking points that my colleagues thought were important. In short, I surrendered all aspects of my much-valued academic freedom for the sake of enacting the role that the school wanted me to play. But I could not fool those self-satisfied profit-hungry MBAs. Like a big and strong but incredibly stupid horse that somehow senses fear in its rider and throws the hapless equestrian into the mud, my huge and inherently nasty class of 200 MBAs somehow intuited my pitiable discomfort and ruthlessly punished me for it.

My scores in the course evaluations reached the lowest nadir attainable. With clear evidence in their comments that the students had maliciously collaborated in their survey responses, I set new records for vindictive student dislike, as reflected in my appallingly miserable teacher ratings.

Indeed, I found this experience so distressing, so embarrassing, and so humiliating that I immediately began contemplating my retirement and moved unwaveringly in that direction for the next three or four years. Fortunately for me – during that interlude, in recognition of my ineptitude in teaching a standardized core course – the school mercifully permitted me to go back to teaching my consumer behavior and commercial communication classes. I again attracted the few compatriot spirits who had somehow found their way into our MBA program plus a number of empathetic souls from other parts of the university. These relatively amiable MBAs and cross-registrants chose me freely for courses that they wanted to take and seemed to appreciate what I offered them. So – all things considered – I rounded out my teaching career at Columbia on an agreeably pleasant note.

But, all the while, I could not help noticing the sacrifices to academic integrity that flourished all around me. Inklings of further trouble had begun to surface during the mid-1990s when Columbia's rankings started to suffer in the sorts of polls conducted by *Business Week* and *US News & World Report*. The *BW* poll included survey responses from each school's graduates. And it turned out that MBA students similar to those who had treated me with such punishing disdain did not possess even enough public-spirited decency and self-preservative common sense to give their own school favorable ratings in a poll that would affect the prestige and marketability of their own academic diplomas. By figuratively cutting off their noses to spite their faces, the actions of these disgruntled students spoke volumes about their inability to treat others with kindness and respect, much less gratitude. At the time, I served as a member of the school's Admissions Policy Committee. And, when pressed with questions about how we might improve the situation, I pleaded the case for recruiting nicer students. Needless to say, my well-intentioned advice fell on deaf ears. But, in fairness, I must admit that – in the fullness of time – the school did seem to succeed in attracting exactly those sorts of MBA candidates who would favor a curriculum composed largely of required standardized core courses whose instructors had homogenized their offerings to reach hitherto unexcelled heights of anti-intellectualism and academic vapidity.

One might wonder what the school could do to address such a problematic situation. One misguided answer hinged on . . . marketing. Specifically, the school began a program to brand itself. It redesigned its stationery, revised its promotional materials, and changed its name from the old "Graduate School of Business at Columbia University in the City of New York" (rather dignified, I always thought) to "Columbia Business School" or "CBS" for short (thereby echoing Harvard's "HBS" while blurring Columbia's identity with that of a major television network). As the Columbia Business School or CBS marched forward, a new dean arrived on the scene in 2004 – this one a brilliant scholar, an economic advisor to presidents (George W. Bush) and presidential candidates (Mitt Romney), and a generally nice fellow with a good sense of humor. The dean's flair for self-deprecating comedy worked overtime in 2010 when Charles H. Ferguson created his documentary film entitled *Inside Job*, a major portion of which he devoted to trashing the Columbia Business School in general and one of its economics professors plus its dean in particular. In an on-screen interview – thanks in part to aggressive editing, I suspect – our generally mild-mannered dean appeared a bit petulant, and Ferguson won an Academy Award for his efforts. As a retiree, I had stopped suffering through faculty meetings, but my friends in attendance at one of these events told me that our dean referred with mock pride to his "Oscar-winning performance." Nonetheless, I suspect that *Inside Job* and the interview in question did little to burnish the brand image of CBS (the school, not the TV network).

Branding CUGSB as CBS fits, of course, with the whole project of running the university in general or its individual schools in particular like businesses. As such, the application of branding strategies to academic endeavors fills me with a certain amount of distaste (left over from days of yore when we knew that a "brand image" inevitably entailed some degree of permissible puffery or purposeful phoniness). Such a strategy reached full flower in (what I regard as) one of the satiric masterpieces of our time – namely, the sublimely ridiculous but musically sophisticated promotional video released by Appalachian State University in 2005 and entitled "Hot, Hot, Hot" (available on YouTube.Com). Opinions differ on whether this delicious parody was originally meant as a serious attempt to enhance ASU's brand image or, rather, was intentionally tongue-in-cheek to begin with. Either way, I regard it as a definitively hilarious send-up of all the trumpery that can result from treating an academic institution as a business.

Speaking of which, we cannot fail to be reminded of the philosophy espoused by Donald J. Trump – namely, that not only his scandalously discredited Trump University but also the United States of America should be run like a business. In this connection, to gain a sense of what Mr. Trump means by the word "business," we might contemplate the long list of atrocities that he is alleged to have committed – shipping jobs overseas, paying starvation wages to foreign employees, refusing to honor debts to suppliers and workers, pocketing big revenues before declaring bankruptcy, an unwillingness to supply tax records, retaining ownership of family businesses so as to defy emoluments regulations, showing rampant xenophobic prejudices against Muslims and Mexicans, displaying egregious disrespect toward women, firing law-enforcement prosecutors in ways that might constitute obstructions of justice, disguising or denying ties with Russia that might put him in a compromised position, inciting an insurrection, claiming he won an election that demonstrably he lost, stealing classified government documents, lying almost every time he opens his mouth, and many others. Whenever DJT is accused of some such nefarious activity, his standard excuse is to claim that it is "good business."

Here, we find the concept of business dragged through the dirt, degraded, and defiled in ways that reduce it to what practically amounts to a form of criminality. Such a perspective cannot help but rub off on the ways in which business is viewed in the modern world. As an illustration of this dismal progression (in a story mentioned in Chapter 11), on a day shortly before I retired, I walked into Uris Hall, right past the spot where the aforementioned now-obliterated inspirational words of Alfred North Whitehead had once shined down on all who entered. Not 30 feet from what used to be ANW's elevated message, I observed the installation of a new school motto in the form of a huge banner that proudly proclaimed, "We will not lie, cheat, steal, or tolerate those who do." Standing directly under this new insignia, I found our dean, so I asked him if he did not think that our sights, our ambitions, our goals, and our aspirations had sunk a bit in the scheme of things to the point where they now reflected a very mediocre standard of excellence. To my surprise, he wholeheartedly agreed with me but said, by way of explanation, that the school had erected the banner in deference to the wishes of the MBA students, who had adopted this rather paltry pledge and wanted it proclaimed for all to marvel at. This seems to be what happens when you let the inmates run the asylum (an insulting figure of speech, no doubt, but perhaps one with an element of truth lurking therein).

The arguments advanced thus far appear as a diagrammatic summary in Figure 13.1. Please pause for a moment to observe and recall how the various factors combine and interact to reinforce one another so as to create the downward spiral that I have described in the present essay. When considered all together, as a self-reinforcing system of mutually supportive mistakes, the syndrome displayed in the figure seems to beg for some sort of problem-ameliorating prescription.

But, wincing as I write this, I must confess that I see no ready solutions for these and the other problems mentioned in the present essay. The tide seems to have turned against us, with a vengeance. To mix metaphors rather flamboyantly, we cannot put the toothpaste back into the tube, and it's too late to shut the barn door. Still, I shall end with a few modest suggestions for minor ways in which we might tweak the current system for MBA education in marketing and other areas of study to achieve admittedly small improvements.

1 Stop running the university in general and its various schools in particular like businesses. Instead, run each school like an academic institution.
2 Stop regarding students as customers. Instead, regard them as channels of distribution, whereby knowledge created by the school is implemented and disseminated throughout society.
3 Stop viewing the business school as a brand to be promoted like laundry detergent or soda pop. Instead, view it as a community of scholars dedicated to the creation of business-related knowledge.

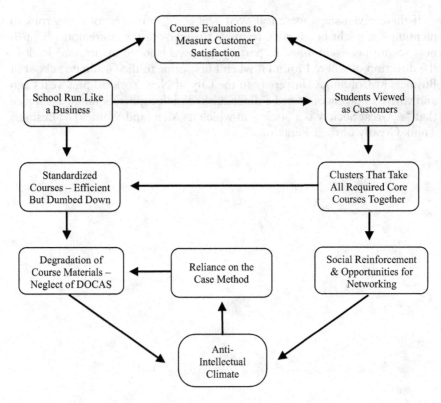

Figure 13.1 Inter-relations among the Main Factors Contributing to the Decline of Marketing Education at One Graduate School of Business

4 Stop asking students to submit anonymous course evaluations. Instead, ask them to sign their names to their student ratings.
5 Stop grouping students into clusters that take all their core courses together. Instead, let them find and choose their own circles of friends with whom to form lasting relationships based on something more than short-term proximity and opportunistic career-enhancing networks.
6 Stop requiring students to take standardized core courses. Instead, let them gravitate toward sections taught by professors whose idiosyncratic teaching styles match their own preferences.
7 Without intruding on their academic freedom, encourage such professors to pursue a broadened conception of the business as a Dynamic Open Complex Adaptive System (DOCAS) that must balance the interests of multiple stakeholders (not just those who own stock in the company) interacting within an environment in ways that pursue long-term survival by seeking a sustainable ecological niche (not just short-term wealth-maximizing profits).

If these seven steps were followed – plus many others too numerous to mention – it might be possible to move the ethos of the contemporary business school (as exemplified in part by my own beloved institution) back in the direction of where I found it when I first came to the Graduate School of Business at Columbia University in the City of New York 50-plus years ago and where I first encountered a distinguished philosopher's exalted assurance that "A Great Society is a Society in which its Men [and Women] of Business Think Greatly of their Functions."

Appendix
Promotional Messages Featuring Experiential Claims – Full List of Over 600 Examples

Consumer Nondurables

Drinks

Braun Tassimo (Hot Beverage System) – "Experience all the irresistible hot drinks you could ever wish for";

Coca-Cola BlaK™ – "Experience BlaK™ . . . . Every sip is an experience";

Critics' Choice (Wine Tastings) – "Part of the New York Wine Experience";

Frontgate Estate (Wine Club) – "Introducing a Rewarding New Way to Experience Wine";

Geerlings & Wade (Wines) – "The Vineyard Experience";

Gevalia (Coffee) – "All You Need for the Perfect Coffee Experience";

Jablum (Coffee from Jamaica) – "Experience Jablum's Blue Mountain Coffee" and "The Coffee Experience Beyond Compare";

LavAzza (Italian Coffee) – "Experience an Italian Classic Since 1895";

Mojito Lab (Paris) – "The Mojito Experience";

Mountain Road Wine Experience – "Mountain Road Wine Experience . . . cooler by several degrees";

Smartwater Sparkling (Bottled Water) – "Elevate Your Experience";

Wine Spectator – "New York Wine Experience . . . Celebrate the Good Life!";

Wine Spectator Wine-Tasting Event – "*Wine Spectator's* New World Wine Experience";

Zagat Wine Club – "Share the Zagat Wine Club experience with friends" and "Wouldn't it be great to share your wine experiences with fellow wine lovers and be able to buy wine with greater confidence?";

Food

Baileys Coffee Creams (Candy) – "The taste could only be Baileys. The experience could only be yours";

Dorritos (Tacos) – "A taste experience like no other";

Fish Farm (French Gourmet Foods) – "Food as pleasure . . . .. The Experience";

Ghiardelli (Chocolate) – "All the ingredients for the most intense chocolate experience";

Hillshire Farm Deli Select (Premium Lunch Meat) – "Made with special touches for a delectably different taste experience!";

Lindt Lindor (Chocolate Truffles) – "Like nothing you have ever experienced";

Matador (Beef Jerky) – "A Revolutionary Snacking Experience";

Oro Dioliva (Olive Oil) – "Experience Complimentary Tasting";

Seabear (Wild Salmon) – "Seafood Experiences to Share";

Health-Care Products

Ambien (Sleeping Pills) – "Experience Ambien CR for yourself";

Glide (Dental Floss) – "Experience the Glide Difference";

Pine Brothers (Cough Drops) – "Not just a cough drop but an experience";

Polident (Denture Adhesive) – "Made the Kiwis an enjoyable experience";

Systane Balance (Eye Drops) – "Experience a Lifetime of Beautiful Eyes";

Vicks VapoRub – "Experience the feeling of free breathing";

Beauty Products

Clairol's Herbal Essence (Shampoo) – "Experience the intensity";

Freeman (Facial Clay Masque) – "Experience the revitalizing benefits of organic perfection";

Lauder's Beyond Paradise (Fragrance for Men) – "Introducing the new experience in men's fragrance";

Line Eraser (Face Cream sold at Kiehl's) – "Experience the Line Eraser with 10.5% Vitamin C";

Noxzema (Face Cleanser) – "Experience the One and Only Noxzema Deep Clean";

Old Spice (Deodorant) – "Experience Is Everything";

Rêve d'Infini (Feminine Fragrance) – "Lift [the flap] To Experience Lalique De Lalique";

Miscellaneous Nondurables

Air Wick – "A Cleaner Fragrance Experience" and "Experience the Limited Edition White Collection from Air Wick" and "Experience the Airwick scented candle";

Charmin (Flushable Moist Wipes) – "Experience the fresher feeling";

Downy and Tide (Laundry Products) – "Experience Downy and Tide Clean Breeze";

Fancy Feast (Cat Food) – "Experience the very latest of the very best from Fancy Feast";

Florida Olive Oil Company – "Olive Oil & Balsamic Vinegar Tasting Experience";

P&G BrandSaver (In-Store Promotions for Tide, Charmin, Crest, Pringles, etc.) – "Experience P&G BrandSaver Live . . . An Exciting Store Event Where You Can Try Samples, Watch Demos & Consult Experts";

Tic Tacs (Breath Mints) – "Entertainment for your mouth";

Tourism

Airlines

Alaska Air Line – "An Entirely New Flight Experience";

Alitalia Airlines – "Experience Italy with Alitalia!";

American Airlines – "Experience the allure of Europe" and "New York's Premium Travel Experience . . . Our premium travel experience gives you the luxury and convenience you expect";

British Airways – "Expectation: A better business class experience";

British Airways Sleeper Service^{SM} – "Experience somnia";

Charlotte-Douglas International Airport (Sign in Men's Room) – "Charlotte-Douglas International Airport Is Committed to a superior customer experience";

Continental Airlines – "Take Your Travel Experience to a Higher Level";

Delta Airlines – "Enhance Your Experience . . . . Relax in Delta Comfort™";

JetBlue Airlines – "The JetBlue Experience" and "Your Ticket to a Great Flight Experience Goes Here" and "JetBlue Fly-Fi® is real broadband Internet in the sky, delivering a robust online experience" and "When you enhance your JetBlue experience with Even More® Space, you can expect . . . Extra room to stretch out and relax" and "The Mint experience on JetBlue gives you the flexibility to sleep, work and relax, so you can be refreshed for the day ahead" and "Allow us to mint you a new travel experience . . . welcome to a newly minted experience . . . thoughtful moments throughout the experience that rejuvenate and engage a weary traveler";

JetOne – "Experience Ultimate Aviation";

Korean Air – "Experience global networking on a whole new scale";

Orbitz – "At the airport . . . Enjoy a hassle-free airport experience with these travel tips from OrbitzTLC";

Singapore Airlines – "Experience the comfort of the most spacious bed in the sky";

South African Airways – "Delivering a Premium African Experience";

Cruises

Alaska Cruisetours – "Unparalleled Experience, Unbeatable Value!";

American Express Mariner Club – "Extraordinary cruise experience";

American Cruise Lines – "You'll experience an award-winning shore excursion";

Blue & Gold Fleet – "Experience Blue & Gold Fleet's New Breathtaking Bay Cruise Adventure";

Celebrity Cruises – "Come experience everything that makes a Celebrity cruise a true departure" and "Modern Luxury: Experience it":

Crystal Cruises – "Start with your personal Crystal Experience" and "Collect the Kind of Experiences that Add to the Narrative of Your Life" and "Experience the Historical & Unfolding Culture of Cuba . . .. Cuba . . . is now accessible . . . to experience the rich history and heritage this beautiful island has to offer";

Cunard (Ocean Liners) – "Experience It Today" and "Experience the very finest the world has to offer with our rich legacy of excellence and impeccable service" and "Celebrate the Golden Age of Ocean Travel. Better Yet, Experience It";

Holland American Line "A classic cruise experience" and "The cruise experience you've been waiting for";

Magellan Residential Cruise Line – "The most extraordinary residential experience ever conceived";

MSC Seaside – "Experience VIP Treatment";

Ponant (Cultural Cruises & Expeditions) – "Savor the experience";

Princess Cruises – "Experience Europe Like Never Before!" and "50 Essential Experiences: The Travel Bucket List";

Regent Cruises – "Experience the World Your Way" and "The Most Inclusive Luxury Cruise Experience™";

Silversea (Cruise Ship) – "Signature sailing experiences include: Intimate performances, lively discussions, interactive events" and "Ultimate Antarctica Experience . . . All-Inclusive Expedition Packages to the Ends of the Earth";

Sitmar Cruises – "The Sitmar Experience";

StarVista Signature Cruises – "Experience Diana Krall . . . on an Unparalleled and Exclusive Entertainment Excursion";

Automobiles

Aston Martin – "An entirely new car experience";

Audi A4 Sedan – "Experience the Audi A4 at your local dealer today";

Avis (Car Rentals) – "Please Tell Us about Your Avis Experience";

BMW – "It's a feeling you can only experience in a BMW";

Buick – "Experience . . . the New Buick" and "Experience Buick Lease";

Cadillac – "This summer, . . . experience a Cadillac for yourself";

Drive Time (Used Cars) – "Experience the New Drive Time";

Enterprise (Car Rentals) – "At Enterprise, we want your rental experience to be perfect";

Hertz (Car Rentals) – "Elevate your next car-rental experience with the best";

Hertz Neverlost (Navigation System) – "Experience an elite level of navigation performance";

Inifiniti – "Experience the Power of Infiniti Now";

Infiniti Q50 – "Experience the all-new Infiniti Q50";

Infiniti Q505 – "Experience Flight from the Driver's Seat";

Jaguar – "Experience the 2011 Jaguar Line-Up at Your Award-Winning Jaguar Dealer";

Jaguar XE – "Experience the XE for yourself at your Jaguar retailer";

Kia – "Get ready for the driving experience of the summer";

Land Rover (SUV) – "The Land Rover Experience" and "Experience the Freedom";

Lexus – "Experience Amazing" and "It's a golden opportunity to experience the Lexus performance" and "There's never been a better time to experience Lexus performance" and "Experience the SUV that dares to go beyond eternity";

McLaren (Automobile) – "Experience the exclusive McLaren 12C through one of our 9 authorized dealerships in the U.S.";

Mercedes-Benz of Brooklyn – "Extraordinary value, world-class service and an unparalleled experience";

Mercedes-Benz of Huntington – "Experience Luxury at Affordable Prices";

Mercedes-Benz of Southampton – "Experience the Difference . . . The ultimate Mercedes-Benz sales and service experience";

Paragon (Car Dealer) – "The ultimate car-buying experience";

Potamkin (Car Dealer) – "Personal Automotive Experience";

Ray Catena (Car Dealer) – "Affordable luxury starts with a 3-step experience . . .. Our Winning Combination: A Complete Ownership Experience";

Toyota – "A carefree driving experience";

Other Transportation

Bay Bus Service – "Experience the Difference";

Bay Ferries (Northumberland Ferries Limited) – "Save Time and Driving. Get the Full Maritime Experience";

Eurail – "Enjoy . . . experience . . . explore";

Holiday Bus – "Experience Excellence";

NY10 (MSNBC) – "Making Your Taxi Experience Better";

Taxi Entertainment Network – "Making your taxi experience better";

Hotels and Resorts

Baymont Inns – "Experience . . . Hometown Hospitality";

Biltmore Hotel, Providence – "Enjoy the historic experience";

Breakers, The (Palm Beach) – "Immerse yourself in a one-of-a-kind experience at Florida's favorite oceanfront resort" and "Celebrate . . . a luxuriously customized experience";

El Dorado Maroma, Mexico – "This Is Not a Resort. This Is an Experience . . .. Experience the First Overwater Bungalows in the Mexican Caribbean";

Exclusive Resorts – "Experience the World Together";

Fairmont Hotels and Resorts – "There's Only One Way to Experience Summer" and "Indulge in the beauty of the Riviera, or experience a world-class golfer's retreat . . .. Book your Fairmont Experience today";

Ginn Clubs & Resorts – "Reinventing the Resort Experience";

Hilton H Honors Gold Membership – "Go experience more";

Horned Dorset Primavera, The – "Experience True Elegance";

Hyatt Regency – "Make Plans Now to Experience Hyatt Resorts Puerto Rico";

Imperial, The – "The Imperial Experience";

Intercontinental Hotels & Resorts – "Experience Adds. Vision Multiplies";

Leela, The – "Experience the true essence of India";

Mandalay Bay, Las Vegas – "The Glow . . . 10% off your entire Mandalay Bay experience";

Mar-a-Lago Club, The – "An Experience Rich in History";

Marina Hotel – "Experience African Hospitality";

Marriott – "One Rewarding Experience Leads To Another";

Martha Washington Inn & Spa, Abingdon, VA – "An unforgettable experience" and "Experience e-mailing from a 200-year-old canopy bed";

MGM Grand Hotel, Las Vegas – "MGM Grand Offers Maximum Food & Beverage Experience";

Mohegan Sun – "A legendary getaway experience";

Niagra Parks (Golf Courses) – "A Legendary Experience . . . The Ultimate Golf Experience";

Ocean Edge Resort – "Only our 400 acre seaside Resort delivers the ultimate Cape Cod experience";

Paradise Island's Atlantis Hotel – "An Experience Like No Other";

Paradisus Palma Real Golf & Spa Resort – "The Paradisus Experience";

Pelican Hill (Resort) – "Give a Pelican Hill 'Experience' . . .. No Other Golf Experience Compares";

Peninsula Hotel, Beverly Hills – "Red Carpet-Ready Experience";

Puntacana Resort & Club – "Experience Puntacana Resort & Club";

Ritz Carlton, The – "Whatever travel experience you're looking for, you'll find it here";

Rose Hall Resort, Jamaica – "A Contemporary Resort Experience Is Coming";

Sanctuary® (Camelback Mountain Resort and Spa) – "Experience a higher level of fun, laughter and renewal";

Sea View Beach House – "An unforgettable vacation experience";

Sheraton Hotels – "Welcome to the Link@Sheraton® experienced with Microsoft® featuring complimentary Wi-Fi, a friendly bar, and comfy seats for more ways to connect whenever you want";

Stowe Mountain Resort – "A Mountain of History & Beauty and the Experience of a Lifetime. . . . Experience Stowe";

SummerBay Resort, Las Vegas – "Experience Las Vegas With a Free Two Night Stay!";

Temple Tower Hotel, Rome – "Experience the Power of the Temple Tower Club . . . experience the glory of Rome";

Trump® National Doral Miami – "You Deserve the Best Hotel Experience";

Waldorf Astoria – "Upgrade your Waldorf Astoria experience with your Visa Signature® card";

Westin Hotel – "Relax, Refresh, and Experience Westin Renewal";

Travel Destinations

Aruba – "Aruba Experience";

Atlantis Paradise Island, Bahamas – "2 Free Dolphin Experiences and Free Full Breakfast Daily";

Bermuda – "Experience Bermuda";

Blue Rush Sports Camp – "Experience the Rush!";

Caribbean, The – "Experience the Caribbean";

Chrysler Building, The – "Experience the Modernization Of An Icon";

Florida – "It's all about the experience";

Florida (VisitFlorida.Com) – "Bucket-List Learning Experiences for the Whole Family";

Florida (MustDoTravel.Com) – "Experience the top 10";

Greece – "Live Your Myth in Greece . . . Starring You . . . Amazing Sights, Diverse Experiences";

Honesdale, PA – "Enjoy the Honesdale Experience!";

Israel – "Where else can a view of the sea be a Biblical experience?";

Lexington, KY – "Your Chance To Experience Lexington, Ky Like a Local";

Los Angeles, CA – "Experience it";

Montauk, NY (Roadside Sign) – "Experience New York";

New Hampshire – "Live Free and Experience";

New York State (Roadside Sign) – "Welcome to New York . . .. Experience . . . Explore . . . Enjoy";

Orkney Islands – "A timeless experience";

Palm Beach – "Experience #ThePalmBeaches for Yourself";

ParcsCanada.GC.CA – "Expériences inoubliables" [unforgettable experiences];

Reversing Falls, Jet Boat Ride (Saint John's, New Brunswick) – "Have You Experienced the Falls Today???";

Saint Edward's Island, Canada – "Come and Experience Canada's Birthplace";

Saint John, Canada – "Urban Experiences";

Scottsdale, AZ – "Experience Scottsdale . . .. Bring your passion for life";

Spring Island, SC – "Get Lost . . . and Find Yourself . . . Through our Discovery Experiences";

St. Mary's, GA – "Experience . . . History, Adventure & Cumberland Island";

Stonehammer (Geopark) – "Experience a Billion Years of Stories";

Sydney, Australia (Experience Sydney and make it a year to remember";

Ulster County, New York – "Experience the Style of Ulster County";

Williamsburg, VA – "When you experience Colonial Williamsburg, it stays with you";

Travel Tours

Central Park Conservancy – "Enhance Your Park Experience . . .. Take an Official Central Park Tour";

Columbia Alumni Association (Travel Tours) – "Experiences of a Lifetime by Private Jet" and "Cuba . . . An Extraordinary People-to-People Experience";

Country Walkers – "Step into the Experience . . . The experience of a lifetime . . . To enhance your Italian experience";

Dolphin Encounters – "The Experience of a Lifetime";

DreamCycle Tours – "Experience Colorado . . .. Experience the grandeur of cycling along the shores of Colorado's Arkansas River";

Far & Wide Tours – "Adventure . . . Discovery . . . Experience . . . Experience the Best of New Zealand";

Frosch (Ken Heit, Independent Travel Consultant) – "The All-Inclusive Experience";

Harvard Alumni Association, Worldwide Travel Programs, Toronto – "Experience the unique underground network of pedestrian tunnels and dine at the CN Tower";

Hop-On Hop-Off Sightseeing Tours – "Experience Washington DC in Full Bloom";

InsightCuba.Com (*JazzTimes*) – "Experience Jazz in Cuba" and "The Havana Jazz Experience . . . featuring hands-on experiences with Cuban musicians and artists";

Inspirato with American Express – "Experience a New Way to Travel";

JazzTimes Tour – "Experience Jazz in Istanbul";

Key Culinary Tours – "Experience the Tastes of Sarasota";

Lindblad Expeditions – "Explorations . . . New Expeditions, Fresh Experiences";

National Geographic Explorer (Expeditions) – "Inclusive Pricing Means Value Plus Experiences";

New York Times Travel Show – "Be Part of the Ultimate Travel Experience";

Northwest Passage Explorer, 2017 – "Experience an Adventure";

Perillo Tours – "Eight unique travel experiences";

Rocky Mountaineer (Railroad Tour) – "Experience an award-winning Rocky Mountaineer rail journey";

Tauck Tours – "Preview the Tauck Travel Experience . . .. It's sure to be one of your most memorable travel experience";

Tauck Tours – "The Difference Is the Way You Experience the Places You Visit";

TotalExperiences.Com – "Total Experiences®: The Ultimate Group Getaway";

Travcoa Escorted Journey's – "Request your complimentary Travcoa catalog to experience the personal touch of an Escorted Journey";

Wine Spectator's Grand Tour – "Experience More Than 200 of the World's Finest Wines!";

Travel Books and Guides

AAA Travel TripTik – "The best travel experience";

AFAR – "Curious. Unconventional. Open to new discoveries. New experiences. And new opportunities . . .. AFAR is about travel the way YOU experience it";

Chopsticks NY – "Experience Japan in New York City";

Jelly Belly Visitor Center – "Experience the Fun!";

Must Do (Magazine) – "Experience the top 10 . . . Beautiful Beaches . . . Delicious Dining . . . Unique Shopping";

Must Do (Internet Visitor Guide) – "Discover. Explore. Experience . . .. Experience it all at www.MustDo.com";

TripAdvisor.Com – "Every experience counts" and "What wildlife viewing experience would you most enjoy?";

Restaurants

American Girl Place – "Experience dining designed with girls in mind!";

B. R. Guest restaurants – "Tell us . . . about your experience today";

Barbao – "Barbao has closed. We are grateful to all who experienced the restaurant with us. Please consider visiting our other restaurant";

Ben & Jack's Steakhouse – "A true New York Experience";

Boucherie – "We would appreciate your feedback about your experience";

Caribbean Xpress – "A Tasty Island Experience";

Ciao by the Beach – "Our passion here at Ciao by the Beach is to help you create special memories with our intimate family dining experience";

CIBO Express (Gourmet Markets) – "An OTG experience™";

Coffee Bean & Tea Leaf, The – "We Apologize the Inconvenience. We Are Closing at 2:00 P.M. Today in Order to Improve the Coffee & Tea Leaf Experience! The Store will Reopen Tomorrow Morning at 6:30 A.M.";

Dirty Dog Jazz Cafe – "Detroit's Best Jazz Experience";

Empire Steak House – "Experience the Taste";

Georgia's Café – "Experience a Taste of Europe";

Limani – "A dining experience like no other";

Megu – "Imperial Oyster Experience";

New Ciao Montauk, The – "The Ultimate Dining Experience";

PizzaHut – "Experience the flavor of now";

Red Lobster – "Creating an Experience that's not just a meal";

Riverboat Bar & Grill (Newton, MA) – "Experience Our New Menu";

Soda Fountain, The (Rosie's Chicken Salad Sandwich) – "This will be a 'riveting' experience";

Spring House Restaurant, Kitchen & Bar – "The Spring House experience is gracious and authentic";

Sushi Yasaka – "Moderate Price Extraordinary Experience";

Swallow East – "A New Kind of Dining Experience";

Ted's Montana Grill – "Experience Nacho Nirvana";

Telecharge (Broadway Ticket Sales) – "Book a dining experience today to enjoy before or after the show!";

Two Rivers Grille – "A New Dining Experience";

Museums

American Museum of Natural History – "Experience the largest animals to ever walk the Earth. Join the museum today" and "Dive In and experience the amazing underwater world of whales" and "An immersive experience in the Hayden Planetarium";

Bard Graduate Center (Decorative Arts, Design, History, Material Culture) – "The Interface Experience: Forty Years of Personal Computing";

Cooper Hewitt Smithsonian Design Museum – "Experience the New Cooper Hewitt";

Intrepid Sea, Air, & Space Museum – "Inspiring experiences for all ages";

Maritime Museum (Halifax) – "Experience History";

Metropolitan Museum of Art (Membership Recruitment) – "Come for the Art. Stay for the Member Experience";

New Brunswick Aquarium and Marine Center – "Experience the Maritimes [sic] Best Aquarium!";

New York Historical Society – "offering a multimedia cinematic experience for museum visitors of all ages";

Consumer Durables

Electronics

Acer® (Laptop Computer) – "Ultimate fun . . . Designed to maximize content enjoyment, providing the same rich multimedia, gaming and web experience you can enjoy on your home PC";

Bang & Olufsen BeoLab 11 (Subwoofer) – "Adding BeoLab 11 to your speaker set-up will greatly improve your listening and viewing experience";

BeoVision Avant HDTV – "Everyone Deserves the Bang & Olufsen Experience";

BlackBerry 10 – "The Blackberry Experience";

Blu-Ray Music – "Experience Jazz Classics on Blu-Ray Audio";

Bose VideoWave™ (Entertainment System) – "To be experienced by everyone and owned by a few";

Dell (Computers) – "Experience Windows 8";

HP (Computers) – "Experience it now at Circuit City";

HP EliteBook Revolve – "Transform to a tablet in an instant to get an intuitive touch experience";

Intel® – "Experience what's inside";

JBL – "Experience a New Standard in Wireless Headphones with the All New Everest Line-Up From JBL";

Jitterbug (Cell Phone) – "Three reasons why the Jitterbug experience is simply better";

JVC (HDTVs) – "The Perfect Experience . . .. JVC's HD-ILA TV is designed to fit your lifestyle – and totally change the way you experience television";

Monitor Audio (Loudspeakers) – "Experience the power and grace of Monitor Audio's Gold GX Series";

My Net™ (HD Routers) – "My Net™ . . . delivers blazing-fast HD Wi-Fi for the ultimate entertainment experience";

Nexus S by Samsung/Google (Smart Phone) – "Nexus S, a pure Google experience . . . Get it FREE today only";

Nintendo (Video Games) – "Experience a New Way to Play";

Nook (Digital Books) – "The Ultimate Reading Experience™";

Panasonic (HDTVs) – "Experience Visual Excellence on a Plasma HDTV" and "Experience the Undeniable Power of Panasonic Plasma";

Playstation⁽ˣ⁾ (Video Games) – "The Ultimate Destiny Experience is on Playstation⁽ˣ⁾";

Polk (Loudspeakers) – "Connect to your TV and get the full experience of an entertainment system";

Samsung (HDTVs) – "The Complete 3D Experience" and "Enjoy a true movie experience, watching colors and details come to life";

Sony Xperia (Cell Phones) – "Experience the best in Sony smartphones";

Sprint/Samsung (Cell Phones) – "Experience 4G";

Toshiba (Computers) – "Experience Windows 8 with Toshiba® computers";

Vertu (Cell Phones) – "Extraordinary Experiences";

Zenith (HDTVs) – "Zenith: Digitize the Experience";

Musical Instruments

Cannonball Saxophones – "It creates one of the most free-blowing experiences you can imagine";

Dakota Saxophones – "Owning and Playing Either Model Will Be the Ultimate Reward and Experience at Any Venue";

Garritan/Yamaha CFX Concert Grand (Virtual Piano) – "Experience the Passion Reflected in Every Detail at Garritan.Com";

JodyJazz DV (Saxophone Mouthpiece) – "The JodyJazz DV is the best playing saxophone mouthpiece you'll ever experience";

Mason & Hamlin (Pianos) – "Experience the new legendary Mason & Hamlin piano";

Yamaha (Digital Pianos) – "Experience the Nocturne Grand";

Neotech Saxophone Straps – "Experience the Innovation";

Zildjian Cymbals – "Experience the Dark-Ride";

Other Durables

Benjamin Moore (Paint) – "Experience Richer Colors in a More Durable Finish . . .. Benjamin Moore "Aura" paint";

Big Green Egg (Grill) – "The Ultimate Cooking Experience";

Bosch Ascenta® (Dishwasher)/Finish Quantum® (Dishwashing Tablets) – "Experience the team for a superior clean";

Cartier (Jewelry) – "Offering the best luxury experience to Cartier clients";

Enlite Bra – "Experience a revolutionary sensation in the Enlite Bra";

Endless Pools – "Experience the freedom of swimming at home";

HunterDouglas/Janovic (Motorized Window Shades) – "Two premium brands . . . One great experience . . . 10 NYC locations";

Inada (Massage Chair) – "The Inada DreamWave™ offers a therapeutic, transcendent full-body massage experience you can enjoy any time, every day in your home";

Mephisto (Footwear) – "For a Comfortable and Effortless Walking Experience";

Neiman Marcus (Jewelry) – "Forevermark Ultimate Diamond Experience";

Nespresso (Espresso Machines) – "Experience the Incomparable Coffee of Nespresso" and "Discover soon a world of unique coffee experiences";

Peloton (Exercise Cycle) – "The Indoor Cycling Experience That Happens in Your Home";

Rockport (Shoes) – "Experience the Style and Comfort of Rockport";

Schweitzer (Sheets and Pillow Cases) – "For the Ultimate Linen Experience";

Sealy (Mattresses) – "Optimum™ is the first mattress to feature cooling gel foam from top to bottom to once again deliver an exceptional sleep experience";

Stressless Seating – "Comfort. Defining your home theater experience";

Tempur-Pedic (Swedish Mattresses and Pillows) – "Experience the kind of sleep you've always dreamed about";

Thermador (Home Appliances) – "This is the transformative experience of Culinary Preservation Centers, exclusively from Thermador";

Trufocals® (Eyeglasses) – "Nothing is better for experiencing the whole field of view";

Walk-In Bathtubs – "The Safer Bathing Experience";

Waterpik® (Shower Head) – "To begin your Waterpik® shower experience we want to give you all of the proper tools to make installation easy and quick";

Events

Broadway and Off-Broadway

Beauty and the Beast (Musical) – " 'Tis the Season to Experience the Magic!";

Broadway Theater Musicians – "Live Music . . . Experience It!";

Broadway.Yahoo.Com (DVD included) – "Here's Your Ticket to the Ultimate Broadway Experience";

Cadillac/Broadway – "Cadillac Invites You to Win the Ultimate Broadway Experience";

Doubt (Play) – "An experience to last you a lifetime";

Jersey Boys (Musical) – "Now, you can experience it for yourself – *Jersey Boys*";

Memory (Play) – "A Rare Theatrical Experience to Treasure";

Once (Musical) – "Come Experience the Magic of *Once*";

Radio City Music Hall – "Experience New York like never before at 'Heart & Light'";

Roundabout Theatre – "Experience The Mystery of Edwin Drood";

Warhorse (Play) – "You only have until January 26 to experience the wonder of *Warhorse*";

Wonderland (Musical) – "Experience Alice through a Whole New Wonderland";

Television and Films

AMC Theaters – "Experience It in IMAX 3D . . . The World's Most Immersive Film Experience";

Arrival (Film) – "It's more than a film. It's an experience";

Avatar (Blue Ray DVD) – "The 3-D Experience comes home";

Awake (TV) – "Experience the Best New Show of the Season . . . *Awake*";

Bambi (Film) – "The classic childhood experience awaits";

Colbert Report (TV) – "Enhance Your Colbert Report Experience. Download the Free Zeebox App!";

Edge of Tomorrow (Film)– "Experience it on IMAX 3D June 6";

Green Hornet, The (Film) – "An Amazing 3D Experience";

Jurassic Park 3D (Film) – "You've Never Experienced Jurassic Park like This";

Lush (Film) – "You've rarely felt more alive in a movie theater than you will experiencing *Lush*";

Magdalene Sisters, The (Film) – "Experience the Year's Most Triumphant Film";

Mao's Last Dancer (Film) – "A Magical Experience You Must Not Miss";

Monster Calls, A (Film) – "Don't miss the most spectacular motion-picture experience of the season";

National Geographic Channel (TV) – "Don't Just Watch TV. Experience It";

Netflix (Customer Service Survey) – "I am satisfied with my Netflix Customer Service experience/I am unsatisfied with my Netflix Customer Service experience";

NYTimes.Com/Experience (Videos) – "Welcome to the Experience . . ..
Watch the Videos that Tell the Stories: NYTimes.Com/Experience";

Pirates of the Caribbean (Film) – "This Friday, experience the film critics are calling the perfect summer movie";

Rescue Dawn (Film) – "Experience the Incredible True Story of One Man's Journey Home";

Spider Man 2 (Film) – "Experience the Movie Event of the Summer";

Spirit (Film) – "Saddle Up and Experience the Spirit of the West!";

Suicide Squad (Film) – "Experience it on Imax";

Sundance Online Film Festival – "To experience the passion and excitement of independent film, just bring your Wi-Fi laptop";

The Help (Film) – "An unforgettable experience";

Tron: The Legacy (Film) – "Now Experience the Movie 3D Was Made For";

Water for Elephants (Film) – "Experience the film that has audiences talking";

Jazz and Pop

AllanHarris.Com – "Allan Harris Experience . . . 'The headwaters of the protean talent that is Allan Harris'";

Artists Collective, The – "Experience a Jammin' Jazz Getaway";

Clef-Verve Count Basie Recordings/Mosaic Records – "Experience Why There Is No Swing Like Basie Swing";

eJazzLines.Com – "Experience the web's largest and most user-friendly catalog of jazz";

Gregory Porter (Singer) – "Experience the Gregory Effect Now";

Gretchen Parlato (Singer) – "Experience the magic";

Jazz Inside (Magazine) – "The Jazz Music Dashboard . . . Smart Listening Experiences";

JazzVoyeur.Com – "jazz voyeur . . . the visual experience";

Jean-Luc Ponty (Jazz Violinist) – "The Acatama Experience";

Jimmy Hendrix (Rock Musician) – "Are You Experienced?";

Litchfield Jazz Festival – "The Experience";

Mike Longo & the NY State of the Art Jazz Ensemble – "One of the Most Enjoyable Evenings of Fabulous Music You Will Ever Experience!";

New Orleans Jazz & Heritage Festival – "To everyone who experienced the healing power of music at Jazz fest 2006 New Orleans says, 'Thank You!'";

RushRecords52@gmail.com – "Thank you for your order. We will make every effort to make sure you have a pleasant shopping experience";

Sandyland (Sandy Sasso, Singer) – "*Sandyland* Is . . . A Joyous Musical Experience";

Sheffield Jazz Recordings – "Experience the Natural Sound of Sheffield Jazz";

Southport Jazz Festival 2003 – "We Give You the Ultimate 4 Day Jazz Experience!";

Classical Music and Ballet

American Ballet Theater – "Experience the Power of Dance";

Carnegie Hall – "Dear Friend . . ... Thank you for attending Carnegie Hall's Bruckner symphony cycle. We hope you had an extraordinary experience . . ... Please help us make the Carnegie Hall experience the best it can be by answering the following question";

Chamber Music Society – "Rediscover the concert experience" and "An Unrivaled Way to Experience Unparalleled Artists";

Metropolitan Opera – "Experience the Met's new *Ring* cycle";

New York Philharmonic – "Welcome to the New York Philharmonic . . . Concert Experience";

Soundspace (92nd Street Y) – "Come experience music at 92Y for yourself";

Town Hall World Cabaret Series, The – "Experience . . . the drama of German Kabarett";

Volodos (Classical Pianist) – "Experience Tchaikovsky's Piano Concerto like never before!";

Other Events

American Express/Discovery Times Square – "Last Chance to Experience . . . Dead Sea Scrolls . . . The Exhibition";

Bodies, the Exhibition – "Real Human Bodies, Preserved Through an Innovative Process . . ... Experience the Human Body Like Never Before";

Brooklyn Expo Center, Worlds Fair Nano NY – "Experience the Future";

CBSsports.Com – "Experience the Next Level of Fantasy Football";

Discover, Times Square (Interactive Attraction) – "CSI: The Experience";

Discovery World at Pier Wisconsin – "Experience Discovery World during our Year of Discovery™";

Dutchess County Fair, The – "Experience a Classic";

Global Extremes – Mt. Everest – "Experience the Pinnacle of Live Television";

Minneapolis Metrodome – "Experience Minneapolis Metrodome";

New York City Marathon – "Experience the mania, apply Nov. 8 and find out if 'You're In' for 2011";

New York Yankees (Broadcasts) – "Experience the Yankees Like Never Before";

NFL (National Football League) – "Win unreal experiences every week";

Power Within, The (Motivational Speeches by William Jefferson Clinton, Michael D. Eisner, and Lance Armstrong) – "Experience the Power Within";

Pro Football Hall of Fame (Contest, Land O' Frost Turkey Breast) – "Win the Experience";

Related Urban Development – "New Yorkers dine out as an entertainment experience";

Ringling Bros. and Barnum & Bailey Circus Xtreme – "Enter a world of Xtreme and experience the highest, fastest, strongest, most daring acts on the planet . . . . Experience the amazement of seeing it live with your whole family";

Rita's Petting Farm – "Hands on Experience with Petting Farm Animals at Rita's Stable";

Shen Yun (Performing Arts) – "Experience the divine";

Walking With Dinosaurs (Presented by Immersion Edutainment) – "The Live Experience";

WSJ+ (Talks, Screenings, and Events Sponsored by the *Wall Street Journal*) – "We are delighted to welcome you to WSJ+, a whole new Wall Street Journal experience . . . .. We are also continuing to expand . . . nationwide, so you can enjoy these experiences in person wherever you are";

Zarkana (Cirque de Soleil) – "Experience the Grandeur";

Education

American Marketing Association – "Experience unparalleled discovery . . . An event you have to experience to believe . . . M.planet";

American Marketing Association, 2007 Winter Marketing Educators' Conference – "Creating Value through Marketing Experiences";

App.HarvardMagazine.Com – "Better Reading Experience";

Asia Society – "Experience Persia's national epic as never before";

Brown University, Pre-College Programs – "Experience College this Summer";

CampusGroups (Event Management System) – "This exciting new initiative should improve the overall user experience . . . for the entire community";

Capsim – "Experience the world's best-selling business simulations while networking with your peers";

Carleton College – "Your gift to the annual fund helps students experience Carleton in their own unique way";

Columbia Alumni Association – "A New Alumni Experience Awaits";

Columbia Business School – "Experience the Joys (visit the site)";

Columbia Business School (From the Dean) – "Please join me for a Town Hall meeting, an open exchange to discuss your academic experience";

Columbia Business School's On-Line Course-Listing Software – "Our ongoing commitment to improving the Angel experience";

Despair Motivational Products – "Finally, you can experience all the pain . . . without the indignity";

Emerald Publishers – "Emerald strives to provide the best experience we can of publishing with us . . . .. We would like to know what you thought about your experience of publishing with Emerald";

Great Courses, The (Instructional Videos) – "Experience the 36 Events That Forever Changed History" and "Experience the Wonders of the Hubble Telescope";

Hands On! (Music Classes for Children) – "A Musical Experience";

Harvard University (Planned Giving) – "Cultivating Connections: Donors Enrich Their Harvard Experience through Giving";

Hollins University – "The Hollins Experience: Personal. Practical. Powerful";

Incarnation Camp – "Sharing the Camp Experience" and "The Authentic Summer Camp Experience";

Irish Whiskey Academy – "Our aim is to deliver a truly unforgettable distillery experience";

Leadership Challenge®, The (Workshop Presented by iLead and Wiley) – "A Unique Experience";

Listening In: The Secret White House Recordings of John F. Kennedy – "Experience History as It Happened" and "The *New York Times* Bestseller that takes you inside the Oval Office to experience history as it happened";

Longwood Gardens – "Experience the spectacle online . . .. The Experience of a Lifetime, Every Time";

Marketing Association of Columbia (The 6th Annual MAC Conference) – "Experience: Elevated, Enhanced and Personalized for Today's Mindful Consumer";

Marketing Science Institute (MSI) – "Beyond the Product: Designing Customer Experiences";

Marketing Science Institute (MSI, Research Priorities, 2012–2014) – "3. Designing experiences, not products. What accounts for experiences that are remembered, interesting, repeated, and valued?";

National Geographic – "Experience the national parks like never before";

New York Botanical Garden – "Experience Nature's Showplace" and "Experience a World of Nature . . . Four Seasons of Every Year";

New York Times Programs of Study – "Learn From Experience";

New York Times, The – "We invite you to continue experiencing *The Times*";

Public Art Fund – "Public Art Fund invites you to experience New York City's iconic statue of Christopher Columbus as never before";

SAGE Publications/*Journal of Macromarketing* – "To help ensure SAGE and Journal of Macromarketing provide the best possible service to their authors, we would greatly value your completion of a short anonymous questionnaire on your experience of publishing in this journal and with SAGE";

Schools & Camps Summertime Spectacular – "An Experience that Lasts a Lifetime";

Teach12.Com – "Experience the Wonders of Ancient Rome";

Teaching Company, The – "Experience the Power and Beauty of English";

TheGreatCourses.Com – "Experience Everyday Life in Ancient Pompeii";

Third Street Music School – "It was really a once-in-a-lifetime experience . . .. My experience at Third Street was so important";

University of Phoenix – "If you prefer a classroom experience, look no farther than your own neighborhood";

University School of Milwaukee – "The Experience of a Lifetime" and "The new USM website . . . now offers hundreds of new ways to view the USM experience";

Wilson Quarterly, The (Magazine) – "Discover the writing of the world's leading thinkers . . .. Experience *The Wilson Quarterly*";

Housing

Aldyn Residences, The/Athletic Club/Spa – "New York's Ultimate Sporting Experience";

Atria – "Redefining Today's Senior Living Experience";

Bald Head Island – "Experience the Exceptional Nature of . . . North Carolina's Premier Second-Home Community";

Champlin Woods Condos – "Experience Better";

City Connections Realty, Inc. – "A Better Real Estate Experience";

Esplanade Senior Residences – "Experience . . . The Esplanade Senior Residences" and "You're Invited to Experience . . . Esplanade";

Estates at Acqualina™, The – "Oceanfront Living As You've Never Experienced It Before" and "Experience Life on the A-List";

Extell Condominium Residences – "Experience the Extell Choice";

Gurney's Residences – "Experience the Gurney's Lifestyle";

Hudson Yards – "Experience the best New York City has to offer";

Hyatt in Briarcliff Manor (Retirement Community) – "Experience Luxury Senior Living";

Oldfield (Private Club Community) – "To Experience It All for Yourself, Only a Personal Visit Will Do";

Osborn Retirement Community, The – "Experience the views";

Reef, The (Residences, Paradise Island) – "Experience the Reef as an Owner";

Residences at the Mark, The – "Experience the cultivated life";

St. Regis Residence Club, The – "Experience the exhilaration of the U.S. Open year after year with Membership in the St. Regis Residence Club, New York";

Town & Country Real Estate (East End of Long Island) – "Experience Montauk";

Village Green – "Experience 311 E 11: Village Green. Live better in every sense";

VIP Realty Group – "Experience magnificent views overlooking Southwest Florida's Gulf Coast";

Watergate, The (Apartment Building) – "Experience the Rebirth of Washington's Premier Address";

World, The (Residences at Sea) – "You encounter rare, tailored experiences in remote destinations and vibrant cultural capitals";

Shopping

Bricks-and-Mortar Stores

A&D Building, New York – "BSH Experience & Design Center";

Amos Pewter (Halifax) – "Shop & Tour Experience";

Art of Shaving, The – "Experience the Perfect Shave";

Best Buy – "The Samsung Experience Shop";

Bloomingdale's (Bed and Bath Department) – "Experience our new bed & bath department, Now Open on 6!";

Bloomingdale's (Vera Wang, Burberry, Tribeca Film Festival, etc.) – "Introducing Our 5 One-In-A-Lifetime Ultimate Experience";

Bloomingdale's/Borghese Mud Treatment – "Experience the Biggest Makeover in NYC";

Brooks Brothers (Clothing Store) – "Experience the standards of Quality and Value";

CVS Pharmacy (Posted Sign) – "In order to provide you with a quick and hassle free experience we ask if you could please give your undivided attention and not talk on your cell phone while being served by a staff member";

Design Within Reach (DWR) – "Design Is a 3-Dimensional Experience";

Essentials (Variety Store) – "Gazillions of Games . . . a Wonderful Toy Experience";

Florida Leather Gallery – "Experience the Style and Comfort of Stressless";

Geox (Shoe Store) – "Experience Comfort Without Compromise";

Gracious Home (Housewares) – "Experience";

Hampton Teak & Rugs – "The Hampton's Newest Home Shopping Experience";

Hardware Designs, Inc. – "A Great Way to Improve Your Cooking (Experience)";

Harry's Shoes – "Come experience an American Original . . . Hush Puppies";

Harvey (Electronics Store) – "Grand. Experience";

Hershey Store (Chocolate) – "This Season, Experience Light and Airy, Melting Bubbles";

Home Depot (Hardware Store) – "Your Opinion Counts! We would like to hear about your shopping experience";

Hunt's Photo & Video Store – "A Picture Perfect Experience";

Laytner's (Home-Furnishings Store) – "Our aim is to improve your shopping experience while bringing you Higher Standards at Lower Prices";

Loewe's (Hardware Store) – "Experience Loewe's. Let's Build Something Together";

Lord & Taylor (Beauty Floor) – "The Ultimate Beauty Experience . . .. Come experience the best of the best firsthand";

Macy's (Department Store) – "Experience 5-star luxury";

Oakley Store – "Experience the latest innovations from the Oakley Design Bunker including sunglasses, apparel, footwear, watches, and accessories";

Ralph Lauren (Clothing Store) – "The Ultimate Experience";

Raymour & Flanigan (Furniture Store) – "Delivering a Better Experience";

RCS (Electronics Store) – "RCS experience";

Rockefeller Center – "NBC, The Experience Store";

Sleepy's (Mattress Store) – "Experience Tempurpedic – the mattress that's changing the way the world sleeps";

Storefront (Ad for Kellogg's Special K) – "Rethink Your Jeans: A Unique Denim Experience";

Sunspots Studios – "Experience this Spectacular Display of Artistry 7 Days a Week";

Tanger Outlets – "You'll find a great shopping experience at Tanger Outlets";

Tile Showcase (Bathroom Fixtures) – "Experience Selection, Value and Service";

Trader Joe's (Grocery Store) – "Customer Experience: A Trader Joe's Love Story";

Verizon Stores (Cell-Phone Store) – "The Verizon Experience";

Walmart – "Walmart is committed to providing you superior customer service and a pleasant shopping experience";

Wyland Galleries (Sarasota) – "Wyland Galleries Experience";

Online Shopping

BelleBooks.Com – "Belle's-Books hope that your experience shopping with us was a pleasant one";

BestBuy.Com – "Experience Limitless Entertainment";

Bonobos.Com – "Today, Bonobos offers the complete online experience for all menswear";

Charles Tyrwhitt (Men's Clothing) – "Dear Morris Holbrook . . . Would you like to tell Charles Tyrwhitt (US) what you thought about your recent experience?";

DollGallery.Com – "The Ultimate Collector's Experience";

FAOSchwartz.Com – "Book an Unforgettable Experience Today";

Frontgate.Com/NYT – "Experience Frontgate Quality";

Go4AllSports.Com – "The Premium Sports Shopping Experience";

Grupo L&L (Amazon.Com Vendor) – "Greetings Morris B. Holbrook . . .. Select the rating that best reflects your experience and add your comments";

Kosher.Com – "Bring Kosher Home . . . delivering the Kosher experience";

Microsoft – "Thank you for shopping with Microsoft . . .. We hope you enjoyed your shopping experience";

MLBshop.Com (Major League Baseball) – "A Fanatics Experience";

More.Com/Experience – "Experience More! . . . Check Out the List of Unique Experiences We're Offering";

ShopHop.Com – "The online shopping experience!";

Starbucks.Com – "Experience more at Starbucks.com";

Stelton.Com – "We hope you enjoy your shopping experience on our website";

SuperMediaStore – "We just want to encourage you to rate your shopping experience with our store by leaving feedback through Amazon.com";

TheRealReal.Com (Online Consignment Shop) – "The Most Rewarding Consignment Experience";

Zabar's.Com – "Ship a N.Y.C. Experience";

Shopping Areas

Anchorage Center – "Grand Cayman's Ultimate Duty Free Shopping Experience";

AOL Time Warner Center – "The most exciting and elegant shopping experience in New York City";
Home Entertainment Show – "Experience the Lifestyle";
Old Hyde Park Village (Tampa) – "Experience the Village";
US Outdoor Sports Center – "Experience Patagonia";

Other Shopping

Fashion & Retail Day (New York City): "Experience NYC";
Premiere Caterers – "Experience the Difference";
Standard Coffee Service Co. – "We deliver the coffee house experience";
TrueCar.Com – "When buying a car, it guarantees savings and a hassle-free experience";

Financial Services

Banks

Chase – "Welcome to a Better Banking Experience";
Citigold® (Citibank Services) – "Experience the Citigold difference" and "An Elevated Citigold® Experience Is Coming Soon";
City National Bank – "Experience the Difference";
Commerce Bank – "Experience America's Most Convenient Bank";
First International Bank of Israel – "You experience the traditional Private Banking of the renowned World Wide Safra Banking Group";
Valley National Bancorp – "Valley offers a unique customer experience at each one of our 198 branches by offering unparalleled customer service";

Credit Cards

American Express Platinum Card – "An Experience That Makes You Rethink Every Other";
Chase Freedom® Credit Card – "Experience Chase Freedom®";
GM Card – "The GM Card experience";
Mastercard® – "Mastercard® is reserving priceless New York experiences just for you";
Visa Card – "Black Card Members Experience More" and "There's nothing better than sharing experiences with the people we love";

Other Financial Services

Fidelity Investments – "Experience the value of fixed-income investing at Fidelity";
Fidelity.Com (website) – "Welcome to the New Accounts & Trade experience! . . . Note: The new site experience will permanently replace the classic experience soon";

Quicken Loans – "For a mortgage experience that's engineered to amaze";

Sage Software – "Experience efficiency that puts time back on your side";

TIAA (Retirement Investments, formerly TIAA-CREF) – "Shorter name. New experience";

VirtualWallet.Com by PNC Bank – "Experience Everything Virtual Wallet has to offer";

Miscellaneous Services

Utilitarian Services

Adobe Flash (Online Download) – "Rate your download experience";

AT&T – "AT&T. A Better 3G Experience";

Caesars Palace – "Total Experiences: A Whole New World of Access for Group Getaways";

DirectTV® – "Experience it yourself";

Intel (Networks that Monitor Road Conditions) – "Rush Hour Becoming a Moving Experience";

iO TV – "Experience DVR on every TV in the house!";

Jenkens & Gilchrist (Lawyers) – "The experience you deserve . . . the Jenkens experience";

Lionmail (Email Provider) – "As part of our effort to improve your experience across our consumer services, we're updating the Microsoft Services Agreement and the Microsoft Privacy Statement";

Microsoft Windows – "One experience for everything in your life";

Mozilla Firefox (Web Browser) – "Firefox automatically sends some data to Mozilla so that we can improve your experience";

Optimum (Cable) – "Experience TV that goes beyond TV";

Public Storage – "Our goal is to provide you with the best customer experience";

Time Warner Cable – "You can have a better TV experience too" and "Experience the ultimate selection of products from TimeWarner Cable" and "Get the ultimate cinema experience with HD Movies on Demand" and "All across America, families are coming back to Time Warner Cable for a whole new experience";

T-Mobile – "Our next-generation broadband experience";

United States Post Office – "Attention Customers: Tell Us about Your Recent Postal Experience at postalexperience.com/pos";

Verizon Internet – "Rev up you online experience" and "You're invited to experience the Internet as it was meant to be" and "Verizon has always set out to provide you with the most powerful and reliable network experience" and "Get More. Do More. Experience More . . .. A TV experience like no other . . .. Connect to a fast Internet experience";

Verizon FIOS (Cable) – "FIOS: A Better TV Experience Is Here" and "Switch to a better entertainment experience" and "At Verizon, we strive to provide you with the best experience" and "Enjoy a bigger, better entertainment experience" and "For an entertainment experience that goes beyond cable, get FIOS TV";

Hedonic Services

Deborah Thompson Day Spa: "Experience the world of Marrakech . . .. It will be an unforgettable spa experience";

eHarmony.Com – "Experience the difference of a site that really cares about helping you find a wonderful relationship";

Exhale® Mind-Body Spa – "Experiences";

Massage Parlor/Spa – "Siesta Key Massage Experiences";

Spa at the Providence Biltmore Hotel, The – "While enjoying your stay at the Biltmore, a complete sensory experience awaits" and "Experience the very best in massage, skin care, nail treatments . . ..";

St. Tropez Tanning Essentials – "Experience the Luxury of St. Tropez Instant Sunless Tanning";

Health-Care Services

American Red Cross – "Experience the feeling of making a difference";

Mount Sinai Hospital – "Patient Experience";

United Health Care – "It's Time for a Better Health Care Experience, New York";

Weill Cornell Medicine/New York Presbyterian – "Experience the Difference a World-Class ENT Physician Can Make";

Other Services

Jewish Center, The – "MJE . . . Manhattan Jewish Experience";

LinkedIn – "Hi Morris, . . . To make sure you continue having the best experience possible on LinkedIn, we're regularly monitoring our site";

New York Times Times Reader 2.0 – "Experience the Next Generation News Reader";

OuterBody.Org (Photo Booth for Voyeuristic Introspection) – Outerbody Experience Lab . . . See yourself from a third person perspective using video goggles and cameras";

Roadway Moving – "A Truly Moving Experience";

Spot Experience, The (Dog Daycare) – "The first luxury experience for your dog" and "The Spot Experience is the first luxury experience of its kind for your dog";

Unlimited Earth Care – "Landscape Design . . . For the Perfect Outdoor Living Experience."

References

Abbott, Lawrence (1955), *Quality and Competition*, New York, NY: Columbia University Press.

Addis, Michela (2023), "Introduction by the Guest Editor," *International Journal of Arts Management*, 26 (1, Fall), 4–5.

Addis, Michela and Morris B. Holbrook (2001), "On the Conceptual Link Between Mass Customisation and Experiential Consumption: An Explosion of Subjectivity," *Journal of Consumer Behaviour*, 1 (1, June), 50–66.

Addis, Michela and Morris B. Holbrook (2010a), "Consumer's Identification and Beyond: Attraction, Reverence, and Escapism in the Evaluation of Films," *Psychology & Marketing*, 27 (9), 821–845.

Addis, Michela and Morris B. Holbrook (2010b), "Dreaming of Artistic Excellence, Popularity, or Both?" in *Marketing the Arts: A Fresh Approach*, ed. D. O'Reilly and F. Kerrigan, London, UK: Routledge, 141–152.

Adler, Mortimer J. (1981), *Six Great Ideas*, New York, NY: Palgrave Macmillan.

Alderson, Wroe (1957), *Marketing Behavior and Executive Action*, Homewood, IL: Irwin.

AMA Task Force on the Development of Marketing Thought (1988), "Developing, Disseminating, and Utilizing Marketing Knowledge," *Journal of Marketing*, 52 (4), 1–25.

Anand, Punam and Morris B. Holbrook (1990a), "Reinterpretation of Mere Exposure or Exposure of Mere Reinterpretation?" *Journal of Consumer Research*, 17 (2), 242–244.

Anand, Punam and Morris B. Holbrook (1990b), "The Convergent Validity of Dichotic Listening and Hemispheric Priming as Methods for Studying Lateralized Differences in Affective Responses," *Marketing Letters*, 1 (3), 199–208.

Anand, Punam, Morris B. Holbrook, and Debra Stephens (1988), "The Formation of Affective Judgments: The Cognitive-Affective Model Versus the Independence Hypothesis," *Journal of Consumer Research*, 15 (3, December), 386–391.

Arnould, Eric J. (2007), "Service-Dominant Logic and Consumer Culture Theory: Natural Allies in an Emerging Paradigm," in *Consumer Culture Theory, Vol. 11 of Research in Consumer Behavior*, ed. Russell W. Belk and John F. Sherry, Jr., Oxford, UK: Elsevier, 57–76.

Arnould, Eric J. (2013), "Rudiments of a Value Praxeology," *Marketing Theory*, 14 (1, March), 129–133.

Arnould, Eric J. and Craig J. Thompson (2005), "Consumer Culture Theory (CCT): Twenty Years of Research," *Journal of Consumer Research*, 31 (4, March), 868–882.

Arnould, Eric J. and Craig J. Thompson (2007), "Consumer Culture Theory (And We Really Mean *Theoretics*): Dilemmas and Opportunities Posed by an Academic

Branding Strategy," in *Consumer Culture Theory, Vol. 11 of Research in Consumer Behavior*, ed. Russell W. Belk and John F. Sherry, Jr., Oxford, UK: Elsevier, 3–22.

Arussy, Lior (2002), *The Experience! How to Wow Your Customers and Create a Passionate Workplace*, San Francisco, CA: CMP Books.

Askegaard, Søren and Linda Scott (2013), "Consumer Culture Theory: The Ironies of History," *Marketing Theory*, 13 (2), 139–147.

Babin, Barry J., William R. Darden, and Mitch Griffin (1994), "Work and/or Fun: Measuring Hedonic and Utilitarian Shopping," *Journal of Consumer Research*, 20 (4, March), 644–656.

Balliett, Whitney (1959), *The Sound of Surprise*, New York, NY: E. P. Dutton & Co.

Banbury, Catherine, Robert Stinerock, and Saroja Subrahmanyan (2012), "Sustainable Consumption: Introspecting Across Multiple Lived Cultures," *Journal of Business Research*, 65 (4, April), 497–503.

Bass, Frank M. and William L. Wilkie (1973), "A Comparative Analysis of Attitudinal Predictions of Brand Preference," *Journal of Marketing Research*, 10 (3, August), 262–269.

Batat, Wided (2019), *Experiential Marketing: Consumer Behavior, Customer Experience, and the 7Es*, London, UK and New York, NY: Routledge.

Batra, Rajeev and Olli T. Ahtola (1991), "Measuring the Hedonic and Utilitarian Sources of Consumer Attitudes," *Marketing Letters*, 2 (2, April), 159–170.

Batra, Rajeev and Morris B. Holbrook (1990), "Developing a Typology of Affective Responses to Advertising," *Psychology & Marketing*, 7 (1, Spring), 11–25.

Beardsley, Monroe C. (1967), "History of Aesthetics," in *Encyclopedia of Philosophy*, Vol. 1, ed. P. Edwards, New York, NY: Macmillan and Free Press, 1835.

Belk, Russell W. (1975), "Situational Variables and Consumer Behavior," *Journal of Consumer Research*, 2 (3, December), 157–164.

Belk, Russell W. (1988), "Possessions and the Extended Self," *Journal of Consumer Research*, 15 (2, September), 139–168.

Bell, Stephen, Morris B. Holbrook, and Michael R. Solomon (1991), "Combining Esthetic and Social Value to Explain Preferences for Product Styles with the Incorporation of Personality and Ensemble Effects," *Journal of Social Behavior and Personality*, 6 (6), 243–274.

Bello, David C. and Morris B. Holbrook (1995), "Does an Absence of Brand Equity Generalize Across Product Classes?" *Journal of Business Research*, 34 (2, October), 125–131.

Berliner, Paul F. (1994), *Thinking in Jazz: The Infinite Art of Improvisation*, Chicago, IL: University of Chicago Press.

Berthon, Pierre, Morris B. Holbrook, and James M. Hulbert (2000), "Beyond Market Orientation: A Conceptualization of Market Evolution," *Journal of Interactive Marketing*, 14 (3), 50–66.

Berthon, Pierre, Morris B. Holbrook, and James M. Hulbert (2003), "Understanding and Managing the Brand Space," *MIT Sloan Management Review*, 44 (2), 49–54.

Berthon, Pierre, Morris B. Holbrook, James M. Hulbert, and Leyland F. Pitt (2007), "Viewing Brands in Multiple Dimensions," *MIT Sloan Management Review*, 48 (2), 37–43.

Bettman, James R. (1979), *An Information Processing Theory of Consumer Behavior*, Reading, MA: Addison-Wesley.

Bevan Julia and Ruth Murphy (2001), "The Nature of Value Created by UK Online Grocery Retailers," *International Journal of Consumer Studies*, 25 (4, December), 279–289.

Bingham, Christopher B. and Kathleen M. Eisenhardt (2011), "Rational Heuristics: The 'Simple Rules' That Strategists Learn from Process Experience," *Strategic Management Journal*, 32 (13, December), 1437–1464.

Bode, Matthias and Per Østergaard (2013), "The Wild and Wacky Worlds of Consumer Oddballs: Analysing the Manifestary Context of Consumer Culture Theory," *Marketing Theory*, 13 (2), 175–192.

Bond, E. J. (1983), *Reason and Value*, Cambridge, UK: Cambridge University Press.

Börjesson, Sofia and Tobias Fredberg (2004), "Jam Sessions for Collaborative Management Research," in *Collaborative Research in Organizations*, ed. N. Adler, A. B. Shani, and A. Styhre, London, UK: Sage Publications, 135–148.

Bourdeau, Laurent, Jean-Charles Chebat, and Christian Counturier (2002), "Internet Consumer Value of University Students: E-Mail-Vs.-Web Users," *Journal of Retailing and Consumer Services*, 9 (2, March), 61–69.

Boyd, Harper W. and Sidney J. Levy (1963), "New Dimensions in Consumer Analysis," *Harvard Business Review*, 41 (November–December), 129–140.

Bradshaw, Alan and Morris B. Holbrook (2007), "Remembering Chet: Theorising the Mythology of the Self-Destructive Bohemian Artist as Self-Producer and Self-Consumer in the Market for Romanticism," *Marketing Theory*, 7 (2), 115–136.

Bradshaw, Alan and Morris B. Holbrook (2008), "Must We Have Muzak Wherever We Go? A Critical Consideration of the Consumer Culture," *Consumption, Markets and Culture*, 11 (1), 25–43.

Bradshaw, Alan, Finola Kerrigan, and Morris B. Holbrook (2010), "Challenging Conventions in Arts Marketing: Experiencing the Skull," in *Marketing the Arts: A Fresh Approach*, ed. Daragh O'Reilly and Finola Kerrigan, London, UK: Routledge, 5–17.

Brown, Stephen (ed. 2006), *Consuming Books: The Marketing and Consumption of Literature*, London, UK: Routledge.

Brown, Stephen (2012), "Wake Up and Smell the Coffin: An Interpretive Obituary," *Journal of Business Research*, 65 (4, April), 461–466.

Brown, Stephen and Anthony Patterson (ed. 2000), *Imagining Marketing: Art, Aesthetics and the Avant-Garde*, London, UK: Routledge.

Brown, Stephen and Sharon Ponsonby-McCabe (ed. 2014), *Brand Mascots and Other Marketing Animals*, London, UK and New York, NY: Routledge.

Brunswik, Egon (1956), *Perception and Representative Design of Psychological Experiments*, Berkeley, CA: University of California Press.

Capon, Noel, Morris B. Holbrook, and James Hulbert (1972a), "Industrial Purchasing Behavior: A Reappraisal," *Journal of Business Administration*, 4 (1), 69–77.

Capon, Noel, Morris B. Holbrook, and James Hulbert (1972b), "Industrial Purchasing Behavior: Some Final Comments," *Journal of Business Administration*, 4 (1), 83.

Capon, Noel, Morris B. Holbrook, and James M. Hulbert (1977), "Selling Processes and Buyer Behavior: Theoretical Implications of Recent Research," in *Consumer and Industrial Buying Behavior*, ed. A. G. Woodside, J. N. Sheth, and P. D. Bennett, New York, NY: North-Holland, 323–332.

Carbone, Lewis P. (2004), *Clued in: How to Keep Customers Coming Back Again and Again*, Upper Saddle River, NJ: Prentice Hall.

Carú, Antonella and Bernard Cova (2003), "Revisiting Consumption Experience: A More Humble But Complete View of the Concept," *Marketing Theory*, 3 (2), 267–286.

Carú, Antonella and Bernard Cova (ed. 2007), *Consuming Experience*, London, UK: Routledge.

Chaudhuri, Arjun and Morris B. Holbrook (2001), "The Chain of Effects from Brand Trust and Brand Affect to Brand Performance: The Role of Brand Loyalty," *Journal of Marketing*, 65 (2), 81–93.

Chaudhuri, Arjun and Morris B. Holbrook (2002), "Product-Class Effects on Brand Commitment and Brand Outcomes: The Role of Brand Trust and Brand Affect," *Journal of Brand Management*, 10 (1), 33–58.

Cluley, Robert and John Desmond (2015), "Why Psychoanalysis Now?" *Marketing Theory*, 15 (1, March), 3–8.

Contardo, Ianna and Robin Wensley (2004), "The Harvard Business School Story: Avoiding Knowledge by Being Relevant," *Organization*, 11 (2, May), 211–231.

Cooper-Martin, Elizabeth and Morris B. Holbrook (1993), "Ethical Consumption Experiences and Ethical Space," in *Advances in Consumer Research*, Vol. 20, ed. Leigh McAlister and Michael L. Rothschild, Provo, UT: Association for Consumer Research, 113–118.

Cova, Bernard, Daniele Dalli, and Detlev Zwick (2011), "Critical Perspectives on Consumers' Role as 'Producers': Broadening the Debate on Value Co-Creation in Marketing Processes," *Marketing Theory*, 11 (3, September), 231–241.

Cunha, Miguel Pina e, Stewart R. Clegg, and Ken Kamoche (2012), "Improvisation as 'Real Time Foresight'," *Futures*, 44 (3, April), 265–272.

Dennis, Noel and Michael Macaulay (2003), "Jazz and Marketing Planning," *Journal of Strategic Marketing*, 11 (3, September), 177–185.

Dennis, Noel and Michael Macaulay (2007), " 'Miles Ahead' – Using Jazz to Investigate Improvisation and Market Orientation," *European Journal of Marketing*, 41 (5–6), 608–623.

DeSarbo, Wayne S., Lehmann, Donald R., Morris B. Holbrook, William J. Havlena, and Sunil Gupta (1987), "A Stochastic Three-Way Unfolding Model for Asymmetric Binary Data," *Applied Psychological Measurement*, 11 (4), 397–418.

Dodds, John C. and Morris B. Holbrook (1988), "What's an Oscar Worth? An Empirical Estimation of the Effects of Nominations and Awards on Movie Distribution and Income," in *Current Research in Film: Audiences, Economics, and Law*, Vol. 4, ed. Bruce A. Austin, Norwood, NJ: Ablex Publishing, 72–88.

Dodds, William B. and Kent B. Monroe (1985), "The Effect of Brand and Price Information on Subjective Product Evaluations," *Advances in Consumer Research*, Vol. 12, ed. Elizabeth C. Hirschman and Morris B. Holbrook, Provo, UT: Association for Consumer Research, 85–90.

Dodds, William B., Kent B. Monroe, and Dhruv Grewal (1991), "Effects of Price, Brand, and Store Information on Buyers' Product Evaluations," *Journal of Marketing Research*, 28 (3, August), 307–319.

Dolata, Mateusz and Gerhard Schwabe (2014), "Call for Action: Designing for Harmony in Creative Teams," in *Advancing the Impact of Design Science: Moving from Theory to Practice, Proceedings of the 9th International Conference, DESRIST*, Cham: Springer, 273–288.

DownBeat (2015), "A Legacy of Beautiful Music," *DownBeat* 82 (6, June), 102.

Earl, Peter E. and Jason Potts (2013), "The Creative Instability Hypothesis," *Journal of Cultural Economics*, 37 (2, May), 153–173.

Engel, James F., David T. Kollat, and Roger D. Blackwell (1968), *Consumer Behavior*, New York, NY: Holt, Rinehart & Winston.

Farley, John U., Morris Holbrook, Mac Hulbert, James Lewis, and Michael Ryan (1975), *Fleet Administration at the Bayea Corporation*, New York, NY: Columbia Business School.

Farley, John U., John A. Howard, and L. Winston Ring (ed. 1974), *Consumer Behavior: Theory and Application*, Boston, MA: Allyn & Bacon.

Farley, John U. and L. Winston Ring (1970), "An Empirical Test of the Howard-Sheth Model of Buyer Behavior," *Journal of Marketing Research*, 7 (4, November), 427–438.

Faulkner, Robert R. and Howard S. Becker (2009), *Do You Know . . .? The Jazz Repertoire in Action*, Chicago, IL: University of Chicago Press.

Fishbein, Martin and Icek Ajzen (1975), *Belief, Attitude, Intention and Behavior*, Reading, MA: Addison-Wesley.

Frankena, William K. (1973), *Ethics* (Second Edition), Englewood Cliffs, NJ: Prentice-Hall.

Frishberg,David(1987),*Can'tTakeYouNowhere*,FantasyFCD-9651-2,on-line@https://www.discogs.com/release/4634159-David-Frishberg-Cant-Take-You-Nowhere.

Frishberg, David (1991), *Where You at?* Bloomdido BL 010, on-line @ https://www.discogs.com/release/11940211-Dave-Frishberg-Where-You-At.

Frishberg, David (undated), *Listen Here: Songs by Dave Frishberg* (Second Edition), Milwaukee, WI: Hal Leonard Corporation.

Frondizi, Risieri (1971), *What Is Value? An Introduction to Axiology* (Second Edition), La Salle, IL: Open Court Publishing Company.

Gallarza, Martina G., Francisco Arteaga, Giacomo Del Chiappa, Irene Gil-Saura, and Morris B. Holbrook (2017), "A Multidimensional Service-Value Scale Based on Holbrook's Typology of Customer Value: Bridging the Gap Between the Concept and Its Measurement," *Journal of Service Management*, 28 (4), 724–762.

Gallarza, Martina G. and Irene Gil-Saura (2006), "Value Dimensions, Perceived Value, Satisfaction and Loyalty: An Investigation of University Students' Travel Behaviour," *Tourism Management*, 27 (3, June), 437–452.

Gallarza, Martina G. and Irene Gil-Saura (2008), "The Concept of Value and Its Dimensions: A Tool for Analysing Tourism Experiences," *Tourism Review*, 63 (3), 4–20.

Gallarza, Martina G., Irene Gil-Saura, and Morris B. Holbrook (2011), "The Value of Value: Further Excursions on the Meaning and Role of Customer Value," *Journal of Consumer Behaviour*, 10 (4, July–August), 179–191.

Gallarza, Martina G., Irene Gil-Saura, and Morris B. Holbrook (2012), "Customer Value in Tourism Services: Meaning and Role for a Relationship-Marketing Approach," in *Strategic Marketing in Tourism Services*, ed. Rodoula H. Tsiotsou and Ronald E. Goldsmith, Bingley, UK: Emerald Group Publishing Limited, 147–162.

Gallarza, Martina G., Irene Gil-Saura, and Francisco Arteaga Moreno (2013), "The Quality-Value-Satisfaction-Loyalty Chain: Relationships and Impacts," *Tourism Review*, 68 (1), 3–20.

Garcia, Antonio J. and Donald Hunsberger (2015), "Reminiscing on Ray," *Down-Beat* (6, June), 136–139.

Gladwell, Malcolm (2000), *The Tipping Point: How Little Things Can Make a Big Difference*, New York, NY: Little Brown & Co.

Gold, Michael and Steve Hirshfeld (2005), "The Behaviors of Jazz as a Catalyst for Strategic Renewal and Growth," *Journal of Business Strategy*, 26 (5), 40–47.

Gould, Stephen J. (1991), "The Self-Manipulation of My Pervasive, Perceived Vital Energy Through Product Use: And Introspective-Praxis Perspective," *Journal of Consumer Research*, 18 (2, September), 194–207.

Gould, Stephen J. (1995), "Researcher Introspection as a Method in Consumer Research: Applications, Issues, and Implications," *Journal of Consumer Research*, 21 (4, March), 719–722.

Gould, Stephen J. (2012), "The Emergence of Consumer Introspection Theory (CIT): Introduction to a *JBR* Special Issue," *Journal of Business Research*, 65 (4, April), 453–460.

Grönroos, Christian (2011), "Value Co-Creation in Service Logic: A Critical Analysis," *Marketing Theory*, 11 (3, September), 279–301.

Grönroos, Christian (2012), "Conceptualizing Value Co-Creation: A Journey to the 1970s and Back to the Future," *Journal of Marketing Management*, 28 (13–14, December), 1520–1534.

Grönroos, Christian and Annika Ravald (2001), "Service as Business Logic: Implications for Value Creation and Marketing," *Journal of Service Management*, 22 (1), 5–22.

Grönroos, Christian and Päivi Voima (2013), "Critical Service Logic: Making Sense of Value Creation and Co-Creation," *Journal of the Academy of Marketing Science*, 41 (2, March), 133–150.

Gupta, Sunil and Donald R. Lehmann (2006), "Customer Lifetime Value and Firm Valuation," *Journal of Relationship Marketing*, 5 (2–3), 87–110.

Hadida, Allègre L. and William Tarvainen (2014), "Organizational Improvisation: A Consolidating Review and Framework," *International Journal of Management Reviews*, DOI: 10.1111/ijmr.12047.

Hall, Everett W. (1961), *Our Knowledge of Fact and Value*, Chapel Hill, NC: The University of North Carolina Press.

Hartman, Robert S. (1967), *The Structure of Values: Foundations of Scientific Axiology*, Carbondale, IL: Southern Illinois University Press.

Hasse, John Edward (2004), "Leadership Lessons from the Jazz Masters," on-line @ www.johnedwardhasse.com.

Hatch, Mary Jo (1998), "Jazz as a Metaphor for Organizing in the 21st Century," *Organization Science*, 9 (5, September–October), 556–557.

Hatch, Mary Jo (1999), "Exploring the Empty Spaces of Organizing: How Improvisational Jazz Helps Redescribe Organizational Structure," *Organization Science*, 20 (1, January–February), 75–100.

Havlena, William J. and Morris B. Holbrook (1986), "The Varieties of Consumption Experience: Comparing Two Typologies of Emotion in Consumer Behavior," *Journal of Consumer Research*, 13 (3, December), 394–404.

Havlena, William J., Morris B. Holbrook, and Donald R. Lehmann (1989), "Assessing the Validity of Emotional Typologies," *Psychology & Marketing*, 6 (2, Summer), 97–112.

Heisley, Deborah D. and Sidney J. Levy (1991), "Autodriving: A Photoelicitation Technique," *Journal of Consumer Research*, 18 (3, December), 257–272.

Hilliard, A. L. (1950), *The Forms of Value: The Extension of Hedonistic Axiology*, New York, NY: Columbia University Press.

Hirschman, Elizabeth C. (1980a), "Attributes of Attributes and Layers of Meaning," in *Advances in Consumer Research*, Vol. 7, ed. Jerry C. Olson, Ann Arbor, MI: Association for Consumer Research, 7–12.

Hirschman, Elizabeth C. (1980b), "Innovativeness, Novelty Seeking, and Consumer Creativity," *Journal of Consumer Research*, 7 (3, December), 283–295.

Hirschman, Elizabeth C. (1983), "Aesthetics, Ideologies and the Limits of the Marketing Concept," *Journal of Marketing*, 47 (3, Summer), 45–56.

Hirschman, Elizabeth C. (1984), "Experience Seeking: A Subjectivist Perspective on Consumption," *Journal of Business Research*, 12 (1, March), 115–136.

Hirschman, Elizabeth C. (1986), "Humanistic Inquiry in Marketing Research: Philosophy, Method, and Criteria," *Journal of Marketing Research*, 23 (3, August), 237–249.

Hirschman, Elizabeth C. (1992), "The Consciousness of Addiction: Toward a General Theory of Compulsive Consumption," *Journal of Consumer Research*, 19 (2, September), 155–179.

Hirschman, Elizabeth C. (2000), *Heroes, Monsters & Messiahs: Movies and Television Shows as the Mythology of American Culture*, New York, NY: Andrews McMeel Publishing.

Hirschman, Elizabeth C. and Morris B. Holbrook (ed. 1981), *Symbolic Consumer Behavior*, Ann Arbor, MI: Association for Consumer Research.

Hirschman, Elizabeth C. and Morris B. Holbrook (1982), "Hedonic Consumption: Emerging Concepts, Methods, and Propositions," *Journal of Marketing*, 46 (3), 92–101.

Hirschman, Elizabeth C. and Morris B. Holbrook (1986), "Expanding the Ontology and Methodology of Research on the Consumption Experience," in *Perspectives on Methodology in Consumer Research*, ed. David Brinberg and Richard J. Lutz, New York, NY: Springer-Verlag, 213–251.

Hirschman, Elizabeth C. and Morris B. Holbrook (1992), *Postmodern Consumer Research: The Study of Consumption as Text*, Newbury Park, CA: Sage Publications.

Hirschman, Elizabeth C. and Morris B. Holbrook (2011), "Consuming the Vampire: Sex, Death, and Liminality," *American Journal of Semiotics*, 27 (1–4), 1–45.

Hoffman, Donna L. and Morris B. Holbrook (1993), "The Intellectual Structure of Consumer Research: A Bibliometric Study of Author Co-Citations in the First 15 Years of the *Journal of Consumer Research*," *Journal of Consumer Research*, 19 (4), 505–517.

Holbrook, Arthur Tenney (1949), *From the Log of a Trout Fisherman*, Norwood, MA: Plimpton Press.

Holbrook, Morris B. (1973a), "A Review of Advertising Research," in *Advertising and the Public Interest*, ed. J. A. Howard and J. M. Hulbert, Washington, DC: Federal Trade Commission, B1–B62.

Holbrook, Morris B. (1973b), "Note on Validity of a Mechanical Measure of Interletter Similarity," *Perceptual and Motor Skills*, 36 (1), 298.

Holbrook, Morris B. (1974), "A Synthesis of the Empirical Studies," in *Consumer Behavior: Theory and Application*, ed. John U. Farley, John A. Howard, and L. Winston Ring, Boston, MA: Allyn & Bacon, 229–252.

Holbrook, Morris B. (1975a), "A Comparison of Methods for Measuring the Interletter Similarity Between Capital Letters," *Perception & Psychophysics*, 17 (6), 532–536.

Holbrook, Morris B. (1975b), *Dissertation: A Study of Communication in Advertising*, Doctoral Dissertation, Columbia University, January. Sponsor: John A. Howard. Copies available from University Microfilms, Ann Arbor, MI.

Holbrook, Morris B. (1976), "Two Ways to Evaluate an Advertising Campaign," *Journal of Advertising Research*, 16 (4), 45–48.

Holbrook, Morris B. (1977a), "Comparing Multiattribute Attitude Models by Optimal Scaling," *Journal of Consumer Research*, 4 (3), 165–171.

Holbrook, Morris B. (1977b), "More on Content Analysis in Consumer Research," *Journal of Consumer Research*, 4 (3), 176–177.

Holbrook, Morris B. (1978a), "Beyond Attitude Structure: Toward the Informational Determinants of Attitude," *Journal of Marketing Research*, 15 (4), 545–556.

Holbrook, Morris B. (1978b), "Effect of Subjective Interletter Similarity, Perceived Word Similarity, and Contextual Variables on the Recognition of Letter Substitutions in a Proofreading Task," *Perceptual and Motor Skills*, 47 (1), 251–258.

Holbrook, Morris B. (1978c), "Effect of Subjective Verbal Uncertainty on Perception of Typographical Errors in a Proofreading Task," *Perceptual and Motor Skills*, 47 (1), 243–250.

Holbrook, Morris B. (1979), "The Role of Subjective Probability in Mediating the Relationship Between Word Frequency and Error Recognition," *Perceptual and Motor Skills*, 48 (2), 617–618.

Holbrook, Morris B. (1980a), "Representing Patterns of Association Among Leisure Activities: A Comparison of Two Techniques," *Journal of Leisure Research*, 12 (3, Summer), 242–256.

Holbrook, Morris B. (1980b), "Some Preliminary Notes on Research in Consumer Esthetics," in *Advances in Consumer Research*, Vol. 7, ed. Jerry C. Olson, Ann Arbor, MI: Association for Consumer Research, 104–108.

Holbrook, Morris B. (1981a), "Integrating Compositional and Decompositional Analyses to Represent the Intervening Role of Perceptions in Evaluative Judgments," *Journal of Marketing Research*, 18 (1, February), 13–28.

Holbrook, Morris B. (1981b), "Introduction: The Esthetic Imperative in Consumer Research," in *Symbolic Consumer Behavior*, ed. Elizabeth C. Hirschman and Morris B. Holbrook, Ann Arbor, MI: Association for Consumer Research, 36–37.

Holbrook, Morris B. (1982a), "Mapping the Market for Esthetic Products: The Case of Jazz Records," *Journal of Retailing*, 58 (1, Spring), 114–129.

Holbrook, Morris B. (1982b), "Some Further Dimensions of Psycholinguistics, Imagery, and Consumer Response," in *Advances in Consumer Research*, Vol. 9, ed. A. A. Mitchell, Ann Arbor, MI: Association for Consumer Research, 112–117.

Holbrook, Morris B. (1983a), "On the Importance of Using Real Products in Research on Merchandising Strategy," *Journal of Retailing*, 59 (1), 4–20.

Holbrook, Morris B. (1983b), "Product Imagery and the Illusion of Reality: Some Insights from Consumer Esthetics," in *Advances in Consumer Research*, Vol. 10, ed. R. P. Bagozzi and A. M. Tybout, Ann Arbor, MI: Association for Consumer Research, 65–71.

Holbrook, Morris B. (1983c), "Using a Structural Model of Halo Effect to Assess Perceptual Distortion," *Journal of Consumer Research*, 10 (2, September), 247–252.

Holbrook, Morris B. (1984a), "Belk, Granzin, Bristor, and the Three Bears," in *Scientific Method in Marketing: Proceedings of the Winter Educators' Conference*, ed. Paul F. Anderson and Michael J. Ryan, Chicago, IL: American Marketing Association, 177–178.

Holbrook, Morris B. (1984b), "Situation-Specific Ideal Points and Usage of Multiple Dissimilar Brands," *Research in Marketing*, 7, 93–131.

Holbrook, Morris B. (1984c), "Theory Development Is a Jazz Solo: Bird Lives," in *Scientific Method in Marketing: Proceedings of the 1984 AMA Winter Educators' Conference*, ed. Paul F. Anderson and Michael J. Ryan, Chicago, IL: American Marketing Association, 48–52.

Holbrook, Morris B. (1985), "Why Business Is Bad for Consumer Research: The Three Bears Revisited," in *Advances in Consumer Research*, Vol. 12, ed. Elizabeth C. Hirschman and Morris B. Holbrook, Provo, UT: Association for Consumer Research, 145–156.

Holbrook, Morris B. (1986a), "Aims, Concepts, and Methods for the Representation of Individual Differences in Esthetic Responses to Design Features," *Journal of Consumer Research*, 13 (3, December), 337–347.

Holbrook. Morris B. (1986b), "A Note on Sadomasochism in the Review Process: I Hate When That Happens," *Journal of Marketing*, 50 (3), 104–108.

Holbrook, Morris B. (1986c), "Emotion in the Consumption Experience: Toward a New Model of the Human Consumer," in *The Role of Affect in Consumer Behavior: Emerging Theories and Applications*, ed. Robert A. Peterson, Wayne D. Hoyer, and William R. Wilson, Lexington, MA: D. C. Heath and Company, 17–52.

Holbrook, Morris B. (1986d), "I'm Hip: An Autobiographical Account of Some Consumption Experiences," in *Advances in Consumer Research*, Vol. 13, ed. Richard J. Lutz, Provo, UT: Association for Consumer Research, 614–618.

Holbrook, Morris B. (1986e), "The Place of Marketing Research on the Business-Research Continuum," in *Marketing Education: Knowledge Development, Dissemination, and Utilization, Proceedings of the Winter Educators' Conference*, ed. Joseph Guiltinan and Dale Achabal, Chicago, IL: American Marketing Association, 11–15.

Holbrook, Morris B. (1986f), "Whither ACR? Some Pastoral Reflections on Bears, Baltimore, Baseball, and Resurrecting Consumer Research," in *Advances in Consumer Research*, Vol. 13, ed. Richard J. Lutz, Provo, UT: Association for Consumer Research, 436–441.

Holbrook, Morris B. (1987a), "An Audiovisual Inventory of Some Fanatic Consumer Behavior: The 25-Cent Tour of a Jazz Collector's Home," in *Advances in Consumer*

Research, Vol. 14, ed. Melanie R. Wallendorf and Paul F. Anderson, Provo, UT: Association for Consumer Research, 144–149.

Holbrook, Morris B. (1987b), "From the Log of a Consumer Researcher: Reflections on the Odyssey," in *Advances in Consumer Research*, Vol. 14, ed. Melanie R. Wallendorf and Paul F. Anderson, Provo, Utah: Association for Consumer Research, 365–369.

Holbrook, Morris B. (1987c), "Mirror, Mirror, On the Wall, What's Unfair in the Reflections on Advertising?" *Journal of Marketing*, 51 (3), 95–103.

Holbrook, Morris B. (1987d), "O, Consumer, How You've Changed: Some Radical Reflections on the Roots of Consumption," in *Philosophical and Radical Thought in Marketing*, ed. Fuat Firat, Nikhilesh Dholakia, and Richard P. Bagozzi, Lexington, MA: D. C. Heath, 156–177.

Holbrook, Morris B. (1987e), "Progress and Problems in Research on Consumer Esthetics," in *Artists and Cultural Consumers*, ed. Douglas V. Shaw, William S. Hendon, and C. Richard Waits, Akron, OH: Association for Cultural Economics, 133–146.

Holbrook, Morris B. (1987f), "Some Notes on the Banausic Interrelationships Among Marketing Academics and Practitioners," in *Marketing Theory, Proceedings of the Winter Educators' Conference*, ed. Russell W. Belk, Gerald Zaltman, Richard Bagozzi, David Brinberg, Rohit Deshpande, A. Fuat Firat, Morris B. Holbrook, Jerry C. Olson, John F. Sherry, and Barton Weitz, Chicago, IL: American Marketing Association, 342–343.

Holbrook, Morris B. (1987g), "The Dramatic Side of Consumer Research: The Semiology of Consumption Symbolism in the Arts," in *Advances in Consumer Research*, Vol. 14, ed. Melanie R. Wallendorf and Paul F. Anderson, Provo, UT: Association for Consumer Research, 237–240.

Holbrook, Morris B. (1987h), "The Study of Signs in Consumer Esthetics: An Egocentric Review," in *Marketing and Semiotics: New Directions in the Study of Signs for Sale*, ed. Jean Umiker-Sebeok, Berlin: Mouton de Gruyter, 73–121.

Holbrook, Morris B. (1987i), "What *Is* Consumer Research?" *Journal of Consumer Research*, 14 (1, June), 128–132.

Holbrook, Morris B. (1987j), "What *Is* Marketing Research?" in *Marketing Theory, Proceedings of the Winter Educators' Conference*, ed. Russell W. Belk, Gerald Zaltman, Richard Bagozzi, David Brinberg, Rohit Deshpande, A. Fuat Firat, Morris B. Holbrook, Jerry C. Olson, John F. Sherry, and Barton Weitz, Chicago, IL: American Marketing Association, 214–216.

Holbrook, Morris B. (1988a), "An Interpretation: *Gremlins* as Metaphors for Materialism," *Journal of Macromarketing*, 8 (1, Spring), 54–59.

Holbrook, Morris B. (1988b), "Consumption Symbolism and Meaning in Works of Art: A Paradigmatic Case," *European Journal of Marketing*, 22 (7), 19–36.

Holbrook, Morris B. (1988c), "Steps Toward a Psychoanalytic Interpretation of Consumption: A Meta-Meta-Meta-Analysis of Some Issues Raised by the Consumer Behavior Odyssey," in *Advances in Consumer Research*, Vol. 15, ed. Michael J. Houston, Provo, UT, Association for Consumer Research, 537–542.

Holbrook, Morris B. (1988d), "The Positivistic and Interpretive Sides of Semiotic Research on Artistic Consumption: Hermes Speaks," in *Marketing: A Return to Broader Dimensions, AMA Winter Proceedings*, ed. S. Shapiro and A. H. Walle, Chicago, IL: American Marketing Association, 494–497.

Holbrook, Morris B. (1988e), "The Psychoanalytic Interpretation of Consumer Behavior: *I Am an Animal*," *Research in Consumer Behavior*, 3, 149–178.

Holbrook, Morris B. (1989a), "Aftermath of the Task Force: Dogmatism and Catastrophe in the Development of Marketing Thought" (President's Column), *ACR Newsletter* (September), 1–11.

Holbrook, Morris B. (1989b), "Farewell Address" (President's Column), *ACR Newsletter* (December), 1–9.

Holbrook, Morris B. (videotape 1989c), *John Howard: A Life in Learning*, Chicago, IL: American Marketing Association.

Holbrook, Morris B. (1989d), "Seven Routes to Facilitating the Semiological Interpretation of Consumption Symbolism and Marketing Imagery in Works of Art: Some Tips for Wildcats," in *Advances in Consumer Research*, Vol. 16, ed. T. R. Srull, Provo, UT: Association for Consumer Research, 420–425.

Holbrook, Morris B. (1989e), "Some Words of Inspiration on Research, Religion, Bach, and Baseball" (President's Column), *ACR Newsletter* (March), 1–3.

Holbrook, Morris B. (1989f), " 'These Foolish Things,' 'The Dear Departed Past,' and the Songs of David Frishberg: A Commentary and Critique" (President's Column), *ACR Newsletter* (June), 1–8.

Holbrook, Morris B. (1990a), "Holbrook's Reply to Pechmann: Prelude and Poem," *ACR Newsletter* (September), 4; also in Holbrook, Morris B. (1995b), *Consumer Research: Introspective Essays on the Study of Consumption*, Thousand Oaks, CA: Sage Publications, 316–317.

Holbrook, Morris B. (1990b), "On Hatching a Program of Consumer Research: An Elephant's Faithful One Hundred Percent," *ACR Newsletter* (December), 15–18.

Holbrook, Morris B. (1990c), "The Role of Lyricism in Research on Consumer Emotions: Skylark, Have You Anything to Say to Me?," in *Advances in Consumer Research*, Vol. 17, ed. Marvin E. Goldberg, Gerald Gorn, and Richard W. Pollay, Provo, UT: Association for Consumer Research, 1–18.

Holbrook, Morris B. (1991a), "From the Log of a Consumer Researcher: Reflections on the Odyssey," in *Highways and Buyways: Naturalistic Research from the Consumer Behavior Odyssey*, ed. Russell W. Belk, Provo, UT: Association for Consumer Research, 14–33.

Holbrook, Morris B. (1991b), "Romanticism and Sentimentality in Consumer Behavior: A Literary Approach to the Joys and Sorrows of Consumption," *Research in Consumer Behavior*, 5, 105–180.

Holbrook, Morris B. (1991c), "What Do MBA's Like?" *ACR Newsletter* (June), 5–6.

Holbrook, Morris B. (1992a), "A Tribute to John O'Shaughnessy on the Occasion of His Retirement," *ACR Newsletter* (September), 10–13.

Holbrook, Morris B. (1992b), "Book Review – *Handbook of Consumer Behavior*," *Journal of Marketing*, 56 (2), 128–132.

Holbrook, Morris B. (1992c), "Just Junior, Dizzy, and Me on the Way to Our Gig," *Marketing Signs*, 1 (14–15), 15–18.

Holbrook, Morris B. (1992d), "Patterns, Personalities, and Complex Relationships in the Effects of Self on Mundane Everyday Consumption: These Are 495 of My Most and Least Favorite Things," in *Advances in Consumer Research*, Vol. 19, ed. J. F. Sherry and B. Sternthal, Provo, UT: Association for Consumer Research, 417–423.

Holbrook, Morris B. (1992e), "Product Quality, Attributes, and Brand Name as Determinants of Price: The Case of Consumer Electronics," *Marketing Letters*, 3 (1), 71–83.

Holbrook, Morris B. (1993a), "Book Review – On *Marketing and Semiotics*: What's Cooking in Denmark?" *Semiotica*, 97 (1–2), 119–146.

Holbrook, Morris B. (1993b), "Comments on the Report of the AMA Task Force on the Development of Marketing Thought," in *Enhancing Knowledge Development in Marketing: Perspectives and Viewpoints*, ed. P. Rajan Varadarajan and Anil Menon, Chicago, IL: American Marketing Association, 19–23.

Holbrook, Morris B. (1993c), *Daytime Television Game Shows and the Celebration of Merchandise: The Price Is Right*, Bowling Green, OH: Bowling Green University Popular Press.

Holbrook, Morris B. (1993d), "Gratitudes and Latitudes in M.B.A. Attitudes: Customer Orientation and the *Business Week* Poll," *Marketing Letters*, 4 (3, July), 267–278.

Holbrook, Morris B. (1993e), "Nostalgia and Consumption Preferences: Some Emerging Patterns of Consumer Tastes," *Journal of Consumer Research*, 20 (2), 245–256.

Holbrook, Morris B. (1993f), "On the New Nostalgia: 'These Foolish Things' and Echoes of the Dear Departed Past," in *Continuities in Popular Culture: The Present in the Past & the Past in the Present and Future*, ed. R. B. Browne and R. J. Ambrosetti, Bowling Greem, OH: Bowling Green State University Popular Press, 74–120.

Holbrook, Morris B. (1993g), "Rereading the Encyclopedias of Jazz: Analyses of Data on the Tastes of Readers, Critics, and Musicians from 1955 to 1970," *Popular Music & Society*, 17 (4, Winter), 83–104.

Holbrook, Morris B. (1994a), "Axiology, Aesthetics, and Apparel: Some Reflections on the Old School Tie," in *Aesthetics of Textiles and Clothing: Advancing Multi-Disciplinary Perspectives*, ed. Marilyn Revell DeLong and Ann Marie Fiore, ITAA Special Publication #7, Monument, CO: International Textile and Apparel Association, 131–141.

Holbrook, Morris B. (1994b), "Book Review – *Pursuing Happiness: American Consumers in the Twentieth Century*," *Journal of Macromarketing*, 14 (1, Spring), 83–88.

Holbrook, Morris B. (1994c), "Ethics in Consumer Research: An Overview and Prospectus," in *Advances in Consumer Research*, Vol. 21, ed. Chris T. Allen and Deborah Roedder John, Provo, UT: Association for Consumer Research, 566–571.

Holbrook, Morris B. (1994d), "Loving and Hating New York: Some Reflections on the Big Apple," *International Journal of Research in Marketing*, 11 (4, September), 381–385.

Holbrook, Morris B. (1994e), "Nostalgia Proneness and Consumer Tastes," in John A. Howard, *Buyer Behavior in Marketing Strategy* (Second Edition), Englewood Cliffs, NJ: Prentice-Hall, 348–364.

Holbrook, Morris B. (1994f), "The Nature of Customer Value: An Axiology of Services in the Consumption Experience," in *Service Quality: New Directions in Theory and Practice*, ed. Roland T. Rust and Richard L. Oliver, Thousand Oaks, CA: Sage Publications, 21–71.

Holbrook, Morris B. (1995a), "An Empirical Approach to Representing Patterns of Consumer Tastes, Nostalgia, and Hierarchy in the Market for Cultural Products," *Empirical Studies of the Arts*, 13 (1), 55–71.

Holbrook, Morris B. (1995b), *Consumer Research: Introspective Essays on the Study of Consumption*, Thousand Oaks, CA: Sage Publications.

Holbrook, Morris B. (1995c), "On Eschatology, Onanist Scatology, or Honest Catology? Cats Swinging, Scat Singing, and Cat Slinging as Riffs, Rifts, and Writs in a Catalytic Catechism for the Cataclysm," in *Proceedings of the Marketing Eschatology Retreat*, ed. Stephen Brown, Jim Bell, and David Carson, Belfast: University of Ulster, 28–47.

Holbrook, Morris B. (1995d), "Romanticism, Introspection, and the Roots of Experiential Consumption: Morris the Epicurean," in *Consumption and Marketing: Macro Dimensions*, ed. R. W. Belk, N. Dholakia, and A. Venkatesh, Cincinnati, OH: South-Western College Publishing, 20–82.

Holbrook, Morris B. (1995e), "Seven Pieces of Wisdom on Consumer Research From Sandy, Quarter, Tommy, Matthew, Paul, Dave, and Dolly: A Love Letter to ACR" (Speech Given on the Occasion of Receiving the Fellows Award from the Association for Consumer Research), in *Advances in Consumer Research*, Vol. 22, ed. Frank R. Kardes and Mita Sujan, Provo, UT: Association for Consumer Research, 16–20.

Holbrook, Morris B. (1995f), "The Four Faces of Commodification in the Development of Marketing Knowledge," *Journal of Marketing Management*, 11 (7, October), 641–654.

Holbrook, Morris B. (1995g), "The Three Faces of Elitism: Postmodernism, Political Correctness, and Popular Culture," *Journal of Macromarketing*, 15 (2), 128–165.

Holbrook, Morris B. (1996a), "Consumption as Communication in the World of *Mrs. Cage*," *Journal of Marketing*, 60 (2, April), 139–142.

Holbrook, Morris B. (1996b), "Market Success as a Criterion for Assessing Player Contributions in Sports Businesses via a Regression-Based Approach Using Adjusted Performance Measures and Quasi-Dummy Variables," *Marketing Letters*, 7 (4), 341–353.

Holbrook, Morris B. (1996c), "On Eschatology, Onanist Scatology, or Honest Catology? Cats Swinging, Scat Singing, and Cat Slinging as Riffs, Rifts, and Writs in a Catalytic Catechism for the Cataclysm," in *Marketing Apocalypse: Eschatology, Escapology and the Illusion of the End*, ed. Stephen Brown, Jim Bell, and David Carson, London, UK: Routledge, 237–259.

Holbrook, Morris B. (1996d), "Reflections on Rocky," *Society & Animals: Social Scientific Studies of the Human Experience of Other Animals*, 4 (2), 147–168.

Holbrook, Morris B. (1996e), "Special Session Summary: Customer Value – A Framework for Analysis and Research," in *Advances in Consumer Research*, Vol. 23, ed. Kim P. Corfman and John G. Lynch, Jr., Provo, UT: Association for Consumer Research, 138–142.

Holbrook, Morris B. (1996f), "Stereography in the Social Sciences: An Application Whose Time Has Come," *Stereoscopy*, Series 2 (27, June), 24–29.

Holbrook, Morris B. (1997a), "Borders, Creativity, and the State of the Art at the Leading Edge," *Journal of Macromarketing*, 17 (2, Fall), 96–112.

Holbrook, Morris B. (1997b), "Camouflage" (Stereograph), *Stereo World*, 24 (2, May–June), 1.

Holbrook, Morris B. (1997c), "Feline Consumption: Ethography, Felologies, and Unobtrusive Participation in the Life of a Cat," *European Journal of Marketing*, 31 (3–4), 214–233.

Holbrook, Morris B. (1997d), "Marketing Across or Beyond, Without or Among, and At or On the Borders: Some Literal, Littoral, And Literary Ideas Whose Times Definitely Have, Probably Have Not, and Maybe Might Have Come" (Keynote Address), in *Marketing Without Borders, Proceedings of the 31st Annual Conference*, Manchester, UK: Academy of Marketing, Manchester Metropolitan University, 811–849.

Holbrook, Morris B. (1997e), "On Reaching, Grasping, Flapping, and Flopping," *Marketing Educator*, (Winter), 4.

Holbrook, Morris B. (1997f), "Romanticism, Introspection, and the Roots of Experiential Consumption: Morris the Epicurean," *Consumption, Markets and Culture*, 1 (2), 97–163.

Holbrook, Morris B. (1997g), "Stereographic Visual Displays and the Three-Dimensional Communication of Findings in Marketing Research," *Journal of Marketing Research*, 34 (4, November), 526–536.

Holbrook, Morris B. (1997h), "Three-Dimensional Stereographic Visual Displays in Marketing and Consumer Research," *Journal of Consumer and Market Research*, 97 (11), on-line @ http://citeseerx.ist.psu.edu/viewdoc/download?doi=10.1.1.196.9485&rep=rep1&type=pdf.

Holbrook, Morris B. (1997i), "Walking on the Edge: A Stereographic Photo Essay on the Verge of Consumer Research," in *Consumer Research: Postcards from the Edge*, ed. Stephen Brown and Darach Turley, London, UK: Routledge, 46–78.

Holbrook, Morris B. (1998a), "Breaking Camouflage: Stereography as the Cure for Confusion, Clutter, Crowding, and Complexity," *PSA Journal (Journal of the Photographic Society of America)*, 64 (8, August), 30–35.

Holbrook, Morris B., Lauren G. Block, and Gavan J. Fitzsimons (1998), "Personal Appearance and Consumption in Popular Culture: A Framework for Descriptive and Prescriptive Analysis," *Consumption, Markets and Culture*, 2 (1), 1–55.

Holbrook, Morris B. (1998b), "Closely Read Books – Marketing Literature, Consumption as Text, and the Leaves from Our Lives: Slow, Slower, and Slowest," *Journal of Marketing*, 62 (3, July), 141–145.

Holbrook, Morris B. (1998c), "Howard, John A.," in *The Elgar Companion to Consumer Research and Economic Psychology*, ed. Peter E. Earl and Simon Kemp, Northampton, MA: Edward Elgar, 310–314.

Holbrook, Morris B. (1998d), "Illuminations, Impressions, and Ruminations on Romanticism: Some Magical Concepts and Mystical Comments from Morris the Catoptric on the Superiority of Stereoscopy in Visual Representations of Marketing and Consumer Research," in *Romancing the Market*, ed. Stephen Brown, Anne Marie Doherty, and Bill Clarke, London, UK: Routledge, 86–124.

Holbrook, Morris B. (1998e), "Journey to Kroywen: An Ethnoscopic Auto-Auto-Auto-Driven Stereographic Photo Essay," in *Representing Consumers: Voices, Views, and Visions*, ed. Barbara B. Stern, London, UK: Routledge, 231–263.

Holbrook, Morris B. (1998f), "Marketing Applications of Three-Dimensional Stereography," *Marketing Letters*, 9 (1, February), 51–64.

Holbrook, Morris B. (1998g), "Stereo 3D Representations in Postmodern Marketing Research," *Marketing Intelligence & Planning*, 16 (5), 298–310.

Holbrook, Morris B. (1998h), "The Dangers of Educational and Cultural Populism: Three Vignettes on the Problems of Aesthetic Insensitivity, the Pitfalls of Pandering, and the Virtues of Artistic Integrity," *Journal of Consumer Affairs*, 32 (2, Winter), 394–423.

Holbrook, Morris B. (1998i), "The Katarche of Catology in Research on Marketing: *Breakfast at Tiffany's*, Stereography, Subjective Personal Introspection, and Cat," *Irish Marketing Review*, 11 (2), 29–38.

Holbrook, Morris B. (1998j), "The Retailing of Performance and the Performance of Service: The Gift of Generosity with a Grin and the Magic of Munificence with Mirth," in *Servicescapes: The Concept of Place in Contemporary Markets*, ed. John F. Sherry, Jr., Chicago, IL: NTC Business Books (American Marketing Association), 487–513.

Holbrook, Morris B. (1999a), "Conclusions," in *Consumer Value: A Framework for Analysis and Research*, ed. Morris B. Holbrook, London, UK: Routledge, 183–197.

Holbrook, Morris B. (1999b), "Explaining the Vividness, Clarity, and Realism of Three-Dimensional Stereoscopy," *Stereoscopy*, Series 2 (37, March), 17–21.

Holbrook, Morris B. (1999c), "Introduction to Consumer Value," in *Consumer Value: A Framework for Analysis and Research*, ed. Morris B. Holbrook, London, UK: Routledge, 1–28.

Holbrook, Morris B. (1999d), "Popular Appeal Versus Expert Judgments of Motion Pictures," *Journal of Consumer Research*, 26 (2, September), 144–155.

Holbrook, Morris B. (1999e), "Reframing Consumers – Commentary," in *Rethinking Marketing: Towards Critical Marketing Accountings*, ed. D. Brownlie, M. Saren, R. Wensley, and R. Whittington, London, UK: Sage Publications, 145–151.

Holbrook, Morris B. (1999f), "What Stereography Can Do for You: The Power of Three-Dimensional Visual Displays in Quantitative and Qualitative Marketing and Consumer Research," *ad.* 2, 512, 30–35 (published by Dentsu, Tokyo, in Japanese).

Holbrook, Morris B. (ed. 1999), *Consumer Value – A Framework for Analysis and Research*, London, UK: Routledge.

Holbrook, Morris B. (2000a), "The Influence of Anxiety: Ephebes, Épées, Posterity, and Preposterity in the World of Stephen Brown," *Journal of Marketing*, 64 (1), 84–86.

Holbrook, Morris B. (2000b), "The Millennial Consumer in the Texts of Our Times: Experience and Entertainment," *Journal of Macromarketing*, 20 (2, December), 178–192.

Holbrook, Morris B. (2000c), "Tupperware, Tommy Moore, Teddy Bear, and Tipper Gore – Pete, Jamie, Stew, Oyster, and Morrie's High School Reunion: Titillation and Titivation in Entelechic Entitulation," in *Imagining Marketing: Art, Aesthetics and the Avant-Garde*, ed. Stephen Brown and Anthony Patterson, London, UK: Routledge, 196–213.

Holbrook, Morris B. (2001a), Entries on "Baker, (Chesney Henry) 'Chet'" (p. 57); "Brubeck, David Warren" (pp. 119–120); "Charles, Ray (Robinson)" (p. 151); "Desmond, Paul" (p. 228); and "Frishberg, David L." (p. 302), in *The Guide to United States Popular Culture*, ed. R. B. Browne and P. Browne, Bowling Green, OH: Bowling Green State University Popular Press.

Holbrook, Morris B. (2001b), Entries on "Game Shows" (pp. 305–308) and "Game-Show Hosts, Hostesses, and Producers" (pp. 308–310), in *The Guide to United States Popular Culture*, ed. R. B. Browne and P. Browne, Bowling Green, OH: Bowling Green State University Popular Press.

Holbrook, Morris B. (2001c), "Market Clustering Goes Graphic: The Weiss Trilogy and a Proposed Extension," *Psychology & Marketing*, 18 (1), 67–85.

Holbrook, Morris B. (2001d), "Oniomania, Ergo Sum: The Complete Guide to Compulsive Buying Disorders" or "Book Review of April Lane Benson – *I Shop, Therefore I am: Compulsive Buying and the Search for Self*," *Psychology & Marketing*, 18 (9), 985–997.

Holbrook, Morris B. (2001e), "Postmodern Consumer Research: Definition, Genesis, Introspections, and Stereopsis," *Diamond Harvard Business Review (Japan)*, 6 (June), 141–145 (in Japanese).

Holbrook, Morris B. (2001f), "Remembrance: John A. Howard (1915–1999)," *Journal of Consumer Research*, 28 (2, September), 337–338.

Holbrook, Morris B. (2001g), "The Millennial Consumer Enters the Age of Exhibitionism – A Book-Review Essay: Part 1," *Consumption, Markets and Culture*, 4 (4), 383–437.

Holbrook, Morris B. (2001h), "The Millennial Consumer in the Texts of Our Times: Evangelizing," *Journal of Macromarketing*, 21 (2), 181–198.

Holbrook, Morris B. (2001i), "The Millennial Consumer in the Texts of Our Times: Exhibitionism," *Journal of Macromarketing*, 21 (1), 81–95.

Holbrook, Morris B. (2001j), "Times Square, Disneyphobia, HegeMickey, the Ricky Principle, and the Downside of the Entertainment Economy: It's Fun-Dumb-Mental," *Marketing Theory*, 1 (2), 139–163.

Holbrook, Morris B. (2001–2002), "ACR Fellows' Bookshelf," *ACR News* (Winter 2001), 34–38, (Spring 2002), 38–40, (Fall 2002), 38–41.

Holbrook, Morris B. (2002a), "Book Review: *Marketing – The Retro Revolution* by Stephen Brown," *Journal of the Academy of Marketing Science*, 30 (3), 262–267.

Holbrook, Morris B. (2002b), "Having Fun with Qualitative Methods or Interpretive Approaches in Marketing and Consumer Research," *ACR News* (Fall), 5–8.

Holbrook, Morris B. (2002c), "The Millennial Consumer Enters the Age of Exhibitionism – A Book-Review Essay: Part 2," *Consumption, Markets and Culture*, 5 (2), 113–151.

Holbrook, Morris B. (2003a), "A Book-Review Essay on the Role of Ambi-Diegetic Film Music in the Product Design of Hollywood Movies: Macromarketing in La-La-Land," *Consumption, Markets and Culture*, 6 (3), 207–230.

Holbrook, Morris B. (2003b), "Adventures in Complexity: An Essay on Dynamic Open Complex Adaptive Systems, Butterfly Effects, Self-Organizing Order,

Coevolution, the Ecological Perspective, Fitness Landscapes, Market Spaces, Emergent Beauty at the Edge of Chaos, and All That Jazz," *Academy of Marketing Science Review*, on-line @ www.citeseerx.ist.psu.edu/viewdoc.

Holbrook, Morris B. (2003c), "Book Review – *How Customers Think: Essential Insights into the Mind of the Market* by Gerald Zaltman," *Journal of Marketing Research*, 40 (4), 498–499.

Holbrook, Morris B. (2003d), "Foreword to Chris Hackley," in *Doing Research Projects in Marketing, Management and Consumer Research*, London, UK: Routledge.

Holbrook, Morris B. (2003e), "Time Travels in Retrospace: Unpacking My Grandfather's Trunk – Some Introspective Recollections of Life on the Brule," in *Time, Space, and the Market: Retroscapes Rising*, ed. Stephen Brown and John F. Sherry, Jr., Armonk, NY: M. E. Sharpe, 171–198.

Holbrook, Morris B. (2004a), "Ambi-Diegetic Music in Films as a Product-Design and Placement Strategy: The *Sweet Smell of Success*," *Marketing Theory*, 4 (3), 171–185.

Holbrook, Morris B. (2004b), "Book Review – *Universities in the Marketplace: The Commercialization of Higher Education* by Derek Bok," *Journal of Macromarketing*, 24 (1, June), 68–74.

Holbrook, Morris B. (2004c), "Gratitude in Graduate MBA Attitudes: Re-Examining the *Business Week* Poll," *Journal of Education for Business*, 80 (1, September–October), 25–28.

Holbrook, Morris B. (2005a), "Ambi-Diegetic Music in the Movies: The Crosby Duets in *High Society*," *Consumption, Markets and Culture*, 8 (2), 153–182.

Holbrook, Morris B. (2005b), "Art versus Commerce as a Macromarketing Theme in Three Films from the Young-Man-with-a-Horn Genre," *Journal of Macromarketing*, 25 (1, June), 22–31.

Holbrook, Morris B. (2005c), "Customer Value and Autoethnography: Subjective Personal Introspection and the Meanings of a Photograph Collection," *Journal of Business Research*, 58 (1, January), 45–61.

Holbrook, Morris B. (2005d), "Marketing Education as Bad Medicine for Society: The Gorilla Dances," *Journal of Public Policy & Marketing*, 24 (1, Spring), 143–145.

Holbrook, Morris B. (2005e), "Marketing Miseducation and the MBA Mind: Bullshit Happens," *Marketing Education Review*, 15 (3, Fall), 1–5.

Holbrook, Morris B. (2005f), "The Ambi-Diegesis of 'My Funny Valentine'," in *Pop Fiction – The Song in Cinema*, ed. S. Lannin and M. Caley, Portland, OR: Intellect, 48–62.

Holbrook, Morris B. (2005g), "The Eye of the Beholder: Beauty as a Concept in Everyday Discourse and the Collective Photographic Essay," in *Review of Marketing Research*, Vol. 1, ed. Naresh K. Malhotra, Armonk, NY: M. E. Sharpe, 35–100.

Holbrook, Morris B. (2005h), "The Role of Ordinary Evaluations in the Market for Popular Culture: Do Consumers Have 'Good Taste'?" *Marketing Letters*, 16 (2), 75–86.

Holbrook, Morris B. (2006a), "Consumption Experience, Customer Value, and Subjective Personal Introspection: An Illustrative Photographic Essay," *Journal of Business Research*, 59 (6, June), 714–725.

Holbrook, Morris B. (2006b), "Does Marketing Need Reform School? On the Misapplication of Marketing to the Education of Marketers," in *Does Marketing Need Reform? Fresh Perspectives on the Future*, ed. Jagdish N. Sheth and Rajendra S. Sisodia, Armonk, NY: M. E. Sharpe, 265–269.

Holbrook, Morris B. (2006c), "On the Commercial Exaltation of Artistic Mediocrity: Books, Bread, Postmodern Statistics, Surprising Success Stories, and the Doomed

Magnificence of Way Too Many Big Words," in *Consuming Books: The Marketing and Consumption of Literature*, ed. Stephen Brown, London, UK: Routledge, 96–113.

Holbrook, Morris B. (2006d), "Photo Essays and the Mining of Minutiae in Consumer Research: 'Bout the Time I Got to Phoenix," in *Handbook of Qualitative Research Methods in Marketing*, ed. Russell W. Belk, Cheltenham, UK: Edward Elgar, 476–493.

Holbrook, Morris B. (2006e), "Reply to Bradshaw, McDonagh, and Marshall: Turn Off the Bubble Machine," *Journal of Macromarketing*, 26 (1, June), 84–87.

Holbrook, Morris B. (2006f), "ROSEPEKICECIVECI Versus CCV – The Resource-Operant, Skills-Exchanging, Performance-Experiencing, Knowledge-Informed, Competence-Enacting, Coproducer-Involved, Value-Emerging, Customer-Interactive View of Marketing Versus the Concept of Customer Value: 'I Can Get It for You Wholesale'," in *The Service-Dominant Logic of Marketing: Dialog, Debate, and Directions*, ed. Robert F. Lusch and Stephen L. Vargo, Armonk, NY: M. E. Sharpe, 208–223.

Holbrook, Morris B. (2006g), "The Consumption Experience – Something New, Something Old, Something Borrowed, Something Sold: Part 1," *Journal of Macromarketing*, 26 (2, December), 259–266.

Holbrook, Morris B. (2007a), "Cinemusical Meanings in Motion Pictures: Commerce, Art, and Brando Loyalty . . . Or . . . De Niro, My God, to Thee," *Journal of Consumer Behaviour*, 6 (6), 398–418.

Holbrook, Morris B. (2007b), "Five Phases in a Personal Journey Through the Troubled Waters of Academic Values in a World of Business: Where's the Beef?" *Journal of Public Policy & Marketing*, 26 (1, Spring), 135–138.

Holbrook, Morris B. (2007c), "Marketing to Pet Owners," *Contact* (Summer), 38.

Holbrook, Morris B. (2007d), "Objective Characteristics, Subjective Evaluations, and Possible Distorting Biases in the Business-School Rankings: The Case of *U.S. News & World Report*," *Marketing Education Review*, 17 (2, Summer), 1–12.

Holbrook, Morris B. (2007e), "Playing the Changes on the Jazz Metaphor: An Expanded Conceptualization of Music-, Management-, and Marketing-Related Themes (Full-Length Monograph)," *Foundations and Trends in Marketing*, 2 (3–4), 185–442 (1–257 in the published version); also *Playing the Changes on the Jazz Metaphor: An Expanded Conceptualization of Music-, Management-, and Marketing-Related Themes*, Hanover, MA: Now Publishers, Inc.

Holbrook, Morris B. (2007f), "The Consumption Experience – Something New, Something Old, Something Borrowed, Something Sold – Part 2," *Journal of Macromarketing*, 27 (1, March), 86–96.

Holbrook, Morris B. (2007g), "The Consumption Experience – Something New, Something Old, Something Borrowed, Something Sold – Part 3," *Journal of Macromarketing*, 27 (2, June), 173–201.

Holbrook, Morris B. (2007h), "The Consumption Experience – Something New, Something Old, Something Borrowed, Something Sold – Part 4," *Journal of Macromarketing*, 27 (3, September), 303–329.

Holbrook, Morris B. (2007i), "When Bad Things Happen to Great Musicians: The Role of Ambi-Diegetic Jazz in Three Tragedepictions of Artistic Genius on the Silver Screen," *Jazz Research Journal*, 1 (1), 99–128.

Holbrook, Morris B. (2008a), "Compromise Is So . . . Compromised: Goldilocks, Go Home," *European Business Review*, 20 (6), 570–578.

Holbrook, Morris B. (2008b), "Consumers Just Wanna Have Fantasies, Feelings, and Fun!!" in *Consumer Behavior: How Humans Think, Feel, and Act in the Marketplace*, auth. Banwari Mittal, Cincinnati, OH: Open Mentis, 653–658.

Holbrook, Morris B. (2008c), "Music Meanings in Movies: The Case of the Crime-Plus-Jazz Genre," *Consumption, Markets and Culture*, 11 (4), 307–327.

Holbrook, Morris B. (2008d), "Pets and People: Companions in Commerce?" *Journal of Business Research*, 61 (5, May), 546–552.

Holbrook, Morris B. (2009a), "A Cinemusicaliterary Analysis of the American Dream As Represented by Biographical Jazz Comedepictions in the Golden Age of Hollywood Biopics: Blow, Horatio, Blow; O, Jakie, O; Go, Tommy, Go; No, Artie, No," *Marketing Theory*, 9 (3), 259–313.

Holbrook, Morris B. (2009b), "CB as I See It: Class and Income," in *Consumer Behavior: Buying, Having, and Being*, ed. Michael Solomon (Eighth Edition), Upper Saddle River, NJ: Pearson, Prentice-Hall, 503.

Holbrook, Morris B. (2009c), "In Memoriam – Barbara B. Stern," *Marketing Theory*, 9 (1), 5–7.

Holbrook, Morris B. (2009d), "Manufacturing Memorable Consumption Experiences from Ivy and Ivory: The Business Model, Customer Orientation, and Distortion of Academic Values in the Post-Millennial University," in *Memorable Customer Experiences: A Research Anthology*, ed. Adam Lindgreen, Joëlle Vanhamme, and Michael B. Beverland, Burlington, VT: Gower Publishing Company, 267–290.

Holbrook, Morris B. (2010), "Book Review of '*Do You Know . . .?' The Jazz Repertoire in Action*," *Contemporary Sociology*, 39 (4, July), 442–444.

Holbrook, Morris B. (2011), *Music, Movies, Meanings, and Markets: Cinemajazzamatazz*, New York, NY: Routledge.

Holbrook, Morris B. (2012), "Catering to Consumers or Consuming the Caterers: A Bridge Too Far . . ., Way Too Far," in *Marketing Management: A Cultural Perspective*, ed. Lisa Peñaloza, Nil Toulouse, and Luca Massimiliano Visconti, New York, NY: Routledge, 489–504.

Holbrook, Morris B. (2013), "The Greedy Bastard's Guide to Business," *Journal of Macromarketing*, 33 (4), 369–385.

Holbrook, Morris B. (2014a), "Consumption Criteria in Arts Marketing," in *The Routledge Companion to Arts Marketing*, ed. Daragh O'Reilly, Ruth Rentschker, and Theresa A. Kirchner, London, UK and New York, NY: Routledge, 194–203.

Holbrook, Morris B. (2014b), "Discipline and Liberation in Consumption," in *Legends in Consumer Research: Russell W. Belk, Vol. 9, Discipline and Liberation in Consumption*, series ed. Jagdish N. Sheth, ed. Craig J. Thompson, New Delhi, India: Sage Publications, 286–290.

Holbrook, Morris B. (2014c), "Morris the Cat or the Wolf-Man on the Upper West Side: Animal Metaphors and Me," in *Brand Mascots and Other Marketing Animals*, ed. Stephen Brown and Sharon Ponsonby-McCabe, London, UK and New York, NY: Routledge, 76–88.

Holbrook, Morris B. (2015a), "Commentary: The Consumer Perspective on Branding," in *Brands: Interdisciplinary Perspectives*, ed. Jonathan E. Schroeder, London, UK and New York, NY: Routledge, 297–308.

Holbrook, Morris B. (2015b), *Legends in Consumer Behavior: Morris B. Holbrook, Vol. 14, Inspirational Applications, Part I: Marketing Education*, series ed. Jagdish N. Sheth, ed. Herbert Jack Rotfeld, New Delhi, India: Sage Publications.

Holbrook, Morris B. (2015c), *Legends in Consumer Behavior: Morris B. Holbrook*, series ed. Jagdish N. Sheth, New Delhi, India: Sage Publications, in 15 Vol., as follows: Vol. 1, *Traditional Decision-Oriented Approaches: Attitude, Information-Processing, and Features-Perceptions-Affect Models*, ed. Joel Huber; Vol. 2, *"Radical" Experiential Views: The Consumption Experience and Customer Value*, ed. Elizabeth C. Hirschman; Vol. 3, *Emotions*, ed. Meryl P. Gardner; Vol. 4, *Esthetics and Tastes, Part I: Art and Entertainment*, ed. Finola Kerrigan; Vol. 5, *Esthetics and Tastes, Part II: Effects of Personality, Class, and Expertise*, ed. Michela Addis; Vol. 6, *Nostalgia and Age-Related Preferences*, ed. Robert M. Schindler; Vol. 7, *Quantitative Methods: MDS, MDA, CCA, and Beyond*, ed.

William L. Moore; Vol. 8, *Qualitative Methods, Part I: Interpretive Approaches*, ed. John O'Shaughnessy; Vol. 9, *Qualitative Methods, Part II: Symbolic Consumer Behavior or Consumption Symbolism*, ed. Alan Bradshaw; Vol. 10, *Qualitative Methods, Part III: Subjective Personal Introspection*, ed. Stephen J. Gould; Vol. 11, *Marketing Applications: Branding, Communications, and Strategy*, ed. Pierre Berthon; Vol. 12, *Macromarketing Applications, Part I: Ethical Concerns, Social Issues, and Animal Companions*, ed. Clifford J. Shultz; Vol. 13, *Macromarketing Applications, Part II: Marketing Versus Consumer Research*, ed. Ronald P. Hill; Vol. 14, *Inspirational Applications, Part I: Marketing Education*, ed. Herbert J. Rotfeld; Vol. 15, *Inspirational Applications, Part II: Scholarship and Creativity*, ed. William L. Wilkie.

Holbrook, Morris B. (2015d), "Morris B. Holbrook," in *Harvard and Radcliffe Class of 1965: Fiftieth Anniversary Report*, ed. John Paul Russo and Linda Smith Summers, Cambridge, MA: Class Report Office, Harvard University, 459–463.

Holbrook, Morris B. (2015e), "Our Debate on Consulting" and "Ode of Concession, Contrition, and Conciliation," in *Legends in Consumer Behavior: Jacob Jacoby, Vol. 2, the Early Years: Attitudes, Brand Loyalty and Perceived Risk*, series ed. Jagdish N. Sheth, ed. L. B. Kaplan, New Delhi, India: Sage Publications.

Holbrook, Morris B. (2015f), "Some Reflections on Psychoanalytic Approaches to Marketing and Consumer Research," *Marketing Theory*, 15 (1, March), 13–16.

Holbrook, Morris B. (2015g), "The Marketing Manager as a Jazz Musician," *Marketing Intelligence & Planning*, 33 (7), 958–965.

Holbrook, Morris B. (2016), "Reflections on Jazz Training and Marketing Education: What Makes a Great Teacher?" *Marketing Theory*, 16 (4, December), 429–444.

Holbrook, Morris B. (2017), "Morris B. Holbrook: An Historical Autoethnographic Subjective Personal Introspection," *Journal of Historical Research in Marketing*, 9 (2), 144–190.

Holbrook, Morris B. (2018a), "A Subjective Personal Introspective Essay on the Evolution of Business Schools, the Fate of Marketing Education, and Aspirations Toward a Great Society," *Australasian Marketing Journal*, 26 (2, May), 70–78.

Holbrook, Morris B. (2018b), "Essay on the Origins, Development and Future of the Consumption Experience as a Concept in Marketing and Consumer Research," *Qualitative Marketing Research*, 21 (4), 421–444.

Holbrook, Morris B. (2020), "The Concept of Consumer Value: Development, Implications, Trajectory," in *Value in Marketing: Retrospective and Perspective Stance*, ed. Marin Marinov, London, UK: Routledge, 9–41.

Holbrook, Morris B. (2021), "Commentary: Consumption Experiences, Customer Value, Subjective Personal Introspection, the Photographic Essay, and Semiological/Hermeneutic Interpretation," *Journal of Global Scholars of Marketing Science*, 31 (4), 663–675.

Holbrook, Morris B. (2023), "Consumption Experiences in the Arts," *International Journal of Arts Management*, 26 (1, Fall), 6–17.

Holbrook, Morris B. (2024), "What for Art Thou, Marketing?" *Journal of Customer Behaviour*, 23 (1), 27–32.

Holbrook, Morris B. and Michela Addis (2007), "Taste Versus the Market: An Extension of Research on the Consumption of Popular Culture," *Journal of Consumer Research*, 34 (3), 415–424.

Holbrook, Morris B. and Michela Addis (2008), "Art Versus Commerce in the Movie Industry: A Two-Path Model of Motion-Picture Success," *Journal of Cultural Economics*, 32 (2), 87–107; this article won the 2010 Werner Pommerehne Price for "best paper to appear in the *Journal of Cultural Economics* (*JCE*) over the two years 2008 and 2009."

Holbrook, Morris B. and Punam Anand (1990), "Effects of Tempo and Situational Arousal on the Listener's Perceptual and Affective Responses to Music," *Psychology of Music*, 18 (2, October), 150–162.

Holbrook, Morris B. and Punam Anand (1992), "The Effects of Situation, Sequence, and Features on Perceptual and Affective Responses to Product Designs: The Case of Aesthetic Consumption," *Empirical Studies of the Arts*, 10 (1), 19–31.

Holbrook, Morris B. and Rajeev Batra (1987), "Assessing the Role of Emotions as Mediators of Consumer Responses to Advertising," *Journal of Consumer Research*, 14 (3, December), 404–420.

Holbrook, Morris B. and Rajeev Batra (1988), "Toward a Standardized Emotional Profile (SEP) Useful in Measuring Responses to the Nonverbal Components of Advertising," in *Nonverbal Communication in Advertising*, ed. Sidney Hecker and David W. Stewart, Lexington, MA: D. C. Heath and Company, 95–110.

Holbrook, Morris B., Stephen Bell, and Mark W. Grayson (1989), "The Role of the Humanities in Consumer Research: Close Encounters and Coastal Disturbances," in *Interpretive Consumer Research*, ed. Elizabeth C. Hirschman, Provo, UT: Association for Consumer Research, 29–47.

Holbrook, Morris B. and Stephen A. Bertges (1981), "Perceptual Veridicality in Esthetic Communication: A Model, General Procedure, and Illustration," *Communication Research*, 8 (4, October), 387–424.

Holbrook, Morris B., Robert W. Chestnut, Terence A. Oliva, and Eric A. Greenleaf (1984), "Play as a Consumption Experience: The Roles of Emotions, Performance, and Personality in the Enjoyment of Games," *Journal of Consumer Research*, 11 (2, September), 728–739.

Holbrook, Morris B. and Kim P. Corfman (1985), "Quality and Value in the Consumption Experience: Phaedrus Rides Again," in *Perceived Quality: How Consumers View Stores and Merchandise*, ed. Jacob Jacoby and Jerry C. Olson, Lexington, MA: D. C. Heath and Company, 31–57.

Holbrook, Morris B. and Ellen Day (1994), "Reflections on Jazz and Teaching: Benny and Gene, Woody and We," *European Journal of Marketing*, 28 (8–9), 133–144.

Holbrook, Morris B. and Glenn Dixon (1985), "Mapping the Market for Fashion: Complementarity in Consumer Preferences," in *The Psychology of Fashion*, ed. Michael R. Solomon, Lexington, MA: D. C. Heath and Company.

Holbrook, Morris B. and Meryl P. Gardner (1993), "An Approach to Investigating the Emotional Determinants of Consumption Durations: Why Do People Consumer What They Consume for as Long as They Consume It?" *Journal of Consumer Psychology*, 2 (2), 123–142.

Holbrook, Morris B. and Meryl P. Gardner (1998), "How Motivation Moderates the Effects of Emotions on the Duration of Consumption," *Journal of Business Research*, 42 (3, July), 241–252.

Holbrook, Morris B. and Meryl P. Gardner (2000), "Illustrating a Dynamic Model of the Mood-Updating Process in Consumer Behavior," *Psychology & Marketing*, 17 (3, March), 165–194.

Holbrook, Morris B. and Mark W. Grayson (1986), "The Semiology of Cinematic Consumption: Symbolic Consumer Behavior in *Out of Africa*," *Journal of Consumer Research*, 13 (3, December), 374–381.

Holbrook, Morris B., Eric A. Greenleaf, and Robert M. Schindler (1986), "A Dynamic Spatial Analysis of Changes in Aesthetic Responses," *Empirical Studies of the Arts*, 4 (1), 47–61.

Holbrook, Morris B. and William J. Havlena (1988), "Assessing the Real-to-Artificial Generalizability of Multiattribute Attitude Models in Tests of New Product Designs," *Journal of Marketing Research*, 25 (1, February), 25–35.

References 269

Holbrook, Morris B. and Elizabeth C. Hirschman (1982), "The Experiential Aspects of Consumption: Consumer Fantasies, Feelings, and Fun," *Journal of Consumer Research*, 9 (2, September), 132–140.

Holbrook, Morris B. and Elizabeth C. Hirschman (1993), *The Semiotics of Consumption: Interpreting Symbolic Consumer Behavior in Popular Culture and Works of Art*, Berlin and New York, NY: Mouton De Gruyter.

Holbrook, Morris B. and Elizabeth C. Hirschman (2015), "Experiential Consumption," in *The Wiley-Blackwell Encyclopedia of Consumption and Consumer Studies*, ed. Daniel Thomas Cook and J. Michael Ryan, Malden, MA: John Wiley & Sons, 271–275.

Holbrook, Morris B. and Douglas V. Holloway (1984), "Marketing Strategy and the Structure of Aggregate, Segment-Specific, and Differential Preferences," *Journal of Marketing*, 48 (1, Winter), 62–67.

Holbrook, Morris B. and J. A. Howard (1977), "Frequently Purchased Nondurable Goods and Services," in *Selected Aspects of Consumer Behavior: A Summary from the Perspective of Different Disciplines*, ed. Robert Ferber, Washington, DC: National Science Foundation, 189–222.

Holbrook, Morris B. and Joel Huber (1979a), "Separating Perceptual Dimensions from Affective Overtones," *Journal of Consumer Research*, 5 (4, March), 272–283.

Holbrook, Morris B. and Joel Huber (1979b), "The Spatial Representation of Responses toward Jazz: Applications of Consumer Esthetics to Mapping the Market for Music," *Journal of Jazz Studies*, 5 (Spring–Summer), 3–22.

Holbrook, Morris B. and Joel Huber (1983), "Detecting the Differences in Jazz: A Comparison of Methods for Assessing Perceptual Veridicality in Applied Aesthetics," *Empirical Studies of the Arts*, 1 (1), 35–53.

Holbrook, Morris B. and Joel Huber (1994), "Detecting the Differences, Indeed," *Empirical Studies of the Arts*, 12 (1), 59–61.

Holbrook, Morris B. and Neville C. Hughes (1978), "Product Images: How Structured Rating Scales Facilitate Using a Projective Technique in Hypothesis Testing," *Journal of Psychology*, 100 (2), 323–328.

Holbrook, Morris B. and James M. Hulbert (1975), "Multi-Attribute Attitude Models: A Comparative Analysis," in *Advances in Consumer Research*, Vol. 2, ed. Mary Jane Schlinger, Ann Arbor, MI: Association for Consumer Research, 375–388.

Holbrook, Morris B. and James M. Hulbert (2002a), "Elegy on the Death of Marketing: Never Send to Know Why We Have Come to Bury Marketing But Ask What You Can Do for Your Country Churchyard," *European Journal of Marketing*, 36 (5–6), 706–732.

Holbrook, Morris B. and James M. Hulbert (2002b), "What Do We Produce in the 'Knowledge Factory' and for Whom? A Review Essay of *The Knowledge Factory* by Stanley Aronowitz," *Journal of Consumer Affairs*, 36 (1, Summer), 99–114.

Holbrook, Morris B., James M. Hulbert, and Michael J. Ryan (1978), "The Extended Matching Hypothesis in Complex Selling Interactions," in *Proceedings of the 86th Annual Conference*, Washington, DC: American Psychological Association, Division, 23, 29.

Holbrook, Morris B. and Takeo Kuwahara (1998), "Collective Stereographic Photo Essays: An Integrated Approach to Probing Consumption Experiences in Depth," *International Journal of Research in Marketing*, 15 (3, July), 201–221.

Holbrook, Morris B. and Takeo Kuwahara (1999), "Probing Explorations, Deep Displays, Virtual Reality, and Profound Insights: The Four Faces of Stereographic Three-Dimensional Images in Marketing and Consumer Research," in *Advances in Consumer Research*, Vol. 26, ed. Eric J. Arnould and Linda M. Scott, Provo, UT: Association for Consumer Research, 240–250.

Holbrook, Morris B., Kathleen T. Lacher, and Michael S. LaTour (2006), "Audience Judgments as the Potential Missing Link Between Expert Judgments and Audience Appeal: An Illustration Based on Musical Recordings of 'My Funny Valentine'," *Journal of the Academy of Marketing Science*, 34 (1, December), 8–18.

Holbrook, Morris B. and Donald R. Lehmann (1980), "Form Versus Content in Predicting Starch Scores," *Journal of Advertising Research*, 20 (4), 53–62.

Holbrook, Morris B. and Donald R. Lehmann (1981), "Allocation of Discretionary Time: Assessing Complementarity Among Activities," *Journal of Consumer Research*, 7 (4, March), 395–406.

Holbrook, Morris B., Donald R. Lehmann, and John O'Shaughnessy (1986), "Using Versus Choosing: The Relationship of the Consumption Experience to Reasons for Purchasing," *European Journal of Marketing*, 20 (8), 49–62.

Holbrook, Morris B., Donald R. Lehmann, and Bernd Schmitt (2016), "Marketing," in *Columbia Business School: A Century of Ideas*, ed. Columbia Business School, New York, NY: Columbia University Press, 81–105.

Holbrook, Morris B. and Karl A. Maier (1978), "A Study of the Interface Between Attitude Structure and Information Acquisition Using a Questionnaire-Based Information-Display Sheet," in *Advances in Consumer Research*, Vol. 5, ed. H. Keith Hunt, Ann Arbor, MI: Association for Consumer Research, 93–98.

Holbrook, Morris B. and William L. Moore (1980), "Assessing the Convergent Validity of Decompositional and Compositional Methods in the Case of Socially Sensitive Perceptions," in *Advances in Consumer Research*, Vol. 7, ed. Jerry C. Olson, Ann Arbor, MI: Association for Consumer Research, 749–752.

Holbrook, Morris B. and William L. Moore (1981), "Feature Interactions in Consumer Judgments of Verbal Versus Pictorial Presentations," *Journal of Consumer Research*, 8 (1, June), 103–113.

Holbrook, Morris B. and William L. Moore (1982), "Using Canonical Correlation to Construct Product Spaces for Objects with Known Feature Structures," *Journal of Marketing Research*, 19 (1, February), 87–98.

Holbrook, Morris B. and William L. Moore (1984), "The Pick-Any Procedure Versus Multidimensionally-Scaled Correlations: An Empirical Comparison of Two Techniques for Forming Preference Spaces," in *Advances in Consumer Research*, Vol. 11, ed. T. C. Kinnear, Provo, UT: Association for Consumer Research, 56–62.

Holbrook, Morris B., William L. Moore, Gary N. Dodgen, and William J. Havlena (1985), "Nonisomorphism, Shadow Features, and Imputed Preferences," *Marketing Science*, 4 (3, Summer), 215–233.

Holbrook, Morris B., William L. Moore, and Russell S. Winer (1982), "Constructing Joint Spaces from Pick-Any Data: A New Tool for Consumer Analysis," *Journal of Consumer Research*, 9 (1), 99–105.

Holbrook, Morris B. and T. J. Olney (1995), "Romanticism and the Wanderlust: An Effect of Personality on Consumer Preferences," *Psychology & Marketing*, 12 (3), 207–222.

Holbrook, Morris B. and John O'Shaughnessy (1976), "Influence Processes in Interpersonal Persuasion," in *Advances in Consumer Research*, Vol. 3, ed. B. B. Anderson, Ann Arbor, MI: Association for Consumer Research, 364–369.

Holbrook, Morris B. and John O'Shaughnessy (1984), "The Role of Emotion in Advertising," *Psychology & Marketing*, 1 (2, Summer), 45–64.

Holbrook, Morris B. and John O'Shaughnessy (1988), "On the Scientific Status of Consumer Research and the Need for an Interpretive Approach to Studying Consumption Behavior," *Journal of Consumer Research*, 15 (3), 398–402.

Holbrook, Morris B., John O'Shaughnessy, and Stephen Bell (1990), "Actions and Reactions in the Consumption Experience: The Complementary Roles of Reasons and Emotions in Consumer Behavior," *Research in Consumer Behavior*, 4, 131–163.

Holbrook, Morris B. and Michael J. Ryan (1982), "Modeling Decision-Specific Stress: Some Methodological Considerations," *Administrative Science Quarterly*, 27 (2), 243–258.

Holbrook, Morris B., Raquel Sánchez-Fernández, and Martina G. Gallarza (2020), "Conclusion: A Personal Look at the Concept of Consumer Value: Meanings, Methods, and Measures," in *La Valeur Perçue en Marketing: Perspectives, Théoriques et Enjeux Managériaux*, ed. Rémi Mencarelli and Arnaud Rivière, Aix-en-Provence: Presses Universitaires de Provence, 203–218.

Holbrook, Morris B. and Robert M. Schindler (1989), "Some Exploratory Findings on the Development of Musical Tastes," *Journal of Consumer Research*, 16 (1, June), 119–124.

Holbrook, Morris B. and Robert M. Schindler (1991), "Echoes of the Dear Departed Past: Some Work in Progress on Nostalgia," in *Advances in Consumer Research*, Vol. 18, ed. Rebecca H. Holman and Michael R. Solomon, Provo, UT: Association for Consumer Research, 330–333.

Holbrook, Morris B. and Robert M. Schindler (1994), "Age, Sex, and Attitude Toward the Past as Predictors of Consumers' Aesthetic Tastes for Cultural Products," *Journal of Marketing Research*, 31 (3, August), 412–422.

Holbrook, Morris B. and Robert M. Schindler (1996), "Market Segmentation Based on Age and Attitude Toward the Past: Concepts, Methods, and Findings Concerning Nostalgic Influences on Customer Tastes," *Journal of Business Research*, 37 (1), 27–39.

Holbrook, Morris B. and Robert M. Schindler (2003), "Nostalgic Bonding: Exploring the Role of Nostalgia in the Consumption Experience," *Journal of Consumer Behaviour*, 3 (2), 107–127.

Holbrook, Morris B. and Robert M. Schindler (2013), "Commentary on 'Is There a Peak in Popular Music Preference at a Certain Song-Specific Age? A Replication of Holbrook & Schindler's 1989 Study'," *Musicae Scientiae*, 17 (3), 305–308.

Holbrook, Morris B. and Clifford J. Shultz, II (1996), "An Updating Model of Salary Adjustments in Major League Baseball: How Much Is a Home Run Worth?" *Journal of Sport Management*, 10 (2), 131–148.

Holbrook, Morris B., Michael R. Solomon, and Stephen Bell (1990), "A Reexamination of Self-Monitoring and Judgments of Furniture Designs," *Home Economics Research Journal*, 19 (1), 6–16.

Holbrook, Morris B., Debra Lynn Stephens, Ellen Day, Sarah M. Holbrook, and Gregor Strazar (2001), "A Collective Stereographic Photo Essay on Key Aspects of Animal Companionship: The Truth About Dogs and Cats," *Academy of Marketing Science Review*, on-line @ http://citeseerx.ist.psu.edu/viewdoc.

Holbrook, Morris B. and Barbara Stern (1997), "The Paco Man and What Is Remembered: New Readings of a Hybrid Language," in *Undressing the Ad: Reading Culture in Advertising*, ed. Katherine Toland Frith, New York, NY: Peter Lang, 65–84.

Holbrook, Morris B. and Barbara Stern (2000), "The Use of Space-Travel and Rocket-Ship Imagery to Market Commercial Music: How Some Jazz Albums from the 1950s, 1960s, and 1970s Burned Brightly but Fizzled Fast," *Extrapolation*, 41 (1, Spring), 51–62.

Holbrook, Morris B., David A. Velez, and Gerard R. Tabouret (1981), "Attitude Structure and Search: An Integrative Model of Importance-Directed Information Processing," in *Advances in Consumer Research*, Vol. 8, ed. Kent B. Monroe, Ann Arbor, MI: Association for Consumer Research, 93–98.

Holbrook, Morris B., Michael J. Weiss, and J. Habich (2002), "Disentangling Effacement, Omnivore, and Distinction Effects on the Consumption of Cultural Activities: An Illustration," *Marketing Letters*, 13 (4), 345–357.

Holbrook, Morris B., Michael J. Weiss, and J. Habich (2004), "Class-Related Distinctions in American Cultural Tastes," *Empirical Studies of the Arts*, 22 (1), 91–115.

Holbrook, Morris B. and Richard Westwood (1989), "The Role of Emotion in Advertising Revisited: Testing a Typology of Emotional Responses," in *Cognitive and Affective Responses to Advertising*, ed. Patricia Cafferata and Alice M. Tybout, Lexington, MA: D. C. Heath and Company, 353–371.

Holbrook, Morris B. and Rebecca S. Williams (1978), "A Test of the Correspondence Between Perceptual Spaces Based on Pairwise Similarity Judgments Collected with and Without the Inclusion of Explicit Ideal Objects," *Journal of Applied Psychology*, 63 (3, June), 373–376.

Holbrook, Morris B. and Arch G. Woodside (2008), "Animal Companions, Consumption Experiences, and the Marketing of Pets: Transcending Boundaries in the Animal-Human Distinction," *Journal of Business Research*, 61 (5, May), 377–381.

Holbrook, Morris B. and Robert B. Zirlin (1985), "Artistic Creation, Artworks, and Aesthetic Appreciation: Some Philosophical Contributions to Nonprofit Marketing," *Advances in Nonprofit Marketing*, 1, 1–54.

Howard, John A. (1963), *Marketing Management: Analysis and Planning*, Homewood, IL: Richard D. Irwin.

Howard, John A. and Jagdish N. Sheth (1969), *The Theory of Buyer Behavior*, New York, NY: John Wiley & Sons.

Huber, Joel and Morris B. Holbrook (1979), "Using Attribute Ratings for Product Positioning: Some Distinctions Among Compositional Approaches," *Journal of Marketing Research*, 16 (4, November), 507–516.

Huber, Joel and Morris B. Holbrook (1980), "The Determinants of Esthetic Value and Growth," in *Advances in Consumer Research*, Vol. 7, ed. Jerry C. Olson, Ann Arbor, MI: Association for Consumer Research, 121–126.

Huber, Joel and Morris B. Holbrook (1981), "The Use of Real Versus Artificial Stimuli in Research on Visual Esthetic Judgments," in *Symbolic Consumer Behavior*, ed. Elizabeth C. Hirschman and Morris B. Holbrook, Ann Arbor, MI: Association for Consumer Research, 60–68.

Huber, Joel and Morris B. Holbrook (1982), "Estimating Temporal Trends in Consumer Preferences Measured by Graded Paired Comparisons," *Journal of Business Research*, 10 (4), 459–473.

Huber, Joel, Morris B. Holbrook, and Barbara Kahn (1986), "Effects of Competitive Context and of Additional Information on Price Sensitivity," *Journal of Marketing Research*, 23 (3), 250–260.

Huber, Joel, Morris B. Holbrook, and S. Schiffman (1982), "Situational Psychophysics and the Vending-Machine Problem," *Journal of Retailing*, 58 (1), 82–94.

Huizinga, Johan (1938), *Homo Ludens*, New York, NY: Harper & Row.

Humphreys, Michael, Deniz Ucbasaran, and Andy Lockett (2011), "Sensemaking and Sensegiving Stories of Jazz Leadership," *Human Relations*, 65 (1, January), 41–62.

Jaccard, James and Gregory Wood (1986), "An Idiothetic Analysis of Attitude-Behavior Models," in *Advances in Consumer Research*, Vol. 13, ed. Richard J. Lutz, Provo, UT: Association for Consumer Research, 600–605.

Jackson, Caroline, Michael Morgan, and Nigel Hemmington (2009), "Extraordinary Experiences in Tourism: Introduction to the Special Edition," *International Journal of Tourism Research*, 11 (2, March–April), 107–109.

Jennings, Keith (2007), "What Jazz Taught Marketing (or Should Have)," *Equity Marketing Newsletter*, on-line @ www.marketing profs.com.

Johar, Gita V., Morris B. Holbrook, and Barbara B. Stern (2001), "The Role of Myth in Creative Advertising Design: Theory, Process, and Outcome," *Journal of Advertising*, 30 (2), 1–25.

John, Joby, Stephen J. Grove, and Raymond P. Fisk (2006), "Improvisation in Service Performances: Lessons from Jazz," *Managing Service Quality: An International Journal*, 16 (3), 247–268.

Kamoche, Ken N. and Miguel Pina e Cunha (2001), "Minimal Structures: From Jazz Improvisation to Product Innovation," *Organization Studies*, 22 (5), 733–764.

Kamoche, Ken N., Miguel Pina e Cunha, and João Vieira da Cunha (ed. 2002), *Organizational Improvisation*, London, UK: Routledge.

Kamoche, Ken N., Miguel Pina e Cunha, and João Vieira da Cunha (2003), "Towards a Theory of Organizational Improvisation: Looking Beyond the Jazz Metaphor," *Journal of Management Studies*, 40 (8, December), 2022–2051.

Keynes, John Maynard (1936, ed. 1964), *The General Theory of Employment, Interest, and Money*, New York, NY: Harcourt, Brace & World, Inc.

Kim, Youn-Kyung (2002), "Consumer Value: An Application to Mall and Internet Shopping," *International Journal of Retail & Distribution Management*, 30 (11–12), 595–602.

Kotler, Philip J. and Sidney J. Levy (1969), "Broadening the Concept of Marketing," *Journal of Marketing*, 33 (January), 10–15.

Kozinets, Robert V. (2012), "Me/My Research/Avatar," *Journal of Business Research*, 65 (4, April), 478–482.

Kyriakopoulos, Kyriakos (2011), "Improvisation in Product Innovation: The Contingent Role of Market Information Sources and Memory Types," *Organization Studies*, 32 (8, August), 1051–1078.

Lamont, W. D. (1955), *The Value Judgment*, Westport, CT: Greenwood Press.

Lanier, Clinton D., Jr. and C. Scott Rader (2015), "Consumption Experience: An Expanded View," *Marketing Theory*, 15 (4), 487–508.

LaSalle, Diana and Terry A. Britton (2003), *Priceless: Turning Ordinary Products into Extraordinary Experiences*, Boston, MA: Harvard Business School Press.

Lebergott, Stanley (1993), *Pursuing Happiness: American Consumers in the Twentieth Century*, Princeton, NJ: Princeton University Press.

Leroi-Werelds, Sara, Sandra Streukens, Michael K. Brady, and Gilbert Swinnen (2014), "Assessing the Value of Commonly Used Methods for Measuring Customer Value: A Multi-Setting Empirical Study," *Journal of the Academy of Marketing Science*, 42 (4, July), 430–451.

Levy, Sidney J. (1959), "Symbols for Sale," *Harvard Business Review*, 37 (4, July–August), 117–124.

Lewis, C. I. (1946), *An Analysis of Knowledge and Valuation*, La Salle, IL: Open Court.

Leybourne, Stephen A. (2006), "Managing Improvisation Within Change Management: Lessons from UK Financial Services," *The Services Industry Journal*, 26 (1, January), 73–95.

Leybourne, Stephen A. (2009), "Improvisation and Agile Project Management: A Comparative Consideration," *International Journal of Managing Projects in Business*, 2 (4), 519–535.

Leybourne, Steve, Gary Lynn, and Morten Thanning Vendelø (2014), "Forms, Metaphors, and Themes: An Introduction to the Special Issue on Organizational Improvisation," *Creativity and Innovation Management*, 23 (4), 353–358.

Loring, L. M. (1966), *Two Kinds of Values*, New York, NY: The Humanities Press.

Mandal, Pratap Chandra (2023), "Social Implications and Criticisms of Marketing: Concerns, Strategies, and Initiatives," *International Journal of Social Ecology and Sustainable Development*, 14 (1), 1–16.

Mano, Haim and Richard L. Oliver (1993), "Assessing the Dimensionality and Structure of the Consumption Experience: Evaluation, Feeling, and Satisfaction," *Journal of Consumer Research*, 20 (3, December), 451–466.

Marshall, Alfred (1920, ed. 1961), *Principles of Economics* (Eighth Edition), New York, NY: The Macmillan Company.

Mathwick, Charla, Naresh Malhotra, and Edward Rigdon (2001), "Experiential Value: Conceptualization, Measurement and Application in the Catalog and Internet Shopping Environment," *Journal of Retailing*, 77 (1, Spring), 39–56.

Mathwick, Charla, Naresh K. Malhotra, and Edward Rigdon (2002), "The Effect of Dynamic Retail Experiences on Experiential Perceptions of Value: An Internet and Catalog Comparison," *Journal of Retailing*, 78 (1, Spring), 51–60.

McDonald, Duff (2017), *The Golden Passport: Harvard Business School, the Limits of Capitalism, and the Moral Failure of the MBA Elite*, New York, NY: Harper Business.

Mead, George H. (1938), *The Philosophy of the Act*, ed. C. W. Morris, Chicago, IL: University of Chicago Press.

Meyer, Alan, Peter J. Frost, and Karl E. Weick (1998), "The *Organization Science* Jazz Festival: Improvisation as a Metaphor for Organizing," *Organization Science*, 9 (5, September–October), 540–542.

Meyer, George W. and Girish Shambu (2010), "The Jazz Metaphor for Management Educators: Making Meaning with Students Through Swinging Improvisation," *Business Education Innovation Journal*, 2 (1), 16–26.

Meyer, Leonard B. (1956), *Emotion and Meaning in Music*, Chicago, IL: University of Chicago Press.

Meyer, Leonard B. (1967), *Music, the Arts, and Ideas*, Chicago, IL: University of Chicago Press.

Mick, David Glen (1986), "Consumer Research and Semiotics: Exploring the Morphology of Signs, Symbols, and Significance," *Journal of Consumer Research*, 13 (2, September), 196–213.

Miller, Daniel (2010), *Stuff*, Cambridge: Polity Press.

Miller, Daniel (2012), *Consumption and Its Consequences*, Cambridge: Polity Press.

Milligan, Andy and Shaun Smith (ed. 2002), *Uncommon Practice: People Who Deliver a Great Brand Experience*, London, UK: Pearson Education.

Mills, Michael Kenneth (2009), "Using the Jazz Metaphor to Teach the Strategy Capstone Course," Proceedings of the 23rd Australian and New Zealand Academy of Management Conference, on-line @ eprints.usq.edu.au/6576/.

Mills, Michael Kenneth (2010), "Using the Jazz Metaphor to Enhance Student Learning and Skill Development in the Marketing Research Course," *Journal of Marketing Education*, 32 (3, December), 300–313.

Minowa, Yuko, Luca M. Visconti, and Pauline Maclaran (2012), "Researchers' Introspection for Multi-Sited Ethnographers: A Xenoheteroglossic Autoethnography," *Journal of Business Research*, 65 (4, April), 483–489.

Mintzberg, Henry (2009), "America's Monumental Failure of Management," *The Globe and Mail*, on-line @ www.theglobeandmail.com/opinion/americas-monumental-failure-of-management/article78356.

Montaigne, Michel De (ed. 1993), *The Complete Essays*, trans. M. A. Screech, London, UK: Penguin Classics.

Moore, William L. and Morris B. Holbrook (1982), "On the Predictive Validity of Joint-Space Models in Consumer Evaluations of New Concepts," *Journal of Consumer Research*, 9 (2, September), 206–210.

Moore, William L. and Morris B. Holbrook (1990), "Conjoint Analysis of Objects with Environmentally Correlated Attributes: The Questionable Importance of Representative Design," *Journal of Consumer Research*, 16 (4), 490–497.

Moorman, Christine and Anne S. Miner (1998a), "Organizational Improvisation and Organizational Memory," *Academy of Management Review*, 23 (4, October), 698–723.

Moorman, Christine and Anne S. Miner (1998b), "The Convergence of Planning and Execution: Improvisation in New Product Development," *Journal of Marketing*, 62 (July), 1–20.

Morris, Charles (1956), *Varieties of Human Value*, Chicago, IL: The University of Chicago Press.

Mukerjee, Radhakamal (1964), *The Dimensions of Values*, London, UK: George Allen & Unwin.

Murphy, Patrick E. and Gene R. Laczniak (2012), *Ethics in Marketing: International Cases and Perspectives*, London, UK: Routledge.

Newton, Paul H. (2004), "Leadership Lessons from Jazz Improvisation," *International Journal of Leadership in Education*, 7 (1, March), 83–99.

Nicosia, Franco M. (1966), *Consumer Decision Processes*, Englewood Cliffs, NJ: Prentice-Hall.

Norris, Ruby Turner (1941), *The Theory of Consumer's Demand*, New Haven, CT: Yale University Press.

O'Shaughnessy, John and Morris B. Holbrook (1988), "Understanding Consumer Behavior: The Linguistic Turn in Marketing Research," *Journal of the Market Research Society*, 30 (2), 197–223.

O'Shaughnessy, Nicholas and Morris B. Holbrook (1988), "What Can U.S. Business Learn from Political Marketing?" *Journal of Applied Business Research*, 4 (3), 98–109.

Oakes, Steve (2009), "Freedom and Constraint in the Empowerment as Jazz Metaphor," *Marketing Theory*, 9 (4), 463–485.

Oakes, Steve, Douglas Brownlie, and Noel Dennis (2011), "Ubiquitous Music," *Marketing Theory*, 11 (1), 91–95.

Oliver, Richard L. (1980), "A Cognitive Model of the Antecedents and Consequences of Satisfaction Decisions," *Journal of Marketing Research*, 17 (4, November), 460–469.

Oliver, Richard L. (1997), *Satisfaction: A Behavioral Perspective on the Consumer*, New York, NY: McGraw Hill.

Olney, Thomas J., Rajeev Batra, and Morris B. Holbrook (1990), "A Three-Component Model of Attitude Toward the Ad: Effects on the Zipping and Zapping of Television Commercials," in *Emotion in Advertising*, ed. Stuart Agres, Julie A. Edell, and Tony M. Dubitsky, New York, NY: Quorum Books, 269–281.

Olney, Thomas J., Morris B. Holbrook, and Rajeev Batra (1991), "Consumer Responses to Advertising: The Effects of Ad Content, Emotions, and Attitude Toward the Ad on Viewing Time," *Journal of Consumer Research*, 17 (4, March), 440–453.

Olsen, Barbara (2012), "Reflexive Introspection on Sharing Gifts and Shaping Stories," *Journal of Business Research*, 65 (4, April), 467–474.

Osborne, Harold (1933), *Foundations of the Philosophy of Value*, Cambridge, UK: Cambridge University Press.

Parasuraman, A., Valerie A. Zeithaml, and Leonard L. Berry (1988), "SERVQUAL: A Multiple-Item Scale for Measuring Consumer Perceptions of Service Quality," *Journal of Retailing*, 64 (1, Spring), 12–40.

Parker, Dewitt H. (1957), *The Philosophy of Value*, Ann Arbor, MI: The University of Michigan Press.

Pavlovich, Kathryn (2003), "All That Jazz," *Long Range Planning*, 36 (5, October), 441–458.

Pepper, Stephen C. (1958), *The Sources of Value*, Berkeley, CA: University of California Press.

Perry, Ralph Barton (1954), *Realms of Value*, Cambridge, MA: Harvard University Press.

Pham, Michel Tuan (2004), "The Logic of Feeling," *Journal of Consumer Psychology*, 14 (4), 360–369.

Pham, Michel Tuan (2007), "Emotion and Rationality: A Critical Review of Empirical Evidence," *Review of General Psychology*, 11 (2), 155–178.

Pine, B. Joseph, II, and James H. Gilmore (1998), "Welcome to the Experience Economy," *Harvard Business Review*, 76 (July–August), 97–105.

Pine, B. Joseph, II and James H. Gilmore (1999), *The Experience Economy: Work Is Theatre & Every Business a Stage*, Boston, MA: Harvard Business School Press.

Pirsig, Robert M. (1974), *Zen and the Art of Motorcycle Maintenance: An Inquiry into Values*, New York, NY: Bantam Books.

Prahalad, C. K. and Venkat Ramaswamy (2004), "Co-Creation Experiences: The Next Practice in Value Creation," *Journal of Interactive Marketing*, 18 (3, Summer), 5–14.

Redondo, Ignacio and Morris B. Holbrook (2008), "Illustrating a Systematic Approach to Selecting Motion Pictures for Product Placements and Tie-Ins," *International Journal of Advertising*, 27 (5), 691–714.

Redondo, Ignacio and Morris B. Holbrook (2010), "Modeling the Appeal of Movie Features to Demographic Segments of Theatrical Demand," *Journal of Cultural Economics*, 34 (4), 299–315.

Ritzer, George (1993), *The McDonaldization of Society*, Thousand Oaks, CA: Pine Forge Press.

Roederer, Claire (2013), *Marketing and Experiential Consumption*, Cormelles-Le-Royal, France: Éditions Ems.

Roederer, Claire and Marc Filser (2015), *Le Marketing Expérientiel: Vers un Marketing de la Cocréation*, Paris: Magnard-Vuibert.

Rokeach, Milton (1968), *Beliefs, Attitudes and Values*, San Francisco, CA: Jossey-Bass, Inc.

Rokeach, Milton (1973), *The Nature of Human Values*, New York, NY: The Free Press.

Rosenberg, Milton J. (1956), "Cognitive Structure and Attitudinal Affect," *Journal of Abnormal and Social Psychology*, 53 (November), 368–372.

Russell, Ross (1973), *Bird Lives! The High Life and Hard Times of Charlie (Yardbird) Parker*, New York, NY: Charterhouse.

Ryan, Michael J. and Morris B. Holbrook (1982a), "Decision-Specific Conflict in Organizational Buying Behavior," *Journal of Marketing*, 46 (3), 62–68.

Ryan, Michael J. and Morris B. Holbrook (1982b), "Importance, Elicitation Order, and Expectancy X Value," *Journal of Business Research*, 10 (3, September), 309–317.

Ryan, Michael J., Morris B. Holbrook, and James M. Hulbert (1978), "A Two-Stage Model of Relative Decision-Specific Stress in the Buying Center," in *Proceedings of the 86th Annual Conference*, Washington, DC: American Psychological Association, Division 23, 28–30.

Samuel, Larry (2003), *The Trend Commandments™: Turning Cultural Fluency into Marketing Opportunity*, New York, NY: Bang! Zoom! Books.

Sánchez-Fernández, Raquel and M. Ángeles Iniesta-Bonillo (2006), "Consumer Perception of Value: Literature Review and a New Conceptual Framework," *Journal of Consumer Satisfaction, Dissatisfaction and Complaining Behavior*, 19, 40–58.

Sánchez-Fernández, Raquel and M. Ángeles Iniesta-Bonillo (2007), "The Concept of Perceived Value: A Systematic Review of the Research," *Marketing Theory*, 7 (4), 427–451.

Sánchez-Fernández, Raquel, M. Ángeles Iniesta-Bonillo, and Morris B. Holbrook (2009), "The Conceptualization and Measurement of Consumer Value in Services," *International Journal of Market Research*, 51 (1), 93–113.

Schindler, Robert M. and Morris B. Holbrook (1993), "Critical Periods in the Development of Men's and Women's Tastes in Personal Appearance," *Psychology & Marketing*, 10 (6), 549–564.

Schindler, Robert M. and Morris B. Holbrook (2003), "Nostalgia for Early Experience as a Determinant of Consumer Preferences," *Psychology & Marketing*, 20 (4), 275–302.

Schindler, Robert M., Morris B. Holbrook, and Eric A. Greenleaf (1989), "Using Connoisseurs to Predict Mass Tastes," *Marketing Letters*, 1 (1, December), 47–54.

Schmitt, Bernd H. (1999), *Experiential Marketing: How to get Customers to Sense, Feel, Think, Act, and Relate to Your Company and Brands*, New York, NY: The Free Press.

Schmitt, Bernd H. (2003), *Customer Experience Management: A Revolutionary Approach to Connecting with Your Customers*, New York, NY: Wiley.

Schmitt, Bernd H. (2007), *Big Think Strategy: How to Leverage Bold Ideas and Leave Small Thinking Behind*, Boston, MA: Harvard Business Press.

Schmitt, Bernd H. (2012), *Happy Customers Everywhere: How Your Business Can Benefit from the Insights from Positive Psychology*, New York, NY: Palgrave Macmillan.

Schmitt, Bernd H., David L. Rogers, and Karen L. Vrotsos (2003), *There's No Business That's Not Show Business: Marketing in an Experience Culture*, Englewood-Cliffs, NJ: Prentice-Hall Financial Times.

Schmitt, Bernd H. and Alex Simonson (1997), *Marketing Aesthetics: The Strategic Management of Brands, Identity, and Image*, New York, NY: The Free Press.

Shaw, Colin and John Ivens (2002), *Building Great Customer Experiences*, Hampshire, UK: Palgrave Macmillan.

Sherry, John F., Jr. (2012), "Poems," *Journal of Business Research*, 65 (4, April), 475–477.

Sheth, Jagdish N., Bruce I. Newman, and Barbara L. Gross (1991), "Why We Buy What We Buy: A Theory of Consumption Values," *Journal of Business Research*, 22 (2, March), 159–170.

Shultz, Clifford J., II and Morris B. Holbrook (1999), "Marketing and the Tragedy of the Commons: A Synthesis, Commentary, and Analysis for Action," *Journal of Public Policy & Marketing*, 18 (2), 218–229.

Shultz, Clifford J., II and Morris B. Holbrook (2009), "The Paradoxical Relationships Between Marketing and Vulnerability," *Journal of Public Policy & Marketing*, 28 (1), 124–127.

Siegel, Eli (1981), *Self and World*, New York, NY: Definition Press.

Simonson, Alex and Morris B. Holbrook (1993), "Permissible Puffery Versus Actionable Warranty in Advertising and Salestalk: An Empirical Investigation," *Journal of Public Policy and Marketing*, 12 (2), 216–233.

Smith, Adam (1776, ed. 1937), *An Inquiry into the Nature and Causes of the Wealth of Nations*, New York, NY: The Modern Library.

Smith, N. Craig and John A. Quelch (1992), *Ethics in Marketing*, Homewood, IL: Richard D. Irwin.

Smith, Shaun and Joe Wheeler (2002), *Managing the Customer Experience: Turning Customers into Advocates*, London, UK: Prentice Hall.

Sorensen, Anne, Lynda Andrews, and Judy Drennan (2017), "Using Social Media Posts as Resources for Engaging in Value Co-Creation," *Journal of Service Theory and Practice*, 27 (4), 808–922.

Sorensen, Nicholas (2013)," The Metaphor of 'The Jazz Band': Ethical Issues for Leadership," *Critical Studies in Improvisation/Études Critiques en Improvisation*, 9 (1), on-line @ www.criticalimprov.com/article/view/1903/2974.

Star, Steven H. (1989), "Marketing and Its Discontents," *Harvard Business Review*, 67 (6, November–December), 148–154.

Stern, Barbara B. and Morris B. Holbrook (1994), "Gender and Genre in the Interpretation of Advertising Text," in *Gender Issues and Consumer Behavior*, ed. Janeen Arnold Costa, Thousand Oaks, CA: Sage Publications, 11–41.

Stern, Barbara B., George M. Zinkhan, and Morris B. Holbrook (2002), "The Netvertising Image: Netvertising Image Communication Model (NICM) and Construct Definition," *Journal of Advertising*, 31 (3), 15–27.

Sweeney, Jillian C. and Geoffrey N. Soutar (2001), "Consumer Perceived Value: The Development of a Multiple Item Scale," *Journal of Retailing*, 77 (2, Summer), 203–220.

Taylor, Paul W. (1961), *Normative Discourse*, Englewood Cliffs, NJ: Prentice-Hall.

Terry, Clark and Gwen Terry (2011), *Clark: The Autobiography of Clark Terry*, Berkeley, CA: University of California Press.

Thompson, Craig J. and Elizabeth C. Hirschman (1995), "Understanding the Socialized Body: A Poststructuralist Analysis of Consumers' Self-Conceptions, Body Images, and Self-Care Practices," *Journal of Consumer Research*, 22 (2, September), 139–153.

Tinari, Frank D. and Kailash Khandke (2000), "From Rhythm and Blues to Broadway: Using Music to Teach Economics," *Journal of Economic Education*, 31 (3, Summer), 253–270.

Tisch, Jonathan M. and Karl Weber (2007), *Chocolates on the Pillow Aren't Enough: Reinventing the Customer Experience*, Hoboken, NJ: John Wiley & Sons.

Tung, Vincent Wing Sun and J. R. Brent Ritchie (2011), "Exploring the Essence of Memorable Tourism Experience," *Annals of Tourism Research*, 38 (4), 1367–1386.

Ucbasaran, Deniz, Andy Lockett, and Michael Humphreys (2011), "Leading Entrepreneurial Teams: Insights from Jazz," Working Paper, The International Society for Business Education, on-line @ www.isbe.org.uk/ucbasaran10.

Vargo, Stephen L. and Robert F. Lusch (2004), "Evolving to a New Dominant Logic for Marketing," *Journal of Marketing*, 68 (1, January), 1–17.

Veblen, Thorstein (1899), *The Theory of the Leisure Class: An Economic Study of Institutions*, New York, NY: Palgrave Macmillan.

Von Wright, Georg Henrik (1963), *The Varieties of Goodness*, London, UK: Routledge & Kegan Paul.

Wallace, W. Timothy, Alan Seigerman, and Morris B. Holbrook (1993), "The Role of Actors and Actresses in the Success of Films: How Much Is a Movie Star Worth?" *Journal of Cultural Economics*, 17 (1, June), 1–27.

Wallendorf, Melanie and Merrie Brucks (1993), "Introspection in Consumer Research: Implementation and Implications," *Journal of Consumer Research*, 20 (3, December), 339–359.

Waltzer, Nana and Andreas Salcher (2003), "Management by Jazz – Creating Innovation from the Principles of Chaos and Order," *Industrial and Commercial Training*, 35 (2), 67–69.

Wang, Yonggui, Hing Po Lo, Renyong Chi, and Yongheng Yang (2004), "An Integrated Framework for Customer Value and Customer-Relationship-Management Performance: A Customer-Based Perspective from China," *Managing Service Quality*, 14 (2–3), 169–182.

Weick, Karl E. (1998), "Improvisation as a Mindset for Organizational Analysis," *Organization Science*, 9 (5, September–October), 543–555.

Weiss, Michael J., Morris B. Holbrook, and J. Habich (2001), "Death of the Arts Snob?" *American Demographics*, 23 (6), 40–42.

Whelan, Susan and Markus Wohlfeil (2006), "Communicating Brands Through Engagement with 'Lived' Experiences," *Journal of Brand Management*, 13 (4, April), 313–329.

Wohlfeil, Markus and Susan Whelan (2006), "Consumer Motivations to Participate in Event-Marketing Strategies," *Journal of Marketing Management*, 22 (5–6), 643–669.

Wohlfeil, Markus and Susan Whelan (2012), " 'Saved!' by Jena Malone: An Introspective Study of a Consumer's Fan Relationship with a Film Actress," *Journal of Business Research*, 65 (4, April), 511–519.

Woodruff, Robert B. (1997), "Customer Value: The Next Source for Competitive Advantage," *Journal of the Academy of Marketing Science*, 25 (2, Spring), 139–153.

Woods, Walter A. (1981), *Consumer Behavior*, New York, NY: North Holland.

Woodside, Arch G. (2004), "Advancing from Subjective to Confirmatory Personal Introspection in Consumer Research," *Psychology & Marketing*, 21 (12, December), 987–1010.

Woodside, Arch G. (2006), "Overcoming the Illusion of Will and Self-Fabrication: Going Beyond Naïve Subjective Personal Introspection to an Unconscious/Conscious Theory of Behavior Explanation," *Psychology & Marketing*, 23 (3, March), 257–272.

Woodward, Michael N. and Morris B. Holbrook (2013), "Dialogue on Some Concepts, Definitions and Issues Pertaining to 'Consumption Experiences'," *Marketing Theory*, 13 (3), 323–244.

Zeithaml, Valerie A. (1988), "Consumer Perceptions of Price, Quality, and Value: A Means-End Model and Synthesis of Evidence," *Journal of Marketing*, 52 (3, July), 2–22.

Printed in the United States
by Baker & Taylor Publisher Services